Praise for the *Best Food* [illegible] …ATIVE

"Not just for foodies! This will delight any[illegible] pleasures of a good read and a good meal. Highly recommended."
—*Library Journal*

"Hughes once again pulls together the year's tastiest examples from the growing field of food writing . . . In an era of celebrity chefs and much-hyped restaurants, this collection is thankfully absent the pretentious musings of restaurateurs and TV stars . . . A collection of strong writing on fascinating topics that will appeal to foodies and essay lovers alike." —Kirkus Reviews

"There's a mess of vital, provocative, funny and tender stuff . . . in these pages." —*USA Today*

"An exceptional collection worth revisiting, this will be a surefire hit with epicureans and cooks." —*Publishers Weekly*, starred review

"If you're looking to find new authors and voices about food, there's an abundance to chew on here." —*Tampa Tribune*

"Fascinating to read now, this book will also be interesting to pick up a year from now, or ten years from now." —Popmatters.com

"Some of these stories can make you burn with a need to taste what they're writing about." —*Los Angeles Times*

"Reflects not only a well-developed esthetic but also increasingly a perceptive politics that demands attention to agricultural and nutritional policies by both individuals and governments." —*Booklist*

"This is a book worth devouring." —*Sacramento Bee*

"The cream of the crop of food writing compilations."
—*Milwaukee Journal Sentinel*

"The book captures the gastronomic zeitgeist in a broad range of essays." —*San Jose Mercury News*

"There are a few recipes among the stories, but mostly it's just delicious tales about eating out, cooking at home and even the politics surrounding the food on our plates." —*Spokesman-Review*

"The next best thing to eating there is." —*New York Metro*

"Stories for connoisseurs, celebrations of the specialized, the odd, or simply the excellent." –*Entertainment Weekly*

"Spans the globe and palate." –*Houston Chronicle*

"The perfect gift for the literate food lover." –*Pittsburgh Post-Gazette*

best Food WRITING 2013

Also edited by Holly Hughes

Best Food Writing 2012
Best Food Writing 2011
Best Food Writing 2010
Best Food Writing 2009
Best Food Writing 2008
Best Food Writing 2007
Best Food Writing 2006
Best Food Writing 2005
Best Food Writing 2004
Best Food Writing 2003
Best Food Writing 2002
Best Food Writing 2001
Best Food Writing 2000

Also by Holly Hughes

Frommer's 500 Places for Food and Wine Lovers
Frommer's 500 Places to See Before They Disappear
Frommer's 500 Places to Take the Kids Before They Grow Up

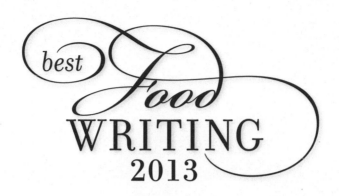

best Food WRITING 2013

Edited by

HOLLY HUGHES

Da Capo
LIFE LONG
A Member of
the Perseus Books Group

Set in 10-point Bembo BQ by the Perseus Books Group

Cataloging-in-Publication data for this book is available from the Library of Congress.

First Da Capo Press edition 2013
ISBN: 978-0-7382-1716-1 (paperback)
ISBN: 978-0-7382-1717-8 (e-book)

Published by Da Capo Press
A Member of the Perseus Books Group
www.dacapopress.com

10 9 8 7 6 5 4 3 2 1

Contents

Home Cooking

To Be a Chef

Introduction

The vegetables were beautiful this year, fat lush heads of arugula and romaine, gleaming taut-skinned summer squash, lusty round beets, impudently tall leeks with loamy soil still clinging to their hairy roots. Every week there were a few horizon-expanding surprises—who knows what I'd have done with those spiky knobs of kohlrabi if the CSA hadn't provided recipes? And the fruit! This was the first year I'd bought a fruit share, too, and I was astonished by how sweet and succulent the berries and peaches were, the cherries delicate and tender, not rubbery like supermarket Bings.

Every week I'd lug home this embarrassment of riches, then panic about using it all. So—what else?—I invested in a mandoline. Each Monday I made a vegetable terrine to cook up the last produce, emptying the crisper drawers for Tuesday's CSA pick-up. Aside from the evening I nearly sliced off my fingertip (so *that's* why they include that finger-guard), I found those meticulous hours of slicing and layering wonderfully meditative. Some combos were better than others, granted, especially before my daughter went full-on vegan and we had to leave out the goat cheese. But making vegetables the main course of our dinner? It seemed like an idea whose time had come.

So this is where we stand in the year 2013: The season of foam and gels has passed, and the Year of the Pork Belly has given way to the Year of Kale. Over the past several months, combing through bookstores and magazines and websites to compile this year's edition of *Best Food Writing,* I've seen the ground shift back towards slow food. Today's true believers are all about farm-to-table sourcing and handcrafted ingredients, and it's tempting to join in.

The mandate to "eat local" has done a lot to level the playing field—as Brett Martin declares in this book's opening essay (page 2), nowadays there is "Good Food Everywhere," not just in a few big restaurant cities. It has also inspired some fine writers to dig deep and reaffirm their faith in the elemental act of cooking—as meditation

(Michael Pollan, page 223), as a way of living life (Edward Behr, page 41), even as a form of prayer (Paul Graham, page 350). Yet I sense that the locavore dogma is due for a pushback. Other voices in this year's book view locavorism with skepticism (Katherine Wheelock's "Is Seasonal Eating Overrated?," page 32), tongue-in-cheek humor (Erica Strauss, "The Terrible Tragedy of the Healthy Eater," page 36), thoughtful re-examination (Todd Kliman, "The Meaning of Local," page 52), and clear-eyed socio-economic reaction (Tracie McMillan, "Why Cooking Isn't Fun," page 48).

I hope that one effect of the local-sourcing movement will last: Giving quality food producers some star power, on a level with chefs. In this edition of *Best Food Writing*, we meet several of them, from all over the country: Erin Byers Murray's Massachusetts female farmers (page 112), Dara Moskowitz Grumdahl's Minnesota cheesemaker (page 119), Rowan Jacobsen's Maine heirloom-apple grower (page 104), Barry Estabrook's Vermont hog farmer (page 142), John Kessler's Georgia cattleman (page 150). Any self-respecting carnivore these days should vicariously slaughter an animal just once (see Tim Hayward's "The Ibérico Journey," page 160), or even better, go hunting with Mike Sula (page 180), Steven Rinella (page 196), and Hank Shaw (page 199), or snail-gathering with Molly Watson (page 129).

Scoring ingredients is only the first step, though. In this Golden Age of Foodism, it's okay to get a wee bit obsessive in the kitchen, especially when a dish carries special significance. Check out culinary mad scientist J. Kenji Lopez-Alt, deconstructing his childhood favorite New England clam chowder (page 212); Tim Carman, resurrecting a lost family cookie recipe (page 240); Michael Procopio, trying to reproduce a favorite restaurant dish that was cut from the menu (page 246); and Bernard L. Herman, lovingly curating a Thanksgiving feast keyed to his family retreat on the Chesapeake shore (page 259).

Farm-to-table sourcing hasn't killed off the four-star restaurant—far from it. Witness the current vogue of multi-course chef's tasting menus, as lamented by Corby Kummer ("Tyranny: It's What's For Dinner," page 19) and played out in real time by Matt Goulding ("Confronting a Masterpiece," page 74). But the rules seem to have subtly changed for top-flight chefs. Joy Manning's skeptical review of Magnus Nilsson's *Fäviken* cookbook (page 236) holds star chefs to a real-world standard. John Swansburg (page 266) profiles Danny Bowien, whose Mission Chinese started as a pop-up; Peter Barrett (page 281) follows Zak Pelaccio as he re-invents himself for a small-town market; and Kevin Pang (page 289) reveals Curtis Duffy as an ex-delinquent redeemed by cooking in high-end restaurants. Eddie Huang's memoir *Fresh Off the Boat* (page 330) credits his family's passion for Taiwan street food as the root of his restaurant Baohaus.

Other chefs profiled this year are working all over the place—cooking in a food truck (Jonathan Gold, page 276) or on a small Caribbean island (Francis Lam, page 309), as a private chef (Karen Barichievy, page 314) or a pizza maker (Chris Wiewiora, page 323).

The line between epicurean ambition and simple home cooking requires constant navigation, as Elissa Altman shows in her memoir *Poor Man's Feast* (page 357). Foodies can be just as interested in Low Food as in High Food, which may be why Dan Barry rhapsodizes about Ding Dongs (page 99), Katherine Shilcutt surrenders to the allure of the McRib (page 95), and Sarah DiGregorio marvels at the healing power of Hood ice cream in a cup (page 371). As Katie Arnold-Ratliff confesses (page 230), our favorite cookbooks aren't always the complicated ones.

Buzzwords like "local," "seasonal," "artisanal," and so on are bound to fade away, as trends always do; what's certain is that our national obsession with all things foodie shows no sign of letting up, especially in the 18-to-30 demographic. As publisher Daniel Halpern remarked in a recent *New York Times* article, "The passion my generation felt about poetry and fiction has gone into food, I think, into making pickles or chocolate or beer." Another *Times* article interviewed 20-somethings in entry-level jobs who spend all of their limited disposable income on dining out in trophy restaurants, instead of on rent or clothes or travel. My college-age kids raptly watch *Chopped* and Guy Fieri's *Diners, Drive-Ins, and Dives* every night during dinner, not because of me—God forbid!—but because that's what their friends are talking about. Only a couple of years ago, snapping a photo of your restaurant meal to post on Twitter would instantly brand you as a food obsessive. Nowadays—for better or worse—it's almost *de rigueur.*

With such an insatiable audience, there are more outlets for food writing than ever, in print and online and on the airwaves. It's an embarrassment of riches, not unlike those overstuffed CSA bags of produce. Cutting through the chatter to find the really good stuff can be a challenge—and that's where *Best Food Writing 2013* comes in. Curating this year's collection has been a bit like assembling a vegetable terrine, building a rich flavor from many different tastes, layered all together. Plunge in and enjoy!

The Way We Eat Now

Good Food Everywhere

By Brett Martin

From *GQ*

To get a handle on the Big American Food Picture, feature writer and essayist Brett Martin travels coast-to-coast, a roving cultural investigator for publications such as *GQ, Vanity Fair, The New Yorker, Bon Appétit,* and *Food & Wine.* His diagnosis? It's all good.

And so here we are, under the arc lights, under the Southern California stars, on a picture-perfect summer evening in America. The kids are arriving, headlights swinging slowly down La Brea, down Beverly. They're cruising, looking for parking, checking out the scene at the car wash and gas station on the corner.

I myself am driving a brand-new, bright-red Ford F-150 pickup truck. This feels important. If you've never been in one of these monsters, it's hard to describe how mighty and right it makes you feel. You understand why men who drive trucks drive like assholes: *(a)* There's a good chance that, despite mirrors the size of a normal human car's hubcaps, they simply don't see other vehicles. *(b)* In some larger, existential sense, all other vehicles have ceased to exist. Driving an F-150 makes you want to run over smaller, lesser cars. It makes you want to invade smaller, lesser countries.

So, with all this fine American muscle rumbling underneath me, I roll up to The Truck Stop. Except, for all its *American Graffiti* trappings, this is no temple to car culture. The pumps are covered. A handwritten sign reads "no gas." The shiny, souped-up vehicles everybody's lining up to see aren't here for a drag race. And those beautiful kids may have youthful hunger in their eyes, but not, it would seem, for young love. A couple, he in black-on-black Yankees cap, she in Snooki sweats and flip-flops, wander arm in arm between the idling trucks. "Ohmigod," she squeals as they approach one. "Those homemade pierogies are uh-mazing." They kiss.

Elsewhere, they're lining up for lobster rolls at the Lobsta Truck; for artisanal Pittsburgh-style "Sammies" at Steel City Sandwich; for salad, of all things, at the Flatiron Truck: butter lettuce and heirloom carrots sliced mandoline thin, tossed with mustard vinaigrette, and topped with pieces of steak marinated in star anise, cooked *sous vide,* finished on the grill, and sent off with a puff of shiitake-mushroom dust. If there's a muse here, an avatar presiding over all this transmutation of energy to young America's stomach from organs slightly farther south, it's the mud-flap girl emblazoned on the most popular truck in the lot. She's a classic: in recline, chest thrust forward, dewy lips lifted and parted to receive—yes, ah yes—a Gruyère and double-cream-Brie grilled cheese sandwich.

But you know this. You've been there, or some version of there. Food trucks have become to food scenes what porcupines are said to be to a forest: a sign that you've got a healthy, vibrant ecosystem at work. And by the time I stood before The Grilled Cheese Truck, midway through a monthlong journey from sea to shining sea, I could already state without equivocation that the nation's food ecosystem was thriving. I'd had magnificent meals in an airport and in a hospital. My coastal urban bigotry had been undermined by amazing eating in small out-of-the-way cities. Just that morning, on a seedy stretch of the Venice Beach boardwalk, where the air hangs heavy with the smell of medical marijuana and white-man's dreads, I had breakfasted on artisanal bread pudding and Blue Bottle coffee from a closet-sized counter squirreled amid the henna-tattoo and cheap-sunglass shops.

It had long since become clear that the fortuitous collision of political, philosophical, health, and fashion movements that together form the Food Revolution had, over the past decade, penetrated nearly every corner of American life. We are now a nation with so many farmers' markets that *The New York Times* has reported that *farmers* are getting a little worried. A nation in which phrases like

"Kosher in Fargo?" or "Filipino in Detroit?"—which once would have been failed pitches for fish-out-of-water sitcoms—are now perfectly reasonable queries on foodie boards. We the people have come to rely on, indeed feel entitled to, good food *everywhere.*

Given the generally blah economic climate, what, it's fair to ask, exactly the hell is going on? How to square the seemingly unstoppable upward trajectory of our eating lives with the supposed downward trajectory of nearly everything else?

The first and most obvious answer is that this is another reflection of the enormous gap between rich and poor. After all, at the same time some of us engage in quests for the perfect *taco al pastor,* obesity and hunger stalk the land—often, in a perverse histori-nutritional anomaly, side by side. Where I live, in New Orleans, is a so-called "food desert" where locals are hard-pressed to buy a fresh lemon, much less a Meyer lemon.

But while the Food Revolution may have started as an indulgence of the boom years, it was just as finely tuned to the crash and sluggish present. It is, first of all, a movement built on entrepreneurs—a generation of countercultural capitalists created, at least in part, by the lack of more traditional, stable work. You start cooking in trucks, don't forget, when you can't afford brick-and-mortar rent. The foods of the movement, meanwhile, though not cheap, tend to be those that soothe: fatty, melty, salty, sweet. Comfort foods. It's no surprise that the flavors ascendant over the past ten years are so often rooted in the cuisines of Italy, Asia, and the American South—places that have long made a virtue of elevating the simple foods of poverty. And the ethics espoused—local, community-based, anti-corporate, anti-industrial—are those of an uneasy population reaching for an idealized past. It just happens to be one of the moment's many dozen paradoxes that the path there is paved with $20 plates of truffled mac and cheese and an endless series of better and better pizzas.

Not long ago, a nice 85-year-old lady from Grand Forks, North Dakota, wrote an earnest review of a new branch of the Olive Garden in the *Grand Forks Herald.* Marilyn Hagerty had been filing reviews for the paper for decades without incident, but this one was picked up and ridiculed by food bloggers. It quickly went viral, becoming another weird semiotic data point in the cyclone of lash and backlash that makes up the electronic food conversation.

In truth, the to-do was less about the provincialism of food than it was about the provincialism of newspapers. But it was notable mostly for how anachronistic it felt. Years ago, Calvin Trillin coined "La Maison de la Casa House" to identify the interchangeable "good restaurant" in any given town. Today's version of that eatery will feature warm, modern design employing lots of wood and recessed lighting. There will be a large bar and a TV, just to hedge its bets with more conservative locals. It will have a blackboard on which are listed the various sources of its ingredients. The menu, too, will read like a 4-H register, so loaded will it be with the names of various farms. It will offer dishes that vacillate between ambition and comfort and probably err on the side of piling too many ingredients on one plate. It will be called something like Market Table Tasting Market, or perhaps Loin, and it will stand a decent chance of actually being good.

That is to say that the coasts and big cities long ago gave up their monopoly on good food scenes. I saw that while eating simple roasted carrots painted with honey at the Red Feather Lounge in Boise, Idaho, and a deep-fried fish head at Jolie in Lafayette, Louisiana. I tasted it in a smoky barrel-aged Manhattan at Frog Hollow Tavern in Augusta, Georgia, and in the Imperial Slam Dunk—a triple shot of Earl Grey tea, brewed with maple syrup and quince paste and topped with a shot of espresso—at MadCap Coffee in Grand Rapids, Michigan, a town once commonly referred to as "Bland Rapids," as if the official nickname, "the Furniture City," didn't convey a sufficient sense of white-breaditude. I could see it in the glistening smoked brisket covered in hickory-hoisin sauce and served on focaccia from the Bone-In Artisan BBQ truck, parked at the farmers' market in Columbia, South Carolina, where one could also buy small-batch artisanal sea salts with a food-pairing guide—surely some decadent edge of food worship.

It's a fair bet that the average supermarket in North Dakota is better today—offering healthier, fresher, and more varied choices—than the same store was in New York City twenty years ago. The idea that there was a fine restaurant to be found in Grand Forks would be less surprising than the notion that all there was to review there was an Olive Garden. We've become a country without a Peoria.

At the Boise, Idaho, airport, a sign welcomed me to the "City of Trees." Out the window I could see nothing but dusty, camel-colored hills with a few straggly specimens sticking up like broken toothbrush bristles. Feeling very small and truckless in my Ford Fusion, I headed downtown.

I had come to Boise because I had heard you could get a great cocktail there. Indeed, considering that there is nothing for 350 miles in any direction and that one of those directions is Utah, it's shocking to report that there's actually something of a cocktail war in effect between two businesses there: the aforementioned Red Feather and The Modern Hotel and Bar, a onetime Travelodge that's been transformed into a boutique hotel. In addition to the *de rigueur* high-thread-count sheets, flat-screen TVs, and an exterior that looks like it's been beamed in from East Hampton, that now means sophisticated food and drink programs.

The latter is run by Michael Bowers. He is a serious 27-year-old gay man with thick-rimmed glasses and a tattoo of modern composer Arnold Schoenberg's name on his forearm. In other words, precisely the kind of person who, until recently, would have automatically migrated to one of the coasts to follow his passions. A local boy whose cocktail experience was once limited to drinking mai tais, Bowers had a scales-falling-from-his-eyes moment over a Ward 8 (rye, grenadine, lemon and orange juices) at the bar Milk & Honey in New York. Instead of staying, though, he returned home committed to bringing Boise serious drinks. He researched recipes on cocktail blogs, learned to shake and stir from YouTube. Most important—because the spread of good food is a conspiracy of producer and consumer—he was confident he would find customers.

He has—though not totally without some necessary education. "The first time we did an egg-white drink, Boise wasn't ready," Bowers says. Both The Modern and Red Feather print drink menus that could double as reference works. Whenever someone orders a boring vodka drink, Bowers politely suggests substituting a Cameron's Kick, a startlingly light and friendly concoction made from scotch, Irish whiskey, lemon juice, and orgeat. Switching scotch for vodka is one decent definition of culinary cojones, but Bowers reports a 99 percent success rate.

Of course, he's not laboring alone in raising the standards of his neighbors. By the time they sit down at The Modern, they've probably already heard the word *mixology* on TV. They've already seen, on *Top Chef*, something like Bowers's technique for drawing the essential oils out of coffee beans by setting them on fire. They've followed blog posts from friends' trips to Portland and Seattle. They're demanding quality even if they've never tasted it before. I recently had a conversation with a discerning eater and drinker who spends a good deal of time on the road. He'd just watched an episode of *Portlandia* for the first time and said, "It's set in Portland, but I see people like that—who are interested in the same things—everywhere I go." Given that the man was John Flansburgh of the hipster-nerd heroes They Might Be Giants, this was a little like Jennifer Aniston reporting that one out of every two human beings is a paparazzo. But he was onto something: Mere geography, as a determining factor in how we dress, what we watch, what we listen to, and yes, what we eat, has all but lost its sway. *Portlandia* wouldn't be especially funny if, in some way, we all didn't live there.

In Boise, I remember eventually sitting before a skyline of empty glasses, each having contained some spirit or combination of spirits Bowers just had to have me try. I remember eating some ethereal gnocchi from The Modern's kitchen. I remember discussing organic gardening at a table containing an MFA student, a philosophy professor, a farmer, and a belly dancer. And I remember finally plummeting into bed with a final thought that I felt reasonably confident had never been thought before: that I'd had such a good time in Boise, I'd have nothing left for Las Vegas.

Vegas! You didn't think we could avoid Vegas? Vegas is such a ruthless beast of commodification—its hungry tendrils relentlessly probing American culture to see what can be turned into fresh dollars—that it is always important. Eating in Las Vegas was once strictly about signifiers of the good life—prime rib! lobster tail! king-crab legs!—at rock-bottom prices. Then the casinos got hip to the fact that high-end food had become something that gamblers would want to spend money on, another badge like Gucci or Chanel; in came the first generation of celebrity chefs, who were handed blank checks, glitzy spaces, and little obligation to be present past opening weekend. The food, while more important than the bad old buffet days, was still secondary to the flash.

And now? I headed for The Cosmopolitan of Las Vegas, branded as the Strip's first hipster casino, which is another way of saying a fifty-two-story memorial to the Death of Hipsterism. I passed by video art of botanical prints in the lobby and rode an elevator playing Devendra Banhart up to the high-end food court area. At Jaleo, José Andrés's tapas and molecular-gastronomy restaurant, I noshed on buttery *jamón ibérico* and wobbly science-fiction-like reverse-spherified olives—the modern answers to prime rib. But across the way, at the dark, quiet bar of a genetically engineered replica of Scott Conant's New York Italian joint, Scarpetta, I ate a tangle of perfectly cooked pasta, topped with a fresh tomato sauce and ribbons of torn basil. Not long ago, nearly anywhere in America, such a dish would have been found on a children's menu, if at all. That it holds pride of place on a menu in the most *au courant* casino on the strip is as revolutionary as finding fine food in one-time gourmet wastelands. It does, though, raise the same question that hovers over the new Korean Steak Tacos to be found at T.G.I. Friday's, or over Domino's Pizza's no-substitution "Artisan" pizzas: Who's winning? Has the Food Revolution really changed the corporate food business, or has it just provided it with new slogans? The cynic in me might assume the latter, but it was the optimist running his finger around the bowl to catch the last bits of sauce at Scarpetta.

It was the same hopeful fool who, not long before, had found himself pushing through Atlanta's Hartsfield-Jackson airport, headed for One Flew South, chef Duane Nutter's upscale eatery tucked into a corner of Terminal E. Walking in was like entering the *Star Trek* holodeck set on Soothing Restaurant World, and once again I was rewarded, this time by a dish I'd never seen before—a deconstructed fish "chowder" in which rich white miso stood in for cream while a large clamshell held the remaining ingredients: celery, potato, and a cube of fatty salmon. It would have been a pleasing revelation anywhere in the world. I was getting used to this. We all are.

Indeed, there is no place left—geographic or institutional—where good food would be noteworthy simply for being unlikely. Well, not quite *no* place. . . . At one point, I found myself in a hospital on the outskirts of Raleigh, North Carolina, surrounded by men in white coats. Each, thankfully, was at the top of his field. One described for me the other's credentials, how he had gone to the very best schools and run a successful practice elsewhere before being recruited to this facility. I was in the very best hands, he assured me, clapping his colleague on the back: "You should taste his cannoli!"

I was standing in the vast kitchen serving Rex Hospital, where Jim McGrody has brought the Food Revolution to the shitshow that is American health care. Around us, McGrody's team of sous-chefs, some of whom attended the Culinary Institute of America, were at work: A cook was grilling yellow squash in batches. Another lifted a tawny, glistening roasted pork loin from an oven while yet another mixed fresh sausage with spinach and rice, to make stuffing.

McGrody has been a lifelong institutional chef, first in the army and then at various universities. It was while working at his first hospital, in Washington, D.C., that he began to believe that the food he was in charge of serving seemed antithetical to anything resembling healing. He began to fantasize about a better way. "Cooks in our hospitals know how to make veal stock. They know how to make pan gravy using the *fond*," McGrody writes in his memoir/manifesto, *What We Feed Our Patients.* "The days of canned peas and three-compartment plates . . . are over."

The kitchen at Rex went a long way toward fulfilling that fantasy. In an office off the kitchen floor, an army of operators fielded orders from patients in the hospital's 433 beds. Each is provided with a room-service-style menu featuring such items as pecan-crusted sautéed chicken topped with maple-butter pan sauce and lime-and-ginger-glazed salmon. A software program alerted the operators to any allergies or other proscriptions: a diabetic ordering four chocolate "mud" shakes, for instance. Even those patients labeled "non-appropriates"—those who can't swallow traditional food—are treated to dignified fare like fresh peas pureed and molded into actual pea shapes, or blueberry panna cotta made from low-fat yogurt. Ingredients were overwhelmingly fresh. Across the board, the notion that healthy and tasty are not mutually exclusive, a lesson that has perhaps had a harder time penetrating the South than many other places, was emphasized—not by lecture but by example. "When I die," McGrody told me, "I want my tombstone to read 'The Man Who Killed Off Fruit Cocktail.'"

It's instinctive that healthful, good-tasting food sourced locally and served lovingly makes sense in terms of healing and investment in one's community. That, of course, doesn't answer why it's been allowed to happen. The fact that McGrody's program has provided a net gain of $1.9 million over three years does. Partly, that represents a savings over the industrial-catering company that previously handled food service. But it also reflects an increase in revenue from patients who choose Rex over other hospitals—just as they might choose Boise's Modern Hotel and its cocktail program over a motel with a sports bar specializing in appletinis. McGrody heard about one who demanded to be taken to the "Rex Carlton." Grassroots locavorism and hidden hipster speakeasies are all well and good; it's when the market speaks through once monolithic, indifferent institutions that we know something serious is afoot.

And so finally east, across the amber waves of grain to New York, the land of my birth. To find a proper example of the Food Revolution in New York City was a challenge, only because the revolution has succeeded so wildly here that it's become the establishment. From the windy shores of the Rockaways, toward which cadres of foodies troop each summer to eat tacos from beachfront shacks, to the once industrial lots of Williamsburg, Brooklyn, now lousy with food trucks, there are few cities in which Good Food Everywhere could be taken quite so literally. Even the Upper West Side, which used to be a reliable object of mockery for its lack of decent eating, has a Momofuku Milk Bar.

The only answer was to venture to the one place I would never go on my own: the very bastion of old, stodgy, arrogant New York, the belly of the beast. I speak, of course, of Yankee Stadium.

I will allow that I write from the point of view of a lifelong Mets fan and Yankee hater. Nevertheless, I think it's fairly objective to point out that the mighty Yankees have lagged behind the city's trend toward good food in its sports facilities, whether Shake Shack at the Mets' Citi Field or the Andrew Carmellini menu unveiled last season at Madison Square Garden. Perhaps this is on the theory that their fans can subsist entirely on a diet of monuments. Whatever the reason, the stadium has stood as evidence that while it is indeed now possible to get good food everywhere, it remains equally possible to get bad food anywhere.

I had never been to the new Yankee Stadium. You enter through an archway in a massive facade at once as oppressive as something from Imperial Rome and as shiny and neon-ringed as a space station. The aesthetic could be called Planet Mussolini. Yet even here, deep in the recesses of the spookily named Great Hall, where one must avert one's eyes lest one be brainwashed by images of DiMaggio, Yogi, and The Mick, among the $9 Bud Lights and the $5 bags of oversalted peanuts, all but ignored though lines stretched everywhere else, there sat a lonesome little booth that marked the end of my journey.

Called Parm, it was a creation of the team behind Little Italy's Torrisi Italian Specialties. The booth looked like any other in the hall, except that if you looked closely, there was an Old World-style display of ricotta-cheese containers and cans of tomatoes on its shelves. Parm offered two sandwiches—meatball parmigiana, and sliced turkey, shredded lettuce, and hot vinegar peppers, both on fresh sesame seed rolls.

I climbed to my seat behind the right-field foul pole. I unwrapped my sandwiches as the national anthem came to a close. Neither was an especially ambitious sandwich—not a slice of hand-cured, kimchi-flavored Kurobuta bacon or hint of reverse spherification to be found. But the lettuce was crisp, the peppers sharp and hot, the turkey fresh. The meatball was light and pillowy, with the funky flavor of real beef. And now the team took the field. And now I took a deep bite of first one sandwich, then the other. And now the umpire took his place behind the catcher; now the pitcher set to throw. And as the crowd rose up, my heart swelled, or maybe it was just my belly. Here on this picture-perfect summer evening. Under the arc lights. America.

The End of Anonymity

By Bethany Jean Clement

From *Seattle Arts & Performance*

As managing editor and food critic for Seattle's alternative weekly *The Stranger*, Bethany Jean Clement is deeply connected to one of America's most vibrant food scenes. In this essay, she asks the million-dollar question: How objective can—or should—a critic really be?

Long ago, in a time before Facebook, anonymous restaurant reviewers roamed the earth. In order to experience restaurants just like anybody else—no special treatment—they telephoned from blocked numbers and made reservations under names that were not their own. They lumbered in as any other diner would, assessing astutely yet nonchalantly the performance of the coat-check girl, the host, the bringers of water, and the offerings of wine; the service was scrutinized while maintaining an entirely pococurante front. Some were rumored to whisper into primitive recording devices hidden in their sleeves. Others relied on memory or on the appearance of a weak bladder, ducking repeatedly into the restroom to scribble notes. And the food appeared on the plate, and it was eaten, and it was paid for in cash or with a credit card under an alias.

In the jungle of New York City, where the *New York Times* reviewer could single-handedly render a restaurant extinct, the burden of remaining unidentified was more serious still. Ruth Reichl famously chronicled her efforts in that role in her 2005 memoir, *Garlic and Sapphires.* She went to an acting coach, acquired a wardrobe of wigs, and dressed as a number of specific characters. She enjoyed an unlimited budget and never visited a restaurant fewer than three times—

generally more—always anonymously. She wrote, "You know what it's like when I'm not in disguise: The steaks get bigger, the food comes faster, and the seats become more comfortable." The presence of a known critic could change the very composition of the furniture—this was serious business. If one needed to wear a mustache, so be it.

But, as Bill Keller noted in the *New York Times* in 2009, "despite all her theatrical dress-ups," Ruth Reichl "was often made by the maître d'hôtel." (One might also imagine that she was sometimes recognized *because* of her costumes—e.g., "Who is that lady in the crazy-looking wig on table 12?") Keller also said that despite subsequent critic Frank Bruni's less dramatic attempts to stay undercover, he'd dined with Bruni "in places where it was clear—from the trying-too-hard service, or the clusters of whispering waiters, or some other tell—that they were on to us." People being "made," the "tell"—it was an undertaking of film noir, and as doomed from the start. When Sam Sifton took the *NYT* reviewer post in 2009, he'd held other posts at the paper; while his photo was removed from the website, it was way too late. Gawker posted Sifton photoshopped into proposed disguises—Harry Potter, Frank Bruni, "that partying dude from Australia." Keller said Sifton would arrive unannounced to review, and noted that "a reviewer's own experience can be cross-checked with intelligence from others. So, while we don't intend to put Sam's face on sides of MTA buses, I'm not going to lose a lot of sleep over this."

Here in Seattle, Nancy Leson—the most powerful person in the industry as the reviewer for the *Seattle Times* for almost a decade—only abdicated her anonymity in 2008, with a "coming out party" revealing her identity on the front page of the food section. The official restaurant-reviewer title was passed on, and Leson became a blogger, excited at the new world open to her "doing in-person interviews with chefs and restaurateurs and getting out to the food and wine events I've long shied away from."

But from the start, Leson's cloak of invisibility had some unavoidable holes. She'd worked waiting tables for 17 years, five of them in Seattle, before she got her journalism degree; as she said in a column in 2000, she was "occasionally 'outed' by friends still in the trade." She was also a freelance writer in the beginning, attending food media events and interviewing chefs in person before anonymity was ever in the offing. She made efforts to stay anonymous, but, she wrote, "many of the city's high-profile chefs and restaurateurs could pick me out of a lineup," and as she acknowledged in print, she was known at favorite places like Marco's Supperclub and Le Pichet. During the 2000 *Seattle P-I/Times* strike, she told me recently, she waited tables at Nell's in Green Lake for a weekend, just for fun, unpaid. Also working there at the time, in the kitchen: Ethan Stowell, now of his own local restaurant empire.

In 2005, when I was a freelance writer, *The Stranger* asked me to interview a Seattle chef about (presciently!) street food. I chose Ethan Stowell. He owned a restaurant downtown called Union that was about as far from street food as you could get. From across the counter of the pass in the swanky, palatial space, he told me he had a thing for the mobile snack-stands of Mexico: "Oysters that have been sitting out for three hours in the sun, the tacos made in a big cast iron bucket on wheels—most people don't eat it, but I do." I'd written a few restaurant reviews, but it seemed silly to be concerned about anonymity—this guy only owned one restaurant, after all, and *The Stranger* had already reviewed it, and what was the big deal with restaurant reviewers being anonymous anyway? It didn't make sense to me, while talking to a chef at his fancy restaurant about his enthusiasm for eating quantities of shrimp from street carts in Mazatlan—that made sense, and that wasn't something that would be the same over the telephone.

Then there was the little problem that Seattle is the size of the head of a pin. Even before everyone's everything was all over the internet, unless you lived under a rock, you could not hide. In 2006, I happened to be sitting at the bar at the Hideout with a friend, and I let my attention drift away up among all the weird and marvelous art on the walls, helped along by a nice cold martini. I reentered reality when my friend sitting next to me said, "That's funny—my friend Bethany writes about restaurants!" Then she leaned back and indicated the man on the next bar stool down: "This is Matt—he just opened a restaurant on Eastlake!" And there was Matt Dillon, the chef/owner of a brand-new place called Sitka & Spruce, before he became one of *Food & Wine*'s 10 best new chefs (2007), opened the Corson Building (2008), and won a James Beard Award for Best Chef Northwest (2012). He said no offense, but that I wouldn't be getting any special treatment if I came in—he cooked for people like he was cooking for friends at his house, which sounded good to me.

When I went to the original Sitka & Spruce in its tiny strip-mall spot, it was already packed. Matt Dillon said hi, and we waited and waited, standing at the tiny counter, because there were only about six tables. Eventually, he sent us a bowl of clams on the house, which (as I wrote in my review) he probably would've done for any group standing at the bar waiting and waiting and basically chewing on their own arms—or as he would've done for friends at his house. But there were no bigger steaks, or faster food, or magically more cushiony chairs. There was just the adorable space, and the sharing (and some hoarding) of plates, and his really wonderful—as in, inspiring moments of wonder—food.

There's not a lot a restaurant can do to significantly improve a critic's experience—either they've got it together or they don't. For *The Stranger*'s reviews, I arrive unannounced, visit with a guest (almost always) twice, and am reimbursed by the paper. Are they going to come out and grate truffles over my head? That would be noticeable—and so, ultimately, are bigger steaks or better service, which can, in fact, be cross-checked with others' experiences. (If online review sites can be useful, it's in gleaning a very general sense of such things from very careful reading.) And restaurants are never going to be able to inject a sense of wonder where there isn't any.

Over the years, I've occasionally accepted invitations to media dinners or events out of (sometimes morbid) curiosity, as well as to investigate places that otherwise would tax *The Stranger*'s definitely not-unlimited budget. When I accept such invitations, that is acknowledged in any writing that might come of it—e.g., the 2010 article "This Is Not a Review of Sullivan's Steakhouse," describing the absurdly lavish "VIP" party that the Texas chain threw itself when it opened downtown. This party had a red carpet, multiple open bars, multiple live bands, oceans of people as dressed up as they get in Seattle, and mini steak sandwiches and crab legs and itty-bitty quiches and etc.—all perfectly tasty, if not at all outstanding. The service was as good as giant-party service gets; they forced a glass of bubbly on you at the very threshold, and if you were too lazy to make your way through the crowd, trays with more drinks and piles of hors d'oeuvres, carried by smiling and attractive people, would find their way to you.

But sometimes even if a restaurant knows a critic is there—even if they know she's coming ahead of time, if *they invited her*—still, they flounder mightily. In 2007, I was invited to dine at Troiani, a cavernous expense-account restaurant downtown. This dinner fell into the morbid-curiosity category; the place had been there for quite a while, and it was run by the same people as the beloved El Gaucho steakhouses, and yet one never heard anything about it at all. It was also the kind of place *The Stranger* would probably never review, even if it were new, which it very much wasn't. The restaurant was empty in a way that felt windswept; you wouldn't have been surprised to see tumbleweeds blowing between the well-spaced tables. Marooned in the far reaches of the place, we glimpsed staff occasionally in the distance. They never managed to bring us a bottle of sparkling water we wanted, and when we ordered a Caesar salad that was to be mixed tableside, there was an unnervingly long delay. Finally, a guy wheeled a cart up to our table, confessed that he'd never done this before and that no one else was there who had, mixed the salad in a way that made you want to get up and help him, and then said he was going to have a smoke. I wish I could say that this is completely atypical of Seattle restaurants' A-game; I cannot. I felt so bad for the salad-mixer and the emptiness, I never wrote anything about it at all. Troiani closed down in 2009.

Selfishly, not being anonymous as a food writer has meant doing much more interesting things. Before Matt Dillon opened the Corson Building, his lovely oasis in Georgetown, he let me poke around the property; I got to see the 1910 building when it was still dilapidated, before the meat-curing room and new kitchen were built, when the foliage was rampant and there was a rusty bedstead instead of raised beds. (Later, I also jotted a few things down during a many-coursed dinner there, eventually causing the woman sitting next to me at the communal table to confess that her name was not actually Barbara and that she was a restaurant reviewer, too. She joked about borrowing my notes.) At events like Gabriel Claycamp's 2008 "Sacrificio" in Port Orchard—the sacrificed one being a pig, killed in front of, then butchered and eaten with the help of, a paying crowd—it just seemed bizarre to be all cloak-and-dagger about it. To talk to Claycamp and the other attendees with transparency about my role seemed only respectful. (I am pretty sure that another food writer, seeming awkward and introducing himself as Del, was there.) At Burning Beast, held for the fifth year this summer, you've got a dozen or more of Seattle's best chefs sweating over open fire pits in an idyllic field; are you going to pretend you're just an especially curious bystander, one who likes to write things down, and then make up a name when they want to shake your hand? Will they treat you so differently back at their restaurants in Seattle that you will be unable to assess whether the place is any good or not?

For a restaurant reviewer to eat what's on their plate in the shadow of their wig, then hand down a verdict in an airless vacuum seems strange when meeting the people involved gives insight into their ethos, their interconnections, even our city as a whole. I interviewed about a dozen local chefs and food writers and cheese-shop owners between 2009 and 2012 for the magazine *Edible Seattle*—interviews at their homes, in which I documented (among other things) the contents of their refrigerators. Ethan Stowell had half a sandwich from Subway. ("It's a bad sandwich—I'm not gonna lie to you," he said. "It's not a good sandwich. It's only five bucks, though.") Zephyr Paquette had a bomb-shelter's worth of home-canned goods, a dog that loved carrots, and a slingshot she was using to shoot corks at the squirrels ravaging her vegetable garden. (Having invaded her home, it was not easy to write later that I did not love the food at her new restaurant, Skelly and the Bean, which closed after less than a year, but it did help me understand the community that helped her build it, and why people like her so very much.)

For another *Edible Seattle* interview, I visited Kim Ricketts, a force of nature who'd put Seattle on the map in terms of food-oriented book events, doing 100-plus dinners and parties and readings with the likes of Anthony Bourdain, Michael Pollan, Patricia Wells, Thomas Keller, Jerry Traunfeld, Greg Atkinson, and Langdon Cook. Her home was as if Martha Stewart actually had good taste; she made baked feta rubbed with oregano, and we drank a lot of wine, and she called the owner of Whole Foods crazy and lightly disparaged the University Book Store and said a lot of stuff no one else ever would. Her husband and one of her kids eventually joined us, sitting around by the fire. For yet another of these interviews, Christina Choi of Nettletown and I sat out on the deck of her Eastlake apartment, talking about growing up in Seattle and her wild-food-gathering days with Foraged & Found and all sorts of things. She'd done a photo shoot for *Seattle Metropolitan* earlier that day, and she insisted I stay for dinner to eat the gorgeous photo-shoot coho salmon with a motley crew of people she maybe only half-knew—an architect who'd made the most beautiful meringues ever seen outside a bakery, a woman who talked about a past job nannying for a very, very rich family during which she'd drugged the children to calm them down (at which only Christina and I looked askance).

Both Kim Ricketts and Christina Choi have since passed away. I was so lucky to get to know them, even just a little—they each had the ability to, in one afternoon, make you feel like part of their family. How could anonymity compare to that?

Tyranny: It's What's for Dinner

By Corby Kummer

From *The Atlantic*

In the three-plus decades that senior editor Corby Kummer has been with *The Atlantic*—earning a slew of writing awards and accolades along the way—he has seen plenty of dining trends come and go. So what's different about this one?

"Dinner? I'm afraid we can't serve you dinner," the waiter at Charlie Trotter's said starchily as we arrived at the celebrated Chicago restaurant. For 25 years, people made special trips from all over the country to brag about the dozens of courses Trotter served on his ever-shifting tasting menus. But as other chefs became more celebrated, the traffic slowed, and Trotter—the first American celebrity chef to build a cult following for elaborate, very long, take-what-I-give-you meals—announced he would be closing for good.

I'd never been to Charlie Trotter's and called the restaurant to ask when in the next six weeks or so they could possibly seat us. After a long time on hold, the man on the phone told me they could fit me in at 5:30 on a distant Friday. We booked our flight, invited Chicago friends who had likewise never been to the restaurant, landed on time, and then were stopped on the runway to wait out a freak thunderstorm—a storm that lasted two full hours, during which we anxiously texted our waiting friends to keep the table.

Keep it they did—but they also, at the restaurant's insistence, ate their way through the eight-course tasting menu. For us, the waiter pronounced when we finally got there, it would be the dessert courses. Or nothing. After a good bit of protestation, the maître d' agreed that we could be served the full meal—at a forced-march pace, all eight appetizers and main courses plus two preliminary and two post-dessert "complimentary" courses. It turned out to be a mercy: we were able to get out in just under three hours.

Mercy is a rare commodity at restaurants like this, where the diner is essentially strapped into a chair and expected to be enraptured for a minimum of three and often four and five hours, and to consume dozens of dishes. Choice, changes, selective omissions—control, really, over any part of an inevitably very expensive experience—are not an option. Course after course after course comes to the table at a pace that is "measured, relentless," as the former *New York Times* restaurant critic Sam Sifton wrote (admiringly!) of Blanca, the latest tasting-menu-only cult restaurant in New York.

When Trotter began, chefs were just breaking out of their backstage supporting roles and putting themselves on display—often literally, in open kitchens. He helped unleash a generation of chefs no longer willing to take orders. The entire experience they will consent to offer is meant to display the virtuosity not of cooks but of culinary artists. A diner's pleasure is secondary; subjugation to the will of the creative genius comes first, followed, eventually, by stultified stupefaction. The animating force radiates outward from the kitchen, with no real chance of countervailing force from the table. The chef sets the rules; the diner (together with the cowed serving staff) obeys. The reason we were initially denied dinner at Trotter's, we later learned, was that it didn't suit the cooks to have us start late. They were making all the courses for all the tables at exactly the same time, and didn't want to break their lockstep pace to accommodate the inconvenient exigencies of customers.

How did the diner get demoted from honored guest whose wish was the waiter's command to quivering hostage in thrall to the chef's iron whim? I found clues in the signed menus on the walls of the guest bathrooms at Trotter's—a history of revered restaurants of the past 25 years, almost all of them in France, the menus inscribed affectionately to Trotter. Paul Bocuse, Frédy Girardet, Michel Guérard, Marc Veyrat—these were the kings of nouvelle cuisine, champions of the techniques of classic cooking married to rigorously seasonal and local ingredients, and lightened to create a supremely elegant dining experience. Many of the menus were degustations, or tasting menus—but tasting menus that were modest in their ambitions. They listed four, five, maybe six courses.

The model Trotter emulated was honorable. Many French chefs built their reputations by naming their restaurants for themselves; they kept control by owning their own places, with the husband running the kitchen and the wife running the dining room and keeping the books—a mom-and-pop model that in this country had been the province of mostly diners and simple spots. In big American cities, financial control of luxury restaurants was in the hands of the manager, who set the tone and attracted the customers. Chefs were employees—invisible and, in the case of the fast-food franchises that began to dominate the American landscape in the 1950s, irrelevant. Even in what many gourmets considered New York City's, if not the country's, best restaurant, Lutèce, the chef-owner, André Soltner, didn't put his name on the door and was famously modest. Nouvelle cuisine brought international media attention to its pioneers, whose names were worth big consulting and franchising fees at Asian—and American—luxury hotels.

Trotter, logically, wanted in on that action. He put his name on the door. He owned his name and his premises. But to that sound, relatively restrained French model he applied a peculiarly American, boosterish, Rotarian spirit. If French chefs made brief handshaking rounds at the end of the meal, Trotter would be more visible than his own maître d', glad-handing everybody in the room and making the chance to be in his presence for the entire meal—a "chef's table" in the previously off-limits kitchen—the hardest reservation in town and, for a while, the country.

Much of this could be explained away as an American form of entrepreneurialism. Trotter's name would be synonymous with the very best: he built a wine cellar with the biggest-name, highest-priced vintages from France, Italy, Germany, and California. He pushed the meticulousness of nouvelle cuisine chefs to a kind of technique-obsessed extreme, making plates as precious as they were pretty. In the most dangerous entrepreneurial touch of all, he took a tire pump to the usual nightly French degustation. If 5 or 6 courses were good, why not 10? Or 12? Or more? He might as well have put gigantic tail fins and hood ornaments on the plates.

Trotter was also a press hound—a relentless self-promoter with a ravenous hunger for fame. Anthony Bourdain has called him the country's first celebrity chef. He may have meant that as praise. In fact, it was the beginning of what can be considered a dining disaster: taking the underside of the French system—the fierce discipline, the screaming in the kitchen—way too far, making a virtue of the red-faced, toque-wearing, will-breaking drill sergeant. Trotter's notorious outbursts in fact led many apprentices to quit his kitchen.

Overboard as his behavior may have been, Trotter paved the way for reality TV, in which hair-trigger eruptions and chef-imposed meltdowns are a gladiator sport. This abuse, long an open secret in French kitchens, spilled over into dining rooms and became a blood sport diners wanted a taste of. The irony is that Trotter, who made Gordon Ramsay's profane and public tantrums possible, was too early to benefit from the television celebrity he likely craved. (The restaurant closed at the end of last August.) But he did leave a lasting legacy: his totalitarian style has become, in many restaurants, the norm. And recently it is enjoying a resurgence.

Unconditional Surrender

The most telling echo of the kind of rampant ego Trotter set in motion in this country was a framed Catalonian menu in a guest bathroom dated 1998: it was from El Bulli and signed by its chef, Ferran Adrià. Starting in the mid-1990s, every ambitious diner had to take a plane and snare a reservation—often in that order, the bleary traveler throwing himself on the maître d's mercy for a cancellation—at two places: El Bulli, a notoriously difficult two-hour drive north of Barcelona, and the French Laundry, a far easier drive from San Francisco to the wine country of Napa Valley. The cuisines at the two restaurants differed in important ways. Thomas Keller, the chef at the French Laundry, was rigorously trained in French technique and incorporated the best of California's artisan food producers into his heavily French, generally heavy (because butter-laden) dishes. Ferran Adrià began as a cook of relatively rustic Catalonian cuisine. But he started experimenting with new techniques and processes that had been the province of the food industry, creating disorienting novelties that acquired a name that he never liked but will forever be associated with: "molecular gastronomy." Adrià wrested the crown of the world's most influential cuisine away from the French and became the chef ambitious cooks had to work for—even knowing that they would be treated like slaves by an exploitative overseer, as Lisa Abend documents in her entertaining book, *The Sorcerer's Apprentices.*

The two restaurants shared something important, though: they extended a typical meal to hitherto unknown numbers of courses—50 at El Bulli, 40 or more at the French Laundry. They didn't give you a choice of what you ate. Adrià and Keller might have begun with similar ambitions: to startle and delight the diner. Adrià wanted to push the sensory experience beyond where it had ever gone, disguising food so that deliberately disoriented diners had to work to recognize a flavor—making hot things cold, soft things hard, solid things powder or air (or, horribly because the technique became ubiquitous, foam). Keller said he was merely overcoming his own palate fatigue, in which his concentration and pleasure eating a dish dropped precipitously after two or three bites. But Adrià and Keller's lasting contribution to the world of restaurants was to shift the balance of power from diner to chef. They demanded unconditional surrender.

I was present at a French Laundry dinner convened by Phyllis Richman, then the restaurant critic of *The Washington Post,* in 1997. The meal became famous because a friend Richman had invited, Ruth Reichl, scooped Richman by quickly writing a column in *The New York Times* declaring the French Laundry to be "the most exciting place to eat in the United States." Richman said that it was "as good as a restaurant gets in this country, maybe as good as a restaurant gets anywhere." I later went back and spent several days and nights in the kitchen to write about Keller.

Besides being impressed by much of the food, though, what we all remembered from that famous dinner was trying to stay awake until long after 1 a.m., when the meal that had begun in the garden at about 8:30—with the signature ice-cream cone of salmon tartare in a savory *tuile* (it became as much a cliché as Adrià's foams)—was drawing to an end. Or so we fervently prayed. The intent was to dazzle, and indeed any tenth of one of these 40-course meals would have dazzled. At the chef-commanded full length, the meal felt like a form of torture.

Could that sort of long, by necessity leisurely meal translate from the flagstone garden of the French Laundry, planted with rosemary and roses, to the sterile mall of the Time Warner Center, in the heart of New York City? Keller opened Per Se in 2004 to immediate rave reviews. But with the taxis of Central Park South flashing their headlights through the restaurant's floor-to-ceiling windows, a very long tasting menu seems endless merely midway through, when thoughts inevitably turn to unanswered e-mails and meetings the next morning. Even people who are willing to sit at the French Laundry for four or five hours, and who find any excuse to wedge in mentions of their dinners at El Bulli, told me they didn't have the patience for Per Se—that what seemed charming in wine country was pompous and overblown in Manhattan. And expensive: with wine, it's hard to get out of Per Se for under $400 a person.

Yet its three Michelin stars and four stars from two *New York Times* reviewers keep Per Se busy—mostly with tourists, who don't have to worry about work the next day and are the only people who can think about sitting through a nine-course lunch. (The restaurant recently added its version of an express lunch, five courses, which makes almost as little sense to a New Yorker.)

When I dined at Per Se recently, the differences from my visits to the French Laundry were notable. There was no one at the check stand to greet me—no visible staff members in the large entry area and bar at all, despite my arriving at the hour of my reservation. If there were New Yorkers in the room, the life had drained out of them. The atmosphere was quiet, reverent, even somnolent. The contrast that makes the French Laundry memorable, with very correct waiters and formal service in a California-casual context, doesn't apply, so the brown-and-beige room just seems cool and somber. The waiter was friendly and relatively informal, but the sommelier was indifferent and condescending to a young French guest who happened to know a good deal about wine and later pronounced himself shocked at the obviousness of the wine choices—for instance, sweet Sauternes paired with foie gras. The parade of gastronomic giveaways before and after dinner seemed shorter and less oppressive than I remembered from California. Nonetheless, when course after course keeps arriving and demands an explanation from the server, genuine or meaningful exchange with one's fellow guests is not a possibility. The focus must be squarely on the food, not the company.

As at Per Se's fellow three-Michelin-star restaurants, technique and precision are what count—not freshness or spontaneity.

Some Per Se dishes did register strongly, not just for the ramrod-straight technique that underpins them all but for the sheer elegance of conception and flavor. Roast lamb with delicate green almonds and intensely flavored cauliflower cream was a triumph, one that will be a taste-memory benchmark. So was the burst of fresh sweet-tart flavor in a gooseberry sorbet with elderberry foam over a toasted corn cake. Impossibly thin and translucent ribbons of cucumber carefully draped over a plate; little green strawberries and sweet melon squares compressed via *sous vide*, a Keller specialty, to give them gem-like tones; squares of pumpernickel also compressed into paper-thin sheets for tiny sandwiches layered like Viennese tortes—much of the food is exquisite.

But exquisite is different from remarkable or transporting. And exquisite can also seem tormented, like so many French gardens. Another guest raised partly in Paris was scandalized by the number of courses: "How is it possible," she asked before the numerous dessert courses arrived, "to eat this much without feeling . . . heavy?" Seen through French eyes, what began as an earnest re-creation of a French model looked like it had passed through Disney World with a stop at Mount Rushmore.

The Apprentices

The counterparts of Adrià and Keller 15 years later are Rene Redzepi and Grant Achatz, who both indentured in Adrià's kitchen—in, as it happens, the same year, 2000. Redzepi, whose Muslim immigrant father met his Danish mother when they were working at the same Copenhagen cafeteria, returned from his time at El Bulli with the idea of overthrowing the Mediterranean ingredients that had world cuisine in a choke hold. So he went foraging in the Scandinavian woods and meadows, and on the Icelandic tundra, for herbs, plants, and wildlife of all kinds to use in ways both traditional and inventive (his latest love is ants). Achatz had been sent to El Bulli by Keller, his mentor—he worked his way up to being sous-chef at the French Laundry (he was in the kitchen the night of my seminal dinner there), and named one of his two sons Keller—and returned with the idea of pushing industrial techniques and ingredients even farther than Adrià had. But he brought to them a stronger sense of design and restraint, and a stronger rooting in French cuisine and technique from his training with Keller. The two apprentices also returned from El Bulli with the philosophy that the chef decides the day's multi-course menu, and the diner gets that, period.

Ten years later, Redzepi's Copenhagen restaurant, Noma, took from El Bulli the title of "world's best restaurant" in a poll of about 900 chefs, restaurateurs, and critics from around the world run by the British magazine *Restaurant.* Noma has kept that title for three years running, just as El Bulli kept it for the previous four years. (In 2003–4, the French Laundry held it.) The list is frequently criticized—most loudly by chefs whose rankings have dropped or who haven't yet made the list—as corrupt and promotional, but it does make people get on airplanes. And now that Adrià has closed the money-losing El Bulli to run a food-research lab and cash in on consulting contracts with the food industry, Noma is the impossible international plat (or rather plats) du jour.

I never made the pilgrimage to El Bulli and never wanted to, having been in Adrià's papal presence on too many occasions. But eating at Noma recently, I felt everything that diners at El Bulli reported in its glory days (and was certain I wouldn't have felt had I gone): the thrill of the new, one spectacularly good dish after another presented in thrillingly fast succession. El Bulli–style whimsy was on the menu: for instance, little flowerpots with baby turnips and carrots embedded in "edible soil" made with malt, hazelnut, and other flours, and butter. El Bulli–style disorientation and surrealism bordering on the sadistic (blood-red meat, raw-looking organs really made of high-tech Play-Doh) were not. But neither was choice.

Achatz's Chicago restaurant Alinea was named the best restaurant in America by *Gourmet* a year after it opened, in 2005. A second restaurant Achatz opened in Chicago last year, Next, sells reservations like theater tickets—pay everything when you book, use it or lose it—in three-month blocks, to coincide with changes in themed menus. After watching all of his Next tickets for an entire year sell out in minutes—at a cost of up to $300 with wine pairings, but much higher when scalped—Achatz and his business partner put seats at Alinea on the same sales system.

This ticketing regime can be seen as the ultimate power grab by a chef: the diner is, like a theatergoer, a passive participant in a spectacle he can either like or lump. It's a dream come true for young chefs on tight budgets, to control food costs and be able to collect revenue. It's less dreamy for diners who stubbornly cling to the antique idea of booking a table when it is convenient for them, not for the restaurant, and persist in hoping they won't lose the price of a meal if they need to reschedule.

In Manhattan, at Eleven Madison Park, the four-star successor to Per Se for the mantle of most fought-over chance to spend a lot of money on a meal someone else decrees, the Swiss-born Daniel Humm has acquired a local reputation as exalted as Keller's. Oddly, I found the cuisine itself a half-thought-through version of the kind of high-style, high-tech experimentation Achatz and Keller and others engage in, with immaculate technique but wan flavors and a use of technology that seemed gimmicky rather than creative.

This became worse when Humm changed from a tasting menu with a 4-or 8-course option to a single 15-course menu at both lunch and dinner, supposedly redefining New York City cuisine with elaborate takes on either locally grown foods or dishes associated with the city. Slices of sturgeon were presented in a giant glass cloche swirling with menacing white smoke from applewood charcoal. "Don't lift the glass," the server warned as she set it down—but later admitted that the fish had been pre-smoked and the show was in fact just for show. The harsh last-minute smoke did lend an urban flavor—as if the fish had come off a New York trash fire. Another server clamped a meat grinder to the side of the table and put into it a long, fat, bright orange carrot with bright greens attached by a tightly wound yellow elastic band. He tried to deny that the ponytail of greens had been re-attached until he admitted that the carrot, which went through the grinder with suspicious ease, had been simmered with olive oil and salt. This was a version of the steak tartare that, his rehearsed patter informed us with sweeping inaccuracy, every New York steakhouse in the 50s and 60s like Delmonico's (which closed in 1923) and the Four Seasons (which opened in 1959) would serve when you came through the door. He put the bright, insipid gratings onto a wooden plate with a dozen or so shallow indentations filled with seasonings for you to mix in at will—an inferior mash-up of the famous Noma egg you fry and stir yourself, and the long fat Noma ash-roasted 24-hour carrot that comes to the table looking like a revolting stick of charcoal but reveals a marvelously sweet, custard-like texture and flavor.

The servers had no sense of whimsy or humor about a menu that depends on humor: they almost ran away when we asked for a wine list, and generally seemed terrorized at being overly garrulous, as the estimable restaurant critic Pete Wells had accused them of being in a *New York Times* "Critic's Notebook" that ran immediately after the menu change. You need to like them, and your guests, to endure the meal: we arrived at 1:00 and were not served our last course until a bit before 5:30. At 4:00, a server disconcertingly began visiting every empty table with a white steam iron, to smooth the tablecloths, and by the time we had paid the check, at 6:00, the tables had begun to fill for dinner.

Worse than bad—which most courses weren't, really—the meal was tedious. Certainly, surprise and delight and originality shouldn't be banished. But in meals this long and ambitious you hope to see the soul of the chef—as you do with Keller and Achatz. In only two of the many courses at Eleven Madison Park did I think I saw Humm's: a seafood stew with bits of bay scallop and apple in a sea urchin and squid custard, subtle, simple, and silken; and an elaborately presented, many-days'-process roast duck served with a dish of fantastically clear and intense consommé, both of them strictly bourgeois and rooted in French technique. Both were food to dream of eating again, food that only someone with Humm's training, background, and staff can produce. True, if chefs don't continually re-invent themselves, their food—especially if they traffic in trendy technology—threatens to look as dated as Trotter's nouvelle cuisine. But as one chef or another seizes the international culinary imagination, Humm seems to be re-inventing himself to chase trends, something he's too talented to do.

The trouble is, chefs don't look to be re-inventing themselves as people willing to cede any control to their customers. Young chefs everywhere are adopting the tasting menu as a way to show off and control costs at the same time—and to signify their ambitions. Few follow the one laudable exception I know: that of Dan Barber, the visionary chef-owner of Blue Hill at Stone Barns, an experimental farm and research center on the lavish Rockefeller estate in Westchester. Some years ago he changed to a tasting menu because, he recently told me, "our menu is dictated by what comes in from the farm in the morning. I don't think people realize that not having a menu here isn't a gimmick. Farmers aren't responding to my menu requests. They're leading the dance. Always."

And fewer still have the talent or artistic vision to sustain a long tasting menu. Trying a diner's patience, though, is an achievement that even a mediocre chef can aspire to. In Somerville, near Boston, the young, self-taught owners of a restaurant called Journeyman made tasting-only menus a part of their business plan, along with the usual local/seasonal/carted-from-the-farm-or-raised-in-our-window-boxes ingredients. When I dined there last year, the inflexibility of the dour, dogmatic servers would have been comical had it not been so infuriating. As more and more restaurants adopt this model, tasting-only menus will empower formerly well-meaning, eager-to-please cooks and servers to become petty despots, and more and more diners will discover that absolute power irritates absolutely.

Service for All!

Even as a new army of fresh-faced Stalins prepares to spread tyranny across the land, at recent dinners at Noma, Next, and even Eleven Madison Park, I saw the seeds of, if not democracy, then perhaps a limited attempt at *glasnost.*

At Noma, the diner feels desired and attended to, in a way that comes across as collegial, not obsequious or didactic. A main reason is that Redzepi sends aproned, working cooks to the table bearing dishes. They'll explain as much or as little as you like about what they give you. They make you feel a part of the action, not just the passive subject of it. At the Sicilian-themed dinner I got tickets for at Next, I saw similar glimmerings of a kind of warmth that has never figured in the severely gray-and-white Alinea. To be sure, there were some eye-roll-inducing touches, like the earnest, handwritten notes to each table signed by the chef and the waiters explaining the philosophy of the meal (dictatorships thrive on theoretical manifestos).

But, shocking from a chef whose presentations have been manicured and tweezed, there were also dishes served family-style and looking positively sloppy. It felt a bit forced, like a seersucker-and-bow-tied dandy putting on a dirty T-shirt and torn jeans. But I was heartened by the effort.

As for Eleven Madison Park, it comes across as less forced than Per Se. This is because of its origins as a restaurant in the empire of Danny Meyer, whose Union Square Hospitality Group has democratized service in luxury restaurants much as the Four Seasons did in luxury hotels. Humm also added the Noma-like touch of sending aproned cooks to the tables, and he himself makes the rounds of tables at every meal.

How far will this as yet very modest evolution go? A lot farther, we can hope. No one wants a return to the reign of the smirking, tip-taking, tyrannical headwaiter, who indeed put the needs of the diner first (the needs of the richest and most famous ones, at any rate)—an era defined by Henri Soulé, of Le Pavillon in the 50s and 60s, and Sirio Maccioni, of Le Cirque in the 80s and 90s. Obsequiousness is seldom far from its twin, contempt. But, ah, how nice it would be if at the world's most celebrated restaurants we could get back to the point where the paying customer picks what and how much she or he eats, guided by helpful but not overbearing suggestions as to what a diner might enjoy most.

Could it be that France, the culinary Forgotten Man, the birthplace of haughtiness, will show us the way forward? I recently came upon two signs it could be trying to fight its way back from the unaccustomed gastronomic shadows by adopting an even more unaccustomed humility. One was a radio interview with Jacques Pépin, the masterly, ebullient, encyclopedic teacher and writer on French food in America, who corrected the host when she asked about the chef as artist. "I never equate a great artist with a great chef," he said with unexpected vehemence. "Food is taste," not art. "A great chef is still an artisan." And in an interview with the *Financial Times,* the Michelin-starred, much-admired Parisian chef Alain Passard replied to a question about whether the customer is always right by saying, "Yes, always. I am there to serve others' commands, and I always do what I am asked to do. I put aside my own concerns when faced with a client who orders a dish cooked a certain way or asks for a certain seasoning."

Pépin and Passard are not quite waving the bloody banner and crying, "To the barricades!" But if they did, a hungry mob with knives and forks would be right behind.

Is Seasonal Eating Overrated?

By Katherine Wheelock

From *Food & Wine*

Food and fashion—and the blurry line between them—are feature writer Katherine Wheelock's main subjects. She has also earned food hipster cred by working at the urban-farm-cum-pizzeria Roberta's in Bushwick, Brooklyn, and is a co-author of the new *Roberta's Cookbook*.

For a couple of weeks last winter, I went on a kale-eating spree. I didn't do this on purpose, exactly. I was making my way through a list of newish New York restaurants I wanted to try, or to revisit because fall had surrendered to winter and I knew their menus would have changed. Most of these places had Dickensian names, names broken by ampersands, or names that sounded like old Vermont family farms. Many had menus freshly jotted on chalkboards, the provenance of the main ingredient in each dish noted. And every last one of them was serving a kale salad. Not long into my dining tour, right around the time I confronted a version with apple and dry Jack at a restaurant a block away from where I'd just had a version with apple and cheddar, I began to regard kale salad the way, as a kid, I viewed my mom's second flounder dinner in the same week: with resentment.

My spree came to an end at a perfectly lovely, smart young Italian restaurant in Brooklyn. It's not that I was looking forward to *carciofi*—I knew not to expect out-of-season artichokes at a place known for its market-driven menu. But I didn't expect to be offered a kale salad. I felt betrayed, sitting there on my stool clutching a season-befitting quince cocktail. I felt like a road warrior so disoriented by sameness, I didn't know what hotel I was in anymore, never mind what city.

What followed my kale bender, as often does benders, was a mild depression. What's wrong with me? I thought. Of all the things to complain about, I was criticizing chefs for systematically removing stringy asparagus from my winter plate and replacing it with the sweetest, tastiest, most environmentally beneficent produce around. The proliferation of seasonally driven menus, albeit a trend mostly still confined to a certain kind of restaurant in a certain kind of town, promised better dining experiences and a smaller culinary carbon footprint for America—a win-win. Come spring, I could count on more chefs than ever to rain morels, fiddleheads and ramps down on me. And I was dreading it.

"I came back from Rome in the spring of 2004 to a rampapalooza," recalls journalist Frank Bruni, the former restaurant critic for the *New York Times*, reflecting on the early days of seasonal fever. "I remember thinking it was great that chefs were exalting the seasons, but also: Do I need to eat this many ramps?"

I remember those days, too. I was practically braiding ramps into headbands, reveling in Mario Batali's embrace of spring produce, in Dan Barber's more priestly devotion to seasonal ingredients, and in the way powerful tastemakers like these chefs were beginning to alter menus all over New York City. Ramp season—and rhubarb, asparagus and strawberry season—was like Christmas. But then Christmas started coming every day. And even more distressingly, seasonally driven menus began to feel less like a genuine celebration of good ingredients and more like some kind of manifesto. "Ramps speak to a lot of different restaurant vanities right now," Bruni says. "They have become more of an ideological, moral statement than a gustatory one."

To be fair to ramps, they didn't start this trend. The 21st-century seasonal-food movement began four decades ago, when Alice Waters founded Chez Panisse in Berkeley. She established the hallmarks of seasonal cooking: locally grown ingredients, simply prepared. These days, the "simply prepared" part is what many critics of slavishly seasonal menus lament. It's not the zeal for seasonal produce that's the problem, they say; it's the lack of imagination that chefs bring to the task of cooking it.

But the point isn't that a dish has to be complicated to be worthwhile, or that a gratifying restaurant experience requires culinary acrobatics that a home cook could never perform. I've had enough plates of first-of-the-season asparagus kissed with grill heat and olive oil to know that the simplest dishes can have the power of a thunderclap. My problem with seasonal menus is homogeny. It's not knowing where I am and whose food I'm eating. It's feeling like the chef cares more about being in sync with the season—and if I'm being paranoid, the culinary zeitgeist—than he or she cares about creating an original dish, or for that matter, pleasing me.

It's still a question worth asking: Is damnably simple food the problem with all this seasonal cooking? The answer, even on the other side of a kale spree, is no. "It's our job to seek out the best ingredients," says Jason Fox, the chef at Commonwealth in San Francisco. "We can't pat ourselves on the back for that and then not take considered steps to turn those ingredients into something magical." When Fox gets his hands on spring's first ramps, he might whip them into a chilled soup garnished with tempura-ed ramp tops, baby fava beans and a dollop of aioli spiked with Meyer lemon. Seasonal, yes. But also totally inspired.

Feeling less like a fool and an ingrate, I began to look at the bright side again—and it proved, of course, to be a big, beautiful bright side. At Chez Panisse, the chefs continue to unfurl hyper-seasonal menus daily. But fried rabbit with sweet-and-sour onions, currants and broccoli? That doesn't make me tired; that makes me hungry. Even if too many chefs let "seasonal" stand in for "good," there are restaurants in every corner of the country doing ingenious work with the best of what's grown around them: Commis in Oakland, California; Le Pigeon in Portland, Oregon; Lantern in Chapel Hill, North Carolina, to name only a few. The chef at the restaurant I work for in Brooklyn changes his menu regularly, without fanfare. You're not expected to applaud him for noticing that celeriac is in its prime—you are expected to applaud him for thinking to marry it with mascarpone, scallions and Piave.

Fingers crossed, we're in the midst of a significant but finite period in the evolution (or perhaps, more accurately, devolution) of American cuisine, moving back to an era before factory farming and before anytime-anywhere produce was the norm. If so, I expect only more seasonal food to come. I also expect, or at least hope for, a rebalancing. Let a reliance on seasonal produce become a given. Let fearless, pioneering restaurants that apply original ideas and techniques to seasonal produce prosper. And equally important, let stellar restaurants without a seasonal flag fluttering out front continue to thrive. We need them to remind us what going to a restaurant is supposed to be about in the first place: pleasure.

When Sara Jenkins opened her second New York City restaurant, Porsena, last winter, she created a minor stir by declaring that the menu wouldn't be especially seasonal. "I buy not-local asparagus in February," Jenkins told me. "Even in ancient times, food was shipped left, right and center. We get so obsessive about things that we tend to make eating a chore. It's one thing we've never really picked up from Europe—how to take great pleasure in eating."

In that spirit, I resolve to stop thinking of eating a cherry tomato in January as the equivalent of smoking a cigarette inside or telling a politically incorrect joke. And the next time I see a grim-faced soul ingesting what's clearly not his first kale salad of the season, I'll quietly slip him the following recommendation: any month but August, the sliced tomato salad at Peter Luger Steak House in Brooklyn (or any steak house, really). And a bowl of seasonally agnostic spaghetti with clams at Porsena, which is no slave to the farmers' market—only to excellent cooking.

The Terrible Tragedy of the Healthy Eater

By Erica Strauss

From *Northwest Edible Life*

From her flourishing Seattle-area organic garden, former restaurant chef Erica Strauss breezily dishes the dirt about her "suburban homestead" lifestyle (yes, she raises chickens too) on nwedible.com, her popular blog site. Here she has fun with the food world's version of political correctness.

I know you. We have a lot in common. You have been doing some reading and now you are pretty sure everything in the grocery store and your kitchen cupboards is going to kill you.

Before Your Healthy Eating Internet Education:

> I eat pretty healthy. Check it out: whole grain crackers, veggie patties, prawns, broccoli. I am actually pretty into clean eating.

After Your Healthy Eating Internet Education:

> Those crackers—gluten, baby. Gluten is toxic to your intestinal health, I read it on a forum. They should call those crackers Leaky Gut Crisps, that would be more accurate. That veggie burger in the freezer? GMO soy. Basically that's a Monsanto patty. Did you know soybean oil is an insecticide? And those prawns are fish farmed in Vietnamese sewage

> pools. I didn't know about the sewage fish farming when I bought them, though, really I didn't!
>
> The broccoli, though . . . that's ok. I can eat that. Eating that doesn't make me a terrible person, unless . . . oh, shit! That broccoli isn't organic. That means it's covered with endocrine disrupting pesticides that will make my son sprout breasts. As if adolescence isn't awkward enough.
>
> And who pre-cut this broccoli like that? I bet it was some poor Mexican person not making a living wage and being treated as a cog in an industrial broccoli cutting warehouse. So I'm basically supporting slavery if I eat this pre-cut broccoli. Oh my God, it's in a plastic bag too. Which means I am personally responsible for the death of countless endangered seabirds right now.

I hate myself.

Well, shit.

All you want to do is eat a little healthier. Really. Maybe get some of that Activa probiotic yogurt or something. So you look around and start researching what "healthier" means.

That really skinny old scientist dude says anything from an animal will give you cancer. But a super-ripped 60-year-old with a best-selling diet book says eat more butter with your crispy T-Bone and you'll be just fine as long as you stay away from grains. Great abs beat out the PhD so you end up hanging out on a forum where everyone eats green apples and red meat and talks about how functional and badass parkour is.

You learn that basically, if you ignore civilization and Mark Knopfler music, the last 10,000 years of human development has been one big societal and nutritional cock-up and wheat is entirely to blame. What we all need to do is eat like cave-people.

You're hardcore now, so you go way past cave-person. You go all the way to The Inuit Diet™.

Some people say it's a little fringe, but you are committed to live a healthy lifestyle. "Okay," you say, "let's do this shit," as you fry your caribou steak and seal liver in rendered whale blubber. You lose some weight which is good, but it costs $147.99 a pound for frozen seal liver out of the back of an unmarked van at the Canadian border.

Even though The Inuit Diet™ is high in vitamin D, you learn that every disease anywhere can be traced to a lack of vitamin D (you read that on a blog post) so you start to supplement. 5000 IU of vitamin D before sitting in the tanning booth for an hour does wonders for your hair luster.

Maxing out your credit line on seal liver forces you to continue your internet education in healthy eating. As you read more, you begin to understand that grains are fine but before you eat them you must prepare them in the traditional way: by long soaking in the light of a new moon with a mix of mineral water and the strained lacto-fermented tears of a virgin.

You discover that if the women in your family haven't been eating a lot of mussels for at least the last four generations, you are pretty much guaranteed a $6000 orthodontia bill for your snaggle-tooth kid. That's if you are able to conceive at all, which you probably won't, because you ate margarine at least twice when you were 17.

Healthy eating is getting pretty complicated and conflicted at this point but at least everyone agrees you should eat a lot of raw vegetables.

Soon you learn that even vegetables are trying to kill you. Many are completely out unless they are pre-fermented with live cultures in a specialized $79 imported pickling crock. Legumes and nightshades absolutely cause problems. Even fermentation can't make those healthy.

Goodbye, tomatoes. Goodbye green beans. Goodbye all that makes summer food good. Hey, it's hard but you have to eliminate these toxins and anti-nutrients. You probably have a sensitivity. Actually, you almost *positively* have a sensitivity. Restaurants and friends who want to grab lunch with you will just have to deal.

Kale: it's what's for dinner. And lunch. And breakfast.

The only thing you are sure of is kale, until you learn that even when you buy organic, local kale from the store (organic, local kale is the only food you can eat now) it is probably GMO cross-contaminated. Besides, it usually comes rolled in corn starch and fried to make it crunchier. Market research, *dahling* . . . sorry, people like crunchy, cornstarch-breaded Kale-Crispers™ more than actual bunny food.

And by now you've learned that the only thing worse than wheat is corn. Everyone can agree on that, too. Corn is making all of America fat. The whole harvest is turned into ethanol, high fructose corn syrup, chicken feed and corn starch and the only people who benefit from all those corn subsidies are evil companies like Cargill.

Also, people around the world are starving because the U.S. grows too much corn. It doesn't actually make that much sense when you say it like that, but you read it on a blog. And anyway, everyone *does* agree that corn is Satan's grain. Unless wheat is.

The only thing to do, really, when you think about it, is to grow all your own food. That's the only way to get kale that isn't cornstarch dipped. You've read a lot and it is obvious that you can't trust anything, and you can't trust anyone and everything is going to kill you and the only possible solution is to have complete and total control over your foodchain from seed to sandwich.

Not that you actually eat sandwiches.

You have a little panic attack at the idea of a sandwich on commercial bread: GMO wheat, HFCS and chemical-additive dough conditioners. Some people see Jesus in their toast but you know the only faces in that mix of frankenfood grains and commercial preservatives are Insulin Sensitivity Man and his sidekick, Hormonal Disruption Boy.

It's okay, though. You don't need a deli sandwich or a po'boy. You have a saute of Russian Kale and Tuscan Kale and Scotch Kale (because you love international foods). It's delicious. No, really. You cooked the kale in a half-pound of butter that had more raw culture than a black-tie soiree at Le Bernardin.

You round out your meal with a little piece of rabbit that you raised up and butchered out in the backyard. It's dusted with all-natural pink Hawaiian high-mineral sea salt that you cashed-in your kid's college fund to buy and topped with homemade lacto-fermented herb mayonnaise made with coconut oil and lemons from a tropical produce CSA share that helps disadvantaged youth earn money by gleaning urban citrus. The lemons were a bit overripe when they arrived to you, but since they were transported by mountain bike from LA to Seattle in order to keep them carbon neutral, you can hardly complain.

The rabbit is ok. Maybe a bit bland. Right now you will eat meat, but only meat that you personally raise because you saw that PETA thing about industrial beef production and you can't support that. Besides, those cows eat corn. Which is obscene because cows are supposed to eat grass. Ironically, everyone knows that a lawn is a complete waste in a neighborhood–that's where urban gardens should go. In other words, the only good grass is grass that cows are eating. You wonder if your HOA will let you graze a cow in the common area.

In the meantime, you are looking for a farmer who raises beef in a way you *can* support and you have so far visited 14 ranches in the tri-state area. You have burned 476 gallons of gas driving your 17-mpg SUV around to interview farmers but, sadly, have yet to find a ranch where the cattle feed exclusively on organic homegrown kale.

Until you do, you allow yourself a small piece of rabbit once a month. You need to stretch your supply of ethical meat after that terrible incident with the mother rabbit who nursed her kibble and ate her kits. After that, deep down, you aren't really sure you have the stomach for a lot more backyard meat-rabbit raising.

So you eat a lot of homegrown kale for awhile. Your seasoning is mostly self-satisfaction and your drink is mostly fear of all the other food lurking everywhere that is trying to kill you.

Eventually your doctor tells you that the incredible pain you've been experiencing is kidney stones caused by the high oxalic acid in the kale. You are instructed to cut out all dark leafy greens from your diet, including kale, beet greens, spinach, and swiss chard and eat a ton of low-fat dairy.

Your doctor recommends that new healthy yogurt with the probiotics. She thinks it's called Activa.

Slow Cooking, Slow Eating

By Edward Behr

From *The Art of Eating*

Erudite, cosmopolitan, and defiantly non-trendy, Edward Behr's food and wine quarterly *The Art of Eating* has influenced the culinary cognoscenti since 1986. In this essay, he sums up his philosophy in a mini-manifesto about authentic food and an authentic life.

The enjoyment of good food and drink in many countries was once the particular preoccupation of the wealthy right wing, of people who had the time and money to indulge in luxuries. Slow Food, whether the organization or the concept, is grittier. In the United States, for instance, there's an allied new wave of young apprentice farmers and food artisans who have little concern for money. Anyone who follows the news closely these days recognizes food as the highly political topic it always was, from government subsidies to the "externalized" costs of industrial farming (such as water pollution) to the content of school lunches to hunger at home and abroad. Food in all its complexity, including its capacity for deliciousness, is a subject increasingly associated with the left wing.

As the North American interest in food and farms has grown, more people have become familiar with the organization Slow Food, which was started in 1986 by leftwing intellectuals in the gastronomically and vinously rich Italian region of Piedmont. (Right away I have to pause and say that I work with people who do or did work for Slow Food, but I'm not much of a joiner, and a few years ago I let my brief membership lapse.) The immediate cause for starting Slow Food was the opening of the first McDonald's in Italy, near the

Spanish Steps in Rome. A few years later, in 1989, the Slow Food movement went international when delegates from 15 countries met in Paris to sign the Slow Food Manifesto.

This short document is rather wonderful. It says: "We are enslaved by speed and have all succumbed to the same insidious virus: Fast Life, which disrupts our habits, pervades the privacy of our homes, and forces us to eat Fast Foods." The manifesto contains a large element of hope: "May suitable doses of guaranteed sensual pleasure and slow, long-lasting enjoyment preserve us from the contagion of the multitude who mistake frenzy for efficiency." And the manifesto proposes just that single solution to the problem: "A firm defense of quiet material pleasure is the only way to oppose the universal folly of Fast Life."

As slogans go, the meaning of "slow food" is perfectly clear. It's the opposite of fast food. The Slow Food mother organization in Italy celebrates the country's traditional regional food, publicizing and arranging support for many individual foods. Those include *lardo di Colonnata* and *alici di menaica.* The first is cured fat back, as prepared in marble coffers in a particular quarrying village above Carrara in Tuscany; the second is cured anchovies, caught in an ancient design of net in just one fishing port 100 miles south of Naples. The symbol of Slow Food is the snail. Slow Food opposes mass production and a high-speed life. It supports what I would call a civilized life.

These days Slow Food talks about Slow everything—even Slow Fish, meaning fish that have been caught in ways that don't result in overfishing or other damage to the environment. But "slow food" also has a lower-case meaning. And a slow life doesn't revolve just around food.

You're living a slow life when you gather seashells along the shore, feed a campfire, visit a nearly empty museum on a weekday morning, talk late into the night, read an ink-on-paper book cover to cover without stopping to do much else, and, I would say, if you take the time to be bored. Part of being civilized is not just being slow but occasionally coming to a stop, establishing a point of reference for the moment when you start moving again. When you stop you aren't really stopping, of course, because that's often when good ideas rise to the surface.

Coincidentally, I started writing and publishing about food in the same year, 1986, that Slow Food started, although at the time I was unaware of the organization. I believed in pretty much the same things: traditional ingredients, traditional methods, traditional dishes. Then as now, I was focused on taste, not on health, entertaining, or some other aspect of food. I was on a back-to-the-land wavelength that assumed superior results came from hand methods and generally from old ways of doing things, which are of course typically somewhat slow. I was opposed to the cheapening effects of industrial production. Yet I had no conscious thought about the importance of speed, fast or slow. If anyone had asked me, I would have said it was pretty self-evident that good work as a rule takes time. I've learned since then, after many visits to cheese makers, bread bakers, charcutiers, market gardeners, olive growers and grape growers and all sorts of farmers, that good work comes from experience and repetition, years if not decades of it.

Some proof that good work takes time lies in traditional handcrafted foods. The best, for instance certain wheels of Gruyère cheese, are still the point of reference for quality in all foods, even if such products are scarce and most of the "artisanal" cheeses that we buy are really made by industrial techniques. When I speak of "proof that good work takes time," I mean that the market generally rewards good traditional products much higher prices. Sticking to the example of cheese, some of the best farm cheese makers, to make more profit from a better product, are going backwards: rejecting silage in favor of pasture and hay, creating "clean" raw milk without the use of sterilizing chemicals on teats and equipment. (The milk contains microorganisms but predominately good ones, enough of them to overwhelm the bad.)

I live in northeastern Vermont, where the view is mostly fields and woods, but my work can be as intense as anyone's and mostly I look at a computer screen. During the warm months, when I'm done for the day, I go outdoors and immediately I relax. In a cliché, I breathe deeply, and I feel my chest expand and relax. I walk into the garden: I hoe, kneel down and pull weeds, maybe thin some seedlings, eat a leaf of lettuce, a carrot, some berries. I may accomplish something, but there's no goal or focus. These are acts of appreciation and pleasure, nothing at all to do with speed or efficiency. They're the *slowest.*

Some of the most delicious food, including some of the greatest dishes, is made using cooking techniques that by nature are slow. Most of these involve liquid–braising, poaching, stewing, soup making. But proper roasting, too, takes time, whether on a spit or in an oven (though the latter is really baking). Some examples of excellent results from slow tactics are a French *navarin* (braised lamb shoulder with spring vegetables, including turnips), oxtail soup (which starts as a braise), braised lamb shanks with whole garlic cloves and bulb fennel, *pieds et pacquets* from Marseille (sheep's feet with packages of sheep stomach), osso buco from Milan, and the beef *brasato* made in different regions of northern Italy.

Of course, those who believe in slow food don't really oppose fast cooking techniques. What's wrong with toast? Or call it *bruschetta.* Certain techniques are inherently fast–sautéing, frying in deep fat, grilling. They apply high heat directly to relatively thin or small pieces of food, and if the cooking goes on too long the food burns. A lamb chop grilled medium rare takes just two or three minutes per side. A classic French omelette takes less than five minutes from cracking the eggs to sliding the cooked omelette onto a plate. Spinach, with the washing water still clinging, can take just a minute to cook through in a wide covered pot, stirred once or twice, a hybrid of boiling and steaming. Peas, green beans, cut-up carrots, turnips, or broccoli put into a big pot of boiling water don't take more than a few minutes. (You can boil spinach, too, but if it's young and delicate, it loses too much flavor to the water.) Then, to have all the good qualities of this quickly cooked food, you have to eat it quickly, before the vegetables lose their utterly fresh taste, before the grilled meat or fish loses juice and the bit of outer crispness.

Slowness really means living at the right speed for whatever you are doing, living more in the present moment, rather than looking always ahead to the next thing: deadlines, bills, future plans. It's not about being inefficient or taking too much time. It's about moving at the right speed.

"Slow" has all the connotations of the words ecological, small-scale, human, just as "organic" used to have for many people. Yet for all that "slow food" is a wonderful phrase, "slow" doesn't have quite the right literal meaning. Better words might be "real," "authentic," "genuine," "decent," "honest," "ethical," all of them difficult to define in relation to food but a lot closer to the mark. In cooking and eating, what's the practical meaning of slow? To me, it's "careful, thoughtful, open, precise." It means you pay attention. A better single word than slow might be "integrity," except that it's a noun and doesn't lend itself at all to a catchy name or a slogan. If we weren't easily distracted by its other connotations, I'd prefer "innocent."

As an opposite to "slow" food, "fast" isn't quite the right word either. Industrial "fast food" is ready-to-eat and quickly eaten, but more important, it's fake, cynical, false, misleading, unhealthy, ill-considered, bad for the environment, bad for workers, bad for all the animals raised under cruel conditions.

The pleasure we find in cooking and eating lies not in being either fast or slow but in being both or in-between at different times. Different speeds are part of food as they are of the rest of life. What we need is balance.

Some slowness helps concentration, unless for example you're driven by adrenaline, like a line cook during the lunch rush. It turns out, if a study I once read about is right, that multitaskers don't have a special ability that the rest of us lack; in fact, they do everything badly. Focus is important. If I run out of shelf space for books and I want to get rid of those I'll never look at again, it doesn't work to skim the shelf–I've tried that. What works is to take each book down and hold it briefly in my hand and mind. I get rid of a lot more books.

Considering that I spend my days writing about food and publishing a food magazine, it's ironical that at the end of the day I often feel I don't have enough energy to cook more than a basic meal, often grilled meat and grilled vegetables with rice or potatoes. My family and I would probably eat out most of the time, if not for the cost, the distances, and the limited choices in the rural area where we live. Americans are cooking less and less. We spend an average of 27 minutes a day preparing food and four minutes cleaning up (to borrow the figures used by Michael Pollan in his writing on the topic). We spent more than twice that amount of time in the mid-1960s. And the reason isn't only to do with time. Fashionable restaurants, from casual to luxurious, now generally pursue minimalist cuisine. In France, the classic sauces have all but disappeared; you hardly find a sauce at all. Maybe we've simplified because we're tired, don't have the time, don't have the attention span. Maybe we're worn out from living with the world's complicated problems. Maybe the "slow" in "slow food" really just means "slow eating," because so few of us cook or want to cook. And if so, I think that's all right.

What about time- and labor-saving kitchen appliances, such as food processors and microwaves? Do they have a place in slow cooking? A labor-saving tool frees you to do something else more important, presumably more important than taking a nap. I write on a computer, which eliminates the many hours I once spent retyping; now I spend more time writing. When the food processor became popular back in the 80s, the idea was not only that it would supply the skills you lacked but you would also have more time to cook fancier meals, involving more chopping, shredding, purées–French meals in particular. Which sounds rather quaint now. Personally, I avoid my food processor, except for making certain purées, because it takes longer to wash, dishwasher or no dishwasher, than a cutting board and a knife do. (Also, I love sharp knives.) For purées, a mortar and pestle give a more pleasing, slippery texture. Cooking and eating are sensory experiences; a food processor only gets in the way. I use a copper bowl and whisk to beat egg whites, just for the pleasure of the process. I can't remember the last time I used an electric mixer. If we still have a blender, I don't know where it is. The best thing about hand tools is that they increase your sensitivity to the physical state of the food, perhaps especially texture. They make you pay close attention. They help you understand the process better, which generally means better results. Often hand tools give more control. My hand-cranked Tre Spade coffee mill gives a more even grind with less powder than my electric coffee grinder does, and that in turn gives less-cloudy coffee whose fine flavors are easier to taste. (We could talk a long time about coffee and the different ways to make it and why.) You cannot make as delicious bread by machine as you can by hand, because the fermentation is everything to flavor, and the best fermentation requires that you check and respond to its precise evolution–another fold, a few more minutes . . .

After you've cooked, "slow eating" may literally come into play. During a meal, when something on the plate is especially interesting to taste, I slow down and zero in–*slow* again.

There's one more thing: you don't eat food without having something to drink, if only water. What about "slow drink"?

The "slowest" drink is local water or, depending on where you live, local wine or beer or something else, such as cider. When liquids are transported from far away—water, wine, beer, soda—there's an environmental cost. It's important to have a few luxuries in life, however, and I admit that for me one of them is imported wine, mostly French. At home, when we open a really good bottle, we tend to sip it more slowly than we do more everyday wine. That's partly because there's more to experience and partly because we don't want the experience to end.

It's obvious that for ideas to surface and for any of us to do our best work, we need time to relax. And some of that time should be spent sitting down and eating with full enjoyment with other people—talking in the easy-going, open atmosphere of the table. Ideas come and information is exchanged that you might never otherwise receive: personal information, stories, unusual facts. An essential refreshment takes place that has nothing to do with the physical one coming from food and drink.

Cooking Isn't Fun

By Tracie McMillan

From *Slate*

Tangled issues of food, class, poverty, and social justice lie at the heart of Tracie McMillan's investigative journalism. As a coda to her provocative 2011 book *The American Way of Eating*, this essay challenges the easy assumptions that many foodies make about how Americans should cook and eat.

It took me until I was 33 to start cooking dinner.

Don't get me wrong—I was no stranger to the kitchen. I had prepared laborious, extravagant meals before, often using exotic ingredients I'd learned about in magazines. My sisters and I had bonded in the kitchen, spending visits preparing elaborate dishes together for hours. Cooking had been everything the food world told me it could be: a way to engage with a community, to travel without leaving home, to respect the local environment, to look after my own health. I nodded along with the eminences of the food world, convinced that their shared conclusion was the pinnacle of truth: Americans just don't cook enough, and we desperately need to cook more. Our health, our civility, our culture depend on it!

And yet, even while espousing the ideals of the communal table and cross-cultural exploration, I rarely cooked dinner for myself in my 20s. Where was the fun in *that*? My sisters and I would groan to ourselves when my stepmother implored us *not* to cook Christmas dinner. (Her reasoning: It was too much work and we could just get Costco lasagna and be done with it.) But when left to my own devices, I would feed myself almost anything so long as I didn't have to turn on the stove. If I had to hazard a guess, I'd say I cooked a meal once a week and otherwise made do with hummus and pita, or cereal, or crackers and cheese and olives. I liked to commune with the foodie writers but not enough to cook every day.

Which brings me to the dirty little secret that I suspect haunts every food writer: When you have no *choice* but to cook for yourself every single day, no matter what, it is not a fun, gratifying adventure. It is a chore. On many days, it kind of sucks.

I might have gone to my grave denying this fundamental truth if I hadn't reported a book that had me living and eating off minimum wage (and less). While working at Wal-Mart in Michigan, I stocked up on bulk items, foolishly using middle-class logic ("great unit price!") instead of working-class smarts ("save enough cash for rent plus small emergencies"). I soon ran out of money and found myself hungry and exhausted, staring down a pantry containing little more than flour, coconut flakes, a few scraggly vegetables, and two frozen chicken thighs. There was nothing about this scene that inspired me to cook. The ingredients were boring. There were no friends bringing over bottles of wine. I had left my glossy food magazines in New York.

But there would be no calling Papa John's for pizza or stopping at Trader Joe's for premade lasagna or a selection of fine cheeses; my $8.10 an hour precluded that. I had two choices: consume raw flour and cauliflower, or cook. By dint of my newfound poverty, I had lost the third option—the escape hatch, really—that most middle-class people take for granted: eating without having to cook. Once subjected to the tyranny of necessity, I found that making my meals from scratch wasn't glamorous at all.

There are many good reasons to cook meals from scratch. Cooking simply at home from whole ingredients is often cheaper, per serving, than heading out to a restaurant—even a fast-food restaurant. Food made at home usually has far less salt and fat than either processed foods or what's on offer in eateries. And, contrary to popular belief, families don't save much time by turning to box meals like Hamburger Helper rather than cooking entirely from scratch. Researchers at UCLA found that, whether using processed foods or whole ingredients, American families spend about 52 minutes preparing their dinner every night.

So the big question is, if cooking from whole ingredients is so easy and cost-effective and healthy, why don't Americans do it more—particularly the low-income ones who are affected the most by obesity? This is a much trickier question than it seems because it implicitly evokes two pernicious myths about Americans' cooking habits that I uncovered in the course of my reporting.

The first myth here is that the poor do not cook. We tend to think that low-income Americans are flooding McDonald's, while more affluent citizens dutifully eat better meals prepared at home. In reality, it is the middle class that patronizes the Golden Arches and its competitors. (That's because fast food may be cheap, but it's still more expensive than cooking at home.) Indeed, beneficiaries of the Agriculture Department's food-stamp program (officially known as Supplemental Nutrition Assistance Program, or SNAP) typically spend far more time than other Americans preparing their meals. (This trend may shift in the future, as some states have begun allowing some subsets of SNAP recipients to redeem their food stamps for fast-food meals.)

The second myth is that cooking is easy. Making food quickly and well is easy once you know how to do it, but it is a learned skill, the acquisition of which takes time, practice, and the making of mistakes. To cook whole foods at a pace that can match box-meal offerings, one needs to know how to make substitutions on the fly; how to doctor a dish that has been overvinegared, oversalted, or overspiced; how to select produce and know how long you have to use it before it goes bad; how to stock a pantry on a budget. Without those skills, cooking from scratch becomes risky business: You may lose produce to rotting before you get the chance to cook it, or you may botch a recipe and find it inedible. Those mistakes are a natural part of learning to cook, but they will cost you and your family time, ingredients, and money without actually feeding you. They also make a persuasive case that cooking is not worth the trouble and that Hamburger Helper is worth the cost.

There's not much acknowledgment of these truths in the current discussion about the benefits of cooking. Instead, we divide ourselves into two opposing camps—"those who cook" and "those who don't care." When the stories we tell about cooking say that it is *only* ever fun and rewarding—instead of copping to the fact that it can also be annoying, time consuming, and risky—we alienate the people who don't have the luxury of choice, and we unwittingly reinforce the impression that cooking is a specialty hobby instead of a basic life skill.

So here's my proposition for foodies and everyone else: Continue to champion the cause of cooking, but admit that cooking every day can be a drag. Just because it's a drag doesn't mean we shouldn't do it—we do things every day that are a drag. We take out the trash, we make our beds, we run the vacuum, we pay the bills. These are not lofty cultural explorations, but they are necessary, and so we do them anyway.

This reality check is exactly what's missing from our discussion about our meals. At least, it's what was missing from mine. Three years after my stint at Wal-Mart, I've gotten over the idea that cooking is fun—or that it is even *supposed* to be fun. Sometimes it's not. It certainly wasn't when I was working at Wal-Mart, especially that first night when I lurched my way around the kitchen and came up with a makeshift chicken curry with cauliflower and onion over biscuits. I grumbled to myself the whole time, but I ate well and physically felt good for several days after without spending an additional penny thanks to leftovers.

Today, my approach to cooking is completely flipped from my pre-Wal-Mart days. I now think of it not as a choice but as a chore—and that's been oddly freeing. I no longer fret over what fabulous recipe I'll make. I don't try to psych myself up, to frame cooking as a fun event with which to entertain myself. (When I find myself whining internally about having to cook, I find the following phrase to be useful: "Suck it up, buttercup.") I remind myself that I do all kinds of things that aren't fun in the name of living a reasonably mature life, and then I cook something from scratch, just like the Mark Bittmans, Michael Pollans, and Alice Waterses of the world suggest.

The Meaning of Local

By Todd Kliman

From *The Washingtonian*

In a city swarming with pollsters and politicians, the D.C. restaurant scene can easily get overheated. Enter the voice of reason: *Washingtonian* dining critic Todd Kliman, who keeps things honest with his monthly restaurant reviews and weekly online chats.

Several years ago, I was at dinner with a friend, a fellow food lover, a man for whom dining out is preferable to virtually every other form of human interaction. The meal was no joy for either of us. It was mediocre and expensive, and I said so with a sigh when the check came.

"It was honest," my friend said, leaping to defend what had seemed to me indefensible.

The chef was known for sourcing locally and from small farmers. He had cultivated these purveyors, had worked with them to come up with products he wanted, and he aimed to present them as cleanly as possible, without engaging in kitchen tricks that might mask the purity of his raw materials. He was honest—in other words, he didn't go in for cheap, processed products and try to pass them off on the dining public. He valued the small farmers who worked so hard to put out high-quality goods. He did things "the right way."

My friend was therefore willing to extend to the chef the benefit of the doubt.

Me, I was peeved that he had squandered ingredients that a chef at a family-run Ethiopian or Vietnamese restaurant, tasked with turning frozen poultry and veggies into tasty dishes, would have regarded as a special treat. Peeved that, not for the first time, a chef seemed to have labored under the notion that credit was given for good intentions.

I've since had countless meals like this and countless conversations with true believers who worry that I'm not grasping the urgency of their message.

In the last 30 years, "local" has evolved from an ideology to a movement to something that looks suspiciously like an ism: more important than any single chef or restaurant—more important, too, than any other philosophy or ideology. It's so ingrained in the world of food today that it's all but impossible to talk meaningfully about food without talking about "local."

And yet what do we talk about when we talk about "local"?

Not nearly enough, it turns out.

A Brief History of Local

In 1971, Alice Waters opened Chez Panisse, the restaurant that would forever alter the direction of food in America. From her kitchen in Berkeley, California, she sought the freshest possible ingredients, often from within a few miles of the restaurant.

Her focus on sourcing locally was, quite literally, a radical statement at a time when factory farming, agribusiness, and chain restaurants had recently cemented their dominance of the food supply. In the world of fine dining, Waters's shunning of luxury ingredients flown in from Europe, white tablecloths, bowing waiters, and snooty maître d's had the same bracing effect that punk rock, bubbling up in the culture at that time, had on popular music.

What Waters was to the West Coast, Nora Pouillon was to the East. In 1979, Pouillon opened Restaurant Nora, on a quiet, leafy block north of DC's Dupont Circle. Twenty years later, it would become the first certified organic restaurant in the country.

The designation requires strict adherence: Ninety-five percent of all products in the kitchen must be organic. Restaurant Nora has been eclipsed in the last decade or so by a slew of places spreading her message with greater urgency and excitement, but it's impossible to deny Pouillon's influence. Ann Cashion, who went on to create the model for the small locally minded bistro at Cashion's Eat Place and later at the original Johnny's Half Shell, got her start under Pouillon, and Ann Yonkers, now codirector of the FreshFarm Markets, worked for her as a recipe tester and cookbook editor.

Pouillon says her motivation was simply to "find a more natural way to do things." As a young and idealistic chef, she was troubled to learn that farmers could be allowed to "contaminate the soil and jeopardize families," so she began driving to farms in Virginia, Maryland, and Pennsylvania, quizzing farmers about their practices.

Jean-Louis Palladin was on a similar quest at the Watergate, determined to unearth the products unique not only to America but also to his chosen patch of the world. Palladin was concerned mainly with distinctiveness, not purity, but he and Pouillon frequently found themselves in the same company.

Pouillon eventually settled on a group of purveyors who were as committed and passionate as she was. She also began organizing bus tours, taking chefs to Pennsylvania to introduce them to the farmers important to her. From these trips emerged Tuscarora Organic Growers, a collective of Pennsylvania farmers that many area restaurants today turn to for their meats and produce.

It wasn't enough, Waters and Pouillon and others argued, for food to taste good. It had to *be* good. A chef might be armed with a battery of techniques to transform his or her raw materials, but if those materials weren't superlative to begin with, Waters wasn't interested. Shopping counted as much as cooking.

It Depends What Your Definition Of "Contiguous" Is

Of the three dozen food-world personalities I interviewed for this article, none could point to an agreed-upon definition of local.

From as far north as Pennsylvania to as far south as Virginia was as close to a consensus as I could find. One chef defined local as his ability to "reasonably" drive to and from a farm in a day, a definition that seemed to provide wiggle room for four or even five hours. Another offered the drive-in-a-day yardstick, without the modifier "reasonably," and I imagined him gunning it deep into the woods of North Carolina for some fresh-killed quail, then turning around and speeding up I-95 in hopes of making it back to his kitchen before his midnight deadline.

Whole Foods defines local differently for each region of the country. DC belongs to the Mid-Atlantic, which includes New Jersey, Ohio, Kentucky, Maryland, Virginia, and Pennsylvania. Until recently, if you shopped at a Whole Foods in this area, where your meat and produce came from was a matter of "contiguity"–anywhere in a neighboring state was considered local.

That meant, for example, that tomatoes from North Carolina were considered local in Arlington stores–because North Carolina and Virginia share a border–while those that traveled a shorter distance from New Jersey were not.

This summer, Whole Foods is changing to a new definition, under which foods grown within about 100 miles or in the same state as the store will be considered local.

But if there's no agreed-upon definition of what local is, that means it can be anything at all, and it's simply how a chef or restaurant or farmer or business chooses to define it. It means the term is essentially meaningless, a point Emily Sprissler drove home rather decisively when I rang her up at Mayfair & Pine, a British gastropub in DC's Glover Park that has since closed.

"America," Sprissler declared, "is my local."

Was she saying local is a limitation?

"I don't find it limiting. I just don't pay attention to it."

A comparison between France and America followed, along with a discussion of economies of scale. "Look, France is the size of Texas," she said. "It's easy to get anything you want there, and quickly, and it's all great. If I'm only going to get products within a hundred miles or whatever, [the definition] is limiting."

Here Sprissler stopped herself, perhaps realizing she'd come dangerously close to branding herself a heretic in the church of local. She began again, choosing her words more carefully: "I'm trying as hard as I can, from toilet paper to tenderloin, to put American products in my restaurant. I'm giving my money to another American so that they can keep their job and put food on their table. I do a miso chicken–there's a company in Massachusetts that makes its own miso, and it's amazing. There's a lot of amazing products out there, and I don't care if they're from Michigan or Wyoming."

She was proud. Proud and defiant and convinced of the rightness of her approach. And she ought to be, both because it was hers and because it seemed a chance to expose her diners to the best artisanally made products from around the country.

But what did it say that she seemed so determined to align herself with the local movement, even as she rejected its core tenets?

Inherently Better?

Let's look at the foundations of the local movement—the arguments that are most often advanced to make the case not merely for its worth but for its necessity:

Local reduces our "carbon footprint."

The phrase is eco-shorthand for the fuel expenditures an ingredient generates before it lands on the table. It's less simple than it sounds, a romantic notion only sometimes supported by the data.

Eggs that have been trucked in from 50 miles away or less are no great environmental stressor, but when the definition of local is as loose as it is, 50 miles is seldom to be counted on.

And not all methods of delivery are equal. One restaurateur told me he's constantly wrestling with questions such as: "Is a large 18-wheeler coming from 80 miles away better than 50 pickup trucks bringing the same ingredients from 50 miles away?"

I told him that sounded like an SAT question.

Right, he said. And with no correct answer.

Local is good for the local economy.

This would appear to be true. As it would be true for giving your money to any small, independently owned business in your neighborhood.

The problem is the notion that this money is a driver of the local economy. You're supporting a person who presumably spends that money locally. But of course, how many of us do? We live in a global, interconnected world where Amazon and others have displaced the neighborhood store, making shopping cheaper, faster, and more efficient.

One thing we can be sure of is that supporting a local producer helps keep that producer in business, and that is indeed a very good thing.

Local equals changing the system.

Local and organic foods currently make up 3 percent of food consumption in America, so it's highly unlikely that those of us who contribute to this small percentage with our purchases are, as political pundits like to say, moving the needle.

You may feel good about your personal actions in a large and indifferent universe. You may salve your conscience in avoiding companies that you consider to be adding to the growing social ills that beset us as a nation. But this isn't the same as altering the status quo.

Local is fresher and better.

Local is not inherently fresher, nor is it inherently better. And it isn't even always the case that when it's fresher, it's better.

I love Rappahannock oysters, and if a restaurant can truck them up from Virginia's Northern Neck just hours after dredging them from the water, I consider that a treat. But I prefer British Columbia oysters, which, though presumably not as fresh—the air time alone is double that of a trip from the Northern Neck—are richer, sweeter, firmer, and more delicate.

Now, local potatoes? Fantastic. They taste like an altogether different species from the trucked-in variety most of us grew up with. Local corn? Ditto. Local tomatoes? Sometimes. I haven't had many local tomatoes that compare to the juicy sweetness of a Jersey beefsteak. Local chickens? From a free-range, hormone-free source like Polyface, absolutely (and if it's a special occasion and I'm not inclined to linger over the pinch of forking over $20 for a roaster, all the more so). From a giant factory farm on the equally local Delmarva Peninsula? Not if I can help it. Local cheese? Rarely.

Consider the Peach

We ought to be talking about "perishability," says Eric Ziebold, the chef at CityZen, a gastronome's paradise in DC's Mandarin Oriental hotel.

For every piece of produce, Ziebold says, there's a "window" of freshness. The window for a ripened peach, for instance, is within the first six hours after being picked. Here he waxes poetic, describing that first bite after pulling one straight from a tree—the texture exquisitely poised between soft and firm, a sweetness that's almost floral, the juice exploding in your mouth and running down your arm. Over the next six hours, the peach begins to degrade. For his purposes, Ziebold says, a peach delivered to the restaurant within 18 hours of being picked is still usable—it might work in a purée or a sauce—though it will have already lost its purity. After 24 hours, it's "pretty much a different piece of fruit entirely."

Ziebold is perhaps pickier than most farmers-market shoppers, and initially I'm tempted to dismiss his words as the obsessive talk of a man who's fanatical about purity and quality. But it occurs to me that that mania to experience a piece of fruit at its ripe and beautiful peak is the reason so many food-loving urbanites flock to farmers markets in season—indeed, that promise is woven deep within the "local" pitch. Better, fresher. If you drop big money on a peach, isn't it fair to expect that the peach—which presumably hasn't had to be trucked great distances and has been harvested not by a mass-production outfit but by the more attentive and loving hands of the small farmer—would be exceptional?

And yet how many farmers-market peaches have you tasted in this area that were worthy of that adjective? I've had many good ones, but I can't remember the last time I had the ecstatic encounter Ziebold describes.

There's a good explanation for that, he says: "If you're a farmer selling in DC, you don't necessarily want to sell a peach that's going to get used that instant. They know that you're going to go back to the office, and they want to give you a little better window. So it's not a tree-ripened peach you're getting."

Closer to the source, he says, it's likely to be a different story: "If you visit that farm and pick up a peach and you don't use it in six hours, it's crap. But if you do use it in six hours, it's the best peach you've eaten in your life."

It never occurred to me that the quality of produce at the urban farmers market isn't the same as the quality of produce at a rural farmers market.

That's one lesson. The other, deeper lesson involves stretching Ziebold's point to its logical conclusion. If perishability is paramount, if tasting things at their freshest is what matters most, then visiting a farmers market isn't the only way to ensure that outcome. In some instances, it might not even be the best way.

"I could get something FedExed that's potentially fresher than a farmers market," Ziebold says.

So can we all. The Internet has opened up sourcing possibilities previously available only to insiders—oysters from Brittany, salmon from Alaska, caviar from Russia.

Of course, the carbon footprint is likely to be considerably higher. More to the point: The romance is clearly missing.

The Literal Fruit of Our Privilege

And romance is not nothing. It's very definitely a something. Local couldn't exist without it.

The wish to connect local food to something larger, to fetishize it as an object of desire, underpins the farmers-market experience and enables its supporters to justify dropping 80 bucks on a single bag of groceries.

Listen to Robb Duncan, who owns Dolcezza—the excellent gelato shops in Georgetown, Dupont Circle, Fairfax, and Bethesda—explain the appeal of going to the farmers market: "You eat this food and it's delicious, and it makes you feel happy to meet this farmer named Zachariah, and he doesn't put any pesticides in his produce, and you walk around as part of this beautiful, beautiful community of people."

This is the farmers market as embodiment of a surviving hippie aesthetic, and for many it's a powerful inducement to spend, whether they came of age in the '60s or, like Duncan, merely wish they did.

There's also the market experience as ratifier of status, in which the notion of simplifying our lives is held out to the busy, scattered urbanite as a glimpse of a new good life and a $4 tomato becomes the literal fruit of our privilege.

I ask Ann Yonkers—who, with Bernadine Prince, has run the area's FreshFarm Markets since 1997—what, beyond the makings of a meal, she thinks her customers come to the markets to buy.

Yonkers is as committed to the cause as anyone in Washington. When FreshFarm began in 1997, there were only about four farmers markets in the area; today there are ten FreshFarms alone. The nonprofit is among the finest purveyors of its kind in the country, with goods coming from 118 farmers and producers.

Yonkers is justifiably proud of this growth and speaks with the tones of an evangelist who believes she has found a path to, if not enlightenment, then happiness. Again and again I'm struck, as we speak, by the way she invests a material good—a cheese, a leg of lamb, a squash—with the aura of the spiritual.

Her customers, she says, aren't just dropping their disposable income on what some might see as luxury items; they're "participating in change." In other words, shopping at a farmers market isn't an upper-middle-class indulgence—or not just. It's also a political act.

I ask if she might share with me some of the ways people can participate in change.

"You can participate in change just by what you eat and buy and who you give your money to," she says. "People come to our markets and they feel empowered."

There's also the matter, she says, of "change for yourself."

Change for yourself?

"Discovering flavor. Just by virtue of how fresh [the products] are." Not new flavors, Yonkers is quick to emphasize—the flavor of familiar things, like melons and potatoes. That these things actually have flavor and aren't the bland, colorless specimens that generations of agribusiness have taught us to accept. "Eating all these different varieties"—like the many different kinds of tomatoes.

Sampling tomato varieties equates with participating in change?

"That's a huge level of change," she says. "The markets have brought back biodiversity, a lot of which was lost in the '50s. We've seen the whole return to grass-fed—and all these reforms as a result of that. Farmers are raising heritage breeds and heirlooms."

I tell her that this particular change, while important agriculturally, seems to me something less than the spiritual change she spoke of when we began talking. I tell her that mostly what I'm hearing from her and others is the opportunity for personal discovery in tasting new foods and cooking differently, and how that personal discovery—valid and worthy in itself—is being framed as a profound social and political act, and thus marketed as something more than it is.

Yonkers acknowledges that a strong sense of the spiritual "runs through the whole movement," then makes an analogy to Catholicism, with its ritualistic consumption of the body of Christ via the Communion wafer. She stops short of saying that taking Communion is akin to shopping at a farmers market, but I gather that for her, and perhaps for her many customers, the experiences are aligned.

"Food," she says, "is holy."

There's Truth, and Then There's Truth

You sit down at a restaurant and open the menu. There's a note at the top: "Proud to support our farmers." Near the bar, you find a chalkboard with the names of all the farms whose products presumably contributed to your meal. The waiter announces the day's specials, noting not only every ingredient for every dish but also the source for that ingredient, as if you just spent the weekend at Path Valley or Toigo Orchards or any of the other farms that are standbys of the restaurant scene. As if you're on intimate terms with the workers who till the soil and plow the fields.

You're not simply supporting the restaurant, you're made to feel; you're supporting a community, an economy, a way of life. You're feeling good: about dinner, about the restaurant, about yourself—hell, maybe even about the world and your place in it.

And why wouldn't you?

Hearing and reading these paeans to local farmers, you'd assume that most of the raw materials that come through those kitchen doors are local, wouldn't you? Perhaps not everything—salt and pepper, for instance, aren't local. But a lot. Three-quarters of all the products, say. Or more than half.

You're assuming too much.

For most restaurants, the answer is around 30 percent. That figure tends to be higher in the warmer months and lower in the colder ones. "In the summertime, 40 to 50 percent maybe," Tom Meyer of Clyde's Restaurant Group says.

Maybe.

Touting a connection to the land and saluting "our" farmers seems a dubious practice when only a third of all the products are from local purveyors. I don't doubt that, from the restaurant's perspective, the 30 percent is more meaningful than the other 70 percent because it took time and effort to procure. All products aren't equal. But if local is something to support, something that matters, shouldn't it matter for the other 70 percent?

One restaurateur says that neither he nor any of his peers is buying items like onions and carrots and celery from local sources. They're making their investment, he says, in "corn and tomatoes—things that make a difference."

A cynic might say: things that get noticed.

Another restaurateur, a man deeply committed to local, confesses that while he sources regularly from more than a dozen purveyors, the milk and cream in his area restaurants aren't local.

Milk and cream? Shouldn't those be the least we can assume comes from nearby farms?

He'd much rather serve locally produced milk and cream in his restaurants, he says, but can't find a consistent source to meet the volume he needs—a problem many restaurateurs also allude to. One local dairy delivery company adheres to such a strict radius that it won't permit its trucks to go a few extra miles to make a drop-off at one of his restaurants.

The channels of distribution for local farmers aren't well developed, in marked contrast to the enormously efficient networks that bring food to supermarkets and chain restaurants. Products that might meet a particular need, at a volume that makes them attractive to chefs, aren't always getting to the restaurants that want them.

These are real concerns and ought not to be minimized. Local requires more work, more thought, and more investment.

At the same time, when you've embraced an ideology that revolves around notions of purity and piety, no one wants to hear about the obstacles that prevent you from being more holy. Excuses will be construed as weakness. You open yourself to charges of hypocrisy if you're anything less than completely faithful in your adherence.

Or, at the very least, to charges of hype.

The fact that distribution is lacking is real. So is the fact that it's possible to source minimally from local farmers and still fly the flag of local.

Lying with Local

Elaine Boland possesses the flinty skepticism of many small farmers accustomed to selling their hard-earned products to urbanites. To talk to her for any length of time is to hear a woman who has grown weary of interactions with people who don't grasp the rhythms of the seasons and the exigencies of life lived close to the land.

She says she "rededicated" her company, Fields of Athenry, in Purcellville, to these older, elemental values after her daughter was diagnosed with Cushing's syndrome, which results from exposure to high levels of the hormone cortisol. Two holistic doctors suggested she try a nutrient-rich diet. The diet helped, and Boland was moved to rethink her operation. If eating high-quality, humanely kept animals could save her daughter, it might save many other lives by preventing those ailments from occurring in the first place. Boland asks if I've ever eaten her meats. I say I have, twice—a lamb shoulder at Vermilion, in Old Town, and a lamb sausage at Haute Dogs & Fries, in Purcellville.

"'Cause I won't sell to most chefs," she says.

Why is that?

Boland goes silent and tells me she fears she'd get in trouble if she spoke her mind. Then, having resolved her inner contradiction, she sighs and says, "A lot of 'em, they buy just enough to use your name on their menu. I don't want somebody ordering two or three chickens off of me and a couple of chuck roasts and putting my name on their menu. When they're probably running 300, 400 dinners a week? You have to be supplementing it with someone else."

I ask how she decides whom she'll sell to and whom she won't.

She laughs ruefully. "I had to learn. I had to learn who was honest and dedicated to this. I learned the hard way."

Today, if a chef expresses interest in featuring her meats, she invites him or her out to the farm along with the kitchen staff. What would appear to be an innocuous meet-and-greet is, in fact, a rigorous screening process, a way for Boland to assess a chef's "level of engagement in talking about whole animal, head to hoof, their love of organ meats, their interest in buying whole animals. There are very few chefs who do that, buy the whole animal. Very few can make the off-product sell, because they really can cook. They'll say to me, 'We don't have to stick to a set menu. We'll figure out how to use the product—don't worry.'"

The screening helps her figure out who is interested in a legitimate relationship, with its give-and-take and dependency, and who is merely interested in taking on a new supplier—or worse, acquiring a bit of fashionable window dressing.

"I don't want to be used," she says, sounding like a twice-jilted lover.

Deep Throat Speaks

A trusted source within the industry, a man I've come to refer to as Deep Throat for the reliable gossip he feeds me, said the practice that

Elaine Boland describes is "more common than you think," adding: "Truth in advertising is one of the biggest issues with this."

Every one of the insiders I spoke with talked about local as doing the right thing, citing its importance for our bodies, our land, our communities, our economies, our farmers. But over the months, I came to distinguish among them as I listened.

Here, for instance, are my notes from a conversation with a young, locally minded restaurateur with a small chain of restaurants:

> "It's always been a big part of our mission and strategy, and it's really exciting to see it start to become a standard in the food space.
>
> "Putting the farmers' names on that board like we do. It's all about transparency.
>
> "We shouldn't get so obsessed with the stricter definitions. That's not the über thing.
>
> "That's what it's all about for us—emotional connection. When our customers see a picture of a farmer and they learn that story. It's about making people feel good about their decision at every touch point."

Now listen to Spike Gjerde, chef and owner of Woodberry Kitchen in Baltimore.

Asked to define "local," he says the word is the basis "for asking some very important questions." Namely: "What are the farmer's practices and what are the impacts on the environment of those practices?"

Gjerde often laments the years he missed in the cause. "I'm 20 years late to this," he says. I hear something of Alice Waters's ethos in his words, particularly when he says that it's not enough to "serve something good."

The "aim of all this," he says, "should be to connect the diner to something larger"—in his case, an appreciation of the Chesapeake, "our Yellowstone, our national treasure." But more broadly, an understanding of where our food is grown and by whom, and a curiosity about how our choices—our dollars—affect the system. "At Woodberry," he says, "we use the restaurant to sell the local products. Conversely, a lot of restaurants are using local to sell the restaurant."

It's not Gjerde's fidelity to a high-church standard of purity that impresses me. It's his understanding of the idea that dinner at a restaurant is a complex interplay of many people, only one of whom is the chef. And that a restaurant has a responsibility to the larger culture.

Perhaps this is why Gjerde doesn't exult over what he has accomplished but continues to torture himself with how he should be doing so much more.

I tell him this sounds like a definition for neuroticism.

Gjerde laughs. "I don't see how you can be engaged in this thing and not be like that."

The Purist's Dilemma

Local has achieved a status unthinkable to many of its earliest adherents, a fact that causes some of them, such as civil-rights warriors or women's-rights advocates, to wax nostalgic over their progress even as they lament that local doesn't mean as much as it once did.

When she opened Cashion's Eat Place in 1995, Ann Cashion says, she took her cues in the kitchen from what her purveyors had on hand, buying whole animals and butchering them herself. The offcuts were troubling to diners; they wanted the chops. They were dismayed at paying top dollar for something they considered scraps, and they couldn't understand her capriciousness—why she kept yanking the chops from the menu.

Cashion is a supporter of Bev Eggleston, who has so often been described as patron saint of the local-food movement that he himself invokes the term, albeit mockingly, in conversation. Eggleston was featured in Michael Pollan's book *The Omnivore's Dilemma,* and there are seemingly as many mentions of his name on menus in Washington as there are beet-and-goat-cheese salads. As recently as five years ago, EcoFriendly Foods, Eggleston's company, sold only whole animals to chefs, but because of growing demand, he recently made parts available to his 50 or so clients from Virginia to New York, having decided "we can't live by our ideals as this point."

He explains: "I'm not as eco-friendly as I would like to be. I wouldn't even call us sustainable—I'd call us resourceful." He uses the analogy of a relationship, citing the compromises necessary to keep a connection going, and says compromise is a reality for many of his clients, too.

Many chefs want to "do the right thing," Eggleston says, but they're under pressure from their bosses who "want to fly the flag of local," yet they bristle at the increase in food costs. Under those conditions, it's easier to "just buy the parts and never even consider the whole animal and what it can do for you."

Cashion suggests this is simply the new reality. The new local. And though it represents progress on the one hand—more high-quality products are on menus than ever before, and that, she says, "improves life for everyone"—on the other hand she thinks something is definitely missing.

What is that?

She pauses for a long moment, then launches into an elegant and impassioned statement of the local ideal, of the give-and-take between chef and farmer, the sense of mutual dependence, the idea that a chef might allow herself to be inspired by the products that arrive at the back door each day, that what hits the table later that night is inconceivable without the input and inspiration of the farmer. Patrick O'Connell, chef at the Inn at Little Washington, a sumptuous respite in the Virginia hinterlands, is even more pointed in lamenting what has been lost.

He attributes the popularity of local to our almost insatiable hunger, in this plastic, commodified culture, for something real and authentic, uncorrupted by corporations. It is, he says, a sad sign of what the past few decades have wrought. The job of the restaurant is to recognize this spiritual hunger. To feed souls as well as stomachs.

"First it was give me something good to eat," he says. "Then it was give me something good to eat and entertain me. Then it was give me something good to eat and take me somewhere I've never been. Now it's prove to me that there is some hope left in the world. Give me a respite from the misery of this world. Let this meal be a sanctuary."

I tell him that sounds like an awful lot to ask of anything, let alone a restaurant.

It is a lot to ask, he says, but isn't this very notion of going beyond embedded in the promise of local, the idea of connecting diners to something larger than themselves? Situating them in time and place? Delivering them to the spiritual?

It seems to pain him, I say, that more chefs and restaurateurs don't regard local with his level of existential seriousness.

"The kind of buzzy stuff that's going on now, I find it kind of tedious and kind of depressing, to be quite honest," he says. "It's contributing to the loss of a sense of place rather than accentuating a sense of place if every restaurant in Washington, DC, has lamb from the Shenandoah."

There follows a lengthy disquisition about chefs who mistake putting out high-quality ingredients on a plate for cooking—"the elevation of those ingredients, through learned technique, into something superlative."

He interrupts himself to say he isn't arguing that the current iteration of local isn't "a good idea for the entire culture and deserving of support."

No?

He sighs. "No. But part of the tragedy of American culture is that we cheapen everything."

A Glimpse of the Future, Part One

The man who, perhaps more than any other, makes me want to believe in the potential of local is Michael Babin. As founder of the Neighborhood Restaurant Group, Babin presides over ten restaurants including Evening Star Cafe, Vermilion, Birch & Barley, ChurchKey, and the new Bluejacket.

The most prominent name in Babin's growing stable is Tony Chittum, the former chef at Vermilion (he's now at the soon-to-reopen Iron Gate Inn, in Dupont Circle) whom many regard as the most passionate, committed supporter of local in our area.

Prior to Chittum's arrival in 2007, Vermilion was a middling restaurant with no discernible focus. Chittum gave it an identity, establishing it as a showcase of the best products from the Chesapeake and the Shenandoah. And while local and artisanal might have become trendy, Chittum's simple, soulful dishes were most assuredly not.

Whether Chittum's arrival spurred Babin to embrace local to the extent he eventually did or Babin would have drifted in that direction anyway is hard to know. But few restaurateurs are more involved in local than he is, and Babin often cites Chittum as inspiration.

One morning last summer, I drove out with Babin to tour a pet project of his, the Arcadia Center for Sustainable Food & Agriculture, a nonprofit operation that manages a small farm near Mount Vernon. It hadn't rained in two weeks, and the crops looked desiccated in the triple-digit heat. Something called "farm camp" was in session; grade-schoolers were learning about crop rotation and–in what sounded like a parody of an urbanite's idea of camp–making pesto.

Arcadia isn't a new idea. Clyde's Restaurant Group runs a farm in Loudoun County. EatWell operates one in La Plata, Maryland. But Arcadia is different, if only because Babin envisions it as something more than a steady source of fresh, local ingredients for his restaurants.

"The farm isn't here to feed the restaurants," he told me. "The restaurants exist to support the farm." Babin is boyish and intense and has the manner of a perpetual grad student, curious and alert to new ideas. A big-city restaurant owner with his own farm on a historic piece of property is a ready-made storyline for a TV show or magazine spread, but it was clear to me that Farm as Symbol held little interest for him.

Thinking he might aid the cause of local by making it more accessible, Babin bought a school bus last year, refitted it with coolers, and had it painted green. The Mobile Market rolled out in May. The bus is loaded up every morning with vegetables and fruits from Arcadia and makes stops five days a week in nine neighborhoods in DC, Maryland, and Virginia that are considered food deserts, lacking the grocery stores and markets of more affluent neighborhoods. Babin called it a "crying need."

What was preoccupying him when I met him was the idea of a large "food hub," a distribution center that would enable more farmers to get their products to more restaurants, and to do so more efficiently. There are more than a dozen of these hubs in Virginia and a few in Maryland. Babin has begun thinking of creating a vast network out of them.

The more forward-thinking members of the movement regard this next-step networking as essential to making good on the enormous promise of local.

Bev Eggleston hopes they'll work toward what he calls "a parallel food system."

"We don't think we can take down Big Agriculture," Eggleston says. "We used to be that naive; we used to think that was possible.

But an alternative transportation system—you can use the analogy of the Beltway. We want to take the pressure off the Beltway, all that traffic. So you have mass transit, you have rail, you have bikes. When farmers are really organized and collaborate, that's what you want. It's not about local; it's about regional and logistical ability. Local isn't moving fast enough for where we need to go. We're moving toward the idea of systems that work versus where things came from."

A food hub, Babin told me, would go some way toward fulfilling that hope. It might even, he said, help bring local out of the realm of the privileged few.

We were standing on a sloping patch of grass that overlooked one end of the property; he gazed beyond a ridge of trees toward a 130-acre stretch of land that he hoped at some point to buy and convert to farmland. I said he didn't sound like a restaurateur or a businessman; he sounded like a social worker who, having achieved a breakthrough with one client, takes on an entire neighborhood.

"People think local is the answer," he said. "It's really the beginning of the answer."

A Glimpse of the Future, Part Two

Mention the word "local" and the image that most often leaps to mind is a farmers market stocked with ripe produce. Or a chef stomping through a farm to pick his own vegetables and herbs for that night's dinner. It most assuredly isn't a diner, especially not a diner with 15 locations—a chain, the seeming antithesis of the movement toward artisanal, fresh, and organic.

A decade ago, I never imagined I'd one day tout the virtues of Silver Diner, let alone hold it up as a symbol of Doing the Right Thing. But times have changed. More to the point: Silver Diner has changed.

From June to July last year, I visited the Greenbelt location of Silver Diner four times for dinner. Among the ten-plus meals I eat out every week, these didn't stand out as particularly memorable—they weren't Culinary Experiences—but I was struck by how much better they were than they needed to be. They were certainly better than what I remembered of the chain some years back, before cofounder Ype Von Hengst overhauled the operation in 2010.

He began sourcing eggs and milk from Amish country—Lancaster,

Pennsylvania. He switched to grass-fed, hormone-free beef and nitrate-free sausage and even added local, dry-aged bison from Monkton, Maryland. Local wines aren't fixtures on menus at many three- and four-star restaurants, yet Silver Diner carries four. There are local beers, too. The last of my four meals included two soft-shell crabs from Crisfield, Maryland, that had been battered and fried and served with a chunky tomato-and-basil salad.

Why make such sweeping changes when no one expects a diner to be anything but a diner? Why attempt such an about-face when there's no necessity?

Von Hengst disagrees. He's vehement. There is a necessity. An urgent necessity.

"I want us to be in business for another 25 years," Von Hengst says. "This is not a fad, this local. Everyone's going to have to get with the program. This is how we're all eating now."

In the first year of his revamp, when he eliminated 35 percent of his old menu, Silver Diner spent an extra million dollars on food, and Von Hengst worried that it might take a few years to attract the customers he needed to sustain the new model. He has since raised prices slightly to cover the higher costs, and his customer base has grown. Local accounted for 10 percent of the menu two years ago but today makes up 30 percent. That might not sound like much, but it's right around average for restaurants that advertise their commitment to local. Von Hengst believes he can bring that up to 40 or 50 percent in five years.

He hopes to work directly with more small farms, to get their products trucked to a central location—an idea not so different from Babin's notion of a food hub. The farmers spend so much of their time farming that they often don't have enough time to spend selling, Von Hengst says. Better that than the other way around, but if there's a centralized source for them and if more restaurants and communities could be exposed to their products. . . .

Here he stops and shares what he hopes is a not-so-crazy dream.

"Bear with me a moment, okay?" All we need to do is connect and organize, he says, and we can turn the local dream into a broader reality. The greatest lesson his work with regional purveyors has taught him is that he wields a power he didn't realize he possessed—a single purchasing decision from Silver Diner, with its volume, can have an enormous effect on the market. Now, suppose other chains—Applebee's, Chili's, T.G.I. Friday's—were to take his example and replicate it on a national scale.

"The Inn at Little Washington and other restaurants that get their good stuff brought to them at the back door every day—that's great," Von Hengst says. "But fine dining is only a small segment of our world—a special class of restaurant that can only be reached by a few. Now, imagine the chains getting in on this with all the people they reach every day and all the volume they do in their buying. Can you imagine the impact?"

The triumph of an idea in this country, Patrick O'Connell says, is the mass adoption of that idea—and its inevitable dilution as it's reinterpreted and bastardized. The corporatization that Von Hengst invites me to ponder is the extension of this principle to the extreme. In a sense, the idea of Silver Diner multiplied by tens and even hundreds stands for the nullification of local as many in the movement like to see it, as a celebration of the authentic, the artisanal, the uncorrupted.

I'm not surprised to discover that Silver Diner itself counts few fans among the movement, though I thought some might be more supportive. Tom Meyer of Clyde's Restaurant Group, who is far from a purist, likens Silver Diner's version of local to "putting Tiffany lamps on the salad bar." It makes the salad bar look nicer, but it forever ruins your image of Tiffany lamps.

That crack is more revealing of the movement's advocates than it is of Silver Diner.

You can say the local movement is about distinctions. You can also say it's about us versus them. You can say it's about spiritual connection. You can also say it's about signifiers of status. You can say it's about doing the right thing. You can say it's about business as usual. You can say there have been great gains in four decades. You can say there remain deep divisions in the food world—divisions the local movement and its advocates were supposed to have paved over. Have and have-not. Foodie and food philistine. Vibrant neighborhoods full of resources and food deserts with precious few outlets for even fresh food.

There's no romance about what Von Hengst is doing. There is realism, however imperfect or impure. A sense—perhaps nascent at this point, but real–of the truly transformative. A glimpse of a future in which local makes good, at last, on its immense latent promise.

If I am to believe–and I want to believe, I do–it will be in this imperfect realism, grounded in the problems of our world and not in a romantic quest for perfection and purity.

A Critical Palate

Confronting a Masterpiece

By Matt Goulding

From *Roads and Kingdoms*

A former food editor of *Men's Health* and co-author of the mega-hit *Eat This Not That* nutrition guides, Matt Goulding indulges his wanderlust appetites as co-founding editor of the digital magazine Roads and Kingdoms, a journal of exotic travel, food, political reporting, and music.

In a mild state of delirium three months ago, I woke up early, opened up three browsers in each of two computers and an iPad, and began furiously clicking. The screens stalled and sputtered and the spinning wheel of death did its foreboding dance of rainbow doom until it felt like the entire Internet was buckling at the knees. But then, suddenly, the skies parted, the wheel stopped spinning, and a calendar with a single green square popped up on one of the nine browsers. This tiny speck of color represented the most coveted table in the culinary universe. One more click and it was mine: no phone calls, no emails, no press credentials—pure, unfettered egalitarianism.

And so here we are in Copenhagen, 90 minutes from what last week was named "the best restaurant in the world" for the third year running by San Pellegrino-sponsored *Restaurant* magazine. (Only el-Bulli, Spain's former reigning king, has held the distinction longer.) Exciting, yes, but I'm not buying it for a second. First of all, never trust a food critic. Second of all, never trust a cabal of critics voting on restaurants many have never been to. Momofuku Ssam Bar is a better restaurant than the French Laundry? Not a single Japanese restaurant in the top 25? These are just a few of the embarrassments of the San Pellegrino list.

But that's not my only source of skepticism. I have read dozens of articles praising Noma's genius, watched global opinion levitate like Apple stock, poured over the Noma coffee table cookbook religiously (cursing the entire time about it being one of the most beautiful and entirely useless texts ever published). It all seems too loose, too ephemeral, as if dinner were being put out by a workshop full of forest nymphs.

And yet, even I find myself using that too convenient shorthand. "Why Denmark?" people ask. "I'm going to eat at the best restaurant in the world," I say. It's too easy, too definitive, too intentionally provocative.

Let's be clear up front. The world needs lots of things: electric cars, an Israel-Palestine peace accord, another season of *Arrested Development*. One thing the world does not need is another Noma article. I will be the 567th critic to file an opinion about this restaurant. I've started and stopped this paragraph a dozen times, but my fingers keep moving. If you've made it this far, I'm sorry for being another voice in the Noma choir. I just can't help it.

How does one prepare for the best meal in the world? Do you train with buckets of cheap caviar and liquefied foie scraps? Do you risk stomach shrinkage with a full-day fast? Or do you follow the lead of competitive eaters like Kobayashi and Joey Chestnut and Sonya "the Black Widow" Thomas and opt for a strict regimen of cabbage and watermelon, mass without the calories, to keep the stomach limber? Perhaps you simply go about your business and hope you arrive at the table ravenous?

I ate a lamb shawarma next to a table of dopeheads in Christiania around noon. That was the extent of my preparation.

"There are no menus. . . . the first part of the meal will come fast and all of it is meant to be eaten with your fingers." This is James Spreadbury, tall, handsome, skinny tie, exceptional Aussie accent. Exactly the kind of guy you want waiting for you on the other side of thosc doors.

1st Course

The meal begins with a few twigs. They've been right there all along, in full camo inside a vase of moss and flowers. Magically a little bowl of crème fraiche appears and we are off. The sticks are made like an eggless pasta and dusted in malt. Washed down with a beer made entirely from birch sap, they taste like dead ringers for real sticks.

2nd Course

A tumbleweed of reindeer moss served on a bed of grass. It weighs slightly more than air and tastes slightly better. And just like that, I feel the pangs of preciousness creeping in already. Am I here to eat or am I here to watch a live performance of Planet Earth?

"I know exactly what you mean. It's like someone is whispering to you but you can't hear it." No, that's not Nathan, my R&K partner and dining companion for the evening. That's René Redzepi, the man himself, chef and owner—the guy who makes Noma Noma. To be fair, he tells me this long after the meal, in a conversation we have by phone, but he then immediately denies it, saying that "generosity is the key of a meal." But he understands my concerns, which says something. Maybe.

If you've seen pictures of the food before, you know what I mean: These plates are hyper-manipulated—down to the last tweezer-placed sorrel leaf—to look like some enhanced version of reality. Nature on steroids. It's what a forest floor might look like for two minutes each spring.

5th Course

"Catch them if you can." It feels like a hollow taunt from the server. After all, it's a mason jar filled with ice. But when you pop the top, there they are, two live shrimp, fresh from a fjord just outside Copenhagen. Every time I make a move, it contorts just enough to throw its body an inch off the ice below. It's still fighting—gently scratching against the roof of my mouth—when my teeth take its life.

"It makes you realize that everything you are going to eat in this meal was alive at some point," says Matthew Orlando, Noma's head chef, a native Californian, and the guy running our meal tonight. "It's not just some piece of meat that comes from the butcher or some vegetable that comes from the green grocer."

At one point, Orlando tells me, 40% of diners at Noma were sending this dish back. Delicious? Sort of. Ballsy? Absolutely.

6th Course

Smoked and dehydrated carrot served on a pitch-black bed of hay ash. "It's how a carrot would taste to a starving man if he found it in the forest, half decomposed, and still loved it." Nathan, globetrotting gastronome, my color man for the evening.

7th Course

A moment of clarity: a single quail egg, cooked sous vide, pickled in apple vinegar, flecked with crunchy shards of salt. It's served in a giant speckled marble egg in which a milky cloud of hay smoke has been trapped. "We use an electric bong we buy in Christiania," says the server with an impish smile.

Turns out that he's not just a server; he's the guy personally responsible for cooking the eggs in a 64°C immersion circulator. One of Noma's greatest contributions to the restaurant world has been putting the cooks themselves in the dining room. They arrive in their checkered pants and brown aprons carrying the food they spend a dozen hours a day prepping and cooking. It's not just the fact that they can add funky little tidbits like the bong anecdote, or that they can break the dish and the cooking process down to a molecular level; it's that the enthusiasm over a dish feels more meaningful when delivered by the hands that cooked it.

Over the course of the night we will meet a good portion of the cooking staff as they each hand-deliver their creations. Some blush like beets, others beam like Scotty, but they all know exactly what they're talking about.

8th–10th Courses

Our table is flooded like some great Southern family picnic. You can't drop a fork without landing on something smoked or cured or pickled. "What happens when you go to a nice restaurant?" Orlando explains later. "You sit down and the waiter comes and asks 'Do you want this? Do you want that?' Then you sit there and you wait for 15 minutes for something to happen. If something doesn't grab onto you right away, then you lose interest. That's why we just hit you. It's our way of saying 'this is not going to be a boring meal.'"

And so the first half hour flashes by in what feels like seconds. After the featherweight food of the first few courses, the flavors begin to match the pace—intensely crunchy, salty, smoky, sharp bites, one after the next.

A crescent moon of crispy pork skin dusted in pine powder and topped with a black currant fruit leather. (Think: stoner meets late-night convenience store, brilliance ensues.)

A finger sandwich, a tile of rye bread filled with lumpfish roe, dill, and smoked cream cheese, and topped with crispy chicken skin. (Think: everything bagel meets chicken nugget, brilliance ensues.)

Cod liver, brined, smoked, frozen, and shaved, dusted with kelp salt, then stacked in a slowly-melting curls atop a milk crisp. (Think: umami madness)

11th–14th Courses

Flower pot. Radish. Dirt. Dig up, crunch down: malt, hazelnuts, dark beer. Grass and yogurt.

Veal neck, hand-shredded into a million microfilaments and wrapped around a spoonful of crème fraiche. Seaweed: oil and powder. A crunchy, creamy marvel. Somewhere upstairs a young prep cook's fingers are bleeding.

A crunchy wave paved with smoked cod roe, dotted with microherbs and topped with broken pieces of brown glass. Those shards are duck chips, not made from the meat itself, but from intensely reduced duck stock, skimmed like scalded milk, then crisped up on the flattop. If this bite of food doesn't give you goose bumps, you are a stone-cold dinner date.

Æbleskiver! Translation: Danish-style donuts served at Christmas time. Only it's May and these battered beauties are stuffed with pickled cucumber and an oily fish fried crisp—his tail and head arching out of both sides of the donut. Nathan starts coughing. Powdered sugar? Powdered vinegar. Salt and sea and vinegar brine, wrapped in the warm, gooey embrace of a perfectly fried donut. Blackout good.

Intermission

And just like that the first wave has crashed right on top of us. The flow of the meal is disarming, both because of its speed and because of the sheer variety of shapes and vessels. Rocks and mounds of moss, flower vases and giant eggs, a shield of vacated mussel shells: the serving vessels mimic the food they carry. The absence of any utensils to speak of only heightens the impact of it all, brings you closer to the food.

As individual bites, some dishes were forgettable and some were magical, but the cumulative effect is pretty stunning. There's no chance for jitters or to even think about how hungry you may or may not be; those butterflies you have when you walk in the door (and if you don't have butterflies, maybe you shouldn't be walking in the door) have their wings clipped by the Noma assault. It's disorienting and counterintuitive and by the time you've inhaled your last granules of powdered vinegar and downed your last drop of birch beer, you realize that your body is buzzing. And that something strange is happening here.

"Did you guys come out to Copenhangen to dine with us?" That's the first question we get from the sommelier. You mean, did we fly 8,000 miles and drop thousands of dollars just to eat one dinner? Seems like a ridiculous question to ask, but as I look around the room and hear the staff talking in Swedish and German and Japanese, maybe not so ridiculous. . . .

"1204 people on the waiting list for this evening. Same day in 2008 (Monday 28th of april) 14 guests in all day. #fuckingfairytale"

This is a tweet sent out by Redzepi moments before being named number one for the third year in a row. That night there was approximately 30 times the number of guests on the waiting list as there were people eating in the restaurant. This year, Noma looks to get something in the neighborhood of a million reservation requests for just 20,000 seats. I thought my mouse click was merely fortunate; I didn't know it was divine intervention.

Part of this crush of interest is out of genuine desire to eat great food, but wasn't Noma serving great food on May 28th, 2008? The weight of that five-word calling card captures the imagination like no other adjective could possibly do: best restaurant in the world.

People don't want to eat in "one of the best" restaurants in the world; it doesn't hold the same weight; it doesn't make as good a doggie bag to take home to your friends and families.

Last year, the day after El Celler de Can Roca north of Barcelona took the second slot behind Noma, I called in the early afternoon and casually made a reservation for five for a week later. In this brave new world, where food is as much a form of conspicuous consumption as Corvettes and chandeliers, second best doesn't quite cut it.

15th Course

Bread and butter. The bane of the fine-dining experience, the filler of stomachs, the destroyer of many a great meal. The blessed breadbasket: It giveth and it taketh away. I swore it off at restaurants with hefty price tags after one too many pre-dessert carbo crashes. But it's sitting there, warm and moist and wrapped in white like a manger child. There is something deeply intoxicating about this loaf; it exhales a warm, sour perfume that feels as ancient as food itself.

I go in for a nibble—just the tip—but end up eating three-quarters of a loaf before Nathan gets back from the bathroom.

A note to other restaurants: I don't want sundried tomato-parmesan bread, black olive bread, walnut-raisin bread. No degustation of breads, please. Give me one loaf, exquisitely made, with the crust crisp and dense enough to break skin and the crumb soft enough to swaddle the wound. Serve it with the best butter you can find, and leave it at that.

Noma understands this. It serves just this one loaf (made with wheat and crushed oats from a small farm in Sweden) along with two magical ramekins: one with rendered pork fat crusted in crispy bits of skin, the other butter made by a small Swedish farmer who whips cultured cream with leftover whey deposits into a transcendent suspension of fat and lactic tang. They call it virgin butter, and indeed, it feels like my very first time. Together, they are the bread and butter by which all others will forever be judged.

Wine and Pine

Ever drink a Douglas fir? Of course you haven't. Until this moment, I didn't know conifers were juiceable. It's the first of five juice pairings, carefully crafted, esoteric cocktails of fruits and vegetables, roots and spices, all designed to go with the high-wire dishes flying out of the kitchen. Celery and celeriac. Carrots and unripe juniper berry oil. Beet and lingonberry. Wines must be retrofitted to dishes based on acidity and spice and sweetness, but by making their own juices, Noma can tweak every last flavor inside the glass to fit the dishes they're being paired with. If there is any advice I can offer, it is this: Skip the wines; order the juice.

17th Course

A single raw razor clam sheathed in an emerald green cloak of parsley, set in a puddle of mussel juice and dill oil that shimmers like ink splotches across the briny surface. A drift of frozen horseradish bites through the sea below. There's a reason why this one has been on the menu since the start. If you asked for Noma in a single bite, this would be it.

18th Course

Wait, what's that sound? I tilt my head towards the din of the dining room. Is it? Could it be? Yes, it is! Laughter, bellowing out from nearly every table in the restaurant. Rumor has it that laughter was banned from Michelin-starred dining rooms sometime back in 1982, but Noma–outlier, rebel, iconoclast–audaciously welcomes it back with open arms.

In all seriousness, laughter is a sound heard too infrequently in nice restaurants. Is it too much to expect that the fun we have be approximately commensurate with the amount we pay? I sure as hell don't want some guy in white velvet gloves delivering me my vol-au-vent of abalone and condor egg, then whispering the ingredients into my ear like a rumor about the queen.

Here's a typical scene from a high-end Euro or Japanese restaurant: Moneyed couples quietly knife and fork their way through course after course of exceedingly beautiful food, occasionally remark on its exquisiteness, and uncomfortably stumble their way through a meal in stilted silence, all the while thinking: "Is this what it feels like to be rich?"

It's all vaguely awkward, even for those who espouse the joys of being pampered. More than that, it's absolutely unfun. I made a promise to myself a long time ago never to drop hundreds of dollars not having fun.

19th Course

A langoustine the size of a smart phone comes beached across an ocean stone. Around it, tiny sea green buttons of oyster and parsley puree. A game of shellfish dipping dots ensues. No pyrotechnics here, nothing screaming "look at me cooking!" That's not the point of this dish. This is one of those dishes you eat at great restaurants where the chef is essentially saying: "Screw you, dude, look at my product." There's not a serious cook in the world who could eat this dish without growing wild with envy.

20th Course

The first real misfire: Chips of dried scallops served with watercress puree and a petroleum pool of mussel juice and squid ink. Too much brine, too much metal–tastes like I've been tossed by a wave and held under a bit too long.

Sometimes you get the feeling that deliciousness is one of a dozen factors a chef considers when putting together a plate, rather than the only–or at least, the primary. That must always be the starting block. Despite what some may say, it wasn't always the primary focus at elBulli (one of Ferran's favorite ingredients, rabbit brains, doesn't scream delicious to most diners), and it isn't at a lot of the places that have followed in its highfalutin footsteps. It's a fragile balance, giving the diners what they want and cooking what you think they need to try. Beef filet or lamb tripe? Chicken breast or cod sperm?

"If we put lamb brain on the menu with cocktail berries, people will probably try it," says Redzepi. "But there's no point in putting anything on the menu if it isn't delicious."

In one respect, you admire the stones on a chef who is willing to put out plates that deeply challenge (and perhaps disappoint) the diner, but it's not enough to bend food into new shapes and textures or conjure up exotic ingredients just because you can. If I can't taste the "why," then what's the point of, say, twisting foie gras like silly putty, or making a potato look like a rock? After eating at Noma, you see that it can be done without disappointing diners. Or making them feel obtuse.

All that being said, allowances must be made for the subjectivity of taste. Culture and rearing have a deep impact on what textures and flavors we find satisfying. Maybe the guy next to me is dunking his scallop chip into the inky puddle with his eyes squinted and his head waggling "yes, yes, yes!"

Requisite Rumination on Foraging

Many of the roots, chutes, rhizomes, leaves, and herbs we are eating tonight are brought to you by the white-clad cooks themselves, who disappear like gnomes into the forest to fill their baskets before service each day. . . .

No one can write about Noma without talking about foraging, and no writer can interview Redzepi without asking him for a demonstration. It seems like a dozen brave scribes have wandered into the forest with René to have him reveal the generosity of Mother Nature. Eater.com coined this new genre of stories the I Foraged with Rene Redzepi Piece (IFWRRP). Nathan and I discuss the possibility of getting Redzepi to go dumpster diving with us in Christiania, but luckily for him, he's at UCLA tonight, giving a speech to an auditorium of Angeleno academics. You lucked out this time, Redzepi.

Søren Wiuff, Denmark's legendary farmer and a major supplier to Noma, has his doubts about Redzepi's crew of forest frolickers. When I visit him at his farm, he tells me that "foraging should be left up to the professionals who do it everyday," not to a team of stagiaires set loose in the forests and along the shorelines around Copenhagen. When I catch up with Redzepi later on the phone, he doesn't disagree: "I feel it would be better if it was organized and done by people who were trained to do it. We are cooks, but the way that it is it's not organized, so we have to do it ourselves. So of course it's shaped our way of thinking about food."

Over the course of the meal, nearly every bite bares something snatched from the wild: an emulsion of sorrel, a tuft of ransom, a thicket of sea spinach. It's not just about looking pretty, or about dropping the f word on diners easily won over by a story; more than anywhere you'll eat right now, the foraged goods at Noma are there for calibrated effect: garlic, acid, spice, bitterness are all enhanced by the Noma scavenge.

22nd Course

A tiny cast-iron skillet arrives at the table screaming hot. Orlando douses it with roasted hay oil and offers up some instructions. "You're going to cook the egg for two minutes. Then you're going to add the butter, stir in the greens, and season it all with salt . . . " We crack the eggs as he returns to the kitchen and just like that, we are cooks in one of the world's best restaurants.

Tsssss. . . . tchaaak . . . chaaaak. Alone with our eggs, heads fuzzy with booze and pine juice, we do our best not to mess this thing up. The oil (infused with roasted hay) spits, the egg (laid by a wild duck with a massive burnt orange yolk) crackles, and the butter (that same glorious stuff that comes with the bread) and ramson and sea spinach (gathered by the chefs) sizzle a glorious tune. You hear it from all sides of the room throughout the evening, but suddenly you're the one making the music.

Later come a pinch of salt, a scattering of fried potato coils, and a generous few spoonfuls of wild garlic sauce. "If you don't like it, it's your own fault," is Orlando's parting shot before the sunset yolk is breached. Eventually, all that is left is the scraping of forks, the grunts of pleasure, and the incoherent mutterings of a man eating the best egg of his life. I've watched ambitious restaurants try to play with sound and taste for years. Normally it's artificial—crashing waves or rustling leaves, a crackling fire piped in from an ipod. It's elevator music; this duck egg, by comparison, is a symphony.

23rd Course

The last savory course of an ambitious tasting menu normally means a hunk of red meat—braised lamb neck, veal breast, beef cheek—but in case you couldn't tell by now, Noma doesn't care much for fine-dining formulae. Instead, a cook brings out a cast-iron pan filled with a massive, sizzling turbot steak, which has been roasted on the bone and basted into submission with an absurd amount of brown butter and herbs. After showing off this fabulously bronzed hunk of fish, it goes back to the kitchen to rest for 10 minutes, just like a good piece of beef. "We didn't think twice about not serving meat," says Orlando.

Nor should they. This is easily the meatiest piece of fish I've ever tasted, as intensely savory and satisfying as the slow-cooked off cuts that you'd normally find at the end of a meal like this. After being carved from the bone, the turbot is slathered with its own roe, buried in a forest of foraged leaves and wild mushroom slices and set afloat in a tea made from dried ceps and berries. The last time I sipped mushroom tea, I spent the better part of the evening in a corner talking to myself, and everything—the sweet watermelon flavor of the fungus, the butter and brine of the roe, the unbelievable savoriness of it all—suggests that tonight might end in a similar manner.

24th–26th Courses

Dessert has come. I think. There is ice cream made from Danish bitters and a disk of yogurt whey frozen solid on top, but there's only the vaguest suggestion of sweetness.

Standard high-end restaurant practice dictates that the dessert stage unfolds more or less in the following fashion: light, palate-cleansing pre-dessert, fruit-driven first dessert high in acidity, knockout chocolate intensity, usually involving chocolate cooked, sculpted, and spiked into various iterations of a general theme. The supporting cast—hazelnuts, passion fruit, tea and herbal infusions—are as predictable as the order in which they will arrive. It's a three-part blueprint that has been baked into the mind of nearly every great chef the world over.

Noma clearly missed the memo. Everything is cold, but nothing is particularly sweet. Redzepi is on the record as not liking sugar, and it shows. In fact, if no one said anything, you might not even know that the meal had hit its savory apex and was now sliding inevitably towards its lightly sweetened conclusion.

After the bitters ice cream comes Pear and Pine: half a pear grilled until blackened, then peeled and served with pickled spruce shoots, pear aquavit, lemon thyme, and a spruce parfait dusted with juniper salt. The last dish is the only one that feels like it was intentionally created to be a dessert: a ruby pool of rhubarb juice with an ivory island of milk curd and tiny archipelagos of brown cheese shortbread. "I'm not sure I understand," Nathan offers after many minutes of silence.

These are complex, esoteric compositions, but as you eat them, you feel like maybe you're missing something. The beauty of the plate, the depth of the description, the excellence of all that has come before this bite leads you to believe that is your own deficiency that has created the letdown—which may actually be true. There is sweetness, yes, but there are many of the same effects that came before it:

bitterness, salt, smoke, acid. In a four-hour, foot-to-the-floor feast, it's a gentle easing off of the accelerator.

You're left thinking: Is this how it ends?

The Bill

The numbers look a little something like this: 26 courses prepared by 40 chefs hailing from 19 different countries served over the course of four and a half hours. Of those courses, 14 of them were stunning, eight were excellent, three were confusing, and one just wasn't good. When it comes to batting averages, that puts Noma in the Ted Williams camp.

The biggest number of the evening? $902.47. That's the pre-tip damage. Staggering, yes, but the hard math paints a much gentler picture: Subtract the wine and juice pairings and the cost per dish works out to be around $11 a dish–what an order of Buffalo wings might run you at Applebee's in Times Square.

The Aftermath

They give us road beers–Noma beers, of course, made exclusively for them by cult microbrewer Mikkeller–for the short stroll through Christianshavn to our little rented apartment. In the canals around the restaurant, boats bob with the shifting tide. Splotches of amber light dance off the water. There is no one out. No one around to notice the stupid smiles on our faces, the triumphant klink of the thick beer bottles, the warm silence of it all.

If you're going to eat at Noma, don't let a cab whisk you back and forth. Take the train to Christianshavn and have a stroll along the canal. Take in the boats, breathe in the sea, let the dim lights of the warehouse district lull you slowly back to reality after a four-hour feast. A meal like this needs to be bookended by quiet, reflective moments, by full consideration for what lies just before–and, eventually, painfully, behind–you.

Food has always been a way for people to tell stories: Pot au feu tells the tale of French housewives transforming scrap meat into luxury through the alchemy of slow cooking. Gazpacho is the story of sunbaked Andalusian laborers looking for a way to take the bite out of the southern Spanish sun. Even luxury bites come with their creation stories: The salmon cornet, the start to every meal at the French

Laundry and Per Se, is the story of a whimsical Thomas Keller and his childhood days at the scoop shop.

But Noma's dishes themselves don't tell concrete stories as much as occupy a vast, interweaving narrative, one that speaks of a new age of cooking. It has most of the hallmarks of great food of the modern age—technical refinery, perplexing combinations, whimsy—but they're strung together in a way that makes them wholly unique. This is not the lovechild of the French Laundry and El Bulli, even if those are the two most readily apparent antecedents to this cooking. This is not molecular gastronomy, modernist cuisine, or even New Nordic. The meal tonight was the first chapter in a novel waiting to be written.

The View from West 12th

By Pete Wells

From *The New York Times*

Even in the Yelp and Twitter era, a thumbs-up or thumbs-down from the chief dining critic of *The New York Times* can be a game-changer. Since assuming the mantle in January 2012, Pete Wells has adopted a nuanced approach: not just ranking stars but really telling the unique story of each restaurant.

If we have a shred of sanity left, those of us who never stop thinking about what we're eating have to wish that once in a while we could turn back the clock. We start to miss the days when you could go out to dinner without all the food talk: the "have you been there yet?" interrogations, the name-dropping of pop-up ramen stands and celebrity milkweed foragers, the tableside decipherings of what is on your plate, moving counterclockwise from the cod milt gelatin resting in a pickled starling's nest.

A yearning for simpler times may explain the Beatrice Inn in the West Village, which has been packed to its low rafters since it opened in November. Graydon Carter said that he and his partners in the restaurant, Emil Varda and Brett Rasinski, wanted it to be "a classic chophouse," a term so dusty that one of the city's few remaining chophouses, Keens, now calls itself a steakhouse.

Everything about the place—the burnished paneling; the leather banquettes in law-firm green; the men waiting tables in white shirts and black neckties; the short and to-the-point menu of Hillary Sterling, the chef since February—broadcasts a return to the days when dinner required no explanation. Sorry, Instagrammers, but you will not be posting shots of your steak or salad, because a footnote on the menu reads "Photography is not permitted."

It might have added, "Please refrain from talking about your food," but there's little danger of that.

After eating squishy goat-cheese gnudi that were bursting with the flavor of warm New York City tap water and were buried under slices of prosciutto almost too thick to cut with a fork, only one remark came to mind: "How's your steak?"

The steak was no conversation piece itself. A New York strip, it had a chewy band of fat at its edge, as if the meat were wearing a protective latex sheath, and the meat was shot through with gristle. My dinner companion and I stared and chewed and thought for a long time. Finally, one of us said, "Well, it *is* medium-rare."

There was nothing to say about a stack of carrots that came with a braised and roasted veal breast except that it shouldn't be possible for vegetables to be both charred and raw. Apparently it is, though, because a steak turned up in the company of blackened and crunchy hen-of-the-woods mushrooms. The desperately undercooked sunchokes with sautéed trout were something of a relief. They were awful, but they were not even a little bit burned.

For dessert there was crème brûlée studded with dried-out apple fragments that might have come from an envelope of instant oatmeal, and an uncreamy scoop of ricotta gelato on a stiff pool of ice-cold honey caramel with chopped walnuts.

This time words came easily. We asked for the check.

Other dishes were unremarkable in a more benign way. Flattened chicken with crunchy, golden skin and a kind of dirty-blond gravy was easy enough to eat. Kale dressed with lemons, chiles and fried garlic was better than that, and so was a salad of watercress and other greens with shaved radish. The strip steak on a later visit was juicier and more tender.

Lamb porterhouse showered with roasted artichoke leaves was very satisfying once I ignored the grainy, salty sauce of dried black olives around it. So were crisp and fresh fried oysters with smoked char roe, as long as I didn't focus too much on a bitter and blandly sweet citrus purée. A dessert with fresh grapefruit and whipped cream on top of lemon curd was refreshing and soothing.

But there I go, talking about the food. The thing to do at the Beatrice Inn is to look and listen.

Two longtime staff members at *Vanity Fair*, which Mr. Carter has edited since 1992, are huddled at a cozy round table. They nod to me because I used to work as a fact-checker at the magazine, drifting away around 1994.

"Everybody is obsessed with Jennifer Lawrence," the man next to me is shouting. Speaking only for myself, I am more interested in Candice Bergen, who left a few minutes ago. And over there is Charlie Rose and his posse. He seems about to doze off, but he looked that way before he started eating.

Sleep would be challenging. Those ceilings multiply the roar. On the plus side, they make short people look like models and models look like church steeples. Everybody is roughly twice as attractive inside these walls. This might explain why, when the Beatrice Inn was a nightclub known for youthful high jinks, the previous owners had to put up signs reminding patrons that it was not all right to have sex in the bathrooms.

Mr. Varda and his partners put a stop to all that. The drug of choice at the Beatrice Inn is now wine, most of it rather expensive, served with laconic grace by Aaron Zebrook. One night he recommended a pinot noir that took me over some rough patches in my meal, and he also led me to a bottle I drank during the one good dinner I had at the Beatrice Inn.

This was back in January, when the chef was Brian Nasworthy, previously a sous-chef at Per Se. Mr. Nasworthy's interpretation of chophouse cuisine was careful, smart and refined, although the desserts were still a punt. His shrimp cocktail played gently poached shrimp against a horseradish-chile gastrique that had the lively hot-sweet-sour-salty tension of a Southeast Asian sauce. He baked oyster mushrooms, salsify and spinach under a textbook hollandaise for a clever take on oysters Rockefeller. It was meant to be a sideshow to an over-the-top-rich Wagyu rib-eye for $150, but came close to upstaging it.

Mr. Nasworthy was dismissed a few weeks later and is now the chef de cuisine at Picholine. Mr. Varda praised his talent but said, "his culinary philosophy did not agree with ours."

Evidently not. The four of us at the table that night had talked about the food on the way home.

Takaya or Leave Ya: Didn't New Asian Get Old, Like, Ten Years Ago?

By Ian Froeb

From *Riverfront Times*

Before becoming dining critic for the daily *St. Louis Post-Dispatch* in June 2013, Ian Froeb reviewed and blogged about St. Louis restaurants for the weekly *Riverfront Times* for six years—long enough to refine the inevitably necessary craft of how to write a negative review.

The calamari looked innocuous enough when our server brought the appetizer: familiarly curled squid rings breaded and fried to a light golden brown, with aioli for dipping. My wife ate a few. I ate a few. We looked at each other.

"Where's the squid?" she asked.

"I don't know," I said and took a close look at one of the rings. It looked like fried calamari, but beneath the fried breading, there seemed to be nothing but . . . more fried breading. "I don't even know how this is scientifically possible."

"It's like it's there. But it's not."

Schrödinger's calamari.

I scraped as much breading as I could from another piece of squid. There was something underneath, after all: a spindly, off-white ring of squid, utterly desiccated. I snapped it in half with my fingers. It went *crunch.* I summoned our server. She examined the evidence. She made a face. The face looked like this: o_0. She said she'd tell the kitchen about the calamari. In the meantime, did we want a replacement order?

We did not.

The spirit of scientific inquiry notwithstanding, it is with some regret that I report that the calamari was the second-worst dish we had at dinner that evening at Takaya New Asian.

Takaya New Asian opened in January as part of the new Mercantile Exchange development downtown. Owners Eric and Jenny Heckman also operate Tani Sushi Bistro in Clayton, a restaurant I liked when I reviewed it in 2008 and to which I've returned several times since, and happily. Yet Takaya is such a spectacular failure that, as Pitchfork once memorably claimed about a new Weezer album, you have to consider whether the older work is as good as you remember.

The problems are apparent as soon as you walk in the door. The blissed-out faux-Portishead lounge music like the soundtrack to a soft-core flick on Cinemax. The open fireplace in the center of the dining room. The cushy booths big enough to hold an entire bachelorette party and the bride-to-be's inflatable replica of Jon Hamm's penis.

Is it 1997? No. Did the hostess, having run out of menus on one of our visits, ask us to share a single copy? She did. Does the menu feature Asian-fusion cuisine? You bet your bulgogi sliders it does.

Those sliders, selected from among the menu's list of appetizers and small plates, were one of the more successful dishes I encountered at Takaya. An order brings three (two, at lunch) miniature sandwiches with marinated steak on brioche buns. The meat was tender and flavorful, gently sweet, though the bread could have been fresher. Another appetizer, Korean-style grilled short ribs, featured a similar marinade—sugar and soy sauce, with hints of garlic—but tougher meat.

Grilled hamachi jaw is a "signature" appetizer. (The menu uses the term frequently—and spells it correctly, unlike "makerel" and "massago.") I thought it logical to try a signature appetizer. Our server took my order. She returned a few minutes later: the kitchen didn't have any grilled hamachi jaw that evening.

Another "signature" appetizer is mozzarella tempura—a fancy term for fried cheese sticks. These are crunchy and gooey but maybe not as salty as you want from fried cheese and, oh, God, I'm critiquing cheese sticks at an upscale downtown restaurant.

There's a sushi selection, which features nigiri sushi, sashimi and the over-the-top Americanized rolls for which Tani is known, such as the "Oh My God" roll, which arrives at your table completely engulfed in flames. At Tani the delicate knifework and no-nonsense presentation of the nigiri sushi impressed me. Here, ragged slabs of fish sat atop rice swabbed with too much wasabi paste. A piece of "makerel" was weirdly juicy, as if plucked from a bin of brine.

Dinner entrées include "specialty" sushi presentations, as well as more conventional—and certainly not "New Asian," however you choose to define that nebulous phrase—dishes, such as teriyaki (your choice of chicken or beef). Among the sushi entrées is "hamachi carpaccio." This, the menu boasts, isn't merely another "signature" dish, but Takaya's absolutely *most* outstanding, must-try dish. I thought it logical to try an absolutely *most* outstanding, must-try dish. Our server took my order. She returned a few minutes later: the kitchen didn't have any "hamachi carpaccio" that evening.

In its place our server directed me to a similar preparation with very thin slices of raw tuna and equally thin slices of avocado fanned around a plate. The tuna and avocado sat in an iridescent puddle of various sauces—soy, ponzu, something vaguely chile-mayonnaise-esque (it was difficult to tell)—that looked like an oil slick and tasted like tuna water.

The worst thing we ate on the night of Schrödinger's calamari was pan-seared sea bass in a garlic-miso sauce. A large hunk of fish sat atop a mound of rice, with a few paltry asparagus stalks doing garnish duty. The fish was inexplicably, mouth-hauntingly bitter—until I turned it over to reveal a crust of diced garlic that had been burnt black.

At least I found an explanation for the sea bass. I still can't figure out the squid. Admittedly, that's not entirely Takaya's fault. On a recent episode of the public-radio Zeitgeist prodder *This American Life*, a reporter obsessively bird-dogged a rumor that (once, maybe) a pork processor somewhere had packaged pig rectums (or, as they're called in the industry, "bung") as "imitation calamari." When the investigation proved fruitless, the reporter resorted to a blind taste test in which he pitted fried calamari against fried bung. One of the two participants preferred the bung.

I was not one of the tasters, and I'm pretty damn sure I've never eaten pig-butt rings à la calamari, but I suspect that in a blind tasting I'd have chosen 'em over the deep-fried squid I ate at Takaya.

I should mention that our server did delete the calamari from the bill. That kind gesture, however, barely dented the total tab: $90, for a dinner for two. Unless you're content with a minimalist selection of nigiri, a meal at Takaya will cost you. Maybe there was a time in St. Louis when merely opening a sleek new restaurant aping a played-out culinary trend was enough to serve as one of the cornerstones of splashy new downtown development.

In 2013, though, it comes off as a load of horse–well, you know. Rhymes with bung.

I Ate My First McRib, and I Regret It

By Katharine Shilcutt

From *Houston Press*

In a boom city like Houston, fine dining can be *so* beside the point. All the better for an iconoclastic voice like Katherine Shilcutt, who began at the alt weekly *Houston Press* as a blogger and kept that brash style throughout three years of *Press* restaurant reviews. She is now features editor at the monthly *Houstonia* magazine.

I made it through 32 years without tasting a McRib. Over three decades spent tasting and eating all other manner of offensive foods—yet a McRib had never passed my lips, until last Thursday. I can't say I regret my meal. It goes deeper than that: a sense that I gave in, sheeplike, to a national phenomenon whose promises—no matter how meager—were always going to fall short of my expectations.

I knew I wouldn't like or even understand the McRib, and was content to go the rest of my life without tasting one. Fast food and I have a strained relationship as it is except for a few soft spots: McDonald's coffee, Whataburger taquitos, Jack in the Box tacos at 1 a.m.

I respect—perhaps even admire—the technology and ingenuity involved in creating an identical meal across thousands of different chain restaurants 365 days a year, 24 hours a day in many cases . . . but the product is rarely something I'm interested in consuming. And those same massive food systems that are, in part, responsible for creating clone versions of Big Macs or Whoppers every single day are also responsible for the woeful industrialization of our agricultural systems and farms. Those fast food chains are, in part, responsible for our nation's deepening battle against obesity, hypertension, diabetes and a whole host of other health issues.

And, quite frankly, the McRib always looked simply disgusting, like a flattened condom stuffed with Ol' Roy-brand cat food and slathered with untrustworthy sauce between two buns that looked like the plastic set that came with my children's grocery store set when I was six years old.

To a Texan, the concept of barbecued pork is reserved for a handful of items: pork butts and ribs, both left on the smoker for hours and neither coated in sticky-sweet sauce. We don't do pulled pork sandwiches here, either, so the idea of a pork sandwich—pulled or not—doesn't appeal to me either . . . especially one from McDonald's.

But I let curiosity get the better of me last week when I logged onto Facebook one morning.

"I would like to see you write a complete review on the McRib," read a request on my wall from frequent commenter Fatty FatBastard. "And it should be the cover story."

"I would like Tard the Grumpy Cat to come and live with me," was my hasty reply. (Luckily Fatty is battle-hardened by all the years spend in the EOW comments section.) "You can't always get what you want." Besides, I argued, I'd never had one before.

Fatty persisted. "See? Then it would be a completely unbiased review."

Less than 24 hours later, I was hitting my third McDonald's of the afternoon and cursing Fatty's real name as I searched desperately for one that still had the damn sandwich in stock. Each one I approached beckoned with a sign heralding the glories of the limited-time McRib, yet a closer look at the signs revealed tiny stickers saying simply: "Sold out."

Along with a keen sense of irritation, my curiosity was growing still stronger. If the stupid sandwiches are sold out everywhere, they must be at least decent—right? People couldn't be buying out the sandwiches if they tasted like Ol' Roy.

Finally, I found myself in the drive-thru lane of the McDonald's on North Main, where a cheerful-sounding Hispanic woman was imploring me through the speaker to add another McRib to my order for only $1.

You have enough McRibs here to tack them on like apple pies? I wanted to yell back at her. *Send them to the other McDonald's so people don't have to waste $20 worth of gas driving around town like pork-crazed assholes trying to find them!*

Instead, I pathetically contemplated actually adding the extra McRib to my order. *It's only one dollar*, I reasoned. *I deserve it.*

I shook my head and snapped out of the disgusting food-as-reward mindset I fall into far too often—a mindset, I might add, that's once again encouraged by deals such as these at fast food chains such as this one. (Besides, the brownie bites I'd added onto my 1 a.m. Jack in the Box order the night before had been woeful. And those were only $1 too.)

Back at the office after nearly an hour on the road, I actually tore into my McRib with a voracity that both appalled and astonished me. A growling stomach was making all of my decisions suddenly, but even after the first few hunger-blinded bites I could tell it had been a mistake.

Here's the thing: The McRib does not taste terrible, except for the fiddly, fleshy little nubbins extruding from the sides that are meant to represent "ribs." In fact—full disclosure—I ate the entire thing.

I felt so hollow afterwards that it was as if my stomach had shifted entirely outside my body, as though my abdominal cavity was rejecting it in shame. This was a terrible thing to have eaten and I had no real excuse to do so. It contained no nutritional value whatsoever and unlike the questionable tacos and other junk food fare I occasionally consume, it didn't even have the benefit of being so delicious as to excuse its negligible health benefits.

The "pork" inside the McRib tastes quite obviously fake. It has a curious spongy texture that allows your teeth to slide into the meat with almost no give whatsoever. It's not like you're eating real meat at all, but something materialized on the Holodeck of the Starship Enterprise or a piece of food that's fast-fading in some airport during the course of the *Langoliers*. It's just . . . weird.

The pickles and onions, with their very real and very appropriate crunch, absolved the meat somewhat of its off-putting texture. But the bread suffered the same fate as the meat, falling apart in my mouth like dust, as if it had never been real in the first place. I spent the next hour trying and failing to understand how there can be any passion around such a dull, lifeless thing. How is there a clamor for the McRib? In what way is it "epic" or "legendary"?

I am left today with the disappointing knowledge that there is a huge segment of my fellow Americans who look forward to this creepy fake meat every year with a hunger that borders on the pathological. I am not judging their taste—taste, after all, is subjective—but rather judging the quality of the food that people have come to revere. This silly, false thing. This vague improvement over potted meat.

I cringe as much as the next person when I hear words like "organic," "artisan," or "craft" overused or, worse, misapplied. But I'd far rather suffer a surfeit of foods in our nation that are leaning towards the *real* end of the spectrum than the fake. Because there is really no excuse for the McRib, and my life is poorer for having tasted it.

Back When a Chocolate Puck Tasted, Guiltily, Like America

By Dan Barry

From *The New York Times*

In November 2012, when snack food giant Hostess Bakeries shut down its ovens, junk food mavens nationwide went into a tailspin. (Not to worry—new owners revived the brand in July 2013.) Leave it to *Times* columnist Dan Barry to catch the guilty spirit of America's Twinkie addiction just right.

There was a time; admit it. There was a time when, if given a choice between a warm pastry fresh from a baker's oven and an ageless package of Ring Dings fresh from the 7-Eleven, you would have chosen those Ring Dings. Not even close.

After opening the tinfoil or cellophane wrapping with curatorial care, so as not to disturb the faux-chocolate frosting, you would have gently removed the puck-shaped treat and taken a bite deep enough to reveal crème—not cream, but crème—so precious that a cow's participation was incidental to its making.

You did not care that this processed food product in your trembling hand was an industrial step or two removed from becoming the heel of a shoe. You already knew that not everything is good for you, and this was never truer than with a Twinkie, a Sno Ball, or a Ring Ding—the Ding Dong equivalent in the Northeast.

To you, they all tasted like, like: America.

Now, from Irving, Texas, comes word of the closing of Hostess Brands, your friendly neighborhood baking conglomerate, the maker of Ring Dings, Ho Hos, Funny Bones and other treats whose names conjure a troupe of third-rate clowns.

"We ceased baking this morning," Anita-Marie Laurie, a Hostess spokeswoman, said Friday morning. This means Hostess, and Drake's, and Dolly Madison, oh my.

Though the bankrupt company attributes its closing to a strike by a union with a mouthful of a name—the Bakery, Confectionery, Tobacco Workers and Grain Millers International—the truth is that the bad-snack market has been in decline for years. All of a sudden, it seems, nosy consumers want to know what it is that they are ingesting, and that's not good if you manufacture edible curiosities like SuzyQs and Raspberry Zingers.

Beyond the heart-aching loss of many, many jobs, a Hostess shutdown doesn't necessarily mean that consumers, particularly the dietetically tone-deaf, have eaten their last Twinkie. Some industry analysts express confidence that as Hostess sells off its assets in this saddest of bake sales, an iconic treat like the Twinkie will be snatched up by a savvy opportunist—perhaps one who might resume production using a novel application for the famously indestructible Twinkie (a loofah sponge you can eat!).

Speaking personally, the news sent me into a panic. A Hostess shutdown would mean an end to certain rare and delicious moments of guilty bliss, those few seconds that come right after devouring a Ring Ding and right before the stomach realizes what has happened.

It would also mean an end to measuring the passage of time by the color of Hostess Sno Balls, those marshmallow-y mounds of cake and gunk that appear to be some kind of confectionary prank. Normally the pinkish color and approximate texture of an eraser, they turn green for St. Patrick's Day, orange for Halloween and lavender for the Easter celebration of the death and resurrection of Christ. Or maybe the lavender just means springtime.

Hurrying to the nearest food store, I barreled past the fruit and fresh produce section, fully aware of the eyes of potatoes narrowing in disappointment, and the heads of lettuce turning away in judgment. I nursed dark, violent thoughts about making a salad, and kept going.

And there, in the supermarket equivalent of the timeout room, were the food chain's nutritional delinquents. Your Hostess cupcakes. Your Funny Bones. Your Yodels. Your Yankee Doodles and Sunny Doodles, the ebony and ivory of cupcakes. And, yes, your Ring Dings. Make that my Ring Dings.

I held a package of two Ring Dings in my hands. Reading the nutrition facts, I took comfort in seeing that the word nutrition was not in quotation marks. I skipped past unimportant details—the 310 calories, the 13 grams of fat, the 37 grams of sugar—and found validation in the 2 grams of dietary fiber.

The package says that's 8 percent—count 'em—8 percent of your "daily values." Whatever that means.

Then I turned my eyes to the block of white type listing the ingredients that help to make the "devil's food cake" resilient enough to be enjoyed in whatever comes after the End of Days. Well, I thought, you can never have too much "sodium stearoyl lactylate," and I headed to the checkout counter with my single item.

Here is the eat-your-broccoli part of the Hostess saga. According to Harvey Hartman, a food-industry researcher and consultant in Bellevue, Washington, the country's food culture is rapidly changing. Consumers want less processed foods, he says, and more information about "the story behind their food"—which might not be something that a Sno Ball would want told.

But Mr. Hartman understands the allure. The careful unfolding of a Yodel or Ho Ho, but only after the frosting has been nibbled away. The scraping of teeth against the piece of white cardboard for that last remnant of a SuzyQ. The connection in a Twinkie, or a Funny Bone, to what he calls the "soulful elements of our past."

That is why, one night this fall, or maybe this winter, or perhaps in the spring—there's no rush—I will wait until the kids are asleep, their tummies content with kale chips and quinoa. Then, basked in the bluish glow of some black-and-white television show, I will eat my faux-chocolate, crème-filled, Bloomberg-infuriating, chemical-rich, bad-for-me, really-really-bad-for-me, all-but-extinct Ring Dings.

Both of them.

Farm to Table

Forgotten Fruits

By Rowan Jacobsen

From *Mother Jones*

As his book titles suggest—*American Terroir, Shadows on the Gulf, The Living Shore, Fruitless Fall*—Rowan Jacobsen is a unique amalgam of science/nature/food writer, bent on a very particular quest: To underscore the connections between our food and our imperiled environment.

Every fall at Maine's Common Ground Country Fair, the Lollapalooza of sustainable agriculture, John Bunker sets out a display of eccentric apples. Last September, once again, they covered every possible size, shape, and color in the wide world of appleness. There was a gnarled little yellow thing called a Westfield Seek-No-Further; a purplish plum impostor called a Black Oxford; a massive, red-streaked Wolf River; and one of Thomas Jefferson's go-to fruits, the Esopus Spitzenburg. Bunker is known in Maine as "The Apple Whisperer," or simply "The Apple Guy," and, after laboring for years in semiobscurity, he has never been in more demand. Through the catalog of Fedco Seeds, a mail-order company he founded in Maine 30 years ago, Bunker has sown the seeds of a grassroots apple revolution.

All weekend long, I watched people gravitate to what Bunker ("Bunk" to his friends, a category that seems to include half the population of Maine) calls "the vibrational pull" of a table laden with bright apples. "Baldwin!" said a tiny old man with white hair and intermittent teeth, pointing to a brick-red apple that was one of America's most important until the frigid winter of 1933–34 knocked it into obscurity. "That's the best!"

A leathery blonde from the coast held up a Blue Pearmain in wonder. "Blue Peahmain," she marveled. "My ma had one in her yahd."

Another woman got choked up by the sight of the Pound Sweet. "My grandmother had a Pound Sweet! She used to let me have one every time I hung out the laundry."

It wasn't just nostalgia. A steady conga line of homesteading hipsters—Henry David Thoreau meets Johnny Depp—paraded up to Bunk to get his blessing on their farm plans. "I've got three Kavanaghs and two Cox's Orange Pippins for fresh eating, a Wolf River for baking, and three Black Oxfords for winter keeping, but I feel like there are some gaps I need to fill. What do you recommend for cider?" Bunk, who is 62, dished out free advice through flayed vocal cords that make his words sound as if they are made of New England slate.

Most people approached with apples in hand, hoping for an ID of the tree that had been in their driveway or field ever since they bought the place. Some showed him photos on iPhones. Everywhere he travels in Maine, from the Common Ground Country Fair to the many Rotary Clubs and historical societies where he speaks, Bunk is presented with a series of mystery apples to identify. He's happy to oblige, but what he's really looking for are the ones he *can't* identify. It's all part of being an apple detective.

In the mid-1800s, there were thousands of unique varieties of apples in the United States, the most astounding diversity ever developed in a food crop. Then industrial agriculture crushed that world. The apple industry settled on a handful of varieties to promote worldwide, and the rest were forgotten. They became commercially extinct—but not quite literally extinct.

Even when abandoned, an apple tree can live more than 200 years, and, like the Giving Tree in Shel Silverstein's book, it will wait patiently for the boy to return. There is a bent old Black Oxford tree in Hallowell, Maine, that is approximately 213 years old and still gives a crop of midnight-purple apples each fall. In places like northern New England, the Appalachian Mountains, and Johnny Appleseed's beloved Ohio River Valley—agricultural byways that have escaped the bulldozer—the old centenarians hang on, flickering on the edge of existence, their identity often lost on the present homeowners. And John Bunker is determined to save as many as he can before they, and he, are gone.

The key thing to understand about apple varieties is that apples do not come true from seed. An apple fruit is a disposable womb of the mother tree, but the five seeds it encloses are new individuals, each containing a unique combination of genes from the mother tree and the mystery dad, whose contribution arrived in a pollen packet inadvertently carried by a springtime bee. If that seed grows into a tree, its apples will not resemble its parents'. Often they will be sour little green things, because qualities like bigness, redness, and sweetness require very unusual alignments of genes that are unlikely to recur by chance. Such seedling trees line the dirt roads and cellar holes of rural America.

If you like the apples made by a particular tree, and you want to make more trees just like it, you have to clone it: Snip off a shoot from the original tree, graft it onto a living rootstock, and let it grow. This is how apple varieties come into existence. Every McIntosh is a graft of the original tree that John McIntosh discovered on his Ontario farm in 1811, or a graft of a graft. Every Granny Smith stems from the chance seedling spotted by Maria Ann Smith in her Australian compost pile in the mid-1800s.

The fine points of apple sex were lost on most US colonists, who planted millions of apple seeds as they settled farms and traveled west. Leading the way was John Chapman, a.k.a. Johnny Appleseed, who single-handedly planted tens of thousands of seeds in the many frontier nurseries he started in anticipation of the approaching settlers, who were required by the government to plant 50 apple trees as part of their land grants. Even if they had understood grafting, the settlers probably wouldn't have cared: Although some of the frontier apples were grown for fresh eating, more fed the hogs or the fermentation barrel, neither of which was too choosy.

Every now and then, however, one of those seedling trees produced something special. As the art of grafting spread, those special trees were cloned and named, often for the discoverer. By the 1800s, America possessed more varieties of apples than any other country in the world, each adapted to the local climate and needs. Some came ripe in July, some in November. Some could last six months in the root cellar. Some were best for baking or sauce, and many were too tannic to eat fresh but made exceptional hard cider, the default buzz of agrarian America.

Bunk likes to call this period the Great American Agricultural Revolution. "When this all happened, there was no USDA, no land grant colleges, no pomological societies," he says. "This was just grassroots. Farmers being breeders." As farms industrialized, though, orchards got bigger and bigger. State agricultural extension services encouraged orchardists to focus on the handful of varieties that produced big crops of shiny red fruit that could withstand extensive shipping, often at the expense of flavor. Today, thousands of unique apples have been lost, while a mere handful dominate the market.

When Bunk lays out his dazzling apple displays, it's a reminder that our sense of the apple has increasingly narrowed, that we are asking less and less from this most versatile of fruits—and that we are running out of time to change course.

Exhibit A: The Harrison apple, the pride of Newark, New Jersey, renowned in the early 1800s for making a golden, champagne-like cider that just might have been the finest in the world. But the Harrison, like most of the high-tannin varieties that make good hard cider, disappeared after Prohibition. (The recent hard-cider revival has been making do largely with apples designed for fresh eating, which make boring cider.) But in 1976 one of Bunk's fellow apple detectives found a single old Harrison tree on the grounds of a defunct cider mill in Newark, grafted it, and now a new generation of Harrison trees is just beginning to bear fruit. It's as if a storied wine grape called pinot noir had just been rediscovered.

The usual argument for preserving agricultural biodiversity is that monocrops beg for monolithic wipeouts caused by pests and disease, while diversity gives you more genetic tools to choose from when you suddenly need them. And, indeed, some of the old apples have genes for resistance to apple scab and other scourges of the modern orchard that are proving useful. (Apples require more pesticides than any other crop, and it's exceedingly difficult to grow modern apple varieties organically.) But don't discount romance. We still have the option, as did previous generations, of experiencing apples with hundreds of different personalities.

Bunk's love affair with apples dates to 1972, when he began farming a hardscrabble plot of land in the town of Palermo, Maine, after graduating from Colby College. That first fall, he noticed the apples ripening all over town, trees that had been started decades ago and were now in their prime, yet mostly went ignored. He began picking them.

"I felt like these trees I was finding in my town, and then eventually all over Maine and other places, were a gift to me by someone whom I had never met, who had no idea who I was, who had no idea that I was ever going to be." Over time, he says, "I started thinking, I got to come to earth and have this amazing experience of all these trees that were grown and bearing, and all these old-timers who would take me out into their fields and show me things and take me on trips down these old roads. And I would knock on somebody's door, and the next thing you know I'm eating with them. It was like gift after gift after gift. And I started thinking, 'Do I have any responsibilities with this? Or do I just soak it up and let it go?'"

So he founded Fedco Trees, which specializes in rare heirloom fruits and vegetables, the goal being to make them less rare. When he finds one of these missing links, he grafts it onto rootstocks at the Fedco nursery and begins selling the trees a few years later. Bunk estimates that over the past 30 years he has saved anywhere from 80 to 100 varieties from oblivion. His forensic methods involve everything from studying the depth of the cavity around the stem, to checking the trunk for grafting scars, to poring over old nursery catalogs and historical records. He hangs "Wanted" posters at corner stores in the towns where the apples originated, hands them out at historical society meetings. A typical poster reads, "Wanted Alive: Narragansett Apple. Last Seen in York County! . . . Originated on the farm of Jacob H Harmon, Buxton, Me., in 1873." Then, beneath a drawing and description of the apple, is the plea, "If You Know the Whereabouts of This Apple Please Contact Fedco." He dreams of finding once-adored apples that haven't been heard from in a century, like the Fairbanks (the pride of Winthrop, Maine) and the Naked Limbed Greening (a big green sucker from Waldo County). His current Holy Grail is the Blake, a richly flavored yellow apple so tasty it is said to have been exported to England in the 1860s. According to old catalogs and horticulture books, the Blake was widely distributed in Maine in the mid-1800s, with flesh that was "fine, firm, crisp, subacid," and a distinctive habit of holding onto its apples after most other trees had dropped theirs. Bunk had been tantalizingly close to a positive Blake ID in December 2011, when an old tree covered with small yellow apples was spotted in a field near Portland, on land that might have been owned by a J. H. Blake in the 1870s, but the tree turned out to be a seedling, the apples didn't quite fit, and the quest for the Blake continued.

One of Bunk's best finds was the Fletcher Sweet, which his research indicated had originated in the Lincolnville area. In 2002, he met a group from the Lincolnville Historical Society. They had never heard of the apple, but they knew of a part of Lincolnville called Fletchertown, which, like many other old villages in northern New England, had since been reclaimed by the forest. A member of the society wrote an article for the local paper saying it was looking for an old apple called a "Fletcher." A 79-year-old named Clarence Thurlow called the paper and said, "I've never heard of a Fletcher, but I know where there's a Fletcher Sweet."

Thurlow led Bunk to the abandoned intersection that had once been the heart of Fletchertown, pointed to an ancient, gnarled tree, and said, "That's the tree I used to eat apples from when I was a child." The tree was almost entirely dead. It had lost all its bark except for a two-inch-wide strip of living tissue that rose up the trunk and led to a single living branch about 18 feet off the ground. There was no fruit, but Bunker was interested. A few months later he returned, took a handful of shoots, and grafted them to rootstock at his farm. A year later, both Clarence Thurlow and the tree died, but the grafts thrived, and a few years later, they bore the first juicy, green Fletcher Sweet apples the world had seen in years. "It's a great apple," Bunk says. "It has a super-duper distinctive flavor." Today, Bunk has returned young Fletcher Sweet trees to Lincolnville.

This is the magic of apples. You can't take a graft of Clarence Thurlow and grow a new one, but his tree was easily duplicated and returned to Maine life. Today, I can take a bite out of a Fletcher Sweet and know exactly what Clarence Thurlow was experiencing as a boy 80 years ago. I can chomp into a Newtown Pippin and understand what Thomas Jefferson was lamenting in Paris when he wrote to a friend that "they have no apples here to compare with our Newtown Pippin."

"It's about apples and it's not about apples," Bunk says of his work. "I talk about the history of apples, but you know what? I'm giving a highly political talk, because it's about our agricultural heritage."

And that heritage is in jeopardy. Not only has the industrial food system confined us to a meager handful of apple varieties, but many of the new apples being released, like the SweeTango, are "club apples"—intellectual property of the universities that bred them. Growers must sign a contract that specifies how the trees will be grown and where they can be sold, and they must pay annual royalties on every tree. The days of farmers controlling their own apples may be numbered, and the idea of breaking that chain of knowledge bothers Bunk. "When you and I interact, our ability to be together on earth is predicated by all the stuff that people did for thousands of years. You and I didn't invent language. You and I didn't invent clothes, roads, agriculture. It's up to us to be not just the receivers of what was given to us, but the givers of whatever's going to come next."

By the end of the Common Ground Fair, I had begun to wonder if there were any more apples to rediscover. Freakish spring weather had produced the worst apple year in a century. Many trees had no fruit at all, and fewer people than usual were bringing Bunk their enigmas. We'd seen several Pumpkin Sweets and Roxbury Russets, along with a bushel of seedlings, but not a single tantalizing lead. Then a handsome young couple walked up to us. They looked vaguely Amish, he in a vest and straw hat, she in homespun linens. "Is there one with 'ghost' in the name?" the man asked. "We recently bought a place in Gardiner that has some really old trees. The 95-year-old previous owner told us the names. One was something like 'ghost.'"

Bunk couldn't think of any heirloom apple with a name even close to "ghost," but a month later he made the trip to check out the ghost apple. As soon as he saw the Gardiner house, he grew hopeful. It was a classic old Cape and barn, and there was a row of some of the oldest pear trees he'd ever seen in the front yard. Fifty-foot crab apple trees shaded the house.

Skinny maples had colonized the land behind the house, but at regular intervals between them, in an orderly grid, he could make out the dark bulk of ancient revenants. It was an old orchard of about 30 trees. Most were dead. Some had gradually lain down on the ground and were now melting back into the earth.

The Ghost, it turned out, was a Snow, the name misremembered.

A bright red Canadian apple cultivated by French settlers in the 1600s, the Snow is fairly common, though it's best known as the mother of the McIntosh. It is named for its snow-white flesh. "Or ghost-white," Bunk mused. He identified a brown, fuzzy Roxbury Russet, the oldest apple variety in America, also not an unusual find. He didn't feel particularly disappointed; most leads go nowhere.

Then, along the back edge of the old orchard, he came upon a gnarled tree that was at least 150 years old. It held no fruit, but on the ground beneath it lay two dozen golden apples. Bunk picked up one and turned it over in his hand. It was round and firm, with prominent russet dots and a splash of russet around the stem. He knew instantly that he'd never before seen this apple, and, with a thrill, he also instantly wondered whether he had just found the Blake at last. Very few truly yellow apples were grown in Maine 150 years ago. But was the flesh "fine, firm, crisp, sub-acid"? He bit into the apple. Check, check, check, check. It would take a lot more detective work to prove this was a Blake, and he would have to return next fall to get some fruit in better condition, but he had a strong hunch that this ghost of the Great American Agricultural Revolution was a ghost no more.

Earth Mothers

By Erin Byers Murray

From *Edible Boston*

As *Edible* magazines proliferate across America, it's a natural fit for them to profile a new breed of independent local farmers and artisans. Case in point: this feature by Erin Byers Murray, managing editor of *Nashville Lifestyles* magazine and author of *Shucked: Life on a New England Oyster Farm.*

"Have you seen a sexier tractor?" Karen Pettinelli grinned as she pulled up the corner of a dusty brown tarp to show off her 60-year-old Persian orange Allis-Chalmers cultivation tractor. The trim, olive-skinned 29-year-old is the founder of Terrosa Farm in Barre—and a member of one of the state's fastest-growing farm demographics: female between the ages of 25 and 40. The US Department of Agriculture's 2007 census reported that female-operated farms in Massachusetts doubled since 2002 and, says Rick Chandler, the state's director of agriculture business training, those numbers are still climbing.

"They've inherited a piece of land that no one else wanted or they're looking for a secondary income. A large number have been career changers," says Chandler. Many of these women are part of a couple, he says, noting, "It's a reversal in the traditional family farm. The men are now playing a support role and the women are in charge."

But land, income and career are only part of it. Women are flocking to the field for the lifestyle—one that allows for hard work with high emotional rewards. Each of the four farmers included in this piece downplayed the rigorous schedules and task-juggling and focused more on what they personally get out of their own farms: personal fulfillment, joy and, most of all, community.

"The community is just as important as the food that we're growing," says Meryl LaTronica of Powisset Farm in Dover. "We're not just growing food. We're growing people."

"For me, community was a huge reason to get into it," says Karen Pettinelli. She's been farming in earnest since she was 19; the Sudbury native was first inspired by Sienna Farm owner Chris Kurth. "We were scheduled to go on a field trip and Chris came into the classroom saying, 'There's going to be a frost tomorrow, we have to pick all the eggplant right now! Who's going to help me?' And I thought, 'Class or that? Count me in.' So I went to pick eggplant with him. And that was the beginning of the end," she laughs.

Farming was never at the front of the suburban girl's mind, especially since her father had grown up on a farm and hated it. "It was a poor farming family so he went to college and then climbed that ladder. He didn't want this life," she says, adding cautiously, "and now, here's his daughter who wants to farm."

Ten years later, Pettinelli says her father is starting to come around. After high school, she worked at Green Meadow Farm for four years, then the Food Project for two. Last season, she reconnected with Kurth to be the assistant farm manager at Sienna; this year, she'll work there part-time while also running her own farm.

Terrosa's first season, 2011, was a rocky one. The original plan was for Pettinelli to farm her family's land in Mendon, where her father grew up, but a carpet of poison ivy covered the two usable acres and completely derailed her plans.

"There it was mid summer: I'd bought a tractor, I was all prepared to do a CSA and I didn't have any land," she says. Her boyfriend, a 29-year-old pig farmer named Floyd Kelley, stepped in and offered her the use of a few acres of land on a neighbor's property in Barre. Pettinelli uses it on the simple terms that she pay the owner in vegetables (the owner pays a reduced tax on the land since it's used for commercial farming).

Kelley grew up on his family's working farm where he now raises pigs, sold under the label Burnshirt Valley Farm. Pettinelli uses Kelley's greenhouse for her seedlings and the two have built a root cellar in the family's unused dairy barn. Despite last season's rough start, Pettinelli sold most of her crop at the Wayland winter farmers market and to the restaurant Armsby Abbey in Worcester.

This summer, she's creating a "holiday" CSA, offering boxes of greens and other produce to be timed with Memorial Day and July 4th—she'll start a winter CSA later in the year. "I like the holiday idea because I know what's in the ground, I know how many members to sign up, I know what they're going to get, and I know how much to charge," she says. The traditional summer CSA model can be stressful for a farmer just starting out, she says. "You're going to do your best but you're always trying to meet expectations, which are different for every single member," she says.

Instead, she prefers to grow crops that get her excited, which right now happens to be a lot of roots and specialty greens like fennel leaf, shungiku, mizuna and tatsoi—all of which require more weed control than pest management. Which brings us back to that tractor. The $5,000 piece of equipment was her biggest investment for a reason: "I get to design my own cultivation tools," she says with a smile.

For 31-year-old Caitlin Kenney, family has been the single most valuable asset to her Plough In The Stars Farm in Ipswich. Her parents raised her on a horse farm, the Ascot Riding Center, where her father also tended a large family garden—which eventually became the first plot for Kenney's farm.

"We spent morning till night outside. I grew up riding, bird watching and just working really hard," says Kenney. She studied international development with a focus on agriculture at UMass Amherst while working various odd jobs in the food world. "I was surrounded by people who said: To do what you really want to do, you have to do it on your own. You have to be brave enough to take that step," she says.

Kenney had several opportunities to travel during her college years and came back understanding that for her, sensory experiences were key. "I wasn't someone who could go to work, then come home and have home be the place where I found joy. I needed it from the moment I woke up to the moment I fell asleep," she says. After school, Kenney worked on a few different farms including Seeds of Solidarity and Brookfield Farm, where she says she "learned how to balance a farming life with strength, perseverance, patience and joy."

Spending two seasons at First Light Farm in Hamilton gave her the confidence to go back and start a farm at home. The challenge then became convincing her father. "He had seen the land around us be developed or mismanaged for any number of reasons," she says. He also had concerns about making a farm profitable but she was able to negotiate with him, agreeing to stay within his original 60-by-40 foot garden plot for her first season in 2010, which provided enough produce to supply a 12-person CSA. "I had to show him there was consistency and that I really wanted to do it. From that, he could see I was dedicated," she says.

Now in its third year, Kenney's farm will serve about 60 members—she's expanded to two acres of land, growing enough vegetables, flowers, fruit and herbs for her members as well as for a few restaurants, including The Market Restaurant in Annisquam. Her CSA has two levels, with the option of a deluxe add-on that might include honey, syrup or local cheese. Because her membership is small, she knows many of her customers personally and often tailors shares to what they want (such as arugula over kohlrabi or tatsoi). "My farm is really personal to me and I want everyone who is involved in it to enjoy it and to choose to be there," she says. Most of her members have come through word of mouth—many of them through the riding center itself.

As for profitability, Kenney says the first few years have been flat—she lives rent free as the caretaker of another farm and has made enough through the CSA and weekly trips to the Newburyport Farmers Market to pay off the irrigation equipment, greenhouse costs, seed, fertilizer and market supplies that she uses each season. Last year, she brought on an apprentice/partner who now runs her market operation, plus she's enlisted work-share volunteers and a few high school students as interns. She's still a few seasons away from bringing in a salary, she says, but her quality of life is what really matters. "Having my own farm, there's just so much purpose. It's completely reshaped how I think about my life," she says. "It's challenging but there is a lot of joy in it."

"I really didn't expect to be a farmer at all," says 33-year-old Christy Kantlehner of Wrentham's White Barn Farm. "I thought I had a black thumb."

It turned out, all Kantlehner really needed was a little confidence. After studying sustainable development at UMass Amherst, she took an internship on a farm out in Oregon where she also worked at a sustainable restaurant and started her first garden. She returned home to Wrentham where her grandparents lived on five acres–land that had been in the family for generations. There was an old horse barn and a back field that had been used for hay, but otherwise the property sat unused.

Kantlehner knew she wanted to do something with the land but took her time gaining the skills to turn it into a full-fledged farm. While waiting tables at Al Forno in Providence, she revived the family garden by growing a small selection of crops and flowers. But she needed more hands-on experience. She took 10 months to travel through Europe with World Wide Opportunities on Organic Farms (WWOOF), a program that connects volunteers with organic farms around the world. Working her way through Switzerland, France and Italy, she picked up Old-World farming techniques while, along the way, a mental picture of her own farming life began to take shape. She spent the trip taking notes, drawing up crop plans and mapping out the best uses for her family's land.

Back at home, Kantlehner took a class through the Department of Agricultural Resources called Tilling the Soil of Opportunity. The course helped her lay out a business plan and a name for the farm–both of which she presented to her family to make a case for her start-up. With their approval, she planted a quarter of an acre in 2008 and made plans to clear and plant an additional three acres by the following year. That first season, she farmed in the mornings, made it to markets on the weekends and waited tables at night. She also lived in her grandmother's house rent-free.

"I didn't pay myself at all and only had volunteer labor but was able to pay back all of my expenses that first year," she says. With her earnings, she bought herself a disc harrow and a manure spreader–both of which she needed to open up the additional field–and spent that winter planning for her first CSA. She also started attending meetings of CRAFT, an Eastern Massachusetts collaborative alliance for farmer training, where she met another young farmer named Chris.

"One thing that was always terrifying for me was that I would be doing this alone," admits Kantlehner. Her vision of a fulfilling farm life included meeting a farm husband–and Chris turned out to be the one. Once Kantlehner shared her farm vision, Chris immediately volunteered to partner up and the two started the CSA in 2009. They were married last year—and are expecting their first child in October.

Today, White Barn Farm has about 75 CSA members and a farm stand, which sells vegetables, flower bouquets and other local products like honey, seafood and coffee. Kantlehner is hoping to use the farm in other ways over the coming years, both as a venue for events (her own wedding took place on the farm last year) and a community gathering place for her CSA members—they sometimes project movies on the side of the barn and invite members to bring a picnic. For Kantlehner, the vision of the farming life and the reality are still very much aligned. "It's amazing how it all worked out," she says.

Like Karen Pettinelli at Terrosa Farm, Meryl LaTronica is totally into tractors. As farm manager of Powisset Farm in Dover, a property owned by the Trustees of Reservations, she's in the fortunate position of having a few of them—as well as a barn to house them and a mechanic when she needs one. In 2006, the Trustees turned the Powisset land trust into a working CSA, something they'd also done with one of their properties in Ipswich. They hired LaTronica, who had apprenticed at Blue Heron Farm and Waltham Fields Community Farm, to be their farm manager.

"It wasn't as if the money would be mine—it all goes back to the Trustees—but as a young person there was no possible way I could buy my own farm and make this all happen," she says. "It was the best of both worlds."

LaTronica grew up in Holliston and came to farming in her early 20s. About a year after finishing college at Simmons, when she was working at Veggie Planet in Harvard Square, she attended a protest against the war in Afghanistan and recognized one of the picketers—Ellery Kimball of Blue Heron Farm, a supplier for Veggie Planet—who held a "Farmers For Peace" sign. "I had been mulling over this idea of farming so I ran over and told her I what I was interested in. A week later I was working for her," says LaTronica.

Her apprentice position with Blue Heron, and later at Waltham, gave her a solid foundation but when LaTronica arrived at Powisset, she was faced with the daunting task of starting a farm almost completely from scratch. There was a large cow barn, which she and her team cleared out and turned into a CSA pickup space, as well as eight acres of fields, which had been plowed but had no other infrastructure in place.

"I got here and they told me, 'OK, you have 90 members signed up.' It was a total whirlwind," she says. Membership has since grown to about 340 members and they've plowed three additional acres. LaTronica now manages the farm with an assistant manager, three apprentices and a number of work-share volunteers; she and two of the apprentices have housing on the property.

Unlike Kenney, Kantlehner and Pettinelli, who are all self-employed, LaTronica is tasked with satisfying a much larger body of overseers. A 100-page document, written by the founders of the farm and managed by the Trustees, guides LaTronica's vision for expansion, further farm development and CSA program growth. This year, in an effort to create more urban partnerships, Powisset will supply vegetables to the ReVision Urban Farm in Dorchester to help fill their CSA shares.

For LaTronica, filling a need in the community is one of the greatest rewards. "Farms have this way of gathering people—they're drawn in by food and the energy," she says, echoing a sentiment that Pettinelli, Kenney and Kantlehner also conveyed.

As the women gear up for another summer, they each expressed hope for a successful season and excitement for getting back in touch with their customers. Though there will be an unknown set of challenges facing them after this abnormally mild winter, they all understand that farming is their own choice and no matter how they came to it as a career, they're grateful to be able to do it. Their motivations, after all—working outdoors, preserving and managing a piece of land, lifestyle, sensory experiences, tractors—are secondary to what is fundamentally a job that feeds and nourishes people in their community. LaTronica sums it up perfectly: "To be in the dirt and be outside and see the world happening . . . I have the best job in the world."

The Cheese Artist

By Dara Moskowitz Grumdahl

From *Minneapolis St. Paul Magazine*

New-Yorker-turned-Minnesotan Dara Moskowitz Grumdahl has championed the dynamic Twin Cities food scene for over 15 years, winning five James Beard Awards along the way. She writes about food, she writes about wine—and naturally, the meeting point of the two: cheese.

What would a great horned owl want with a lamb? Just the brains, really. One will fly in over the flock of dairy sheep and grab a young lamb in its talons, then make like a zombie, and fly away. Eagles eat the whole lamb. So do black bears, wolves, and the primary problem, coyotes.

But to lamb guardian and artisan cheesemaker Mary Falk, co-owner of LoveTree Farmstead in Grantsburg, Wisconsin, the predators that target her prized Trade Lake sheep—the creatures that provide the milk from which she makes her exquisite cheese—aren't the true danger. The real danger lurks in the cities, where people don't understand what complex ecology means, where people think you can kill your way to abundance and pleasure. Because if your pleasure is cheese, you should know that Falk makes what many call some of the finest cheese in the United States—maybe even the world. And she does it by nurturing a complex ecology of top predators, gentle grazers, and many much smaller creatures. "The University of Wisconsin sent a guy out here who was doing a predator count in the state," she says. "He counted ours and said we were crazy."

Falk doesn't look crazy. She looks like Jane Fonda playing the role of a farmer who has been out in the sun all day. Her hair is the color of honey, her eyes like a light-green leaf in a sun-dappled forest. She came to the Twin Cities as a radio host, and she has the perfect voice for it, gravelly like Kathleen Turner's, the kind of voice that makes you lean in to hear more. And when she laughs, her voice broadens and deepens into a welcoming boom. It even does this when she's telling a rueful tale, like the time she let coyote hunters on her land and they mistakenly took out "the alpha bitch," disrupting a long-established hierarchy. "She had been running things around here for 10 years, managing two packs of coyotes, keeping them away from the sheep. Once she was gone, all hell broke loose. We went from having perfectly well-behaved coyotes, as those things go, to civil war."

There are many reasons for the great number of predators on LoveTree Farmstead, where Falk and her husband, Dave, have been raising dairy sheep since 1989. The St. Croix River isn't far, and it's a major reserve for great birds such as bald eagles and red-tailed hawks. The land around LoveTree holds eight lakes that act as a water road to the river, attracting all sorts of critters, and there is a string of state forests and wildlife reserves just north of LoveTree. Then there's the fact that Dave and Mary *like* predators, insofar as they support the grand balance of nature. That's why they keep half of their 130 acres as their very own "wildlife refuge." This gives trumpeter swans, osprey, otters, and several less benign animals free run of the spring-fed ponds and rolling hills covered with lavender clouds of bluestem and yellow sparks of birdsfoot trefoil.

To combat the predators without actually waging full-scale war, Mary has assembled a sort of Dr. Doolittle–style SWAT team of protective animals. There are the lookouts: tall, shaggy llamas who spy predators at the perimeters no matter which way the wind is blowing. If the llamas see something, they let the guard dogs know. Mary's guard dogs are a special crossbreed of Spanish Ranch Mastiffs, American-bred Italian Maremmas, and Polish Tatras. They are the size of a timber wolf and are fiercely committed to their lambs and ewes, among whom they live 12 months a year. On any given day, these impressive dogs can be seen poking their heads up a few inches above an ocean of wool, like seals in the sea. They can easily take down a coyote, and they can make a wolf think a lamb is more trouble than it's worth.

The final members of the SWAT team are the border collies, who take on crowd management in the event of an attack, rounding the sheep into a tight flock.

By nature, the LoveTree dairy sheep don't flock; they eat, outside, year round, making the sweet milk that Mary gathers and turns into cheese. On Saturdays, she sets up shop at the St. Paul Farmers' Market and sells cheese to people who, curiously enough, have no idea that they are buying some of the best-tasting cheese in the world.

The Taste of Genius

Tami Lax is the founder of Madison's Slow Food chapter and owns two of Madison's best restaurants: the famous white-tablecloth Harvest and the casual Old Fashioned Tavern. Before that, she was the chief buyer and forager for an even-more-famous Madison restaurant, L'Etoile. That's where she met Mary.

"To this day, I've never had a cheese culinary experience like the day I met Mary," she remembers. "I was at L'Etoile, and she brought in all these little samples. I don't want to say it was life-changing, but I was absolutely speechless at every sample of cheese. The word 'genius' is the first thing that came to my mind, and it's the word that has stayed."

As the chief cheese buyer for her restaurants, and a former American Cheese Society judge, Lax has tasted as many Wisconsin cheeses as anyone. "Mary's easily one of the top three cheesemakers in Wisconsin, there is no doubt in my mind," she says. "The originality of what she does—each of her cheeses has such a unique flavor profile. Such depth, such texture—her cheese is always a mind-blowing experience for me, even years later."

Steven Jenkins, another fan, wrote the book on cheese, literally. His 1996 book, *Steven Jenkins Cheese Primer*, is the definitive reference for Americans who want to understand cheese. "Mary is the most talented, drop-dead cheesemaker of my career," he proclaims. "Her Trade Lake Cedar is an American treasure. What she does to get her sheep's milk—my God. Her sheepdogs have to protect that flock from eagles, bears, wolves—it's a wild wonderland. That she's not a superstar and as rich as some bogus so-called 'celebrity' chef is criminal."

Jenkins's beef with celebrity chefs is this: He feels that artisans like Mary do all the work, and chefs get all the credit. "All chefs do is pick over and buy what artisans and retailers have spent 20 years working on." In Jenkins's view, these poseur chefs are aided and abetted by "hackneyed food writers who keep talking about terroir. What lunacy this idea of striving for terroir is! Cheese is either well made or it's not. It's either made by somebody who has that magical spark or it isn't. You can't actively imbue your foodstuff with terroir. That happens by God and the supernatural, and it's a natural outgrowth of your talent as a cheesemaker."

Terroir is indeed a popular idea in food right now, and it looks to be growing in importance. The idea is this: If a food is from a specific place, and only that place, it will taste of that place. What makes Italy, Bordeaux, and Wisconsin different are the plants, trees, soil, bedrock, rain, rivers, ponds, and lakes there, all the way down the life chain to the tiny microscopic molds and microflora that, incidentally, make cheese possible.

The idea of terroir finds its fullest flower in wine writing: Austrian riesling vines plunge their taproots 40 feet under the ground to retrieve water, and in the process somehow come back with the taste of slate. That idea of terroir is almost entirely responsible for the difference between $10 and $400 wines. But terroir is a critical underpinning of cheese as well. For instance, Roquefort, the famous blue cheese, came about because of the specific natural interactions of a certain little part of southern France, called the Larzac Plateau, where there is a plain of red clay that isn't much good for tilling but is very good for grazing. Sheep were fed there, and their milk turned into cheese, which was stored in natural limestone caves of the region that happened to provide an excellent medium for growing a wild, bluish mold indigenous to those caves, a mold now named *Penicillium roqueforti*, which is cultivated and distributed worldwide.

Cheddar cheese came from a similar but different interplay between the milk of cows from a certain part of southwestern England and wild molds in the caves of the Cheddar gorge. Gruyere cheese has the same story in Switzerland. Today, around the world, and especially in the United States, most cheeses are a sort of 40th-generation carbon copy of that original moment of lightning in a bottle: They're made with commercially cultivated strains of the original molds and bacteria and milk that has been pasteurized, then named after that original tangle of animal, plants, and cave.

An American Original

To make an American cheese with the significance of Roquefort, Cheddar, or real Swiss Fribourg Gruyere is not easy. It requires three things: one, a belief that making such a cheese is possible; two, the willingness to do what it takes to make it happen; and three, an essential erasure of the modern world.

LoveTree Farmstead is where Mary effectively erases the modern world. There are the wolves and great horned owls, of course, but more germane to cheese production are the untilled, herbicide-free, pesticide-free fields of wild grasses, nettles, sedges, and assorted plants on her land. The dairy sheep rotate through the fields, contained by mobile electric fences—her one concession to modernity. The Falks move the sheep into one meadow, with their attendant animal SWAT team, then the sheep and lambs advance, often standing single file like a herd of munching Rockettes, slowly chewing. At the end of the day, the Falks retrieve them, milk them, and then move them into another field.

I toured these fields with Mary one day—fields with names such as Little Eden and Beer Can Stand—and with each footfall a hundred little bugs would hop and skitter: grasshoppers, crickets, odd little leaf jumpers. It sounded like we were walking through a bag of potato chips. "A guy from the USDA came out here to take soil samples for a statewide census of what's living in the soil," Mary says. "He said we had more worms than anybody."

It's easy to imagine why. Many plants need animals to distribute their seeds by physically carrying them through their digestive tracks or on their fur and by tamping seeds in the soil with their feet, piercing the top crust of soil and pushing the seeds into the earth. In the LoveTree fields, chomping, pooping sheep play the roles that deer and bison did on the prairie. Then the sheep turn those wild plants into milk. The milk retains the taste of fringed blue aster,

Indian paintbrush, and purple prairie clover, making it much different from the milk of cows raised in Switzerland or California or on a confinement dairy-cow lot down the highway.

Mary gathers that milk and, in its raw state, separates the curds and whey.

The importance of making cheese from the raw milk of ewes who graze one particular patch of land can't be underestimated. Humankind's understanding of the microbiome—the cloud of bacteria, yeast, protists, and fungi that circulate in, on, and all around us, from the deepest cave to the top of the tallest building—is in its infancy. Recently, scientists from the Human Microbiome Project announced that each and every one of us has 100 trillion microbial things living in and on us, turning food into usable nutrients, moisturizing our skin, and defending our lungs against invaders. Without them, we'd be dead.

Without the right ones, or enough of them, we might just be sick. Research into whether our microbiome plays a critical role in human health is just beginning, but preliminary research suggests it plays a role in everything from obesity to asthma and autoimmune diseases. Research into the flavor complexities of aged foods such as prosciutto, salami, wine, and especially cheese suggests that microbial complexity correlates to the complexity of the finished product's taste. But how does the native complexity of a stand of predator-filled woods in northeastern Wisconsin affect the taste of cheese?

To find out, Mary had her husband take out part of a hill with a Caterpillar. It was a red clay hill, and Dave is comfortable doing things like that, because he used to build silos for a living. "She looked at me and said, 'We're going to put cheese underground,'" Dave remembers. "I had never heard of that."

Once the hill was gone, Dave constructed a concrete room with ventilation leading out to the woods. Over the years he took that hill apart with a Caterpillar several more times, eventually discovering that the best shape for a cave was round, like a silo. It's best because of the way the air circulates, in a circle up to a ventilation hole, and for the way the moisture drips down from a pitched, round roof, keeping humidity even throughout the space.

When Mary shapes her individual cheeses, she brings them to her cave to age. (The whey from the cheese production is also blended into the guard dogs' food, perhaps strengthening the dogs' attachment to their flock.) Many of Mary's cheeses are pure sheep's milk, but some are a blend of sheep's milk and her outdoor-pastured cows' milk. The cows are descended from a Scottish Highland-Angus-Jersey cross and are majestic animals with soaring horns that make them look like bulls, but they're actually milkable ladies. In the cave, the young cheeses are hand-rubbed—a treatment that encourages a rind to form on the outside—and are then flipped every day or so, sometimes for weeks, sometimes for many months, depending on Mary's own personal sense of when a cheese is ready. It is inside this humid, refrigerator-like, woods-connected silo of a cave that the cheeses become what they will become.

What they become is absolutely unique, a true American original cheese unlike anything that has ever been made, or tasted, on earth. Her Trade Lake Cedar looks like a rock or mushroom; the rind tastes earthy and ashy, an umami non-fruit world of hay and mineral, whereas the interior is tangy and chalky and meadow-like. Her dry Gabrielson Lake tastes a little like Parmigiano-Reggiano, but is freaked with little crystals of concentration and tiny red lace points of mold.

The cheeses come and go, and Mary often makes one-of-a-kind batches that reflect some event on the farm, some week of too much milk or too little. "When I think of Mary's cheeses, in terms of a world analog, what comes to mind are principally the cheeses of Sardinia and the Pyrenees," Steven Jenkins tells me. "Though Mary's are more graceful and unctuous." And they're essentially only available to people in the Minneapolis and St. Paul metro area. But she isn't very well known, even among foodies. In fact, an informal poll of people I know outside of the restaurant industry suggests that almost no one has heard of LoveTree.

"It's funny, there's a sort of Minnesota paradox when it comes to something on this level," says Lenny Russo, chef at Heartland and owner of the only market to which Mary will sell. "The Minnesota paradox is, people who live here think it's the best place in the world, even if they've never been anywhere else. At the same time, there's this inferiority complex, where something not from here immediately gets a leg up. If you say this is one of the best cheeses in the world, there are a lot of people here who just won't believe you. But they'll pay a super-premium for something from France or Italy that essentially comes from a factory. This indigenous inferiority complex is what will probably keep her from succeeding the way she should. If she was making this cheese in California or New York, she'd be world-famous."

But Mary isn't even as famous here as she should be. The only places to buy LoveTree farm cheeses are at the St. Paul Farmers' Market (year round), Heartland Market, the summer Kingfield Farmers Market, and the LoveTree farm, at their new farm store. You can also taste them at the LoveTree farm on Pizza by the Pond days. Every Sunday, from 2 pm to 8 pm all year long (weather permitting), Mary trades in her shepherd's crook for a pizza peel and melts some of her LoveTree cheeses on top of her four-day-fermented pizza dough, made with flour from Great River Organic Milling, just down the river, and mixed with a sourdough culture developed from her cheese.

Before the pizza-farm events, she forages for such idiosyncratic toppings as fiddlehead ferns or wild wood nettles, or she trades ingredients with neighboring farms or friends from the farmers' market. Try the plain cheese–it's as bold a plain-cheese pizza as you'll ever have in your life. I've also tried the wild watercress, which tastes like something straight from Sardinia, iron-y and green and fresh. I've also had the Old Man Dave, which comes with different sausages from the day's farmers' market or is topped with meats from a neighboring farm, Beaver Creek Ranch, and vegetables from nearby Burning River Farm. The pizzas are delicious, but more than that, they're exquisitely true to their place. The whole scene reminds me of one of those ridiculous magazine features where writers are eating some salad of wild-foraged greens and locally grazed but unnamed cheese on an island in Corsica that no one could ever get to. But this is in Wisconsin, not too far from a Dairy Queen. The pizza oven is located in another part of the hill that Dave bulldozed, then lined with tire bales, built out with logs from the property, and roofed.

The Politics of Cheese

I talked to Mary in the pizza enclosure one hot day, as some strange beetle gnawed loudly on a log overhead, occasionally sending down a shower of sawdust. She was terrified about the raw milk crackdown that's happening nationally and in Wisconsin. She's convinced that they're coming for the cheesemakers next.

Currently, raw-milk cheeses are allowed in the United States if they're 60 days old or older. She'd of course like to be making younger cheeses, as she has now and then and sold as "fish bait: not fit for human or animal consumption." She has sold it at the St. Paul Farmers' Market, where presumably avid fisher-people snap it up. "We don't have much money or many material things. All we have is what comes from nature," she says. "And that's a good thing. All you have to do to have raw milk and raw milk cheeses is regulate it. I'm not afraid. My milk is much cleaner than pasteurized milk."

The way the state of Wisconsin regulates its milk is by counting absolute numbers of bacteria, the standard plate count. Milk, after it has been already pasteurized, can have an SPC of 20,000 bacteria per milliliter. Milk destined to be made into cheese is allowed to have an SPC of 1 million bacteria per milliliter. Mary says her raw milk is consistently measured with an SPC of less than 10,000 bacteria. If any, or all, of these numbers sounds high, you might have an incorrect notion of how many bacteria actually surround you and everything you see. Adults have two to three pounds of microbes—that is, bacteria, yeast, and other tiny creatures in and on us—at all times; they're also currently in your garden and on your walls and on everything you can see, except the moon, sun, and stars. Heavily pregnant women's whole microbiome changes, with digestive microbes moving to the birth canal; the act of being born is also a biological christening with necessary bacteria.

The way Mary sees it, good cheese does not repudiate its connection with nature; rather, it is the land from which it comes, from the wolves and eagles to the invisible microbes, that makes the caves of France taste like the caves of France and the caves of Wisconsin taste like the caves of Wisconsin. "I remember that first time I felt the cheese in the vat: What is that? That's the curd firming up. And that understanding: This is the milk I have, so how can I get to the flavor I want? Why are people so afraid of nature?"

She launches into a complicated scientific argument about how the cheese-making process destroys pathogens, about how the fact that food has microbiology at all is a foreign idea to many. We understand antibacterial soap, but we don't understand that without the microbiome of bacteria on our very own hands, our skin wouldn't work; it would crack and split. We understand killing bacteria in food. We don't understand that bacteria are not an outside thing, they are part of the thing–they are part of the wolves and the flowers and us. She leans back and listens to a blue heron baying from a nearby pond. "But I don't know if most people even understand where cheese comes from," she muses. "It's easier to be afraid than to learn something. Between the politicians and the coyotes, I prefer the coyotes."

A Snail's Tale

By Molly Watson

From *Edible San Francisco*

The San Francisco area is fertile territory for curious foodists like Molly Watson, a freelance feature writer, recipe developer, blogger (thedinnerfiles.com) and local foods expert for about.com. You never know where culinary curiosity can lead you—in this case, it all began with escargots.

As I stood over our kitchen sink scrubbing slime and bits of snail poo out of a plastic bucket I did not feel heroic. I did not sense the triumph of the urban forager feeding her family with found edibles. I had no swell of locavore pride in preparing tiny creatures plucked from my yard. I did not even give myself a pat on the back for being such a dedicated food writer.

Instead, I knew that despite my fears, I couldn't be too bad of a mother if I was willing to purge snails for my son.

Shortly after this last Christmas, my 9-year-old son and I were lucky enough to find ourselves walking past L'Escargot Montorgueil, an old Parisian restaurant with a giant bronze snail hanging over its awning. The previous day he had been stunned by the fact that a steak and fries is a widely available lunch option, and now he saw that snails were on offer. He can be an adventurous eater and our trip to Paris was bringing out the best in him.

It was morning, so the restaurant was closed. But when a friend and I planned the menu for our New Year's Eve feast, I mentioned my son's newfound fascination with escargots. Our friend's French pride kicked into high gear and he insisted on buying the specimens himself.

The day of the party, he handed me an aluminum tray with a stiff white paper lid bedecked with the Le Grandgousier sticker on top. These weren't just snails, they were the best escargots from the snazziest *traiteur* on the Rue St-Honore. Inside were three dozen fat tan snail shells, each about two inches across and filled to the rim with bright green butter. We baked them in the oven for the recommended 15 minutes and brought them to the table already adorned with baguettes and a bottle of Montrachet.

As the other adults helped themselves to a few shells and sipped their wine, the snail buyer focused on my son, watching him pick up the first shell, dig around with a toothpick (for we had no designated two-pronged escargot forks), pull out a fat squiggle of gray meat dripping with seasoned butter, pop it in his mouth and chew. I'm not sure whose eyes lit up more brightly with delight when it became clear that the long-awaited taste of escargot lived up to so much expectation.

"Mom," he said, "you should write a story about snails!"

Both the French and the Americans at the table laughed. No no, they all asserted, California garden snails aren't the kind you eat.

But they are. They are exactly the kind (or, to be exact, one of the kinds) you eat. In fact, according to UC Davis, California has brown snails (*Helix aspersa*) because a Frenchman brought them here in the 1850s in order to make escargots (we were actually tucking into *Helix pomatia*, the other snail species commonly eaten in France, which tend to be bigger and have distinctive tan shells). Heliciculture didn't take off in the Golden State, but like so many others before and since, the mollusks loved it here.

In Search of Helix Aspersa

Once upon a time, our garden was full of snails. Big fat dudes who left slime trails across the concrete stairs and hid under deck chairs and along the sides of plant containers. I went on a crusade that consisted of leaving saucers of beer all over the place. The snails drank and the snails drowned. And they haven't returned. It ends up that, like the French, raccoons are fond of eating snails. We definitely have raccoons—they dig up the ground cover under the gravel sections of the yard looking for treats and leave their scat on the cocoa shells I use to mulch the center garden plot.

In short, I have no snails in my garden. This is, as most San Franciscans know, usually considered a good thing. It's not, however, such a great thing if you're writing a story about harvesting snails from your garden. Lucky for me, others are not so lucky, so one early March night I grabbed a flashlight and a large bucket and my son donned his camping headlamp and we headed out into the dark of a friend's yard and garden that we had been promised was infested with snails.

Snails are largely nocturnal and like things damp and dreary. Thus, they really dig foggy San Francisco. They like to hang out on the underside of succulents and stalk-y or long-leafed plants. Since it was dark, we found plenty of them just crawling about on rocks and sidewalk edges.

If you know there are snails in your garden, make things easy on yourself: Set up a board on some rocks or bricks or whatever will keep it a few inches off the ground over some soil in a shady part of your yard. Check it in the morning. Chances are there will be scads of snails clinging to the underside of the board.

At first the snails we saw seemed way too small. Their shells were less than half the size of the snails we ate in France. Then, we started noticing how big the snails were outside their shells. The phrase "bite-size morsels" came to mind. We started picking them up and dropping them in the bucket. In quick order, we had five dozen snails to take home.

The Tending of Snails

We covered the bucket, set it in the corner of my study—a place that stays cool and dark—and threw in a few stalks of fennel. My son went to bed. I sat down to read but had to retreat upstairs. The noise of the snails crunching on the fennel was distracting. Hilarious and distracting.

For the next nine days we fed them herbs, then cornmeal, then nothing in a process called "purging" to clean the snails from the inside out. The whole process can easily be sped up to five days. The key points are:

- Choose a container from which the snails cannot escape but in which there is a free exchange of air. A bin topped with a screen weighed down with a brick works, or a container with a plastic lid that snaps on and into which you have poked some holes is good. I used a plastic bucket with an old pair of black tights as a lid (legs of the tights cut off and tied closed). The tights had the advantage of being something that I could dampen each day to help keep the container slightly damp without having standing water in it. A large glass jar with holes punched in the lid lets you see just how much slime and poo they produce. Whatever container you use, sprinkle the snails with a bit of misty water each day after you clean the container, but make sure there isn't a bunch of standing water on the bottom.

- Keep the container in a cool, dark place. That's what snails like. I wouldn't keep them outside. Both raccoons and skunks love to eat snails and who wants to bother with building a raccoon-proof snail bucket?
- To purge the snails, start by feeding them greens and herbs for a day or two. This lets you know what you're starting with. Then feed them cornmeal or oatmeal for a day or two. Since this diet turns their poo white, you'll know other stuff is out of their systems. (Note: Gordon Ramsay recommends giving them carrots for this stage, since it turns their poo orange!) Then give them nothing for a day or two before cooking them. (Note: Some people skip the starving stage, finding it cruel. I saw how much poo these little things make; I didn't want to eat snails full of it.) Some people chill their snails before cooking them–sending them into a fake semihibernation. I found no difference in the taste or texture of the snails that I had chilled versus those I had not.
- Clean the container daily. You may be tempted to skip a day, thinking it won't be that bad. It will be. It will be more than twice as gross. Part of the ick factor comes from the poo, of course, but just as much (if not more) comes from the slime snails leave all over everything. Two days worth of slime takes more than twice as long to clean and scrub out than does one day of slime. Trust me.
- Before you clean their container, transfer the snails to a large bowl or other container. You might want to keep the tempo-

rary container covered. A snail's pace isn't quite as slow as it's made out to be.

Snail Cookery 101

You would think you could now just cook them, but turning snails into something not just edible but tasty and appealing is just a wee bit more complicated than that. There is parboiling, removing their shells, and then a quick cook in acidulated water to de-slime them. I tried skipping this last step and just cooked them with plenty of acid. I ended up with an inedible slimy mess that looked not unlike vomit.

Whether you're making traditional Burgundian escargots or another snail dish, the first steps of cooking snails are the same: Bring a pot of water to a boil. Add plenty of salt. Rinse off the snails—making sure they are poo- and slime-free before you start! Dump them in the pot and cook them for about 3 minutes. Drain the snails and rinse them with plenty of cold water. Use tweezers or a small fork to pull the snails out of their shells. Be warned that there will be more mucus involved here. In some cases a lot more mucus.

On the upside, when you pull the snails out most of them will stretch out as you pull and then spring back into a curlicue shape in a most pleasing and delightful way. On the downside, some of the snails will look like globs of gray diseased snot because they will be coated in so much mucus.

While you're removing all the mollusks from their curly shells, bring a pan filled with ½ water and ½ distilled white vinegar to a boil. Plop in the deshelled snails and boil them until they are slime-free, about 3 minutes. A snail you pull out of the water should not feel slimy and you will probably be able to see bits that look like tiny specks of curdled egg in the water—that's the mucus that's cooked off the snails. Drain the snails and, obviously, rinse them in plenty of cool water to get all the bits of cooked slime off of them. The snails are now ready to be cooked in a recipe.

I made traditional garlic butter–slathered escargots as well as a salad with crisped pancetta and sautéed snails. Snail lovers found them sweet and tender; I found them somewhat mushroom-like but, honestly, thoughts of slime and poo would not leave my head long enough for me to enjoy them.

My son, however, had no such trouble. He swiftly ate a dozen from their shells. Then, when I found a dish of eighteen un-shelled snails that I had accidentally left in the oven after the photo shoot, he downed those too.

When the big one hits or my son asks with verve, I am prepared, if necessary, to tackle buckets of slime and poo again. For the moment, though, I prefer my snails packed up in a neat ovenproof tray with a pretty French sticker on top. Better yet, I'll take them sizzling hot and set in front of me by an aloof but efficient Parisian waiter.

Yes, We Can: Supporting Our Farmers, Preserving the Harvest

By Kim O'Donnel

From *EcoCentric*

Former *Washington Post* food blogger Kim O'Donnel now lives in Seattle and marches to a different drummer: Writing vegetarian cookbooks for carnivores (*The Meat Lover's Meatless Cookbook*) and blogging on seasonal produce for the environmental website EcoCentric.com. She shares here the passion for preserving that led her to found the Canning Across America collective.

I am a little piggy that goes to market, and I do so dutifully every Sunday (often twice during growing season). I am hip to what grows when, but without soil to call my own, I rely on the agronomical know-how and stewardship of folks who know a whole lot more about growing food than I do.

Usually, I survey the weekly offerings, then hone in on what looks good and inspires me to cook. It goes without saying that I care about where my food comes from and how it's grown and raised, and that I prefer farmers' market stands to supermarket aisles. But even with my reusable bag chockfull of heirloom this and organic that, by and large my experience is little more than an exchange of money and goods, with some conversational pleasantries thrown in for good measure.

Until now.

Summer in Washington is typically the dry season, but this year was historically parched, creating conditions that fueled explosive wildfires in one of the state's rich agricultural centers. We city mice watched the flames on the local news in mid-August and our coastal sunsets had grown hazy, even so far away from the scene.

That same week, I set out for one of Seattle's mid-week farmers' markets and stopped by to see what was on offer at the River Farm Organic Produce stand. As I gathered cucumbers and deliberated over melons, farmer Eric Welsch told me and another customer that his house in Ellensburg, Washington (about 75 miles east of Seattle) had just been destroyed, a casualty of the wildfires, and that he and his wife, Liz Goronea, had had just 20 minutes to evacuate. Their 50-acre farm, which has been in Goronea's family since 1976, was untouched, and everyone was safe. But as those who grow and eat seasonally know all too well, the produce doesn't wait, and here they were at the height of the growing season, which meant rebuilding would have to wait. For now, Eric and Liz, who is pregnant, were sleeping on the floor in their office.

My arms full of their melons, I suddenly lost my footing and was unable to utter anything remotely comforting or intelligent in response to Welsch's crumbling news. He was clearly still in shock, quiet and somber, yet he stood tall in the face of a horrible situation and carried on.

I quickly paid for my items and told him I'd see him at market on Sunday. Uttering those few words–See you on Sunday–I know exactly what I can do to help: Keep showing up.

Sunday comes and I tell Welsch I'm gearing up to make marinara sauce. Last year, I put up about nine quarts of sauce that proved to be so delicious and gratifying I nearly cried when I opened the last jar in March. With plans to double this year's pantry allocation, I ask him if they grow Roma tomatoes, which is what I used the previous year. He walks me to the other side of the stand and shows me something called a Stupice. "It's a Czech heirloom," Welsch tells me. "And it makes killer sauce."

I would need 25 pounds, I say.

He smiles.

At that moment, the speed-dating transactions of farmers' markets past made way for a two-way committed relationship. We were in this together.

I spend several hours the next day heating and crushing tomatoes, then passing them through a food mill to remove the skins and the seeds. I divide the nearly translucent crimson puree into two pots, add onion and garlic and simmer for two hours, a slow and steady transformation from the raw to the cooked. There is no checking e-mail or updating my Facebook status. This is a messy, physically demanding endeavor that requires my full attention. The air is heavy with sweet tomato perfume, and the windows are fogged up, like a protective layer of insulation from the outside world. Could this be my new way of a moving meditation?

The sauce has thickened and is now ready to move into jars, where it will live, some of it for months, after a short dip in a monster-size pot of boiling water. To each quart jar, I add lemon juice and salt, then ladle in the sauce. I wipe the rims, place the lids and screw on the rings, then lower the jars into the canning cauldron. Forty-five minutes later, I have nine quarts of Stupice sauce, a delicately sweet, sun-kissed tribute to Welsch and Goronea's hard work.

Sunday morning comes again, the last one of September, and my husband and I greet Welsch. I spot more of his juicy little tomatoes, packed in 20-pound boxes, Mother Nature's penultimate love apple shout-out for the year.

The produce doesn't wait. Make the time.

I'll take a 20-pound box of the tomatoes, I tell him. Plus five.

He nods and calculates the price, and I write a check for 50 bucks for all of our goods. He nods again and says thank you, and I feel his gratitude in my bones.

Once again, I set aside the electronic devices and all other business, don a smock and do-rag and dive into the harvest before me. Six hours later, I've got nine more quarts of sauce. My husband notes we have enough to enjoy two quarts per month until June.

Now it's my turn to be grateful.

Marinara Sauce and Putting It Up in Jars

Adapted from *Put'em Up!* by Sherri Brooks Vinton, with water bath processing steps from *The Meat Lover's Meatless Celebrations* by Kim O'Donnel

Makes 7 to 9 quarts.

25 pounds plum tomatoes, washed and sliced in half (aka paste tomatoes; or Stupice, the Czech heirloom recommended by farmer Eric Welsch)
1 pound storage onions, finely diced
4 garlic cloves, peeled and minced
3 tablespoons bottled lemon juice per quart
1 teaspoon Kosher salt or 3/4 teaspoon fine sea salt per quart

Tools

Food mill, wide-mouth funnel, jar lifter (aka canning tongs), canning rack, a pot deep and wide enough to fit a canning rack and quart jars, with lid on, ladle.

Note: I highly recommend canning with a partner, so that you can share the work load, equipment and cost of ingredients and supplies. For solo voyagers, estimate 6 to 7 hours, from start to finish. As a team of 2 or 3, estimate 4 to 5 hours, particularly if you have two food mills on hand. If you need to brush up on the basics of water bath canning, here's a cheat sheet.

Method

Place 5 pounds of the tomatoes in a large non-reactive pot. Bring up to a lively simmer over medium heat, crushing and stirring the tomatoes occasionally to release their juices.

Add an additional 5 pounds of tomatoes and repeat, continuing to crush and stir as you go. Repeat with the remaining tomatoes until all are crushed and boiling. (Note: You may need to divide tomatoes among two pots.)

Reduce the heat and simmer the tomatoes for 15 minutes. Run the tomatoes through a food mill in batches to remove skins and seeds.

Return the tomato puree to the pot(s). Add the onions and garlic and bring to a simmer. Cook over low heat, stirring occasionally until the sauce is thickened, 1½ to 2 hours. (Note: Avoid tall, deep pots if possible; the sauce cooks more evenly in pots that are wide and more shallow.)

Meanwhile, prepare the jars for processing using the water bath method:

Use quart jars with the two-part lids sold by Kerr and Ball

brands. Wash the rings and lids in hot soapy water and rinse well. Set aside.

Use a pot that is deep and wide enough for a canning rack. Make sure the lid of the pot is still able to sit on top with the rack inside. Arrange the quart jars in the canning rack. Add water to the pot until it is at least 1 inch above your jars. Cover and bring the water to a boil. Keep the jars in the boiling water until ready to process.

Remove the hot jars one by one from the boiling water to a kitchen towel-lined "staging" area. Keep the pot covered and the water boiling.

Add the lemon juice and salt to each quart jar. Rest the wide-mouthed funnel on top of a jar and ladle in the sauce, leaving ½ inch of headspace. With a nonmetal chopstick or other flat-edged item, release trapped air by running along the inside edge of the filled jar.

With a kitchen towel, wipe clean the rim of each jar. Place the lid on top, then gently screw on the ring (not too tight). Using a jar lifter (aka canning tongs), return the filled and covered jars to the boiling water.

Cover and process for 45 minutes. Turn off the heat and with the jar lifter, transfer the jars, one by one, to the towel-lined area. Listen for the "ping" of each jar, a sign that you have a proper seal.

Allow to cool for at least 12 hours. Remove the rings. Check once more for a proper seal by lifting each jar by its lid. Label and date the jars and store in a cool, dark place; the sauce will keep for up to one year.

The Meat of the Matter

Hogonomics

By Barry Estabrook

From *Gastronomica*

In his 2011 book *Tomatoland*, investigative journalist Barry Estabrook delivered a harrowing crash course in the true economic and social cost of supermarket tomatoes. Next up: The true cost of supermarket pork chops.

The best pork chop I have ever eaten came from a hog raised at Flying Pigs Farm about 225 miles due north of New York City. The animal that produced my chop was a rare, heritage breed, either a Tamworth, Gloucestershire Old Spot, or Large Black. It spent its life in the open air and on pasture. After a quick turn over the coals, the meat was so rich, porky, and succulent that the pleasures of all other chops paled. Ever since, I have flatly refused to buy the wan, watery factory-farmed offerings in supermarkets. On the downside, my Flying Pig chop cost fifteen dollars a pound.

In an era of eight-dollar-a-carton organic eggs and accusations of foodie elitism set against the background of an evolving two-tiered food system—healthy food for the Prius set while the rest of the nation subsists on empty calories and dreary, mass-produced meat and produce—there is one question anyone concerned about sustainable food should ask: How can such a high price be justified?

Because I live less than two hours from Flying Pigs Farm, I took my query directly to the source. I wanted to ask how the farmers who produced my chop justify charging $15.00 a pound on the very day when the same cut from the folks at Swift Premium could be had for $3.49 at local grocery stories. I wasn't going to settle for feel-good, aesthetic answers. I wanted hard facts. Dollars and cents.

As I crested a hill on a little-traveled road leading up to the farm, I realized that maintaining unbiased resolve about Flying Pigs was going to be tough. If you had to imagine a picture of hog (or human) heaven, the farm would be close. A nineteenth-century house with stone-walled flower beds and weathered rail fences stood across the road from a red barn. To one side, a trail disappeared up a hill into a deciduous forest. On the other, the land rolled down to the Battenkill River, one of the Northeast's most famous trout streams, renowned for its clear, swift water. The spread was the epitome of what well-heeled New Yorkers envision when they hear the term "country place" (a fate that nearly befell the farm). Only it wasn't investment bankers and Wall Street lawyers who were soaking in the view or meandering along the edge of the forest, but scattered herds of black pigs, reddish brown pigs, and pigs that had the spotted markings of overstuffed Dalmatian dogs.

The owners of Flying Pigs, Jennifer Small and Michael Yezzi, an attractive couple in their forties, ushered me inside their bright, fully restored living/dining room to give me my crash course in Hogonomics. Having kicked off rubber boots in the vestibule, they were sock-footed and in jeans, he wearing a red-and-black checked flannel shirt, she a gray boat-neck sweater. Their two young children were at school. Small and Yezzi were barely out of college when they bought the two-hundred-acre farm from developers in the late 1990s. Since 2000, they have been raising pigs. Their operation is typical of most farms in the United States in that at least one of the owners–in this case Jennifer–has an off-farm job. Michael devotes all his working time to the operation, which produces about 750 pigs a year.

"People assume that there will always be farmers around," said Small. "And even though farmers are very talented, thoughtful, and entrepreneurial, if they can't earn a decent wage, then there won't be any left to feed you." The bottom line, they said, is that a dozen years after the first trotters touched their land, meat production at Flying Pigs is financially viable, though not generating mountains of cash. All the profits are reinvested in buildings and equipment.

The Price of a Piglet

The financial facts of life for the rare, heritage pig that produced my fifteen-dollar chop began decades, if not centuries, before it was born. The sows that produce piglets for modern factory farms have been bred for one thing: the ability to produce large litters of ten or more. Essentially, the sow is a piglet machine, efficiently milling out 2.5 litters every year for the three or four years that she will live—if it can be called a life. Commercial sows tend to be ill-tempered and will fight. To prevent injuries, they are confined in gestation crates. Each six-hundred-pound animal is penned in a metal cage that is too small for her to turn around in. She must sleep on her chest. Temple Grandin, the well-known livestock welfare expert at Colorado State University, has said, "Basically, you're asking a sow to live in an airline seat." Shortly before giving birth, the sow is moved into a slightly larger farrowing crate where she can lie on her side—barely—to nurse her piglets, which live in an eighteen-inch-wide caged area separated from the sow by bars that allow the young to suckle, but prevent the mother from accidentally rolling over and crushing them, or coming in contact with them in any other way.

Heritage pigs, on the other hand, were bred to retain the ability to give birth independently and possess the instincts necessary to be good mothers without reliance on gestation and farrowing crates. They were also selected for their genial temperaments. In the days when pigs still roamed barnyards at will and had to be fed and mucked out manually, no farmer wanted to work around quarter-ton creatures with vicious dispositions. Because producing huge numbers of offspring was not a priority, heritage sows tend to have smaller litters than their commercial cousins—typically, eight or so a litter, although some varieties give birth to half that many. "So right off the bat, you have a 20 or 25 percent difference between the output of a commercial 'pink pig' and one of ours," Yezzi said. Furthermore, Flying Pigs' sows are not confined to crates. Allowing sows to have the freedom to live normal lives carries the unfortunate cost of having the occasional piglet smothered by its mother, further reducing the rate of successful reproduction.

Not only do factory pigs produce more pigs per litter than heritage pigs, they produce more litters per year. It's common to wean commercial piglets at age three weeks or even earlier, when they weigh about twelve pounds. In the industry, this practice is called "early weaning," and Yezzi says it can be detrimental to the health of the piglets, which have to be housed in climate-controlled buildings and fed a special diet supplemented with drugs to survive. Weaning brings the sow back into heat within a few days, and after another four months in her gestation crate, she produces another litter. That works out to two litters every ten months.

Flying Pigs piglets live with their mothers and nurse for two to three months, until they weigh between twenty-five and forty pounds. When they are a couple of weeks old, they begin to nuzzle at the feed troughs of the mature pigs, slowly weaning themselves. A sow left to nurse her brood until the natural age of weaning requires thirteen to fourteen months to produce two litters, meaning commercial sows produce 20 percent more piglets per litter and produce litters 30 percent more often than pigs allowed to breed naturally. Given those numbers, I could understand why a heritage piglet costs Yezzi and Small about 120 dollars, while twelve-pound early-weaned commercial piglets cost factory farmers only about fifty dollars each, and at forty pounds sell for about seventy dollars. Even before the hog that produced my chop had been released on Flying Pigs Farm's pastures, my chop was worth twice as much as the one mass-produced by Swift.

Growing Pains

In addition to being offspring-producing dynamos, pink pigs have been bred to grow fast and convert feed into meat efficiently. They are helped along, if you want to call it that, by some marvels of modern factory farming. First of all, they do their growing inside warehouse-like barns typically holding two thousand hogs, all of the same age. The growing pigs are kept in groups of about twenty in pens that allow each animal between five and eight square feet on which to live out its life—an area measuring two feet by four feet, maximum. With no way to move freely, they don't burn off precious calories with exercise. Their food often contains animal byproducts. Those can consist of feathers, heads, feed, and viscera from poultry processing plants and excess baby chicks from hatcheries. They can also include slaughterhouse waste such as hog hair, tendons, ligaments, entrails, bones, and blood from cows and pigs. Occasionally, commercial hogs are fed spent restaurant grease and rejected ingredients from packaged snack food factories—batches of overdone corn chips, defective candies. Not particularly healthy, but highly caloric.

Artificial lighting and climate control assure that the pigs live under optimal growing conditions all year round. They receive daily rations of antibiotics, not to keep them from becoming sick, but because low-level (subtherapeutic) drug administration makes livestock grow a few percent faster than they would normally. Mechanical augers transport food to their troughs; slats in the floor allow their excrement to fall into pits below, where machines move it away. Human presence is all but unnecessary. Liberty Swine Farms, for instance, an Indiana operator, produces about twenty-two thousand pigs a year with only eight employees. One employee's salary is spread over 2,750 pigs. Jennifer Small recalled visiting a commercial hog barn in Illinois housing thousands of animals. No humans were there. It was as if the entire barn was on autopilot with mechanical devices handling all the husbandry duties of a traditional farmer. "It was eerie," she said.

Six months after it is born, a factory hog has gone from a creature you can cradle in the palms of your hands to a 250-pound porker that is ready for slaughter. But at Flying Pigs Farm, a pig takes between eight and nine months to reach a similar weight, longer during the cold season when the animals have to burn calories just to stay warm. Human contact is a constant factor in a Flying Pig's life. Yezzi and Small go out of their way to make sure that their pigs are docile and accustomed to human contact, not for sentimental reasons or to make pets of them, but because becoming used to humans reduces stress, and unstressed pigs are easier to handle, grow better, and produce better meat.

Thousands of factory animals can be crowded into a single barn that occupies a fraction of an acre of land, but the four hundred or so hogs found on Flying Pigs Farm at any time have the run of twenty to thirty acres. An acre is about the size of a football field. Yezzi has three full-time employees, plus one part-timer, and an employee's salary can be spread over only 170 pigs, not the 2,750 at the Liberty facility. Employees at Flying Pigs have to deliver feed to the pigs daily by tractor and wagon. To prevent the spread of parasites, Yezzi never keeps pigs on the same patch of ground for two years in a row, so he actually has forty to sixty acres of valuable land tied up as pig pasture. The pigs live in groups of five to a couple dozen, depending on their size, in roomy paddocks enclosed by electric fencing. Each group has a feeder, water spigot, and portable metal hut in which to take shelter. Workers move the huts, hoses, feeders, and fencing to fresh pasture every two weeks in the summer. In the cold months, they insert wooden platforms inside each hut so the pigs don't have to lie on cold, wet ground. Straw, which can cost a dollar a day per hut, is placed on top of the platforms to help the pigs stay warm. Yezzi's crew has to be vigilant and clean out the huts whenever the bedding becomes even slightly moist—pigs are notoriously susceptible to pneumonia. Every morning and evening someone visits every hut and rouses its residents and makes them get up and move about. "We check for illness," said Yezzi. "If an animal is slow rising or has its tail and ears down and is looking mopey, we move it into the barn for closer observation and treatment if necessary."

The only time a Flying Pig hog receives medication is when it becomes sick. Antibiotics are not given as part of the daily regimen of healthy animals, even though they will not grow as fast as regularly treated pigs. And because of the presence of animal byproducts and other chemicals that Jennifer describes as "gross" in commercially formulated feeds, Flying Pigs Farm uses a custom formula of corn and soybeans mixed at a local grain mill, a step that costs sixteen thousand dollars a month. Being on pasture, the couple's pigs are always active, rooting, running, and mounding together fifty-strong in pig piles on chilly days. All of this activity gives their flesh color and texture lacking in commercial pork. They forage while on pasture, but Yezzi says that the benefit to that is not so much the weight gain, but that they are kept active and interested. Foraged food also adds flavor to their meat.

The Day of Reckoning and Beyond

Efficiency being the watchword, a two-thousand-pig commercial barn gets filled all at once with animals that are the same age. When the hogs reach slaughter weight, the barn is completely emptied, as all of its former residents are trucked off to slaughter. The large slaughter facilities that commercial pigs go to can kill and butcher more than a thousand pigs an hour, a process that inevitably leaves a few animals alive and sentient when they are dipped in vats of scalding water for hair removal, according to People for the Ethical Treatment of Animals. Unskilled and often ununionized (and undocumented) workers wield knives along a disassembly line, repeating a single cut all day long, rather than performing the skilled job of butchering an entire animal. The "kill fee" at a big plant is between ten and twelve dollars per carcass. According to United States Department of Agriculture (USDA) statistics, an unskilled slaughterhouse worker earns a little over eleven dollars an hour. A Vermont study showed that trained meat cutters in the area near Flying Pigs earned sixteen dollars an hour.

Flying Pigs pays a kill fee of fifty dollars per animal. How commercial hogs and Flying Pigs' animals die is as different as how they are raised. Yezzi loads between ten and twenty pigs a week into his truck and drives them to a USDA-certified slaughterhouse about ten miles from his farm. They arrive there the evening before they are due to be killed and are housed together in their own enclosure overnight. Spending the evening among pigs they know calms them and relieves the stress of transport. Excessive stress at the time of slaughter can ruin the flavor and texture of pork. With no fear of humans, they remain calm until they are killed one at a time by the facility's owner, who processes a maximum of thirty pigs a day. This not only assures as humane a death as a pig bred for human food can get, but allows the on-site USDA inspector to examine each carcass individually, taking all the time needed, an impossibility in a mega-plant where a thousand pigs an hour stream past on a conveyor system. In addition to paying the kill fee, Yezzi spends up to two hundred dollars per carcass, nearly twice the going rate, to have a professional butcher cut it to his exact specifications.

Yezzi has a tremendous advantage over many other small-scale meat producers in that there is a USDA-approved slaughterhouse just down the road. Before it opened, he or one of his employees had to drive for over an hour to the nearest facility, wait there until the animals were off loaded, and return home—twice a week. It represented a tremendous cost in fuel and labor that he no longer has to bear. His fuel bill is further reduced because he burns recycled vegetable oil from nearby Williams College and other sources.

Every Thursday, Yezzi picks up his meat. He hits the road for the 225-mile drive to New York City between six and eight o'clock in the evening, arriving at about one o'clock Friday morning. He crashes at a friend's apartment (another money-saving measure that other small producers don't enjoy) and gets up at six o'clock to make deliveries to his restaurant customers. Two hours later, he arrives at one of the three farmers' markets he attends each week in the city. But even as customers line up for his pork, Yezzi is still incurring expenses. Renting a space at a market costs seventy-five dollars a day. He has to hire sales help in the city to tend his booth for an additional hundred to hundred and fifty dollars a day—about 5 percent of his gross sales. Late Saturday afternoon, he packs up and drives back to the farm to get ready for the next group of pigs.

As you may have guessed, even before I undertook my hard-edged financial analysis, I had already made up my mind that the taste of rare, heritage-breed pork was worth it to me. Sure, it's expensive. But we are all supposed to be eating less meat, so my answer to those who say that grass-fed beef and pastured pork are elitist luxuries would be, "Eat less meat and when you do make it the good stuff. Your wallet will be no worse off, and your circulatory system and conscience will thank you." Now I can add, "And take some comfort knowing that the extra money is spent on better production practices."

There wasn't any fine print on the label of my package of Flying Pigs chops to explain all the extra costs that had gone into producing them. It said only, "Premium pork from the Battenkill River Valley."

The fine print on the label of those $3.49 a pound Swift Premium chops that were "guaranteed tender" said: "With up to a 12 percent solution of pork broth, sodium citrate, and natural salt." Huh? "Natural salt?" "Sodium citrate?" A little research revealed that the supermarket chop had been "enhanced," which means the meat was injected with a saline solution to remedy its lack of taste and dry texture. By my objective calculation, that factory pig corporation charged more than forty cents a pound for salty water. Did I feel ripped off? You bet.

The Upstart Cattleman

By John Kessler

From *The Atlanta Journal-Constitution*

Back in the saddle as chief dining critic of the *Atlanta Journal-Constitution*, John Kessler only occasionally can steal time for long-form feature writing, like this in-depth profile of a cutting-edge meat producer. Knowing all the stories along the food chain—that's what makes Kessler such a vital voice.

It took a mere 20 minutes from the time the coal-black, 1,100-pound heifer ambled through a raised door into the slaughterhouse until two sides of beef, hanging on hooks, disappeared into the cooler. The cow entered a small chamber with high, grass-green walls that enclosed her like a shoebox around a loafer. She looked around curiously with big, brown, avid eyes—first left, then right, then up at a captive bolt pistol pointed at her head. And that was it. One wall lifted and she collapsed onto the kill floor.

The six men working inside this small abattoir—no bigger than a studio loft apartment—made quick work with knives and saws, the first cut straight into her heart, stopping it cold. Soon, one fellow delivered this still-warm organ on a rolling steel cart to a white-coated USDA inspector who eyeballed it closely and ticked a mark on his clipboard.

Will Harris III, the owner of White Oak Pastures, drew a knife from his belt holster, neatly bisected the heart and cut a cube from its center. "Sweetest meat you'll ever try," he said, popping the red morsel into his mouth. It was not yet 9 a.m.

With his 240-pound frame and Stetson hat capping a sun-creased face, Harris looks like the kind of hardcore cowboy dude who'd think nothing of a little raw offal for breakfast. Yet despite the country-road gravel in his voice, he doesn't always sound the part. He loves to quote George Washington Carver on the order of nature and Michael Pollan on the dangers of industrial food production. He takes enormous pride in the organic certification that his pastures and vegetable garden have received and in the new solar panels he is installing.

Others have taken notice, too. Harris' farm has become a waypoint for Florida-bound tourists who stock up on his grass-fed meats. Hungry humans take their meals in a newly completed open-air dining pavilion just down a hill from the abattoirs called "Pasture to Plate." For now it serves as a lunchroom for his employees, who sit by beating fans along two picnic benches. Soon, it may welcome visitors, visiting chefs and culinary students who want to experience life on a working farm. Like he does many nights, Harris plans to meet his family here and microwave the leftovers for dinner.

Row by row, Harris is breaking the mold on farming in Georgia. His organic grass-fed cattle are slaughtered with methods animal welfare advocates call commendable, and steaks from his beef are cooked and plated in Atlanta's finest restaurants. Whole Foods prominently features White Oak Pastures beef in its stores. And Harris, with 85 employees and what seems like half of Early County working for him, is now doing for chicken what he's done for beef: raising pasture-fed birds and slaughtering them more humanely.

But 15 years ago White Oak Pastures wasn't anything like this and Harris, a fourth-generation Georgian farming land owned by his family since the Civil War, seemed destined to farm the same way his father had, and his father before that. Harris' father—a harsh, unyielding man—pushed the farm as far as he could, pumping any and all chemicals into the earth and into the animals to turn acreage into meat. Armed with an animal science degree and a quick mind, Harris set out to best his father, and he did.

But then, one day, without consulting anyone, he just stopped. He stopped feeding his cattle a mixed ration of grain and powdered dietary supplements they digested poorly, and he stopped implanting estrogen pellets behind their ears. He stopped buying bull semen and instead bought bulls. He stopped loading weaned 7-month-old calves into 53-foot-long double-decker hauling trucks to travel 1,400 miles in their own filth to a feedlot. Soon, he stopped spraying his pasture with pesticides and fertilizing them with ammonium nitrate, and as they turned brown and died, he knew he was risking everything. But he kept going.

"The thing is, those fields were already dead," Harris says as he climbs into his beat-up 1995 Jeep Wrangler to make the evening rounds of the property. As he does every night, he brings a double-barreled shotgun and a bottle of Yellow Tail shiraz along for the ride. The sun slants with a hot, eerie stillness as the Jeep chuffs over a green hill and a flock of speckled guinea fowl, which look like giant potatoes with tiny heads and stick legs, disperse.

He casts a steady hazel-eyed gaze on visitors and avows he truly loves the animals—not just his dogs and horses, but also all the mooing, baaing, clucking and quacking things that roam so freely over the thousand acres of his storybook pretty farm. These are the same creatures that will one day find themselves headed for the two slaughterhouses on site. They are the lifeblood of this whole operation, and Will Harris is their badass Old MacDonald.

"Let me tell you a story," Harris says, which in his south Georgia accent sounded like "stirry." He had more than 1,000 acres to cover this evening. There was time to tell it, and it was a good stirry.

Tough Love, History Guide a Young Farmer

Harris shakes his head as his Jeep lumbers over the four-lane divided highway the Georgia Department of Transportation has been building through the center of White Oak Pastures. "Here's your tax dollars at work," he mutters.

Getting the cattle from one side of the road to the other would be no easy feat, so GDOT agreed to build a tunnel under the raised highway. One good thing came from this mess: When bulldozers cut into the pasture abutting the road, they uncovered a clearly distinct stratum of soft, brown topsoil above the hard, red clay. "Fifteen years ago, this wasn't here," Harris says.

Nor were the other markers of healthy organic soil: the mushrooms that sprout so suddenly on the pasture after a night's rain; the black dung beetle that scurries from a cow patty when Harris crushes it with the toe of his leather boot.

But in 1866, when his great-grandfather arrived, the land was even richer. James Edward Harris was a Confederate who assembled and conscripted his own cavalry to fight the Union soldiers back from central west Georgia. After the war, the bank repossessed the farm and freed the slaves, who joined their former master as sharecroppers. Together, they traveled to homestead this new property in Early County—about as far south as you could go in this part of Georgia before the forested red clay hills give way to the flat landscape and sandy earth of the coastal plain.

Every Saturday the Harrises butchered enough meat—one cow, two or three hogs and several chickens—to last the family and the sharecroppers through the week. They raised their four children in a simple two-story log cabin, among them Will Carter Harris, who most likely took possession of the family farm upon his father's death in 1909. The younger Harris married Beulah Bell, the sheriff's daughter and a formidable woman who had a reputation for working black farm hands harder than anyone in the area. They built a new home next to the log cabin.

The family stepped up their production of beef, pork and chicken to sell in nearby Bluffton. They butchered the animals before dawn and made near-daily deliveries. They also opened a commissary beside their house where they sold dry goods and cigarettes alongside vegetables and meat.

The beginning of the Great Depression was doubly hard on the farm, as Will Carter Harris was rapidly losing his eyesight to cataracts. According to family lore, Beulah one day hopped in the family's Model T, drove to the schoolhouse and withdrew her only child to come work on the farm. He was 8.

Will Bell Harris spent his days riding around in a horse-drawn carriage with his father. He was the bossman's eyes, and his mission—reinforced over and over by both parents—was to inform on farm hands and cowboys who weren't pulling their weight. He learned to be feared from an early age.

This third-generation Harris grew into a big man, tall and heavyset, with a dour disposition. As one of his granddaughters recalls, "He was always very quiet except when he was cussing."

Harris wasn't just a good cattleman, he was a local legend who could produce more meat per acre than anyone around. He got rid of the hogs, chickens and crops, and focused solely on cattle.

"My daddy was a man's man and he was a profane man," Harris recalls. "You could cuss around Daddy when Mama wasn't there, but if you cussed at him, that became disrespect."

When he was 12 years old, Will Harris III learned the distinction. He was helping his father corral some cattle that had escaped through an open gate and were wandering all over the road. His father, frustrated with his son's progress, gave the stud horse the boy was riding a surprise crack of the whip. When the horse bucked, Harris exclaimed, "Goddammit, Daddy!" before he could stop himself. The cattle could wait: His father ordered his son down off the horse and whipped him. He never made that mistake again.

Will Harris Breaks the Family Mold

Will Harris III, the first in his family to complete college, studied animal science at the University of Georgia School of Agriculture when fertilizers and antibiotics were revolutionizing American agriculture.

After the war, both pesticides and antibiotics became more commonplace, and farmers discovered a fringe benefit with the latter. Not only did antibiotics keep animals from getting sick, they made them larger and fatter when administered routinely.

In 1947 a giant federal munitions plant in Muscle Shoals, Alabama, switched from making bombs to making chemical fertilizer, and the government began actively promoting ammonium nitrate to farmers as a way to increase crop yields and keep pastures green. Food policy historians, such as Michael Pollan, cite this as a turning point in American agriculture and beef production. With chemical fertilizers came an abundance of cheap grain. By the mid-1950s, Midwestern markets and packinghouses had risen to newfound prominence and were supplying the majority of American beef.

Cattlemen like Harris' father would raise the calves until they were old enough to wean, about 6 or 7 months, and then ship them off to concentrated animal feeding operations–feedlots–to finish out their lives.

In 1959, the National Academy of Sciences assembled the brightest minds in agriculture for a conference at Purdue University titled "Beef for Tomorrow" to discuss the rapid changes in the industry and a two-thirds increase in per-capita beef consumption since the prewar period. The conference objective read: "Authorities in industry and government have clearly indicated what this means to the producer of beef–he must produce more, more efficiently."

At UGA, one of Harris' professors, A.E. Cullison, wrote an influential textbook called *Feeds and Feeding* that detailed formulations for the total mixed rations (TMRs) that were increasingly replacing grass and hay as cattle feed. Because ruminants like cows and sheep don't have the stomach acids to digest the corn and soybean meal in TMRs, they also needed routine antibiotics and drugs to combat acidosis, bloat, heartburn, liver abscesses and the host of other problems that awaited them.

Armed with this education, Harris went to go work for the family farm intent on putting his stamp on it. That proved difficult.

"Mostly what I did was bump heads with my father," Harris recalls. "We could hunt, fish and eat together. But we were both alpha male, and when we went to work, it was really problematic."

Then there was Jenni–the middle of the three girls Will and his wife, Von, were raising in a new home they built next to his father's. She tottered around behind her father in a favorite pair of coveralls from the age of 4, accompanying him as he gave feed to the cattle in their confinement pens at the crack of dawn.

"My grandfather and I did not have a good relationship," Jenni, now 25, recalls. "I was the tomboy, the son my father never had, and my grandfather resented me terribly."

If Jenni wanted to tag along on the yearly visit to the video cattle auction at the county extension office–an event she says "was like the county fair"–her grandfather wouldn't go.

Alzheimer's disease soon started to mute her autocratic grandfather's bark, and as he slipped into a fog of dementia, her father started to rethink his family's farm.

"There was no epiphany," Will Harris III says, though he began reading books about the American farming system he wasn't assigned in ag school. He was particularly struck by *The Unsettling of America*, Wendell Berry's 1977 book that argued agribusiness was destroying the cultural and family context of farming. It made him wonder what kind of system his father had prescribed to, and what kind of legacy he was leaving for Jenni and his other daughters.

He also began thinking about animal welfare in a different light. "If you weren't intentionally inflicting pain and suffering on the animal, it was considered good animal welfare," he said, reflecting a common sentiment among livestock breeders. "By that thinking, if you chain your kids to the TV and feed them a steady diet of potato chips, you're not hurting them."

One day as he was sending 80 calves off in a double-decker hauling truck, the thought occurred to him that the just-weaned animals on the bottom would make the cross-country drive with urine and excrement raining down on them.

Harris realized that he had become so focused on taking the cost out of production that he no longer considered the animals.

He formulated this thought: "Not allowing animals to express their instinctive behavior is working against nature." It stayed with him.

Harris Finds a Market at Atlanta's Woodfire Grill

When Jenni was 11, Harris sat her down and said he needed to talk to her about her future and the future of the farm. He had been reading about organic farming and wanted to try it. Things weren't going to be like they were in her granddaddy's days.

The next year was a disaster. Without any topsoil to hold the grass in place, it washed away in the rain and dried up in the summer heat. Harris had to buy hay just to keep his cattle fed, and he lost money. The thousand acres turned brown and rangy–an eyesore amidst the verdant row crops that surrounded the farm.

"The weeds were eating up my ass in the pasture," Harris recalls. Cattle wouldn't eat the foot-high stalks of pigweed that had taken tenacious root, but sheep would. So Harris bought a herd and took his first step away from the cattle monoculture his father had built.

While Harris still shipped calves off to western feedlots to make ends meet, he increasingly finished them on pasture and hay and took them to local slaughterhouses to be ground for hamburger. He marketed this ground beef relentlessly–handing out samples in food stores and fairs.

He realized that any real customer base for his product wouldn't be folks in southwest Georgia who wanted to stock their freezers, but rather Atlantans involved in the burgeoning "good food" movement. So he signed up to attend a dinner that Atlanta's Slow Food chapter was holding at Woodfire Grill, one of Atlanta's A-list restaurants.

"What did they call that group? A 'convivium?' " Harris chuckles.

"Man, I was dreading it like a trip to the dentist. That dinner was $45! I had never eaten in a restaurant nicer than a Shoney's and just pictured those people as a bunch of arrogant stuffed shirts."

Instead he found his target audience and his impetus to keep pushing. Julie Shaffer, then the local Slow Food leader, says, "It was so encouraging to find someone in our state who was trying to farm animals in such a humane and sustainable way. I felt proud to know him."

Harris saw there was a market for more than frozen hamburger. Atlanta chefs and regional Whole Foods markets wanted grass-fed steaks. He toured the state looking for a slaughterhouse that could process the animals economically, skillfully and humanely. It didn't exist.

So he secured more than $2 million in loans from banks, Whole Foods and a Georgia Department of Agriculture outreach program and set out to build his own processing plant. He hired Temple Grandin, an animal scientist whose autism helps her better understand animal psychology and create less stress for them at slaughter.

"People ask me how I can care about animals and be involved in killing them," says Grandin. "What I believe is we've got to give animals a decent life—one that's worth living."

Grandin insists it doesn't take her mind to see what makes cattle happy. "Let those girls out of their stalls in spring, and they just start running all over the place, udders bouncing along."

Harris completed the slaughterhouse in 2006 with the plan to process his own cattle to the tune of 30 a week.

"Those were the dark days," says Harris. With such a small production, he couldn't keep his costs down enough to make his beef even remotely competitive with the conventional product.

"In one year I went from being comfortable, never having taken a loan, to thinking, 'I've really screwed this up.'"

So he worked out deals with more than a dozen nearby cattlemen. If they'd agree to take their pastures organic, he'd pay more than they could earn from the feedlot brokers. He stepped up production fivefold.

Harris Returns Family Farm to Prosperity—and Its Past

The trip from the old Harris homestead to Bluffton leads past a flock of aggressive, curious turkeys that come running from their roosts when they hear the Jeep's engine. These aluminum-sided shelters line up like row houses and they can be moved about like hotels on a Monopoly board, letting the turkeys root for grubs and beetles and fertilize the ground before they arrive at the next destination.

"You might want to cover your nose," Harris warns as he drives past the bone yard. Thirty head of cattle are slaughtered every day, and their bones—still pink and slick with the bits of meat and tissue that would get processed into so-called "pink slime" elsewhere—come here to dry. They will eventually get ground into bone meal for the compost used in his one-acre organic vegetable garden.

Like many old farming towns in the South, Bluffton today presents little more than a collection of homes in various states of care and decrepitude. There are no longer any schools, and the town post office is scheduled for closure. Turn off the main drag with its water tower and long-neglected park, and you come upon the town cemetery where the elder Harrises lie. After that, it's row crops—peanuts as far as the eye can see.

What pulse remains may be due in large part to Harris. White Oak Pastures sells nearly $20 million of naturally raised meat annually and employs 85 people who pump their $2.3 million in annual salary into the local economy.

His business acumen and his environmental stewardship have earned accolades. He was selected as Georgia's Small Business Person of the Year by the US Small Business Administration in 2011. The Georgia Conservancy named him as its 2012 Distinguished Conservationist of the Year for his efforts in promoting sustainable and organic farming.

When Harris first switched to sustainable farming, "some people down in this area probably thought he lost his mind," says Butch Wiggins, president of the Bank of Early, who loaned Harris the money for his abattoirs. "I don't think they think he's crazy now."

Harris turns into a craggy pasture, and as the Jeep hits an unseen pit, Harris jerks the glass of shiraz in his right hand, which sloshes close to the rim without spilling. "That was close," he laughs. He has clearly had practice.

Most of the 100 or more mama cows and calves stand in a companionable cluster as they munch on rye grass and red clover.

Harris scans the perimeter to look for any cows that have just given birth. When the time comes, they wander off to a secluded hiding spot where they can bond with their newborns. One eventually appears by the trees edging the pasture, still and wary, with a calf standing by her side. Judging by the still-visible placental matter, the calf is but hours old.

Are these happy cows? They are certainly curious and bright-eyed, with glossy coats. Miyun Park, the executive director of the Global Animal Partnership, a nonprofit charity group that rates farms based on animal welfare, says so. "I've been to farms and ranches across the country and around the world–some for profit and some not for profit. The life afforded to animals at White Oak Pastures far surpasses many of them. They're given an opportunity to be cattle and sheep and goats."

The log cabin that James Edward Harris built is long gone. But the house where Will Carter Harris then Will Bell Harris lived is an active construction site. Workers are building a new wraparound patio with an extended roof line. It looks like the kind of porch that can accommodate quite a few rocking chairs.

"I really do not want to run a bed and breakfast, but we're going to need a guest house," he chuckles. "This might as well be it."

These days agritourism isn't just a matter of apple orchards and corn mazes. Visitors on their way to Florida beaches stop by White Oak Pastures–a member of the Georgia Grown agritourism association–nearly every day to load up on grass-fed strip steaks, hamburger, chickens and lamb. Jenni Harris–a dynamo who now directs marketing for White Oak Pastures–fields requests from visitors who want to tour the grounds, hold the baby chicks, poke their noses into the garden greenhouses. Or the abattoir, which she will permit.

But first the old homestead needs, much like the pasture that surrounds it, to be restored. "My parents modernized," Harris chuckles, with more than a hint of irony in his inflection. "They put shag carpets on the hardwood floors, installed fluorescent track lighting and covered the poplar siding with vinyl. I'm trying to return it to the way it was in the early 1900s, when my granddaddy lived here."

The Ibérico Journey

By Tim Hayward

From *The Financial Times*

English food writer Tim Hayward is a busy fellow indeed—freelancing for *The Guardian* and the *Financial Times*, broadcasting on the BBC, running a bakery in Cambridge, and editing *Fire & Knives*, a quarterly journal of new food writing. But there's always time to go chasing the world's most delectable ham.

It's dark, very dark indeed, with thick cloud blanking the sliver of moon. The farmhouse sits squat and black on the peak of the hill, and only the headlights reveal it as we rattle up the track. There are four of us in the Jeep and we've come to see something die.

In rural Spain, pigs are still killed the traditional way as part of a family event called a *matanza*—literally "a slaughter." The family members would gather so that when the animal was killed, there would be enough willing hands to process everything that could be preserved, as quickly as possible. Then, the store cupboard stocked until the next killing, that which couldn't be laid away was consumed on the spot—a brief celebration of plenty before returning to the hard life of the farm.

I'd come to Extremadura—along with Simon Mullins, co-founder of the Salt Yard Group of Spanish and Italian restaurants in London, and Ben Tish, the group's executive chef—to watch a little piece of cultural history played out and to participate. But we'd also come to see a slaughter more real than most will ever experience. There is a natural inquisitiveness about death. There's a moral aspect for a meat eater in connecting with the living animal that has to die for you, and there's the challenge: how will you handle yourself? Witnessing the process has become a rite of passage for a certain kind of serious food lover, so we'd come to join a family matanza, we'd come to learn about Ibérico pigs, but, at the core of it all, we had come to see something die.

"Quique" Asparrago owns Señorío de Montanera, one of the principal producers of Ibérico hams. His family also owns Finca Alcornocal in the Province of Badajoz, deep in Extremadura. It's a fortified farmhouse encompassing a courtyard and surrounded by acres of squat scrub oak trees, around which the handsome black pigs root. The finca is way off any utility grid, and at night the arrhythmic wheezing of the geriatric diesel generator is the only thing keeping us anchored in this century. Tonight we'll sit around a fire built of vast oak stumps and drink lethally strong "gintonics," but at six in the morning we'll kill the pig and by the end of the day it will be salchichón, chorizo, morcilla and hams.

A few pigs due for slaughter have been isolated in a pen as we walk out at dawn to choose one. The animal is weighed, a rope is tied round its hind leg and we all walk back to the farmhouse together, the pig gambolling unnervingly like a large dog on a leash as the slaughterman wrestles with the rope.

Outside the gate of the finca somebody has set up a low table, something like a picnic bench but only a foot or so off the ground. Two local women have arrived from the village, one holding a plastic washing-up bowl. They are not introduced to us and stand off from the main group. Antonio Blas is the *matarife*, or slaughterman, who has come from the Montanera factory for the day, along with a couple of hands to help out. As the pig is led to the table our little team stands, awkward, and there is an embarrassed pause.

Then things move quickly. Four farmhands grab the pig, taking a leg each, lift it on to its back on the table and then roll it over onto its side. Blas whips a short length of rope around its snout, neutralising its ferocious little tusks and giving him purchase to control the position of the head. The pig is, of course, squealing, but although we've been told that it sounds "like a child" or "a human cry," it doesn't seem that way. It is bewildered, furious, it grunts and puffs and, to make the obvious error of anthropomorphising, it sounds indignant.

Blas has pulled a knife from his holster. It's a regular butcher's blade with a bright plastic handle. He cuts a 5cm slash in the tough, loose skin across the throat—which, weirdly, doesn't seem to bother the pig at all—then switches his grip on the blade with an adroit flick and slides it through the cut, vertically down into the pig's chest. He twirls the blade from side to side, wrecking main vessels on either side of the windpipe, withdraws with the first gout of blood and then drives it in again.

One of the women has moved in close, elbowing the men aside to get her bowl under the animal's neck. Enormous amounts of blood are gushing out now, hitting the bowl hard and splashing up to soak her arms and chest. Blas has withdrawn the knife and is holding the head to direct the blood flow. There is still immense muscular strength in the pig as it fights and wrestles, but it has nowhere to move. The men lean their weight into it like a scrum; dynamic, full of power, but locked still.

Everyone wants to know that it's fast and painless. Of course I check my watch. The creature gives up fighting about two minutes after the knife goes in. I have no way of knowing how painful it is to have the vessels around one's heart severed, but the main drive for the animal in its final minutes seems to have been a kind of odd, almost determined rage, rather than panic.

The men push two scaffold poles under the table and carry it like a stretcher into the barn. The body rolls a little as they gently lower the litter to the floor. It is still steaming in the cold air and a bunch of grass has been used to plug the gash in its neck, but it has lost all its intense muscular tone. It's difficult to express the absoluteness of the change; from a condensed ball of raw, angry power to a soft mound of flesh that seems it will almost pour off the bench if the litter bearers don't carry it with extreme care.

A bottle of brandy appears and everyone takes a steadying slug.

An Ibérico pig has a full coat of bristly black hair which has to be removed before butchering. Ben Tish and I are handed a propane flamethrower and a scraping knife. As the farmhands turn the body to expose it to the flame we sear and scrape. The smell of burning hair is strong, but somehow not unpleasant. After about a quarter of an hour of work the pig is pink (apart from its characteristic black hooves), and has ceased to look like something that should be running around a yard, instead resembling something that might occupy a butcher's hook.

Blas steels a shorter, more effective-looking blade and begins to cut. He removes the head, cutting carefully between the vertebrae. He splits the pig along the belly, from the anus to below the throat. Using just the knife he cuts through the cartilaginous link at the front of the pelvis and, with the help of two of the farmhands, opens the pig like a book. The viscera are dragged down, out and into a plastic bowl. Blas puts the heart and kidneys aside and the women separate the intestines—still blue-green in colour from half-digested acorns—which they will spend the next few hours washing and scraping clean at the tap. These will be the skins for our sausages.

With the pig empty and open, Blas begins removing pieces. The legs are removed, tied with string and hung on a couple of ancient-looking hooks. Using the short knife he works from the inside out, teasing out each muscle or group—a process we refer to as "seam butchery." English butchery traditionally uses saws and cleavers to cut the carcass into joints, which are a logical division of the meat in a geometric sense but make little accommodation for the physiology of the beast. A British "shoulder" is a square joint containing muscle, connective tissue and bone in a kind of arbitrary sandwich. Blas instead separates more physiologically distinct pieces of meat, handing each to an assistant to place in the scrubbed wooden troughs, called *artesas,* ranged along the walls.

Ben is looking for particular cuts today. The *secreto* is a flat sheet of muscle from under the shoulder blade, light pink and marbled with fat like toro tuna belly; the *pluma* is the tip of the loin. Both are uniquely Spanish cuts. Both are routinely diverted to the lucrative Japanese market.

The speed and efficiency of Blas's knifework is almost too fast to follow, but in short order the artesas are full of sorted meat and he's lifting the last remaining piece, the cleaned spine, from the spread hide. He snaps it in half with his hands like a stick of celery and throws it into a trim bucket. As he turns away, one of the men rolls the skin and places it in a separate plastic bag.

Somebody has set up a cheap garage barbecue in the corner of the barn, and lunch is picked from the piles of meat and grilled over the coals.

There's something reassuring about the way each stage of the process seems to happen without any appreciable leadership. You're aware in every move that you're watching something that's gone on in much the same way for centuries. Two of the hands carry in an ancient mincer bolted to a table and we begin to crank the trimmings through, creating, over an hour or two, several buckets of sausage meat. The bowl of blood is brought back in and we mix it with meat and spices before packing it into the cleaned intestines to make morcilla. Ben and I have been so drawn into the processes that we hardly notice that we're now entirely soaked up to our elbows in blood.

And suddenly it's over. The farmhands are warming themselves by the dying barbecue with shots of brandy, the artesas, now filled with sausages, have been carried away, the floor has been scrubbed, the mincer dismantled and oiled and we carry the *salchichones* and morcillas across the darkening courtyard to the *hogar*, an outdoor kitchen built around an open hearth where they will hang to dry.

On two large hooks hang the hind legs of the pig, neatly trimmed, a rope around each black hoof ready for our trip to the curing factory tomorrow.

Ibérico ham is some of the most highly prized and expensive charcuterie in the world. It's made only from the hind legs of the black pigs of the region—which is why they are sometimes referred to as *pata negra* or black foot hams—which have been fattened on *bellota*, the acorns of the Extremadura's scrub oaks.

In the morning, as the sun rises, we are barrelling over the Extremadura in another Jeep. This time, as we pass the vast orchards and catch sight of the small herds of pigs rooting freely for acorns, we can't help but see them a different way.

The factory at Sierra de Barbellido is a brutal concrete cube set on top of the tallest hill in the area. It looks exposed—a feature that's vital to ham production, as we'll see inside. We're met by Rafael Navarro, the plant manager, who will walk us through the production process.

The skin is removed from the haunch, leaving only enough at the slender bottom of the leg to show off the all-important hoof and to take the stamps which mark our ham's place and date of production. During trimming the joint is massaged to remove any remaining blood from the main femoral vessels. The legs are layered in sea salt in large numbered plastic baskets designed to be moved by fork lift. The baskets are filed in a huge climate-controlled room, where a computer keeps track of every batch. Salting takes roughly a day per kilo of ham, although other atmospheric factors and the quality of the fat layer can cause this to vary.

By the time salting has finished it has penetrated 2cm into the surface of the meat, but the core near the bone is still essentially raw. Each ham will have lost 30 percent of its moisture by weight, making it an inhospitable environment for the bacteria which cause decomposition and allow lactobacilli to thrive. For the next 90 days the hams will proceed through three fridges with high levels of humidity. During this time the salt distributes throughout the meat and lactic fermentation begins. As the hams leave the last fridge they are coated with a pelt of white and green moulds. (The white mould is a variety of penicillium and will eventually colonise the entire surface of the ham.)

Now the hams move to the top of the building, where they will hang for approximately three years. Today, in midwinter, the temperature is about 5C, but during the summer it will rise to 30C. The factory is higher than the surrounding country and windows can be opened or closed in any direction to take advantage of moist Atlantic winds or to block the drying Northerlies. This, however, is the only control exerted as the meat passes through the annual cycles. By the end of the third year the fat has oxidised to a rich yellow colour and the moulds are brown and white. Finally the hams are moved to the bodega, or cellar, where they hang for several more years. The temperature here shifts only between 10C and 14C and the hams settle, mature and become entirely brown.

Throughout our stay Ben has been putting aside pieces of meat for dinner. First comes the ham. This one came from a pig just like ours, but has aged for four years from the 2008 matanza. Ben shows me how to drape each slice over the back of my hand so it warms to blood heat and the fats begin to soften and liquefy.

Next comes a spectacular mixed grill of "double cooked" ribs (slow-roasted then finished on a grill), heart, liver, kidneys, loin and cured belly. Then, finally, the dish that's perhaps the test of our commitment. We Brits can be squeamish about pork, terrified by a history of unclean rearing practices, disease and poorly understood cooking methods. We particularly have a problem, almost at a cultural level, with undercooked pork.

Ben brings to the table a beautifully seasoned, immaculately constructed Ibérico pork tartare, topped, in the traditional manner, with a raw egg. It has been a long couple of days–physically hard, emotionally punishing and bewildering on every level. Yet we've followed a process which we, as lovers of food, can appreciate has been "clean," in both a physical and moral sense, throughout. The healthy, free-ranging animal has been reduced with inspiring skill and by traditional means to some of the most desirable meat in the world, and we've seen the whole process through.

There is not a moment's pause as we dig in.

Beer and Smoking in Danville, Illinois

By Alan Brouilette

From *Blood-and-Thunder.com*

Barbecue cook-offs are a magnet for weekend food obsessives—a title that comedy writer and e-zine food editor Alan Brouilette might have claimed before he went to Danville. That was before he met his match. . . .

We were just outside Danville on the edge of the cornfield when the nerves began to take hold. Weeks before, in a mood of fine strong confidence, I determined that months of covering barbecue competitions had provided enough wisdom that I was ready to get my own two hands dirty. It was time to take action. Stop watching the parade of pits and pork and *engage.* It was important that I dig in and do it myself. It was necessary: Rub the meat. Smoke the meat. *Cover the story*. I cast about for a suitable venue for this escapade, and settled on a KCBS competition in the town of Danville, Illinois, an hour and a half away at lawful highway speeds. I recruited a team of assistants and fronted $250 in cash for the entry fee. We reserved the weekend and thought no more of it.

The morning before the contest I began to prepare. Proper equipment is important. We had five bags of charcoal, thirty pounds of meat, two high-tech probe thermometers, three coolers, four folding tables, five lawn chairs, a collection of knives, an assortment of sweatshirts, a box of cigars, a bottle of whiskey, a case of beer, a sack of pecan wood, and a whole galaxy of rubs, sauces, marinades, mustards, vinegars, salts, peppers, stocks, pans, infusions, foils, and plastic tubs. We needed all that for the competition, mind you, though once you get locked into a serious barbecue collection the tendency is to push it as far as you can.

We opened the whiskey and began loading the rented flatbed trailer. Considering our inexperience with this sort of undertaking, I would say we did well. I had the foresight to rent an open trailer with two wheels and high sides that we could tow with an SUV, freeing us from the need to cram three vehicles with grease and smoke and kitchenware. We lashed the backyard smokers to the trailer railings and used the coolers and charcoal to wedge them in place. We pulled away from the house with total confidence, and made it nearly two hundred yards before our careful knots unraveled. This was no time to panic. Our expedition was resilient. We stopped the car in the middle of a white suburban street and reorganized using construction straps while jabbering at one another about inertia and vibration. The police did not arrive while we repacked, which was wise. We were in a state of high excitement, which can be interpreted by the cop mind as indicative of drug use and miscreant behavior. We were ill-prepared to convincingly explain that only one of those was at hand, so it was a relief to begin rolling again.

We made it to Danville in the nick of time and rolled down Vermilion Street, Danville's main drag, with "No Vaseline" playing loudly. Ice Cube is a musician that announces your presence with authority. We were here to brook no guff from the locals. We had come to compete. To win. To take the prize away from some bumpkin and his Weber kettles and swagger out of town with a couple of local girls staring sadly as our trailer grew smaller in the distance. We quoted Bill Murray often . . . "Cinderella story . . . outta nowhere . . . "

This was my stated goal. In truth, of the seventeen teams, my best-case goal was to finish anything other than dead last.

The team next to us had an RV complete with sponsorship banners and a smoker larger than our trailer. The team across from us had a display of trophies, several of which were taller than the shortest of us. This was unnerving. The chimney-box they used merely to start their charcoal fires was nicer than all of our equipment combined and their smokers may have cost as much as the Honda Pilot in which we had arrived to the competition. We began to consider the possibility that we were overmatched. We parked with some difficulty—parallel parking a fifteen-foot two-wheel flatbed trailer is a difficult proposition even with a hand not unsteady with nerve—and rushed quickly to the cooks' meeting, a gathering of the grim-faced men and women who comprised our competition. I had attended these meetings before, but always in the service of journalism. Today I was no journalist. Today I was a *participant.* We were addressed by Danville's mayor, who smiled a great deal and reminded me of the actor Troy McClure. He welcomed us to Danville and was very nice. The contest's organizer spoke. We were humming with adrenaline at this point, and impatient while she went on about quiet times and KCBS rules and souvenir t-shirts. We had not come for t-shirts. We had come for *trophies.* I signed a piece of paper agreeing to abide by all the rules and took away the four white-foam clamshell boxes that marked us as serious competitors. "Beer & Smoking in Las Vegas" was emblazoned on our entry form. I swelled with pride. A name is important. A name announces to the other teams that you are not someone to be trifled with. You are no backyard nebbish who brags to the nearest lawnmowers and gutter-cleaners that you make the finest ribs on the block. You are a *serious competitor.* You deserve *respect.*

We took our clamshells back to our cooksite and began to plot. It was crucial to the success of our plan that the brisket go on around 9 p.m. The pork butts could wait until midnight. We opened the first round of drinks and lit cigars; an important step in the preparation of quality competition barbecue. We scurried around our cooksite, unpacking and assessing our circumstances. It had grown dark, and we realized we were hungry. We rooted through the coolers for dinner, but found only a bag of pretzels and some Combos left from the trip down. In our haste to pack all the things we needed to dominate the competition, it had slipped our minds that we would require a meal or two before our meat was ready to feast upon. Thus it was that, at nine p.m. and surrounded by fine barbecue cooks from all around the Midwest, I found myself on the telephone in an argument with a sour employee of Papa John's about delivering pizza to a parking space on Vermilion Street. He insisted that a physical address was necessary, and that I was not making a reasonable request in urging him to deliver to "the green Honda Pilot parked two hundred feet north of Main Street." I saw the strategic need to concede to this rigid corporate policy and pretended I was a late-working drone at the law firm across the street. The driver arrived forty-three minutes later, and I intercepted his dogged effort to deliver pizza to a closed law firm by vigorously explaining the complexities of the situation until he fled.

We began preparing the brisket. I had visited a meat-cutter in Chicago, and we were well-supplied with animal flesh. One whole untrimmed brisket, two monstrous pork butts, four slabs of fine St. Louis cut spare ribs, and sixteen pale chicken thighs on the bone. We stripped the brisket from its Cryovac packaging and rubbed it with yellow mustard. The mustard is flavorless, but ensures the spices adhere. We expertly covered the brisket in a spice mixture of my own devising. I had packed enough brown sugar and kosher salt to rub a dozen briskets, and to the salt and sugar were added seasonings of a dozen types. When rubbing something that will be smoked for more than twelve hours, there is no room for subtlety. You need *bold flavor.* There were chiles of several types, a large hit of garlic and black pepper, and several exotic paprikas. We viciously punctured the meatslab with the Jaccard tenderizer. The Jaccard is a savage thing; brass knuckles with steel teeth. It chewed the brisket a hundred times before we wrapped the thing in plastic and left it to absorb the flavors of the rub.

The temperature was dropping, chilling everything. I fired the first of the two smokers, to warm the inside in advance of the brisket. The fire was a welcome presence, adding the light smell of pecan smoke to the air and warming those with the fortitude to stand close enough. We felt the need for more beer before repeating the rubbing process with the butts. The butts received much the same physical treatment, but we adjusted the ingredients. You cannot just shake a few spices over competition barbecue meat. You have to *season* it. You have to *build* a *flavor profile.* Salt is a critical aid to the osmosis of flavor, but pigmeat has an affinity for sweetness. We accounted for this by adding pomegranate molasses to the mustard and increasing the sugar in the rub as we invented. Pomegranate molasses! I felt clever for having thought of this exotic component. We crusted the pigmeat heavily with seasoning before rolling it in plastic and setting it aside to wallow in its flavor-mud.

We had some downtime now while the smoker heated and the meat absorbed. I seized this opportunity to visit with our neighbor. The banner on the RV next to us read "82's BBQ" and I stepped next door to watch the captain prepare his own meat, bearing an extra beer as a gift to our neighbor. Jasen and his wife Leslie talked barbecue with my team for hours that weekend, speaking of other competitions they had seen, helping us acclimate to the rigors of competition, and even sharing a secret or two. Leslie led us to the nearest grocery around eleven when we ran out of whiskey and paper towels. They were so kind to us that we grew suspicious. If they hoped to become close to us and steal our barbecue secrets, they were in for a nasty surprise. If they had malevolent intention it would be much effort for nothing, because, like a great knuckleballer, our secret weapon was that we didn't know what we were going to do either.

No matter. High time to chamber the brisket and prepare the ribs. The brisket slid cleanly from the eleven feet of plastic-wrap it had taken to contain the thing into the chamber of the Pitmaster, where it would rest and cook for the next thirteen hours. Jasen and I were drinking beers and discussing high adventure when we began to wear the uncomfortable facial expressions of men when each thinks the other has farted. Eventually the smell grew powerful enough that we confessed our repulsion, and, each denying the deed, began to seek the source of the stink. A terrible realization dawned: My team members had opened the first Cryovac package of ribs and unleashed a hellish stench.

Stay calm. *Maintain.* This is no crisis. This is a speed-bump. Competition does not always go as planned. It is those who can overcome setbacks that succeed. You are prepared for this. You built in redundancy. Open the other package of ribs.

Stench! From the second package! *Now* we have a crisis. *Now* the men will be truly separated from the boys! It is midnight in Danville, and we have *no ribs.* Failure to compete in all four categories is both a disgrace and a disqualification. This cannot stand. I ran at top speed toward the stark lights of the all-night grocer two blocks away. The twenty-four-hour grocery is often a depressing place at midnight, filled with whores and thieves and dopers desperate for cookie dough and Cool Whip. I forgave the place all of it tonight, for there were four half-frozen slabs of "baby back ribs" remaining in the meat section.

Baby back ribs are the choice of no true barbecue competitor. They are small and dry out easily and provide little meat compared to the true American masculinity of spare ribs. Tonight they would be pressed into service. Bad ribs are better than none at all, and those of us casting about for pork ribs at midnight in Danville could not afford to be choosy about the cut.

My ribs and I—and a pint of rum I felt necessary to treat the oncoming chill—raced back to our competition site, where I found my team giggling like children about the meat's disposal in a trash bin a thousand feet downwind of us. "You fools!" I shouted, "stop this. We have a *crisis to avert.*" We unpacked my treasure and prepared it, peeling membranes by feel and coating the ribs with the same rub-mixture with which we had encrusted the butts. By this time we were coming to realize that it would have been wise to bring a construction lamp, but we forged through the darkness in the knowledge that what were were doing was right, that we were the undiscovered gem of the contest. We were totally confident in our methods. We *believed.* We had no special secret or revealed wisdom. We were rolling on the high of rookie hubris, the stories in our heads full of "Rookie Team Shocks Danville Competition" headlines and shining trophies.

It was around this time that Jasen told us that, of the seventeen teams in the contest, eleven were nationally ranked.

This put a small dent in our swagger, and we pressed him for details.

"Those guys over there," he said, indicating a camper-trailer that had a smokestack emerging from the back of the trailer, "are ranked number two in Brisket nationwide."

"The one on the end," he said, pointing at a mobile kitchen that looked like something a wealthy oilman would tow to tailgate at a college football home game at his alma mater, "was the number-four ranked barbecue team in America for the whole of last year."

I considered this. He continued to reel off a lavish list of honors accumulated by the eleven major players at the contest. We began passing the bottle of whiskey from man to man as the situation came to look less and less hopeful for the four of us. I began to despair. We needed an infusion of confidence.

"So what you're saying," I asked, "is that this competition is as though the local community college decided to hold a basketball tournament and eight members of the ACC showed up?"

He agreed that this was a fair comparison.

"So there are really two competitions here," I said. "There is the one among the top eleven teams, and then a lesser competition for spots twelve through seventeen?"

It was so.

It was one thirty in the morning, when the soul is hibernating, and the cold is breaking over you like waves, and the darkness swallows hope and motivation in equal measure. This called for a motivational speech. For a man in charge of a team to draw the best from them, to move them with his words, to restore their merit and motive with fine strong words. Time to speak. Time to *rally the troops.*

Unfortunately, one of our number had already rolled himself in blankets and passed out in a lawn chair. He was not just asleep, he was a *goddamn vegetable.* This was ultimately a good thing, though because it allowed the two of us still awake to focus on the cigars and whiskey and to use the bravado those provide in men to talk ourselves back into the idea of staying up all night in pursuit of victory.

The temperature had dropped below the point of bearable, and I realized that it would have been wise to bring blankets or a tent. Too late for creature comforts! We had *work* to do. We moved the two smokers closer together, putting the fireboxes a few feet apart to maximize warmth. We then lit the second smoker; we needed the hot boxes prepared by 3am to smoke the pork butts properly. It was forty-three degrees on-site, and we needed the smokers to hold 225 degrees if we were to maintain hope. We loaded them with charcoal and pecan and opened the airvents wide to facilitate the combustion process. The warmth the two fireboxes provided was enough to sustain us. We put the butts on around 3am. My second teammate elected to attempt a so-called disco nap, and climbed into the Pilot for warmth. Within moments his snoring caused the green SUV to shake as if a bear had become trapped inside and gone into a panic.

Usable smokers start around $150 and go up to prices you might see paid for a fine Thoroughbred racehorse. The primary difference among the type we used, the offset-firebox type, is in the amount of effort and attention required to maintain a constant temperature: The more money you pay *for* the smoker, the less attention you have to pay *to* the smoker. Our two smokers each retailed for around $150. A good general leads his men by example. If my team needed sleep; their captain could not. I opened a small vial of electric dynamite called "Five-Hour Energy" and sent the contents sizzling into my nervous system.

And then because we had another of the little grenades, I sent it after the first, hoping to burn through the cold and the dark.

I vibrated my way through the next three hours with my heart pounding a John Bonham drum solo while I monitored the readouts of the twin probe thermometers that kept me in tune with the atmosphere inside the black barrels. Add a little wood, open the vents, watch the heat soar, trim the airflow, watch it slowly drop, repeat. I would wave in quiet solidarity to my fellow night-tenders as we rode together in the starlight. How I envied those with the means to sleep indoors, secure in the knowledge that their rich-man's smokers would hold temperature through the hours only beasts and long-haul truck drivers should see.

At some point the beer was gone.

The sky lightened around 6am and a friendly woman with an enormous smile walked down Vermilion Street inviting the teams to breakfast. I kicked my team from their slumbers to prep the chicken thighs. I stripped the skin from the sixteen thighs and slashed the fat out from underneath while my teammates mixed a brine. The ratio of salt to sugar to water in a brine is critical. A miscalculation in the ratios can ruin everything. We had to be careful. Brining requires absolute goddamn *precision.* We would be making two gallons of powerful chicken brine, and one of the things we had forgotten was a measuring cup.

Don't panic. All is well. We just have to *convert.* We may have omitted the measuring cup, yes, but stop worrying! We have a *teaspoon.* All we need to do is some goddamn *math.* Twenty-four teaspoons of kosher salt and thirty-six of brown sugar per gallon of water. This mathematical calculation made us feel like scientists. Then to get the salt and sugar to dissolve into the gallon of cold water quickly, we had to mix it with our fingers. If not for the whiskey and the beer and the coffee and the Five-Hour Energy and the cold medicine someone had bought during the night to ward off mucus, we would have been miserable with cold. But we forged ahead, dropping the skinned thighs into the brine while saving the skins to wrap back around the juicier thighs after the brining process was complete. This was *primal.* Is there another undertaking in which you would save the flayed skin of a creature to rewrap around its dead flesh after soaking it in chemicals to improve the flavor? We were twisted enough to rejoice in such savagery, and call ourselves brilliant for it. I was not ashamed of us then; we were in the grip of competition. No advantage was too grotesque.

Those of us who had been up all night were in the mood for coffee and donuts. The competition provided weak coffee, but I needed a strong drink. I walked across the street to the "Java Hut" for a large red-eye. A red-eye is a roiling broth of caffeine comprised of near-equal parts brewed coffee and espresso. The potion gives a king-hell rush on a normal morning but was just enough to keep me upright today. A donut also. I had had enough of cold pizza and raw meat; warm pastry and sugar soothed the stomach I had angered with alcohol and stimulants.

The rubbed and seasoned emergency ribs went into the smokers next, which required a game of Meat Tetris. We had to fit all of the meat into the two smokers while ensuring even heating; a challenge in the best of times. We were buzzing now, moving as one, with a single purpose: *Adhere to the schedule.* The schedule rules barbecue competitions like a cruel Nazi dominatrix with a whip and a stop-watch. There is no quarter from the clock. Many teams will appease this vicious goddess by posting the schedule outside near the smoker, like Texas farmers hanging coyotes from fenceposts. We had nothing to hang a schedule from, and relied on cellphone alarms and focus. 8am: Ribs go on. The next will be the chicken, at 10:30. We return our focus on the coffee, and begin preparing our clamshells. This is easy: Beds of greenleaf lettuce. I will have no truck with chopping a million sprigs of parsley.

The cold wet chicken comes out of the brine at 9:30, and we begin patting it dry. I pause in my Hannibal-Lecterish wrapping of the meat in its own scraped skin to demand music. A cold September morning in central Illinois calls for plenty of pounding bass to get the blood flowing. We load up a playlist filled with references to shaking booties and capping asses and the city of Compton in California and get to business on the birds. We season the thighs with flavored salts only, relying on the molasses and sauce to flavor the sole bite most judges will take. Outside of a bloody bite of rare birdflesh, there is little more off-putting on a chicken thigh than the grit of dry seasoning on moist dark meat. We are careful and attentive. That's something we have lasered in on by this point: attention to detail. We have no other choice: In our current state, which combines serious sleep deprivation with advanced caffeination and mild hangovers, we have only two settings, Seriously Hyperfocused and Off. We must choose the former as we cannot allow the latter. Vigilance.

Okay. All the meat is in. The boxes are ready. The knives are sharp. The tables are sparkling clean. You could *lick* our tables safely, even after the gory horrors of the chicken. We are *ready. Poised.* The team is moving as one now. We are *in the zone.* We have an hour before the first turn-in. Desperate to not lose momentum, we light fresh cigars and add rum to the coffee. We are loose and ready. We are anxious as dogs to have a shot at the meat.

We are also unnerved, for the brisket has been hanging at 145 degrees for many hours. We had been warned this would happen, that brisket "plateaus" before rocketing up to the 195 degrees at which we pull it off and rest it. I pull out my cellphone and text the Big Woodie team, who affirm this phenomenon. My pulse quickens: We are *out on the edge* now. "Timing is critical!" I shout at a passing family. If our brisket is not complete by one-fifteen, we will be submitting *undercooked brisket.* I did not stay up all night, jangling from the double-shot of Five-Hour Energy, to submit an undercooked brisket. I monitor the temperature in the smoke chamber closely and rail at God and physics.

The chicken is due in at noon. Six pieces, one for each of the American citizens with a judge's certification from KCBS. We choose to submit eight. Let them pick from a box of plenty. This is goddamn *America*, after all. Gluttony matters. Overstuffing the box is a sign of *prosperity.* The judges will respect prosperity; it makes them think we had so much magnificent product to submit that we could not bear to choose only six. We choose from the sixteen candidates the eight pieces most pleasing to the critic's eye and arrange it in the box. Artfully, artfully; it would not *do* to give away our nervous inexperience with a sloppy arrangement. The box is away, run into the judging area on feet floating on hope. We seize the opportunity, in the down time, to taste the chicken.

Shock. Awe. This is goddamn *staggering*. These chicken thighs have outpaced not just anything I thought we could make, but anything I thought could be made of chicken thighs at all. They are juicy and tender and so flavorful I begin to wonder if I am hallucinating, if I will look up from a bite of this extraordinary birdflesh to see a lizard lumbering toward me from Jasen and Leslie's RV, a dead chicken of its own hanging from slavering jaws. *Maintain.*

The ribs are next. We begin to slice them apart with a sharp folding knife and are foiled. The goddamn cheap factory-farm ribs, the ones that replaced the spoiled mess, are themselves awful. They are crosshatched with chunks of knuckle and cartilage, and tough as shoes. What edible meat there is is delicious, but it is like eating the meat from a rabbit's foot—all tiny bones and morsels.

Nothing to be done. While these ribs are a sure last place, no ribs at all is a disqualification. We man up, determined to own our mistake like adults. Like proud *Americans.* We retouch the veneer of sauce with an artist's paintbrush of molasses, and stack them prettily in the box. Presentation counts, and we may do well aesthetically with these hideous cartilaginous fingers until someone bites into them.

The brisket is rising again. 178 degrees. It has one hour to go.

Pork is next. We pull off the butts from the smokers to rest before pulling, and begin to strip the bark from the swine to test the flavor profile. Holy god. The flavor of the butts' outside is astonishing. *How did we make this black magic?* It is dark and rich and smoky and sweet and piggy all at once. My head swims. I cannot begin to imagine how we did this, though I could recount every step from slicing open the Cryovac to tasting this bit of pigskin.

"Sorcery!" I shout to a child staring hungrily at my cutting board. He flees.

We pull the butts into shreds with two savage torture-forks, season the pulled meat, and pile twelve ounces of it majestically in the foam container. We are salivating like starving mongrels at the sight of this meat. The judges cannot help but do the same, we reason. They are flesh and blood and appetite. They are human. They will swoon. They will be entranced. They will *lust for our butts.*

That last notion causes us, so tired that everything is much funnier than it should be, to have to sit down. "Lust for our butts!" we shout, laughing maniacally, like men who have been sniffing ether for hours rather than pecan-wood smoke.

The brisket is a photo finish. We watch the temperature climb and the clock tick the way that men strapped into Old Sparky watch the clock and the phone with equal trepidation. Finally the governor calls—195 degrees! We have ten minutes. We gently separate the flat from the point with a machete sharpened for the purpose. One of the team bought the machete from a fat Samoan, which is a good sign. The flat of the brisket is sliced to the thickness of a Camel cigarette, while the point is returned to the grill to sear before we chop it into burnt ends. We taste the brisket, and we are turned to gods.

We did this. Humans. Men. Those of us who stayed up all night made the chest-muscle of an ordinary cow into this slice. We have created something otherworldly. We chop and taste the burnt ends, and we realize that if we do not rush this entry to the judges at highway speeds, we will consume it all in minutes, like hungry wolves shredding the carcass of a jackrabbit.

We slice the brisket with care, arranging six slices of tender flesh around the six handsome succulent chunks of burnt ends. It pains us to give up so much delicious brisket. We begin to discuss how anyone could possibly have made a superior brisket that day, or ever. But I have been up for more than thirty hours, and the job is done. I collapse in a chair, head lolling, and find involuntary oblivion for two hours.

The sun stabs me in the eyes so painfully I briefly wonder if I have been assaulted by a deranged cook wielding the Jaccard tenderizer. I force myself awake. I have slept two hours to little effect. I am exhausted. The team has organized us somewhat, but we still have a lot of packing and cleanup to do. I rise from the chair, joints screaming, and begin restocking the trailer.

Good god, there are a lot of empty bottles.

We scrape the hot coals from the smokers and drain the grease as best we can. The coolers are lightened considerably, but we again make use of their rectangular bulk to block the smokers in place as we strap them to the trailer rails. The wood and charcoal are gone. The cooked meat is packed in coolers with ice. We hitch the trailer to the Pilot and walk stiffly to Temple Plaza, a tiny park on Vermilion Street that serves as the awards site. Local worthies in suits are speaking, but I ignore their jabbering. I am thinking about our trophies. Our meat, save the ribs, was magnificent. We had triumphed. We had *barbecued.* We *surpassed expectations.* I was proud as could be already, and this made me believe we could compete with the big boys. Seventeen teams. Surely we were in the top ten. I had tasted our barbecue, and it was better than anything I had ever had. I believed it better than anyone had ever had.

The woman who organized the contest began to call out winners. She would call out the top ten finishers in each category. As fine a job as we had done with our meat, I prepared myself for how I would react when she called out "*Beer and Smoking in Las Vegas!*" I would walk up, accept the envelope and the trophy, and nod modestly at the photographers from the local newspaper and the teams who stared enviously at my prize. There will be no hooting and waving. Act like you've been there before. *Dignity.*

She never called us.

All of that sublime, *ambrosial* meat, and not a single top-ten finish in *any* category? I began to fume. Some Nazi swine had rigged the contest. This was predetermined, like professional wrestling or Nixon's election. We had been robbed of a rightful prize. I was jabbering like an ape when I received the complete rankings and final scoresheet.

NOT LAST! NOT LAST! HOLY SHIT! NOT LAST! SIXTEENTH OF SEVENTEEN! HOLY SHIT! NOT LAST!

"Beer and Smoking in Las Vegas" has a future here. I have refining to do. Practice. *Analysis.* My team needs to be strengthened with specialists. I need to improve the equipment and the planning. I must practice. I have *work* to do. But it can be done. I was dehydrated and exhausted and hungover, and just sick enough to be totally confident.

Chicken of the Trees

By Mike Sula

From *Chicago Reader*

Like Elmer Fudd confronting Bugs Bunny—"you know this means war"—feature writer and restaurant reviewer Mike Sula launched a campaign against garden-ravaging squirrels, a tale ideally suited for the pages of this offbeat alternative weekly. In the end, what Sula really bagged was a James Beard award.

It starts every summer with the first ripening tomato. Maybe it's the early blush on a squat Cherokee Purple, or the lighter stripes of a Green Zebra turning pale yellow, or a lime Bush Beefsteak going gradually olive, then pink, then red. The effects of the sun on this single fruit carry the promise of summer, and the subtle message of whether it will be a good season for tomatoes, or even whether it will be a good summer overall. I watch the weather forecasts and gently squeeze with my fingertips to calculate the precise day I'll pluck it.

But without fail—sometimes the very day before I plan for this auspicious moment—I'm foiled. I'll climb to the roof to find the fruit's smooth surface violated, chiseled and gnawed by a honed set of incisors. The marauder is insolent and indiscriminate. Sometimes the fruit is discarded, half eaten, on the roof. Other times it remains hanging on the vine. Now this tomato becomes a sign of war. And the hostilities will have begun in my annual jihad with *Sciurus carolinensis*, aka the eastern gray squirrel. It's a war I've never won.

Last year the skirmishing started over a prolific yellow cherry plant. In late July I began to find the sweet mutilated marbles discarded two stories down on the front step. Others were cached in the soil of my cilantro bed. I found corpses every day until the escalation on August 1, 2011, when a low-hanging, pleated-red Brandywine was punctured and left hanging for the flies.

But the assault on my orange Roman Candle paste-tomato plant was Pearl Harbor.

For years I'd grown my tomatoes in buckets on the rooftop. It wasn't the best way to grow them, and my landlord didn't like it, but it's what I could do with the space. It worked if the conditions were right—just not for paste tomatoes. The restricted environment of the bucket isn't good for these varieties, and by late spring the tips of the new green fruit would be withered by blossom-end rot, a calcium deficiency that took most of them out. I don't bother with paste tomatoes anymore, but I'd mistakenly purchased the Roman Candle seedling.

By midsummer, against all expectations, healthy green fingers began lengthening off the vines and I began to entertain impossible hopes of a novel, thick, yellow sauce tossed with freshly cut noodles. The most promising of these specimens turned a vibrant shade of banana by August 8—when near dawn it was attacked, ripped from the vine, savaged in its lower quarter, and mounted on the parapet of the roof like a severed head.

I stood staring at the enemy's trophy, the familiar impotent rage rising. But the impulse to fall to my knees, gnash my teeth, and howl at the gods was stayed this time by a resolution I'd made earlier that spring. The squirrels may take my tomatoes and spit them back, but they would not go unanswered. The time had come to close the circle of life.

At some point we stopped eating squirrels in this country. Certainly the very first Americans ate them in abundance, as did the first European settlers, who cleared the ancient forests and issued bounties on the rodent plagues that ravaged their crops; in colonial Pennsylvania authorities offered hunters three pence per squirrel killed. It was the colonists' skill in bagging them with their long-barreled rifles that gave them an edge on the Redcoats during the Revolution.

In the mid-1800s mass squirrel cullings occurred in Indiana, Ohio, New York, and Kentucky. They often took the form of hunting contests in which thousands of animals were killed. Surely those squirrels wound up in the pots of community feeds. Different regions have different names for the massive stews simmered for harvest celebrations, some of which are still held today: the Brunswick stews of Virginia, the burgoos of Kentucky, the booyahs of Wisconsin, and chowders of southern Illinois. The recipes were similar, a thick, slow-cooked mishmash of meats and vegetables, more often than not featuring squirrel as the most important protein source. A well-circulated formula for Kentucky Burgoo Stew in the 1939 cookbook *Fine Old Dixie Recipes* calls for an astonishing 600 pounds of squirrel meat, "1 doz. to each 100 gals."

City swells didn't turn their nose up at squirrel either, even though it's a member of the order *Rodentia* and cousin to *Rattus norvegicus*, the reviled plague bringer and urban menace otherwise known as the Norway rat. In Chicago in 1879, among the broiled sandpipers and black bear hams on the multispecies menu of the Grand Pacific Hotel's 24th annual Great Game Dinner, there were four preparations of squirrel, including black, gray, and an ornamental "Fox Squirrel in Arbor." On the eve of the Great Depression, the *Chicago Daily Tribune*'s Jane Eddington offered a recipe for Brunswick stew, which called for three cleaned, washed, and jointed squirrels. She acknowledged the difficulty the average urbanite might encounter sourcing the rodent, suggesting chicken, lamb, or veal as substitutes, though coyly noting, "I know of people who shoot squirrels almost in the boundaries of some of our cities, even the largest ones."

Even after the advent of processed and frozen foods, and disarticulated plastic-wrapped meat parts chilling under fluorescent lights, Americans kept eating squirrel, though you'd have to know a hunter to get any. A 1967 collection titled *Game Cookery* claimed that "each year well over 25 million pounds of this delicate meat appear on the tables of American households." That same year the Illinois Department of Natural Resources reported that hunters in the state had picked off over 2.5 million.

Even the venerable godfather of American cuisine approved. "Squirrel has been written about rapturously for years," he wrote in his *James Beard's American Cookery*. "And it has long been associated with elegant dining as well as with the simple food of the trapper and the nomad. Fortunately it is plentiful." Beard's recipe for Brunswick stew called for two to three squirrels, veal stock, and a half cup of Madeira.

But somewhere along the way, squirrel declined in popularity as a game animal, replaced by bigger quarry, such as deer and turkey, whose numbers had grown in the countryside as the number of humans dwindled. Mainstream views on squirrel eating began to drift toward disdainful—it became something hillbillies and rednecks did. In the late 90s a pair of Kentucky neurologists posited a link between eaters of squirrel brains—a time-honored delicacy among hunters—and the occurrence of a variant of Creutzfeldt-Jakob disease, a theoretical but terrifying new mad squirrel disease. (Peer review later deemed this connection unlikely.) And though noted woodsman and Motor City Madman Ted Nugent devoted a few pages of his wild game cookbook *Kill It and Grill It* to "Limbrat Etouffee" in 2002—written with a vengeance he typically reserves for sitting Democratic presidents—when the 75th-anniversary edition of *Joy of Cooking* was published four years later, for the first time in the book's history it didn't include an illustrated how-to for pulling the skin from a squirrel.

Squirrel eating may be making a comeback, however, at least among those with au courant appetites for sustainable, healthy, and locally sourced meats. CNN.com's food blog Eatocracy has encouraged readers to seek out sources of squirrel meat—"more earthy and sumptuous than the darkest turkey." Hunting and foraging authority Hank Shaw has spilled plenty of ink on this "gateway" prey, an abundant animal that hones the hunter's skill for bigger game. It's delicious too, he argues, its pink flesh more dense than a rabbit's, which takes on the nutty flavor of whatever it's been eating.

But think of Squirrel Nutkin, Rocket J. Squirrel, and Princess Sally Acorn. How could one eat such an adorable, puckish animal, so easily anthropomorphized? Ask British food writer and broadcaster Hugh Fearnley-Whittingstall: "I do not argue that we have an inalienable right to eat meat," he writes in *The River Cottage Cookbook*. "I do say however that, if we are going to make meat part of our diet, then wild meat is, for me, the least morally problematic of all. All meat is the product of a killing, and those of us who kill for the pot are merely taking responsibility for the manner of that killing. A squirrel may have a cuteness factor that makes some people shudder at the sight of its back legs crackling on a grill. But if those people have ever seen young calves and lambs playing in the fields, then why have they not applied the cuteness argument to their own carnivorous habits? For I have found that most of the people who seem to be upset by the eating of rabbits, squirrels, and the like are not vegetarians but town dwelling carnivores."

One early Saturday morning last August I was sitting at the bottom of a dry creek bed in southern Indiana with a small shotgun staring straight up into the trees, listening to a squirrel I couldn't see cutting on a nut. The branch on which it ate was almost directly above me some 30 yards. In the forest's otherwise echoing silence it sounded like two quarters rubbing together on the edges.

I'd been awake since before dawn, creeping around the woods with 19-year-old Forrest Turner, a horse trainer and aspiring agriculture student who'd grown up hunting squirrels, turkey, and deer in these woods. He'd already shot about 15 to 20 squirrels since the season started. We'd stepped as lightly as possible, staring up at the canopy slowly coming to light, looking for motion in the branches, and watching for acorn and hickory shells as they dropped from the sky. Much earlier we stood under a tall oak, and with a small shotgun I took my first and only shot on a squirrel directly above me. I missed. Over the course of the morning we'd stalked close to 15 gray and fox squirrels, and while Turner got a few shots off himself, we had no luck. Near midmorning, we were ready to call it a day, until we heard the telltale sound above us and gave it one more try.

I'd never hunted anything in my life, and Turner, an enthusiastic guide, wanted me to get my first squirrel. He left me in the creek bed and went off to pursue others. But as the sun rose higher it became apparent my prey wasn't going to offer me a shot. Turner returned and moved up the bank beyond the tree to flush it out. Taking aim with his scoped .22, he fired off two rounds in quick succession. The second connected, and the squirrel tumbled off the branch and fell to the bank, rolling down the slope almost to my boots. He'd shot it diagonally through the abdomen and the small eastern gray attempted to drag itself away through the leaves with its forelegs. I tried to put it out of its pain with a heel to the head but it wouldn't go easily. Turner finished the job, picked it up, and handed it to me in time to feel its pounding heart slow to a stop.

You can see why it's preferable to shoot a squirrel in the head, both for the sake of the animal and its meat. If that's a challenge for Turner, and a near impossibility for me, imagine what it's like to compete in the Great Washington County Shootout, an annual friends-and-family contest for which hunters are required to use long, heavy, single-sighted flintlock muzzle loaders, working reproductions of the same cumbersome rifles the American colonists used.

I shot one of these guns that afternoon at the home of Zen Caudill, a retired Seymour, Indiana, firefighter and the Shootout's host. He'd built his log-walled house and almost everything in it from the trees and stones surrounding the land at the bottom of the sylvan hollow where it sat. When Caudill hunted squirrels as a boy in Kentucky it wasn't for sport. It was to put food on the table. But he'd done well for himself—and he'd done it all by himself—a rigorously independent badass if there ever was one.

He packed the rifle with powder and shot and handed it to me. It was nearly as tall as I am, ridiculously heavy, with a hair trigger. As I took aim at a small hillock it went off before I could steady it. The chances of me hitting a nimble, camouflaged squirrel at any distance with this thing were almost nonexistent.

Caudill fabricated most of the guns used in the contest himself, and the hunters and their family members gathered at his spread at noon to count their kill, busting each other's chops as they arrived. "I see that one's got tire prints on him," one fellow shouted to another who'd brought in a single fox squirrel. The rules are simple: gray squirrels, which are craftier and tougher to get than foxes, carry a higher score, as do head shots over body shots. A head shot to a gray trumps all. Some dozen hunters took 17 squirrels that day, a mix of grays and the larger, slower foxes. As the men sat around eating fried chicken and potato salad, many complained that, so far, it had been a bad year for squirrel hunting in southern Indiana. Squirrels stay put in hickory trees, and the older ones chase the younger ones down to the lower branches. But hickories hadn't been producing so well last year. Walnuts were doing OK, but squirrels take the tougher nut to higher branches of satellite trees to eat, making them harder targets. In previous years the group had collectively taken as many as 70 squirrels in a single morning.

After lunch, they gradually rose and gathered around 69-year-old

Jay Mellencamp—the uncle of the rock star—who took out his hunting knife and began skinning squirrels to confirm the head shots. No one's won more of these competitions than Mellencamp. His name has been engraved on the wooden winner's plaque eight times since 1987, when the Shootout began. He won the previous year's contest with a single head shot to a gray squirrel, but he didn't bag any that day.

Mellencamp was also a frequent champion of the skinning contests the group held in years when the collective kill was higher. That's why everyone stood back while he made a cut under the tail of each squirrel, planted his boot on it while gripping the hind legs, and peeled off the hide like a wet sock. He finished in less than ten minutes.

Caudill didn't do so well either that morning. He'd hit two grays in the body, but his adult son Matt got two head shots and won the day. Matt and his friend Nathan Knoblitt made short work of cleaning them, slitting their bellies open and whipping out their viscera.

I asked Knoblitt why Mellencamp cut off the heads when he was skinning them. Doesn't anybody eat them? "It tastes like every nut in the forest. It's full of flavor," he affirmed, but lots of folks stopped eating them for fear of mad squirrel disease. He then looked me straight in the eye and his face abruptly twitched and froze in a contorted rictus. I looked around uncomfortably and felt relieved when he started laughing.

Pretty much every squirrel recipe you can find is written on the assumption that cooks will obtain wild country squirrels like the ones the Indiana hunters sent me home with: animals fattened on acorns, hickory nuts, walnuts, and perhaps the odd nest egg or two. Nowhere does anyone advise the consumption of their far more fearless and omnivorous urban brethren. Why is that?

First there's the question of diet. City squirrels, faced with a relatively scarcer supply of tree nuts, supplement with the bounty of gardens and bird feeders, or scavenge what we cast away. They're rats with good PR, as the saying goes.

Rats at least know fear. City squirrels, on the other hand, know that the municipal code prevents you from drawing a bead on them with a muzzle loader. This emboldens the sort of bad behavior a

Washington County squirrel wouldn't dream of. A squirrel (or maybe it was two) ran onto the field during two sold-out games of the National League Division Series at Busch Stadium in Saint Louis last fall—and scampered across home plate while the Cardinals' Skip Schumaker was at bat in the fifth inning of game four before leaping into the stands. One afternoon a few summers back I followed a furious rustling into the kitchen and found a plump squirrel perched atop the counter tearing into a bag of peanut M&M's. While my cat dozed in a corner, it stood on its hind legs and confronted me with a hideous moaning, quacking call—QUA-QUA-QUA—before retreating through the hole it had torn in the window screen. I can count dozens and dozens of them along the path of my morning run, recently blocked by a bushy-tail nibbling on a piece of toast.

Would eating a Dumpster-diving rodent addicted to cold pizza, hot dogs, and tomatoes be any worse than eating a battery chicken that lives its life in a square-foot space sustained on slaughterhouse waste and antibiotics? Do they pick up any diseases or parasites their country cousins don't?

"Most problematic issues can be taken care of by thorough cooking, so eating is going to be the least of your worries," says Steve Sullivan, curator of urban ecology for the Chicago Academy of Sciences and a specialist in the urban squirrel. He heads up Project Squirrel, a "citizen science" study that invites participants to log squirrel sightings on its website with the aim of gaining insights into the larger local ecosystem.

Sullivan didn't recoil when I asked if him if there was any reason not to eat city squirrels. Speaking strictly theoretically, he said it wouldn't be a bad idea at all—with proper management.

"People cry about how much corn it takes and how much land it takes to make a cow," he says, "and especially pigs, with their excretory fluids in our waterways and things. Well, squirrels don't have any of those issues. So why would we not be using those, say, from the health, environmental, ethical standpoint? I don't see any reason not to, other than this cultural hang-up."

The gray squirrel is remarkably prolific, Sullivan pointed out, sometimes breeding twice in a year with litters ranging in size from two to four pups. And it's resilient. "Squirrel populations can withstand relatively high levels of harvest without a significant decrease in abundance because of compensatory reproduction," biologists Michael A. Steele and John L. Koprowski write in *North American Tree Squirrels*, the authoritative work on the subject.

There are lots of complicating variables, but "one of the rules of thumb," says Sullivan, "is you can harvest something less than 80 percent of the squirrel population every year and have it bounce back." Roughly 80 percent of all squirrels don't make it past their first year, with most dying from predators and starvation. "They're selected for reproduction rather than longevity, unlike, say, elephants," he points out.

There's even a possibility, though purely hypothetical, that reducing the eastern gray squirrel's numbers in the city would improve biodiversity by encouraging the fox squirrel—which tends to get pushed around by the gray—to move in.

Sullivan is, in theory at least, a dauntless omnivore. There are plenty of invasive and overpopulated plant and animal species in and around the city for which persuasive arguments could be made for promoting them in our diets: Asian carp, Louisiana crayfish, and garlic mustard greens, to name a few. "The fact of the matter is that we have made a cultural decision to self-limit protein," he says. "That's a very arbitrary decision, and it's silly, ultimately. We have all these other options. Let's use 'em!"

Sullivan doesn't suggest this without caution. He points to the familiar case of the passenger pigeon, once so populous that its flocks blotted out the sky. The species was driven to extinction by habitat loss and hunting, and the last one died in captivity in 1914.

"We as humans have an amazing ability to destroy everything in our path," he says. "As a preindustrial and then industrial society we had a strong need for regulation of firearms and hunting and things like this within our cities. As cities have evolved, as species have adapted, as landscapes have stabilized, we've come to see that there are certain species that do really well amongst us: deer, Canada geese, squirrels, rabbits, raccoons, and opossums. If we could really get over the cultural hang-ups, darn it, we should be eating rats too. And I'm excited about the idea of changing regulations and helping people realize that consumption of wild-born, wild-grown meats is OK, and harvesting of said meats in an urban environment is something we can do in a regulated way, safe for humans and humane for the harvested animal. We can't just have an anarchical harvesting of any game, under any circumstances, in any place. But I don't see why we can't have a regulated harvesting regime of all game of all species in all places, with the understanding that some species will be taken off the list."

The state Department of Natural Resources could regulate the harvesting of urban squirrels for food much in the way it does rural ones: issue licenses and set a daily bag limit (currently five) and seasonal possession limit (ten).

But even if it did, a squirrel is not a deer or a turkey, and though it may taste somewhat similar, it isn't a chicken either. Adult gray squirrels rarely grow over two pounds. Is there enough meat on a squirrel to satisfy any appetite? "A lot of people in the world would look at that carcass and say, 'Hey, that's a bonanza,'" Sullivan suggests.

My job as a food writer takes me to a lot of restaurants that serve rich foods that are hardly necessary, let alone healthy if eaten in excess. And that includes lots of meat. Two years ago I made a concerted effort to change my diet when I was off duty. I mastered portion control, and when not on the job I started eating mostly vegetarian. In that time I lost 35 pounds and I can once again touch my toes without losing my breath. I still love it, but don't crave meat as much anymore. I'm satisfied with less when I do eat it, and I appreciate it more. I'm not even close to endorsing a vegan diet. But collectively Americans, whose per capita meat consumption in 2011 was 216 pounds, could stand to eat a bit less.

But if I were to lose this swell gig, I'd need to replace the meat. If it came to that, why couldn't city squirrel be a plentiful, healthy, and nondestructive option?

Well, there are laws standing in the way. In Illinois the eastern gray squirrel is a protected species, along with domestic pigeons, striped skunks, bats, and dozens of other mammals and birds. It is illegal to hunt squirrels with a gun outside of the state-mandated season from August 1 to February 15, and it's illegal to trap them anytime for hunting purposes. And obviously it's illegal to hunt at all within the Chicago city limits—even if it's an animal that's gnawing through your power lines, chewing into your attic, and scrabbling above your head at five in the morning.

So what recourse do you have if squirrels are tormenting you? The city's Animal Care and Control department will remove nuisance wildlife from homes, but only if an officer actually sees it on the premises, which typically precludes removal of the squirrels and raccoons lurking in your attic or walls. In extreme circumstances department officials will leave a trap, and if they catch anything they'll take the animal to a wildlife rehabilitator, says Officer Carey Logan. "But we don't have the manpower to monitor those traps."

A private company with the proper state-issued permits to trap and remove wildlife can take care of that, but it's going to cost you. Brad Reiter of Critter Control of Chicago, the local franchise of the country's largest wildlife removal firm, says he traps more squirrels than any other animal, about 2,000 a year. But that can be expensive. Armando Martinez of Pest Control Chicagoland says if there's more than one squirrel involved, a typical job including house repairs can cost anywhere from \$500 to \$2,000.

For anyone who doesn't take the killing of animals lightly, it should be pointed out that squirrels (and raccoons and skunks and bats and birds) trapped by removal specialists aren't typically relocated to some paradisiacal nature preserve. They're euthanized. And unlike the squirrels that were ravaging colonial cornfields, nobody's making burgoo out of them.

Popular culture is awash in dystopian survivalist fiction and film—*World War Z*, *Contagion*, *The Road*, to name a few recent examples. For the kids there's *The Hunger Games*. This appetite for apocalyptic anxiety in our diversions is curious, because these are scenarios that with some imagination don't seem any less frightening than those discussed in the documentary *Collapse*, in which former LAPD cop and prominent chain-smoking doomer Michael Ruppert asserts that the earth's resources have reached their peak ability to sustain industrial society. Grow a garden, he counsels. Save your seeds. The shit is coming down.

Why shouldn't we be at least a little bit paranoid? Last fall the Greater Chicago Food Depository released a report stating that 20.6 percent of Chicagoans are food insecure, meaning over half a million people in the city are unsure where their next meal is coming from, or they're not getting enough to eat every day, or they don't have any place to get it. Not long after, Wall Street reported its worst quarter since the 2008 meltdown, Tyson recalled 131,300 pounds of ground beef in 14 states, and a Listeria outbreak ensued after Colorado-grown cantaloupes were shipped to 25 states, sickening 146 people and killing at least 30. Last month an Associated Press survey of economists, think tanks, and academics reported the U.S. poverty rate is at its highest since 1965—and thanks to this summer of drought, the US Agriculture Department says food prices will rise 3 to 4 percent. Right now, we're unable to pay our mortgages, find jobs, or fill the gas tank. How much longer until we're unable to feed ourselves?

Meanwhile, Alderman Lona Lane wanted to ban chickens in the 18th Ward, collective-food-production incubator Logan Square Kitchen closed in May after enduring 19 inspections over the prior two years from city inspectors who couldn't or wouldn't understand its business model, and police routinely harass pushcart vendors who support their families by cutting up fresh fruit and sprinkling it with lime juice and chili powder. The city remains hostile and uncomprehending toward small-scale private and commercial food producers precisely at a time when the economy needs them the most.

What if a real catastrophe occurred and trucks stopped delivering cases of pink-dyed farmed salmon fillets and barrels of ketchup-flavored corn syrup to Costco? Could you feed your family in the middle of a teeming, hungry metropolis? What would you do? What could you do? Would you turn away a meal of squirrel or pigeon or rat if you could catch it? Could you catch it?

Last December the *Seattle Times* reported that a local woman had begun regularly trapping and eating the squirrels that had been invading her home. In Washington it's legal for homeowners to trap and euthanize animals that are causing property damage (though the American Veterinary Medical Association considers her method of dispatching them—drowning—to be inhumane).

Thinking on the fringe: if things got really bad, could I feed my family on city squirrel? Build up a stash? Maybe make cross-rooftop trades with the neighbors—squirrel meat for matches, flour, and cooking oil?

The chef led me through the kitchen and onto the sun-dappled patio behind his restaurant. A meticulous student of southern food history, he took a dead squirrel by the tail and nailed it to a wooden railroad tie braced against the brick wall.

"Americans have gotten really, really weird about food in a very short period of time," he said. "Obviously, working in restaurants I work with a lot of immigrants, and they're not afraid of bones or weird animal parts."

He's not afraid of them either. He grew up hunting and eating squirrels. After a hunt it was nothing to cook up the squirrel heads along with the legs and saddle, crack open the skull, and eat the brain. When I asked if he would show me how to clean a squirrel he readily agreed.

He got started by cutting through the base of the tail, above the anus just until he hit skin, then cutting around the haunches of the hind legs and pulling on them hard until the hide peeled off, down to the forelegs and head. After working the "britches" off the hind legs he laid the squirrel on a table on its back, cut off its tiny penis and testes, and made an incision from its crotch to its neck.

"These organs are good stuff," he said, isolating the heart, liver, and kidneys from the rest of the respiratory and digestive tract. I hadn't planned on that. But after his demonstration I felt obligated to keep them. And the head too, though I knew it was going to take some fortitude to get over that hurdle.

At home I washed the carcass, clipped off the paws, and tried to singe the stray hairs that remained on the flesh. They were persistent, but I got most of them and put it all in a bag in the back of the refrigerator. Pink in plastic, except for its head, the squirrel had made the aesthetic and psychological metamorphosis from animal to meat. But maybe not completely. Later I was startled by what sounded like the rustling of the bag, as if the squirrel had come back to life. But it was only the coffee I'd left boiling on the stove. A not-unappetizing musky, meaty smell clung to my hands and cutting board.

A few nights later I took the meat out of the freezer and cut it into pieces, which I dusted in salt-and-pepper-seasoned flour. I seared it off and braised it in beer for an hour. It tasted like chicken thigh, lean and not at all tough after the long, slow cook. The eyes had turned a milky zombielike white, but still I pulled off a morsel of cheek meat as the cat watched, licking her lips.

I wasn't yet ready for the brain, but I did sauté the heart, liver, and lungs. I burned them, so they were bitter, but the heart was the most palatable, with an almost beefy flavor.

Suffering no apparent ill effects, I saw no reason not to make a case for squirrel meat among my friends and colleagues. And I felt confident I could skin enough squirrels for a dinner party.

For an animal nobody is supposedly cooking anymore, its culinary versatility is well documented online and in the stacks of the Harold Washington Library Center. If you're hankering for smothered squirrel in pan gravy, homesteader's squirrel with cream gravy, crock-pot squirrel, Hmong-style squirrel stew with eggplant, squirrel pie, squirrel dumplings, squirrel and broccoli casserole, squirrel curried, fricasseed, or barbecued, squirrel cakes, squirrel purloo, or the infamous squirrel melts, the recipes are at your fingertips. But of all those I found—apart from simple panfrying—burgoos and Brunswick stews seem the most common application. Maybe that's because the squirrel's relatively low meat yield demands a one-pot dish that can be extended with a variety of other meats and vegetables.

I was able to source a steady, humanely killed supply of city squirrels—I won't say where. I was just under the possession limit for squirrels in Illinois. It was time to make burgoo.

"The favor of your company is requested," read the invitation, "for the most local of harvest meals." I sent this to a healthy mix of 30 eaters both adventurous and particular, and set a date. On the menu: juleps made with the mint growing from my compost pile, coconut curry simmered with the mysterious squash that had taken over the backyard, dinosaur kale, cornbread, and the main event: a thick burgoo, featuring "heirloom tomato, tree nut, and alley-fattened wild caught game."

I didn't expect nearly all of the invitees to accept, but evidently curiosity about urban squirrel's viability as a protein source isn't merely a weird, solitary obsession. A few days before the event I defrosted and cut up the legs and saddles, seared them off in a pot, and deglazed it with Madeira, à la James Beard. I sauteed diced bacon, onions, and garlic, added homemade chicken stock and the squirrel pieces, and braised them slowly.

After three hours or so, the squirrel meat was falling off the bone, so I carefully removed the carcasses, let them cool, and then meticulously separated the meat from its tiny skeletal remains. It was painstaking work, and I was certain a few small fragments remained behind, but in the end I had nearly three-and-a-half pounds of shredded, mostly boneless squirrel flesh. I added it back to the pot along with vegetables and herbs from my garden and the Green City Market—the last of my tomatoes, thyme, corn, potatoes, lima beans, and a few small hot chilies—and let it simmer until the vegetables began to break down. Then I cooled it. (Many recipes advise that a night in the refrigerator and then a slow reheating the following day helps the flavors harmonize.)

Acting on the advice of my butcher I made a paté with the offal, searing the diced hearts, livers, and kidneys, flambéing them briefly in bourbon, and mixing them into a pork and bread crumb matrix before pressing it into a terrine.

When the day arrived my guests brought their own contributions—garage-cured Serrano-style ham from a Slagel Farms pig, a classic midwestern relish tray with chopped liver, olives, pickles, and crudités, Michigan apple pies, and, just in time for Rosh Hashanah, a honey cake from a pastry chef. There was Chicago beer and Indiana bourbon, and I smoked a massive lamb shoulder, mutton barbecue being the traditional accompaniment to burgoo.

Low and slow cooking had deepened the stew into a roasty reddish brown, all the vegetables softening but for sweet, crunchy corn. Conventional burgoo wisdom says that when it's thick enough for the spoon to stand up in the pot by itself, it's ready. And with that, most of my guests dove in.

After the heads braised in mirepoix and sherry, a friend demonstrated with a nutcracker the proper technique for extracting a squirrel brain from its cranial cavity, and a half dozen of us popped them into our mouths. They looked like oversize walnuts and tasted slightly creamy, almost like a soft, roasted chestnut. We pulled out the tongues and cheeks, which contained the most concentrated expression of squirreliness. One guest described the meat from the head as "nutty"; others compared it to pork, duck, or lamb. To me this seemed like the very essence of the rodent. If squirrels grew to the size of pigs, you'd really have something.

I don't think folks were being overly kind when they praised the stew. Out of two gallons of burgoo, at the end of the night I was left with only a cup and a half. In short, with the help of a lamb shoulder and some vegetables, squirrel meat can indeed feed a crowd. If it was just me and my family we could survive on it for a week.

"It was so good that I got kinda depressed," my neighbor e-mailed later. "There are so many people who don't get enough protein and here is this menacing squirrel, there for the taking." She's a prolific gardener herself, with her own squirrel problem.

Some guests pointed out that the flavor of the squirrel itself was diminished or subsumed by the stew or muted by the spices in the paté. "I was expecting a more gamy flavor like an elk sausage or something," one reported. "But I thought it was more comparable to a turkey or duck."

"If I hadn't known in advance," said another, "I doubt I would have been able to tell. But I tasted the cheek and even that, while incredibly delicious, tasted like something between pork and lamb. I never would have guessed it was squirrel in a blind tasting."

Most guests communicated a general surprise that city squirrels didn't taste like the wild muskiness of bigger wild game. I don't think that's an indication that it was overseasoned. I think it's because squirrel doesn't have an assertive flavor to begin with, at least not one that corresponds with its brazen behavior.

Proverbially, it tastes like chicken.

Tasting Notes: Heart

By Steven Rinella

From *Meat Eater*

In *Meat Eater*—a sort of prequel to his 2007 book *A Scavenger's Guide to Haute Cuisine*—outdoors writer and TV host Steven Rinella describes the roots of his rugged hunting/trapping/fishing lifestyle in his Michigan boyhood. The coming-of-age ritual following his first deer kill was not for the squeamish.

First-deer rituals come in many forms, and usually involve some kind of eating or drinking. The movie *Red Dawn* popularized the ritual of downing a cup of blood dredged from the deer's chest cavity. Others say you should bite out a hunk of raw heart. A friend of mine from Montana described being forced to eat a slice of raw liver topped with a sprig of sagebrush. In Scotland it's a ritual to smear the hunter's cheeks with the blood of his first deer. When I hunted there and killed a red deer, the guy I was hunting with smeared his hand with blood and reached toward my face. I explained that I'd killed many deer before. "Not in Scotland," he said, and then gave me a swipe on each side of my face.

We didn't have any particular ritual in my family, as my dad wasn't big on symbolic acts of bravado. But he was big on eating deer hearts, the fresher the better, and when the heart came from my own first deer the meal was treated with even more respect than usual.

I killed it with a lever-action Winchester rifle, a year before I was old enough to do it legally. (Back then, you had to be twelve to hunt deer with a bow and fourteen to hunt them with a gun.) It was late in the morning, and we were doing something called a drive. Basically, a bunch of "pushers" head into an area where deer are known to bed during the day, and a "stander" positions himself where he thinks the deer will pass through as they run out. In this case, the bedding area was a deep ravine with a brushy creek bed at the bottom. My two brothers and a buddy of ours were the pushers who had to go down there and bust the deer out. I was the stander, and it was my job to hide on a hemlock-covered ridgeline that angled down into the ravine and provided a good vantage point to see what was going on below.

I saw the deer coming from way off. I expected it to pass below me as it followed the creek, but instead it broke away from the bottom and turned right up my ridgeline. It kept coming and coming, closer and closer. It didn't even know I was there until it was so close that we could have conversed in whispers. It then stopped behind a bent-over tree. All I could see was its head and a bit of its throat. I aimed for the throat but hit the jaw. The deer fell hard and then scrambled down the side of the ridge in a somersaulting flurry of legs. I was right there behind it when it reached the bottom of the ravine. I kept expecting it to die, but suddenly it regained its feet and started to make some progress. I was carrying a Green River beaver skinning knife on my belt like the mountain men did. I pulled the knife and threw an arm around the deer's neck and laid it down on its side like a cowboy in a roping competition. Then I put the tip of the knife into the deer's neck and sliced its jugular. Only later, after my brother pointed it out to me, did I realize that I could have just shot the thing a second time.

I used that same knife to gut the deer, which weighed damn near what I did. When I was done I dug through the entrails to find the sac—it's called a pericardium—that holds the heart. I could feel the warm firmness of the heart inside, about the size of a man's fist. When I sliced through the sac the heart slid out into my hand as though something were being born rather than killed. It wasn't until later that I would read about how some indigenous hunters fed the hearts of their quarry to their young children, so that the children would inherit the strengths and attributes of the animals they relied on. But I did know I was holding the core of a creature, the essence of its life, and that its life was far bigger and more meaningful than any squirrel's. It was impossible not to see just how serious the business of killing was.

I took off my blaze-orange vest and wrapped the heart in it and put that into my day pack. My brothers then helped me drag the deer up out of the ravine and across a bunch of farm fields and through some windrows to where we'd parked that morning. At home my dad showed me how to take a thin-bladed fillet knife and carve out what are known as the great veins at the head of the heart. This left the heart looking deflated and a little hollowed out. I then started slicing the heart crosswise into slices about three-eighths of an inch thick, beginning at the narrow, pointy end. At first the slices were round and solid, like if you sliced a tree limb. But as I got deeper into the heart I began to hit the open pockets of the ventricles. These pockets started out small, just big enough for a pinky to fit through, but deeper into the heart they were so big that the slices looked as hollow as crosscut slices of a bell pepper.

My dad often deep-fried game in an electric fryer with a basket, but on this day we put a pan on the stove and filled it with a quarter-inch of oil. While the oil heated we spilled out some flour on a dinner plate and then dredged each of those slices through it. They sizzled when they hit the pan, and the oil came bubbling up through the holes of the ventricles, and the edges of the slices curled away from the heat. We took them off when they were crispy on the outside, though not so crispy that the juices didn't still run with a little blood.

In general we weren't allowed to put catsup on deer meat. My dad said it ruined the flavor. But with heart he made an exception. The meat was a little rubbery but snapped like a good hot dog when I bit into it. The flavor was similar to liver, though it wasn't as strong. And there was something kind of metallic about it, too, but in a pleasing way. In all, it was a strong and identifiable flavor that I would grow to love, and that I would enjoy for many years to come. Yet it would never become something that I'd want to eat every day or even every week. Why not? It's kind of hard to say. It was too . . . *something*. Perhaps the best word is one that some Vietnamese used to describe a meal of dog meat that we were sharing. They called it a "hot" food. Not hot like temperature or spicy hot. But hot as in volatile, in that you could feel it burning into your soul.

An Awful Mercy

By Hank Shaw

From *Honest-Food.net*

Former political reporter and ex-line cook Hank Shaw is not just a hunter, he's also a forager and gardener, a recipe developer (check out his new cookbook *Duck, Duck, Goose*), and philosopher of living off the land, as "an omnivore who has solved his dilemma." So what goes through such a hunter's mind when he has a deer in his sights?

Nothing in this world is certain, except death. The Reaper comes for us all in the end. Sometimes that end is horrible, violent and cruel. Sometimes it is a lingering, painful path to rot and ruin, pockmarked with despair and regret. Most of us cannot bear to contemplate this. But in those secret moments when we do allow ourselves to envision our own departure from this world, we ache for it to come swiftly, cleanly. Such a death is the ultimate mercy, the ultimate kindness.

Three days ago, on a cold and rainy hillside in Wyoming, I delivered that ultimate kindness to a dying fawn. And in the hours since, I have been unable to shake the image of that young animal from my mind—nor have I been able to fathom the seeming courage with which it faced me, a handservant of the Reaper.

I'd come to Wyoming in search of antelope, one of my favorite game meats and one I'd not had the privilege of eating since I shot my last 'lopes in 2006. My friend Sheamus and his friends Allen and Tad invited me along on their antelope hunt, and I eagerly accepted.

Allen and Tad were old hands at hunting pronghorn, and were good enough to do it consistently on public land.

But when we went to buy our tags at the sporting goods store in Caspar, we found that the area where Allen had planned to hunt was sold out. So Sheamus and I had to buy tags for a neighboring region, one none of us had ever seen. Sheamus is a chef more interested in meat than horns, and since I already have the skull of a big buck antelope on my wall, we each bought tags that allowed us to kill an antelope doe or fawn instead of a buck.

Into the truck we went, full of hope. Antelope hunting in Northern Wyoming is not the toughest endeavor in the world. There's probably a higher concentration of pronghorn there than in any other place in North America. They are everywhere. The trick, however, is finding them on land you have permission to hunt.

The country we were driving through was sweeping and stark. For starters, these are the high plains. They begin at 5000 feet and go up from there. The wind is constant. Red rock cliffs fade into scrubby shortgrass prairie. Deep coulees hold mule deer, creek bottoms whitetail deer and turkeys. Look around and you are overwhelmed with a sense of beige. Everything is beige: The grasses, the hillsides, the antelope.

And sure enough, we found antelope. Lots of them.

Tad checked a nifty GPS device he had that showed us which was public land and which was private. Again and again and again, the answer was the same: Private. Hours passed.

Finally, Sheamus spotted a lone pronghorn bedded down on the side of a grassy hillside. Tad checked his GPS. "Green light! We can shoot him!" I was up first, so I slipped out of the truck, rifle in hand.

I needed to cross a road and get over a fence before I was legal to shoot—all in plain view of the sitting antelope. My heart hammered against my chest, and only a little of it was because of the altitude. I knew this was probably my only chance to get an antelope and I did not want to mess it up.

But surely the pronghorn would run off if I got close to it? I decided to try something that's always worked with other animals: I walked along the road away from it, not looking. For whatever reason, not looking directly at animals seems not to spook them when I do it. I crossed the fence a few yards down the road and jammed a few shells into my rifle. I glanced to my left, up the hillside. The antelope was still there. So far so good.

I looked at the antelope through my scope. My heart sank a bit: It was a little boy fawn, not a fat doe as I'd hoped. But some meat is better than none, I reckoned. I also realized that from where I was sitting, this would be a long shot. I don't much like long shots, so I decided to walk away from the pronghorn again to get myself around a little knob, where he could not see me. I could get much closer to him by coming up from behind the knob and shooting down from the top.

I worked my way around while Sheamus and crew watched from the truck. As I got closer, I dropped to my knees. When I reached the lip, I crawled. The fawn should be just below me, I thought. But he wasn't. *Had he walked away while I was behind the knob?* I could just imagine everyone laughing at me in the truck. Letting me belly crawl over cactus for nothing.

Where the hell had this antelope gone? I looked to the right, and there he was, this time much closer. He was still bedded down, looking at me, calmly chewing grass. I was stunned. No animal should be that calm with a predator so close. *Why didn't he get up?* Then it dawned on me.

Something was wrong with this fawn. Something serious.

Was he sick? Injured? I looked through the scope again. There he was, looking for all the world like he was just chewing his lunch on any other Monday afternoon. And he was still looking at me.

For a moment I thought I ought to just walk up on this antelope to see what he would do. Maybe he was just young and foolish, maybe I could teach him to fear humans. But I didn't. I didn't do that because, quite frankly, I wanted the meat. If I don't kill a deer or some other sort of venison each year, I don't eat red meat. I've lived this way since 2004, and I am not about to stop.

So I did what I set out to do. I set the crosshairs of my rifle on the best target I had available: The spine at the base of his neck. My pounding heart bounced the crosshairs mercilessly until I took a long, deep breath to calm myself. The last image I had before the world exploded was that fawn looking directly at me.

I did not see the antelope die, but I heard the thud of the bullet hitting him. When I looked up, he was stone dead. I chambered another round just in case he got up, and walked towards him, about 100 yards away. As I drew closer, I saw an odd dark patch near his foreleg. *What?! Had I just shot him in the leg? Then why is he dead?*

Standing over the dead pronghorn, I was at first struck by how small he was. Probably born in June, he could not have weighed more than 50 pounds. Then I saw what the dark patch was. Something, probably a coyote, had almost completely torn off this poor fawn's foreleg. It was hanging only by a small bit of muscle and skin. A horrible wound, a fatal wound.

The yearling had not run away because he couldn't. But three-legged animals can certainly stand, and many can walk. So why had he not stood up and even tried to escape? Was he addled by his injury, which looked to be only a couple days old?

I knelt down and put a tuft of grass in his mouth as a sign of respect; it's a German tradition, a final gift of food to the fallen.

By the time I stood up, Sheamus was walking up the hill to help me out. We carried the pronghorn in silence and carried him back toward the truck. I skinned and quartered him quickly. We remarked that he was almost the exact size and color of a baby goat. "That's gonna be some good meat," Tad said.

He's right. Holly and I will probably get six meals from that little antelope. But I can't stop thinking about its fate. I know in my heart I did the right thing. Not every hunter would have chosen to use his tag on such an animal. And had we left him, the yearling would have died of starvation or, more likely, have been torn to pieces by the coyotes when they returned for him in the night.

My brain tells me that this fawn did not know this, that he could not possibly look his death in the eye serene in the knowledge that with his leg in ruins, a bullet was the best of all possible ends. My heart says otherwise. And I can only hope to show such courage when the Reaper comes for me.

Home Cooking

Guess Who's Coming to Dinner

By Gabrielle Hamilton

From *Bon Appétit*

There are chefs who can write and writers who can cook, but Gabrielle Hamilton—chef-owner of New York City's Prune restaurant and author of the memoir *Blood, Bones and Butter* (2011)—rocks the hyphen better than anyone: she's won James Beard awards for both. A great companion for a culinary road trip . . .

You think road trip and you imagine a dog-eared atlas, a bag of Cheetos on the shifter, feet up on the dash—time and opportunity, both, ostentatiously yours. I've had that road trip. This one, though, starts at the airport at 5 a.m. to get my photographer friend Penny and me to Birmingham, Alabama, in time to "catch the light." I've had to arrange babysitters, school backpacks, and restaurant staff issues to get this six-day stretch of open road. Penny, the one understandably most concerned with catching the light, is equally unrelaxed as we get in the rental car.

Ironically, we're heading out on the road to get . . . "home." Home cooking. Not the roadside diner kind, and most emphatically not the homey stuff that restaurant chefs are peddling these days, with their "house-made" *salumi*, bacon, pickles, bitters, honey, gin, charcoal, mead, candles, and aprons. Little exhausts me quicker. I'm looking for the habits and the eccentricities of the true amateur.

I've been working on a cookbook for Prune, my restaurant in New York, and the question of the home cook comes up often as I aim to be hospitable and useful to my perceived reader. So I've begun to wonder, who, exactly, is the home cook these days, and what and how is he or she cooking? If I ask readers to measure by weight rather than volume, to tackle something that feeds 30 and takes a whole weekend, or more simply, to season with nothing more exotic than salt and pepper, will my book quickly end up in the remainder bin?

The only way to discover the truth of this imagined home cook is to get into the home kitchen. And so I invited myself over for dinner in seven homes across five Southern states, all connected to friends, and all agreeing to ignore my chef self, the photographer with me, and the magazine I am writing for, and to just cook as they usually do.

Day 1: Birmingham, Alabama

Soon after we land, Penny and I are at the lake house of Nicky Barnes with what I've come to call—lovingly and with a wink—"the doctors' wives." It's way more complicated than that, including the fact that one of the doctors' wives is no longer married to "the doctor," and that Jorja, the friend for life who invited me to dinner, isn't cooking, isn't married to a doctor, and we are not even in her home. What's important is this: The women who *are* cooking, Nicky and Lisa, each have four children, cook in their homes at least four nights a week, and have the means to buy whatever groceries they need.

When Penny and I arrive (plenty of daylight!), there is pimiento cheese. I read the handwritten recipe, admiring its awesome specificity of ingredients (*Duke's* mayo, *Kraft* Monterey Jack, *Mt. Olive* brand pickles, but just for the juice), and the charming absence of specificity when it comes to how to make the stuff. There are no measurements, and the instructions are clumsily out of order; it's a classic home "recipe," attributed to a friend as simply "Margaret's Pimento Cheese." For the main course, we have excellent turnip greens from the Junior League of Birmingham cookbook, and a roast chicken dish with tomatoes, basil, and balsamic vinegar that Lisa cooks very well, with natural ease. It's a relief to see she isn't faking for this magazine or chef-ifying for the chef.

I'm struck by Nicky's handwritten, scribbled-over, paper-clipped kitchen notebook, some equivalent version of which we will find in every home we visit. In Nicky's case, it's tidy, short yellow sheets, mapping out the week's meals so that she knows exactly what to get at the store. I had wondered if mothers are still keeping these kinds of books, which—it sounds so archaic, and even antifeminist, to say—

might someday be passed on to their daughters at their weddings. I am gladdened to see that they are, and even gladder, in Nicky's case, that hers will be passed on to one of her four sons!

Day 2: Sullivan's Island, SC, and Savannah, GA

In the very early morning, Penny and I slip out of the lake house where we've spent the night—each with our own guest room, bathroom, and fresh bar of Lever 2000—get the GPS programmed, and hit the road. By mid-afternoon (slanting golden sunlight!), we're in South Carolina, arriving at the Sullivan's Island home of Ginny Deerin to cook "joyfully for oneself," as she put it to me in an e-mail. Ginny is a Katharine Hepburn-esque empty nester who cooks for herself so emphatically that she has conceived of, and been encouraged toward, a cooking-for-one television show. I am thrilled to meet a woman like her, since, as anyone who regularly cooks for oneself can attest, it is not that joyful a proposition.

Ginny's philosophy is actually much like my restaurant cooks' approach to family meal: It's the dovetail between *What have I got that needs to be used up?* and *What do I feel like eating?* Except that Ginny truly enjoys the added inspiration of looking through cookbooks, magazines, and websites. So for her it's not only *What have I got?* and *What do I feel like?* but also *What would Melissa Clark at nytimes.com do?* On this particular day, she has dug up sesame seeds, rolled oats, an ear of grilled corn, and a knob of ginger.

Her fast and loose attitude toward called-for ingredients is a blast of genuine home cooking that I am giddy to see in action. This is perfect data if you are in the midst of writing a cookbook and want to know how your end user feels about your strict ingredient list. In our case, the biscuits Ginny wants to bake are supposed to be made with buttermilk. She doesn't have buttermilk, so she pulls out a small container of milk. The milk, though, is a full two weeks past its expiration date. Undeterred, and unwilling to make that trip to the store for an ingredient she lacks, she gives it a deep sniff, deems it viable, and adds it to the dough after a further souring with a tablespoon of vinegar.

Another recipe we are cooking with calls for sorghum syrup, which she also doesn't have, so she uses maple. The cookies she wants to make require twice the amount of rolled oats she has. They also call for pine nuts, but she has only pecans, and again, only half of what's listed. Ginny uses liquid measuring cups for dry ingredients and her 40-year-old electric egg beater instead of a shiny Kitchen-Aid mixer, and every single thing we cook together—whether pork loin, biscuits, root vegetables, or cookies—gets thrown into the 450-degree oven. She just turns it on and goes!

In Ginny's happy hustle is the quintessence of home cooking. Here is the voice and the eccentricity of an unintimidated, joyful home cook.

She has a sturdy sensibility that, at a couple of junctures, reminds me of the cooking I grew up with in rural Pennsylvania. I have consumed more than my fair share of "perfectly good" past-date milk, soured with vinegar and repurposed. And I have eaten more bruised, wilted, molded-over treasures from the pantry than anyone I've ever met, because my mother fed a family of seven with the same ingrained mentality as her French wartime parents, constantly making more than there was with what there was—albeit with professional-grade skills. It's only serendipity that what I grew up eating—bones, claws, stinking cheeses, vegetables pulled from our garden—has come into vogue in the food "scene."

Penny and I drive in the deepening black of the Southern night until we arrive in Savannah. We speak into an intercom, then punch in a security code, and the heavy gate slowly pulls back and lets us in to drive beneath enormous live oaks. Mrs. Laurie Osteen, her husband, Chris, and their impeccably well-groomed youngest daughter greet us at the door of their majestic riverfront home and lead us into the kitchen. On the highly polished counter, typed and formatted, are three pristine copies of the recipes that Mrs. Osteen will cook for us.

Chicken simmers in Riesling while Mr. Osteen expertly makes us gin and tonics, which I consider as much a part of home cooking as the glistening white three-tiered coconut cake practically levitating under its glass dome on the counter. We have a comfortable and lively dinner on the porch, drinking the same Riesling in which the chicken was braised, made more seamless by the fact that Mrs. Osteen considered two important factors for the meal: reliability and ease. She's made that delicious chicken a hundred times, and it requires nothing of the hostess that might hijack her away from the table, where the best stories are told. When the cake is served, I am held rapt by the tale about how Mrs. Osteen may have killed the local priest with it (he was diabetic; what to do?). Do not let that deter you from making it. It is worth the peril.

Day 3: Davie County, North Carolina

The next lunch finds us at the Cooleemee Plantation House, located between Mocksville and Lexington, North Carolina. When we arrive for the family potluck that my friend Jay has arranged, there is a woman frying chicken in two cast-iron skillets. Stephanie is in street clothes, with a regular apron, but she's using restaurant-style kitchen tongs and an insta-read thermometer. It doesn't register as odd, because I am so attracted to the golden chicken, as is Penny, who's got her camera out in seconds. But then I admire the tiny beans another woman is stirring, and she says, "I don't ever cook butter beans that are but any bigger than a squirrel's ear."

It's a charming thing to say. Almost rehearsed.

She pops a knob of fat in another skillet, slides it into the oven, and taps the door shut.

"Bacon fat?" I ask, eager to get the exact details of everything I will be eating.

"Yes, that's Benton's fat, which has a different flavor profile than Nueske's, which, of course, I use for other things."

What home cook talks about the nuances of the "different flavor profiles" of cult bacon makers? And why is that woman probing her fried chicken with a health department-approved thermometer? I start to worry. Meanwhile, Penny looks genuinely happy for the first time on our trip. We've got good light, handsome food, and a house that enjoys US National Historic Landmark status.

"GH, this is awesome!" she says as I ferry dish after dish onto the porch for her to shoot. While she whistles in photographer heaven, I slide down into a silent writer's ditch.

"There's no story here," I whisper. "These people are foodies. *Chefs!* I. Am. Dying." Penny giggles at my suffering. I am awed by the food—it's impeccable—so much so that I ask for every recipe, eat everything on the table, and have third helpings of the chicken. But it's researched, perfected, and way too articulately explained. In place of handwritten recipes, two of the potluckers generously give me their published cookbooks! I ask Jay what happened to our abiding idea of home cooks at a family potluck.

"They chickened out," he explains. "And I didn't want to let you down."

Day 4: Chapel Hill, North Carolina

I am slightly wary of professionals the following day when we arrive at the Alexanders' in Chapel Hill for a lunch of shrimp and grits. Lex is a professional, but I already know that. He spent 30 years in the retail end of the food business, including sourcing items for Whole Foods Markets to brand. I invited myself over expressly to see what his cooking would be like given his uncompromising respect for exceptional and responsibly sourced products, but I don't want two ringers in a row. Thankfully, I am put at ease when I see his wife, Ann, chop the flat-leaf parsley and then wash it, rinsing the flavor down the drain. (A professional would wash first, dry well, and then chop, just moments before using.)

So I let myself loose in the pantry and, as I expected, there is excellent chocolate, tomato chutney, an Italian fish sauce. The grits Lex is stirring come from a mill in nearby Graham. Their cooking represents exceptionally well something I have seen throughout the trip: a hybrid use of grocery-store convenience products combined with from-scratch elements to create a dish. The only difference here is that the convenience products are of the highest quality. And it reads in the bowl. Thc Alexanders' shrimp and grits–complex and deep and wholly satisfying–take the blue ribbon.

Day 5: Berryville and Nellysford, Virginia

We have breakfast the following morning in Virginia's Shenandoah Valley with the unmistakably genuine Jean "Maw Maw" Hinson, whose home lies in the middle of horse pasture in Clarke County. Maw Maw is waiting for us in her immaculate kitchen, a Teflon pan of Depression-era tomato gravy on the stove, covered with a glass lid.

When it comes time to prepare the Hungry Jack pancakes that go with the gravy, Maw Maw laughs with a little shrug. She is happy to welcome us, but also amused and a bit baffled at what she could possibly have that a magazine would want. "I'm not sophisticated," she says. When she presents the tomato gravy, she shrugs again and adds, "It's not even a recipe, really. It's just two ingredients—the two ingredients we had growing up. We grew tomatoes and we had a cow, so we had butter."

The way those ingredients work together—the sweet, bright, acidic tomato with the soft, creamy butter—stops us in our tracks. After decades of tasting long-cooked, deeply reduced tomato sauce with a paste base or, conversely, the almost inviolable summer pairing of heirloom tomatoes with fruity olive oil, Maw Maw's ripe tomatoes, gently and briefly simmered with sweet butter and served on pancakes like a fruit, knock us out. The gravy is exceptional. Haunting. Of all the excellent cooking we've eaten on this trip, this is the certain thing I will be cooking from now on in my own home.

We end our road trip an hour away in the Rockfish Valley, with dinner at the home of stonemason James "Fuzzy" Monnes. The property sits on a hill, terraced with substantial vegetable gardens. Hand-built cabins and sheds are nestled throughout, all lopsided, all piping chalky pastel-blue smoke from their wood stoves and fireplaces. There's an instant affection here. Maybe it's the fact of Fuzzy's smiling and Technicolor wife, Cathy, with her glowing red hair and turquoise eyes and her golden shawl. Or maybe it's his luminescent daughters, Mary Pearl and Sally Rose. The latter opens her arms and says, "Welcome to Appalachia!"

"Welcome to 'The Monnestary,'" Fuzzy adds.

Sally Rose gives a tour of the property, a kind of homesteading, back-to-the-lander "estate" that includes a well-fenced chicken coop and a walk-in refrigerator where a keg of local beer is kept. "We have three brewers around here and we rotate," Sally Rose explains.

The wood-burning *forno* that Fuzzy built after a trip to Italy anchors the outdoor common space, which has another fireplace, a couch, and a prep table. It's like sitting in a living room, but surrounded by trees and honoring fire and hearth—in the community sense of the word—rather than television. When I e-mailed Fuzzy to ask what he might cook, he wrote, "We are focused on stuff we've grown and caught, shot or harvested off our land [or close to it]. One thing for sure, there will be a blackberry pie involved . . . the freezer's full of berries from last summer."

His ethos might have huge currency these days, but for him it's as pragmatic, thorough, and unsnobby as it gets. While Fuzzy's preparing the venison and tending to the pesto pizzas in the *forno,* Cathy brings us hot and creamy potato-leek soup.

Dutifully documenting the recipes, I inquire about her soup.

"So, Cathy, what did you do here?" I ask, holding my beautiful little bowl.

She ticks off the "recipe," counting on her fingers, in incomplete sentences, like an average grocery or to-do list:

"Grew the leeks.

"Grew the potatoes.

"Made a vegetable stock."

I crack up, imagining the published recipe whose first two steps call for growing your own leeks and potatoes!

A recipe like Cathy's may not make it into a magazine, but when I go back to my cookbook (and my imagined reader) in New York, I will remember it. I started this trip by writing a lot of e-mails, encouraging people to be authentically themselves in their kitchens. And I end this trip having been given permission to do the very same. I thank Maw Maw for letting me know that I can include some of my own two-ingredient recipes without feeling the need to complicate them. And I thank the Osteens for reminding me how tradition and a good, funny story can make a meal more than just what you eat. I thank "the doctors' wives" for their pragmatic reliance on store-bought convenience products, like some I use at the restaurant, and for letting me see that my devotion to specific brands is equal to theirs. I can call for esoteric ingredients knowing full well that Ginny isn't going to buy them but that she is going to make the dish anyway—joyfully!—and that the Alexanders will already have them in their pantry. I now know from the professional potluckers that the home cook is not the only imagined reader: There will be cooks out there with scales and thermometers. And I know that I can ask the reader to do some heavy stuff, like build a fire or wrangle a whole animal or make something difficult from scratch—something that the folks at "The Monnestary" won't think twice about.

Turns out I'm a home cook, too; I just happen to cook in a restaurant.

How to Make Real New England Clam Chowder

By J. Kenji Lopez-Alt

From *SeriousEats.com*

In his weekly Food Lab column on the blogsite Serious Eats, MIT grad J. Kenji Lopez-Alt obsessively deconstructs recipes for the home cook. He gives new meaning to the term "food geek"–but really, who wouldn't want this guy for your lab partner?

If you've spent any amount of time in coastal New England, you've probably noticed how generously awards are bestowed upon clam chowders. Now I've never met the folks who run these award factories, but I take issue with any organization that passes out praise like flyers.

Having spent my entire life traveling through New England, I've grown accustomed to the fact that nine out of ten "award-winning!" or "#1 voted!" clam chowders are going to arrive at the table either thick as paste, bereft of clams, or packed with clams so rubbery they make your jaws bounce, and unfortunately, most home recipes don't turn up results that are much better. And if finding great chowder in its birthplace is difficult, you can imagine what it's like *outside* of New England.

When done right, clam chowder should be rich and filling, but *not* sludgy or stew-like. Its texture should be creamy without feeling leaden, like you're sipping on gravy. Tender chunks of potato should barely hold their shape, dissolving on your tongue, their soft texture contrasting with tender bites of salty pork and briny clam; god help the clam shack that dare serves rubbery clams in their chowder!

The flavor of a clam chowder should be delicate and mild, the sweetness of the pork complementing the faint bitterness of the clams, accented by bits of celery and onion that have all but dissolved into the broth, fading completely into the background. A good grind of black pepper and a bay leaf or two are the only other seasonings you need, unless you count the requisite oyster crackers as seasoning. I know some Yankees who do.

The Precedents

Chowders have a long, complex, and relatively apocryphal history that can be traced back to the fish and seafood stews eaten in coastal England and France. Like many old dishes, the name of the food stems from the word for its cooking vessel, a large cooking pot or "cauldron," known in French as a *chaudiere*. Or perhaps it comes from the old English term for a fishmonger, *jowter*, which had been in use in Cornwall since at least the 16th century.

Whatever the etymology, its history can be traced across the Atlantic to the fishing towns of New England–Boston, Mystic, Nantucket, New Bedford–where the European dish was adapted to work with sea journey-friendly staples like onions, potatoes, and salt pork or beef, along with local ingredients like cod, oysters, and clams.

About a decade ago, I had a job as a cook at B&G Oysters in Boston's South End, a fancy-pants seafood shack run by Barbara Lynch. It was there that I first started taking a serious interest in chowder-making, there that I realized that chowder is *not* just the sludgy stuff I'd been raised to believe it was. We made our chowder in the manner of a fancy restaurant–cooking and seasoning each element individually, combining, pureeing, straining, adding, mixing, until our broth was intensely flavored and light, our clams were perfectly tender, and every vegetable cooked just so.

It was delicious, but it's decidedly *not* the way a traditional chowder is made; a poor man's food meant to take few ingredients and even less effort. I remember thumbing through a copy of *50 Chowders*, by Jasper White, in which he unearths New England's oldest-known printed recipe for chowder, from the September 23rd, 1751, edition of the *Boston Evening Post*:

> Because in Chouder there can be not turning;
> Then lay some Pork in slices very thin,

Thus you in Chouder always must begin.
Next lay some Fish cut crossways very nice
Then season well with Pepper, Salt, and Spice;
Parsley, Sweet-Marjoram, Savory, and Thyme,
Then Biscuit next which must be soak'd some Time.
Thus your Foundation laid, you will be able
To raise a Chouder, high as Tower of Babel;
For by repeating o'er the Same again,
You may make a Chouder for a thousand men.
Last a Bottle of Claret, with Water eno; to smother 'em,
You'll have a Mess which some call Omnium gather 'em.

Aside from the interesting technique of layering ingredients in a post to stew them and the very Victorian use of spices, the recipe essentially reads "put things in a pot and cook them." One thing you'll immediately notice is that dairy is conspicuously absent from the recipe. Instead, the chowder got its thickness and richness from soaked biscuits. (Note that in this usage, biscuits most likely refer to tough, cracker-like hardtack, not the fluffy leavened biscuits of the American south).

Slowly, as dairy became cheaper and more readily available in the region, it began making larger and larger appearances in chowder, at first simply being used to moisten the biscuit, before eventually completely replacing it as the primary ingredient outside of clams, pork, and aromatics. These days, the biscuits live on in the form of oyster crackers, which as any true chowder-head can tell you, should be added liberally to your bowl and allowed to soften slightly before consuming.

So which is the best way to cook chowder? Can the dump-and-simmer method be improved upon by some modern technique, or is there something to the classic that gets lost when fiddled with too much?

I decided to break it down element by element and really figure out what it is that makes clam chowder tick.

Building a Base

Most basic recipes for clam chowder call for rendering down some form of salted pork (bacon or salt pork usually), sweating onions and celery in the rendered fat, a touch of flour, followed by milk, potatoes, chopped, and occasionally bottled clam juice. It all gets simmered together with a bay leaf or two until the potatoes are cooked and the broth is thickened. It gets finished with a bit of cream, or perhaps some half and half.

Right off the bat, there are some issues I have with this process—flour-based roux can be pasty, and cooking the clams as long as the potatoes is a surefire path to rubbery clams. These issues would all need to be addressed. But first things first.

The Pork

There are a few salted pork options at the supermarket:

- **Sliced Bacon** is the most widely available, and what most folks buy for breakfast. It works in a chowder, but I find the smoky flavor of bacon can be a little overwhelming for the delicate clams. Thin slices also achieve an unpleasant texture as they simmer in the broth. A better option is . . . -
- **Slab Bacon**, cut into ½-by ¼-by ¼-inch *lardons* (that's fancy French for "chunks") is a much better option. I like the meaty chunks you end up with in the broth. They match the texture of the clams, making the whole dish more cohesive. But again, its smokiness can be distracting, which leads us to . . .
- **Salt Pork**, which is simply salted and cured un-smoked pork fat and meat. It can be made from three different parts of the pig—belly, side, and back. The further up the back you go, the fattier the salt pork gets. I find the fat back to be a little *too* fatty, turning soft and greasy in the chowder. Better is to look for salt pork with an equal mix of fat and lean.

With any form of pork, **the key is to go low and slow** so that the fat renders out completely without letting the pork burn. This gives you a great base in which to sweat your vegetables.

Of course, you can also go completely pork-less—there is plenty of precedent for that.

The Aromatics

Onions, celery, and bay leaf are the traditional flavorings here, and I found no reason to stray from them. I tried a few versions with things like carrots, thyme, leeks, and garlic, but in all cases found them to be distracting, taking away from the inherent chowderiness of the broth. It simply didn't taste like childhood to me with the alternatives.

The Clams

Here we begin to see a bit of micro-regional variation. Just as eastern North Carolina barbecue differs from western North Carolina Barbecue, so does New England clam chowder made in Cape Cod differ from that made in, say, Mystic, Connecticut. The variation largely comes down to the size of the clam used.

Clams are slow-growing bivalves, and their size can vary tremendously depending on the age at which they are harvested. Under the best conditions, a clam can grow up to quahog size in 3 to 4 years.

At a good market, you might run into the following types of live clams:

- **Countnecks**, the smallest size legally harvested. They are not too common.
- **Littlenecks**, the next size up, and what you are likely to encounter at a raw bar, or on top of a Connecticut pizza.
- **Topnecks**, one size bigger than a littleneck, but not as large as a cherrystone. The term is very rarely used–you're more likely to see them lumped in with either the littlenecks or the cherrystones at the fish market or in a restaurant.
- **Cherrystones** are quite large–usually around 4 to 7 to a pound–and are used primarily for stuffing and baking. Finally . . .
- **Quahogs** (pronounced *KO-HOG*) are the largest, sometimes weighing as much as half a pound or more. Round where I grew up, they're known as "chowder clams," and it's for good reason–their large size makes them very easy to process for chowder, and not great for much else.

On the Cape, most chowders are made exclusively from quahogs–they're inexpensive, and very meaty. Smaller littlenecks and cherrystones are better reserved for more expensive uses like raw bars and baking.

But does that mean that we ought to be stuck using them at home?

I cooked batches of chowder side-by-side, using variously sized clams and found that in the end, cherrystones and littlenecks were actually superior to quahogs, offering a more tender texture.

Fresh Clam Alternatives

Ok, I get it. Some people just can't get fresh clams where they live. Is it the end of the world? Not really. Many restaurants—reputable ones who make great chowder, at that—use canned or frozen chopped clams to great effect. Clam juice can also be an effective way of adding in some clam flavor—even when the fresh guys are available. I prefer frozen chopped clams to minced canned clams.

Whatever clams you choose to use, there's still the question of the best way to cook them.

Clam-Coaxin'

For fresh clams steaming is the method of choice. By adding a bit of liquid (plain water or clam juice work fine) to the pot after sweating my aromatics and adding the clams, I could get the suckers to steam open in a matter of minutes. I pull them out of the pot as their shells pop open, draining their liquid into the pot, then removing the flesh with a spoon before roughly chopping it.

In no time, you should have a pot full of flavorful clam liquid, and a pile of chopped clams on the side. Adding the clams immediately back to the pot is a mistake I've often made in the past. Clams are finicky little suckers. They'll go from sweet and tender to overcooked and rubbery in the blink of an eye, and cooking them for as long as it takes to soften a pot of potatoes is a one-way ticket to Rubber City.

The solution? **Save those clams for the end.**

I chop up the clams, transfer them to a strainer set over a bowl (to collect any juices that drip out from inside), then set them aside until just before serving the chowder. If you're using canned or frozen clams, this is even easier—just dump the clams straight in during the last minute or two of simmering.

Sickening Thickening

Now comes the real deep philosophical questions. How do you

thicken a chowder properly? Currently, I'd been using a roux-based option. That is, a little flour cooked in the rendered bacon fat used to bind together and thicken the chowder as it simmers.

It's a method that works, if a smooth, homogenous liquid is all you're after. But it also creates that "award-winning" sludge effect, where the chowder becomes so thick and goopy that the flavors—those delicate flavors of clam and pork—are muddied. There has to be a better way.

My next thought was to use the thickening power of potatoes to act as a binder. I knew that starchier potatoes like russets are more likely to break down into a broth than waxier potatoes like reds or Yukon golds, but I gave all three a shot.

Russets were the way to go. They not only thicken the best, but they also have the most tender, potatoey texture in the finished dish. That said, with the elimination of the roux, *none* of the chowders came out particularly successfully. They inevitably ended up with a greasy, broken appearance and an off-putting curdled texture.

Why does this happen?

Well, a chowder (and all non-non-fat dairy, for that matter) is what we call an emulsion: It's a stable mixture of two things that generally don't like to mix very well, in this case water, and fat derived both from the milk/cream, and from the pork. As a general rule, fat molecules like to stick together, while water molecules like to push them as far away as possible. In order to get a smooth, creamy chowder, you need to figure out a way to get them to play nicely together and integrate.

When you pour your milk out of the carton, it comes out as a homogenous, creamy mixture. This is because it's gone through a process called homogenization, in which the the milk is forced at high pressure through a super-fine mesh. This breaks the fat into ultra-tiny droplets, each one of which gets completely surrounded by water molecules, preventing them from rejoining.

Think of the fat as a small group of 49ers fans stuck in a bar in Baltimore. Let them in as a group, and they'll stick together. But let them in one at a time, and it becomes much more difficult for them to find each other, leading to a more homogenous mix in the bar.

Now, let's say that a few of those 49ers fans happen to find each other, forming a small group. Suddenly, that group is much more visible to the rest of the 49ers fans, causing them to get drawn towards it. Eventually, you'll find that very rapidly, your balanced mix is broken, your 49ers fans once again forming a distinct blob in the sea of Ravens fans.

Similarly with an emulsified liquid, disturbing this careful mix even slightly—by, say, heating it—can cause the fat to rapidly separate out from the liquid. What's worse is that once a bit of fat starts to coalesce, it can quickly trigger *all* the fat to coalesce. So how does one keep an emulsion stable?

One way is to use a roux, which adds flour particles to the mix that physically impede fat droplets from coalescing. But we've already eliminated that option.

What about using the potatoes better?

At first, I tried adding a few very thin slices of potato to the mix, figuring they'd break down into individual starch granules relatively rapidly in the broth.

It didn't work. The chowder was still broken.

All right, what if instead of waiting for the potatoes to break down naturally, I give them a bit of mechanical aid? I cooked up another batch, this time forcing the potatoes through a potato ricer and whisking the resulting puree into the broth. No good. The broth was lumpy, off-puttingly grainy, and to top it off, *still* broken.

Next, I figured that perhaps my cooking method had something to do with the broth constantly breaking. I know that vigorous heating can cause cream to separate. I also know that the exact ratio of cream to milk, and when in the process the cream is added, can have a big impact on how its fat and water content behaves.

I attempted a dozen more versions, adjusting milk to cream ratios (broken), starting some with just milk and finishing with cream (still broken), using slightly lower amounts of roux (pasty-tasting up until the roux is nearly eliminated, in which case, broken), using only broth to cook the vegetables and finishing with cream and milk, and all the variations in between.

Failure after failure after failure.

It's not that any of the chowders were *bad*, per se. Certainly the flavor of the broth was superior to the vast majority of restaurant versions, and the texture of the clams and potatoes was spot-on. It's just the liquid that suffered appearance and texture-wise without the roux to hold it together.

Then I realized: Perhaps *preventing* it from breaking is not the way to go about this. Why not just let the darn stuff break, and fix it later?

For my next batch, I made a chowder using the most succesful technique I had attempted thus far, cooking the potatoes and vegetables in milk and adding the cream at the end. This time, instead of just stirring the chopped clams into the broken end result, I strained the chowder through a fine mesh strainer and dumped the liquid into my blender, figuring that the violent mechanical action of the blender should be powerful enough to break up those fat droplets, as well as to pulverize a few of the potato cells that may have made their way in there, releasing their starch and helping to keep the mixture homogenous.

It worked like a charm. What came out of the blender was a rich, creamy, perfectly smooth liquid that tasted of clams, pork, and dairy. Not too thick, not too thin, not pasty in the slightest. I poured the liquid back over my strained solids, added the chopped clams, reheated the whole deal, and seasoned it.

Am I overcomplicating things here? Perhaps. But I don't think so.

Indeed, I believe that if a traditional dish can be improved using modern techniques and equipment while still maintaining their historic and cultural core, then it is our *duty* to do so. Chowders have been changing steadily for the past several hundred years, which, incidentally, means that anyone who tells you "that's not *real* clam chowder" or "chowder needs this or that" is, frankly, full of it. Why should we now choose to freeze chowders in time, when more than ever before, we have an understanding of the hows and whys of cooking?

What ended up in my bowl was more than just the platonic ideal of my childhood Cape Cod memories, it was a dish with a real sense of history about it. Some folks have tried to argue that barbecue is the only true regional American cuisine, the only dish with an identity in both time and place. Well, I have a bowl of chowder here that begs to differ.

The only detail remaining? Oyster crackers. Chowder *needs* oyster crackers. It simply wouldn't be a *real* clam chowder without'em.

New England Clam Chowder

½ pound salt pork or bacon, cut into ½-inch cubes
2 tablespoons butter
1 medium onion, finely chopped (about 1 cup)
2 stalks celery, finely chopped (about 1 cup)
1 cup water or clam juice
2 ½ pounds live cherrystone or littleneck clams (see note above)
1 quart whole milk
1 ½ pounds russet or yukon gold potatoes, peeled and cut into ½-inch cubes
2 bay leaves
Kosher salt and freshly ground black pepper
1 cup heavy cream
Oyster crackers, for serving

Combine salt pork and ¼ cup water in a heavy-bottomed stock pot or Dutch oven. over medium heat, stirring occasionally, until water has evaporated and pork has begun to brown and crisp in spots, about 8 minutes. Add butter, onion, and celery. Continue to cook, stirring occasionally, until onions are softened but not browned, about 4 minutes longer. Add clam juice or water and stir to combine.

Add clams or quahogs and increase heat to high. Cover and cook, opening lid to stir occasionally, until clams begin to open, about 3 minutes. As clams open, remove them with tongs and transfer to a large bowl, keeping as many juices in the pot as possible and keeping the lid shut as much as possible. After 8 minutes, discard any clams that have not yet begun to open.

Add milk, potatoes, bay leaves, and a pinch of salt and pepper to the pot. Bring to a boil, reduce to a bare simmer, and cook, stirring occasionally, until potatoes are tender and starting to break down, about 15 minutes.

Meanwhile, remove meat from inside the clams and roughly chop it. Discard empty shells. Transfer chopped clams and as much juice as possible to a fine mesh strainer set over a large bowl. Let clams drain, then transfer chopped clams to a separate bowl. Set both bowls aside.

Once potatoes are tender, pour the entire mixture through the fine mesh strainer into the bowl with the clam juice, rapping the strainer with the back of a knife or a honing steel to get the liquids to pass through. Transfer strained solids to the bowl with the chopped clams. You should end up with a white, semi-broken broth in the bowl underneath, and the chopped clams, potatoes, salt pork, and aromatics in the separate bowl.

Transfer liquid to a blender and blend on high speed until smooth and emulsified, about 2 minutes Return liquid and solids back to Dutch oven. Add heavy cream and stir to combine. Reheat until simmering. Season well with salt and pepper. Serve immediately with oyster crackers.

Step Two: Sauté Onions and Other Aromatic Vegetables

By Michael Pollan

From *Cooked: A Natural History of Transformation*

Ever since his 2006 bestseller *The Omnivore's Dilemma*, Michael Pollan has become the one food writer most Americans know by name. In his steady evolution from environmental journalist to gastronome, *Cooked* is his most culinary book yet.

Sundays with Samin—our usual day together—always began the same way, with her bursting into the kitchen around three in the afternoon and plopping a couple of cotton market bags onto the island. From these she would proceed to pull out her cloth portfolio of knives, her apron, and, depending on the dish we were making, her prodigious collection of spices. This notably included a tin of saffron the size of a coffee can. Her mom sent her these eye-popping quantities of saffron, which whenever a recipe called for it Samin would sprinkle as liberally as salt.

"I'm soooo excited!" she'd invariably begin, in a singsong, as she tied her apron around her waist. "Today, you are going to learn how to brown meat." Or make a soffritto. Or butterfly a chicken. Or make a fish stock. Samin could get excited about the most mundane kitchen procedures, but her enthusiasm was catching, and eventually I came to regard it as almost a kind of ethic. Even browning meat, an operation that to me seemed fairly self-evident if not banal, deserved to be done with the utmost care and attention, and so with passion. At stake was the eater's experience. There was also the animal to consider, which you honored by making the very most of whatever it had to offer. Samin made sure there was also a theme undergirding each lesson: the Maillard reaction (when browning meat); eggs and their magical properties; the miracle of emulsification; and so forth. Over the course of a year, we made all sorts of main course dishes, as well as various salads and sides and desserts. Yet it seemed our main courses always came back to pot dishes, and we probably cooked more braises than anything else.

Much like a stew, a braise is a method of cooking meat and/or vegetables slowly in a liquid medium. In a stew, however, the main ingredient is typically cut into bite-sized pieces and completely submerged in the cooking liquid. In a braise, the main ingredient is left whole or cut into larger pieces (with meat ideally left on the bone) and only partially submerged in liquid. This way, the bottom of the meat is stewed, in effect, while the exposed top part is allowed to brown, making for richer, more complex flavors as well as, usually, a thicker sauce and a prettier dish.

Samin and I braised duck legs and chicken thighs, roosters and rabbits, various unprepossessing cuts of pork and beef, the shanks and necks of lamb, turkey legs, and a great many different vegetables. Each of these dishes called for a braising liquid, and at one time or another we used them all: red wine and white, brandy and beer, various stocks (chicken, pork, beef, fish), milk, tea, pomegranate juice, dashi (a Japanese stock made from seaweed and flaked bonito), the liquid left over from soaked mushrooms and beans, and water straight from the tap. We also made dishes that were not, technically, stews or braises, but were built on the same general principle, including *sugo* or ragù (or ragoût), bouillabaisse, risotto, and paella.

More often than not, the general principle called for a foundational dice of onions and other aromatic vegetables, which I would try to get ready before Samin showed up. And more often than not, Samin would take one look at the neat piles of chopped onions, carrots, and celery on my cutting board (the height of said piles conforming to the prescribed ratio of 2:1:1) and tell me to rechop them, because my dice wasn't fine enough.

"In some dishes, a rough dice like that is fine." I tried not to take offense, but I didn't think of my neat cubes as "rough" at all. "But in this dish, you don't necessarily want to be able to see any evidence of the soffritto," she explained. "You want it to melt away into nothingness, become this invisible layer of deliciousness. So . . . keep chopping!" And so I did, following her example of rocking a big knife back and forth through the piles of diced vegetables, dividing and subdividing the little cubes until they became mere specks.

On the subject of sautéing onions, another operation I wrongly assumed to be fairly straightforward, Samin had definite opinions. "Most people don't cook their onions nearly long enough or slow enough. They try to rush it." This was apparently a major pet peeve of hers. "The onions should have no bite left whatsoever and be completely transparent and soft. Turn down the flame and give them a half hour at *least*." Samin had been a sous-chef in a local Italian restaurant where she had sixteen young men working under her. "I was constantly walking down the line, turning down their burners, which were always on high. I guess it's some kind of guy thing to crank your flame all way to the max. But you need to be *gentle* with a mirepoix or soffritto."

Whether you "sweated" your onions at a low temperature or "browned" them at a higher one yielded a completely different set of flavors in the finished dish, Samin explained. Her ultimate authority on such matters was Benedetta Vitali, the chef she had worked for in Florence, who wrote a whole book about soffritto, called—what else?—*Soffritto*. "Benedetta makes three different soffrittos, depending on the dish—and all of them start with the exact same onions, carrot, and celery. But it can be made darker and more caramelized, or lighter and more vegetal, all depending on the heat and speed you cook them at." (In fact, the word "soffritto" contains the key cooking instruction: It means "underfried.")

Spend half an hour watching onions sweat in a pan and you will either marvel at their gradual transformation—from opaque to translucent; from sulfurous to sweet; from crunchy to yielding—or go stark raving mad with impatience. But this was precisely the lesson Samin was trying to impart.

"Great cooking is all about the three 'p's: patience, presence, and practice," she told me at one point. Samin is a devoted student of yoga, and she sees important parallels in the mental habits demanded by both disciplines. Working with onions seemed as good a place to develop those habits as any—practice in chopping them, patience in sweating them, and presence in keeping an eye on the pan so that they didn't accidentally brown if the phone rang and you permitted yourself a lapse in attention.

Unfortunately, not one of the "p"s came easily to me. I tend toward impatience, particularly in my dealings with the material world, and only seldom do I find myself attending to one thing at a time. Or, for that matter, to the present, a tense I have a great deal of trouble inhabiting. My native tense is the future conditional, a low simmer of unspecified worry being the usual condition. I couldn't meditate if my life depended on it. (Which–believe me, I know–is the completely wrong way to approach meditation.) Much as I like the whole concept of "flow"–that quality of being so completely absorbed in an activity that you lose the thread of time–my acquaintance with it is sorely limited. A great many boulders get in the way of my flow, disturbing the clarity of the mental waters and creating lots of distracting noise. Occasionally when I'm writing I'll slip into the flow for a little while; sometimes while reading, too, and of course sleeping, though I doubt that counts. But in the kitchen? Watching onions sweat? The work just isn't demanding enough to fully occupy consciousness, with the result that my errant, catlike thoughts refuse to stay where I try to put them.

One thought I did have, watching the onions sweat before we added the carrots and celery to the pan, took the form of an obvious question. Why is it that onions are so widespread in pot dishes? After salt, I can't think of another cooking ingredient quite as universal as the onion. Worldwide, onions are the second most important vegetable crop (after tomatoes), and they grow almost everywhere in the world that people can grow anything. So what do they do for a dish? Samin suggested that onions and the other commonly used aromatics are widely used because they are cheap and commonly available ingredients that add some sweetness to a dish. When I gently pushed for a more fulsome explanation, she offered, "It's a chemical reaction." I soon discovered that that's her default answer to all questions about kitchen science. Her second is "Let's ask Harold!" meaning Harold McGee, the kitchen-science writer who, though she had never met him, nevertheless serves as one of the god figures in her personal cosmology.

But what *kind* of chemical reaction? It turns out a comprehensive scientific investigation of mirepoix remains to be done; even Harold McGee, when I wrote to ask him about it, was uncharacteristically vague on the subject. The obvious but incorrect answer is that the sugars in the onions and carrots become caramelized in the sauté pan, thereby contributing that whole range of flavor compounds to the dish. But Samin (like most other authorities) recommends taking pains *not* to brown a mirepoix, whether by reducing the heat or adding salt, which by drawing water out of the vegetables serves to keep the browning reaction from kicking in. The caramelized-sugar theory also doesn't account for the prominent role in mirepoix and soffritto of celery, a not particularly sweet vegetable that would seem to contribute little but water and cellulose. What all this suggests is that there must be other processes that come into play in sautéing aromatic vegetables besides caramelization (or the Maillard reaction), processes that contribute flavors to a dish by other means not yet well understood.

One afternoon in the midst of slowly sweating a mirepoix, I risked ruining it by doing some Internet research on what might be going on in my pan just then. I know, I was multitasking, failing utterly at the "p" of presence, possibly patience as well. I found a fair amount of confusion and uncertainty about the subject online, but enough clues to conclude it was likely, or at least plausible, that the low, slow heat was breaking down the long necklaces of protein in the vegetables into their amino acid building blocks, some of which (like glutamic acid) are known to give foods the meaty, savory taste called "umami"—from the Japanese word *umai*, meaning "delicious." Umami is now generally accepted as the fifth taste, along with salty, sweet, bitter, and sour, and like each of the others has receptors on the tongue dedicated to detecting its presence.

As for the seemingly pointless celery, it, too, may contribute umami to a pot dish, and not just by supplying lots of carbohydrate-stiffened cell walls and water to a mirepoix. My web surfing eventually delivered me to an article in the *Journal of Agricultural and Food Chemistry* written by a team of Japanese food scientists and titled, fetchingly, "Flavor Enhancement of Chicken Broth from Boiled Celery Constituents." These chemists reported that a group of volatile compounds found in celery called phthalides, though completely tasteless by themselves, nevertheless enhanced the perception of both sweetness and umami when they were added to a chicken broth. Way to go, celery.

Abstracted soul that I am, patiently cooking a mirepoix became much more interesting, or bearable at least, now that I had a theory. Now, knowing what was at stake, I paid close attention to the satisfying sizzle—the auditory evidence of water escaping from the plant tissues—and then, as it subsided, to the softening of the vegetables, indicating that the scaffold of carbohydrates that held the cell walls rigid was breaking down into sugars that it was up to me to keep from browning. I now understood that, even before I introduced the meat or liquid to the pot, the depth of flavor in my braise, the very savoriness of it, hung in the balance of these gently simmering onions, carrots, and celery.

One more scientific fact contributed to my deepening admiration for mirepoix and soffritto, and especially for the onions in them, which this fact single-handedly rendered considerable less irritating. It seems that adding onions to foods, and to meat dishes in particular, makes the food safer to eat. Like many of the most commonly used spices, onions (garlic, too) contain powerful antimicrobial compounds that survive cooking. Microbiologists believe that onions, garlic, and spices protect us from the growth of dangerous bacteria on meat. This might explain why the use of these plants in cooking becomes more common the closer you get to the equator, where keeping meat from spoiling becomes progressively more challenging. Before the advent of refrigeration, the bacterial contamination of food, animal flesh in particular, posed a serious threat to people's health. (In Indian cooking, recipes for vegetarian dishes typically call for fewer spices than recipes for meat dishes.) Purely through trial and error, our ancestors stumbled upon certain plant chemicals that could protect them from getting sick. Onions happen to be one of the most potent of all antimicrobial food plants. That the flavors of such plants "taste good" to us may be nothing more than a learned preference for the taste of molecules that helped to keep us alive.

What this suggests is that cooking with these aromatic plants may involve something more than simply overcoming their chemical defenses so that we might avail ourselves of a source of calories other creatures can't. It's much more ingenious than that. Cooking with onions, garlic, and other spices is a form of biochemical jujitsu, in which the first move is to overcome the plants' chemical defenses so that we might eat them, and the second is to then deploy their defenses against other species to defend ourselves.

Cooking with Friends

By Katie Arnold-Ratliff

From *Tin House*

Most cookbook reviews come out when a book is first published, yet the real test may be how much it gets used over the years. Katie Arnold-Ratliff—a novelist (*Bright Before Us*) and senior editor at *O: The Oprah Magazine*—testifies to the staying power of one not-so-obvious cookbook.

Among the gifts awaiting me on Christmas morning 1995 was a cookbook entitled *Cooking with Friends*—"Friends" as in *Friends*, the former Thursday-night NBC tent pole now in weeknight syndication, which the most honest of us will admit to watching when nothing else is on. (Or when emerging from a bad trip: a friend of mine once successfully reoriented herself to reality by watching an episode and repeating the mantra "Monica is the clean one; Chandler is the mean one.") I liked the book in 1995 because I liked the show (I was thirteen), but I like it now because its recipes are low-impact and surprisingly good. It's full of meals that are doable on weeknights, or when you have a bad cold. This food is not splashy or innovative. It's solid. It's the toothsome coffee cake you eat in pajamas, or the sturdy lasagna you serve your brother-in-law. It's the leftovers you actually eat the next day, nothing being lost in the reheat.

CWF arrived under the tree just as I was getting really serious about food, the way some girls get really serious about boys or ponies. I watched the entire *Great Chefs* franchise on PBS, nerded out hardcore on my *Julia Child: Home Cooking with Master Chefs* CD-ROM, and developed an enduring nonsexual crush on Susan Feniger. Right there with me for all of this was my Aunt Karen—the woman who exposed me to both high-end kimchi and fried-baloney sandwiches, the woman who taught me to like sashimi at eight years old but who kept Frosted Flakes around for when I stayed over. She taught me to appreciate the highbrow stuff and the trashy crap in equal measure.

So I knew enough to discern that *CWF*'s recipes were exceedingly basic. What I didn't know yet was that, whether or not we food snobs want to admit it, it's simple fare and not fancy-pants cuisine that lingers most indelibly on the tongue. For example, I had a spectacular meal at Daniel two years ago, but when I say "spectacular," I'm just queuing up a mental reel of each dish. I remember the sweetbreads and duck terrine and oysters with seawater gelée in my head, not my mouth. But I can instantly taste the eight-dollar plate of arterially apocalyptic food I had at Cracker Barrel a while back—the mouthfeel of the Dumplins™, the juicy give of the fried okra, the shattering crust of the Chicken Fried Chicken. Ask yourself what *means* more to you, what you can most easily conjure—Le Bernardin's buttery black bass or your aunt's stuffed bell peppers (and my aunt makes a mean stuffed pepper)—and you'll get my point.

The *Friends* cookbook lands squarely in the middle of these two extremes and draws inspiration from both sides, which is why it's great. I've moved from apartment to apartment, relocated across the country, sold off God knows how many tired old books for cash—but I've hung on to *CWF* for nearly two decades. (Though I will admit to having thrown away the dust jacket, lest anyone see the title.) I've made the pine nut cookies, and the Onion Tartlets à la Monica, and the dated but tasty Peaches Poached in Red Wine with Lemon and Fennel. I've baked Marcel's Banana Bread (named, of course, for Ross's capuchin) at least a dozen times, and—God help me—the Trendy Tiramisu. I doubt I told my husband this, but for our first Thanksgiving together, I re-created the book's entire holiday menu, from the cranberry-orange relish to the apple crisp. And each time I used a recipe, I sifted through background blurbs about each star ("Lisa Kudrow, who has a degree in biology from Vassar . . . "), ancient cast photos (one nearly weeps to see the young, larger-nosed Jennifer Aniston and the poignantly fresh-faced Matthew Perry), and, in the margins, quotes from the first season ("Ugly Naked Guy's got gravity boots!").

After all, this cookbook isn't really a cookbook—or at least, it is one only incidentally. It's a marketing conceit, designed to provide an easy holiday gift for a niece or neighbor (or daughter, evidently). In fact, its whole raison d'être seems to have been the Christmas season of 1995, for which the book was rushed into print. So says Bryan Curtis, who green-lit the project as the vice president of marketing at Rutledge Hill Press (and who was charmingly unfazed by my barrage of questions about a tie-in to a show that ended eight years ago). "We'd done a number of TV-themed cookbooks," Curtis told me. "*Aunt Bee's Mayberry Cookbook, Mary Ann's Gilligan's Island Cookbook, Alice's Brady Bunch Cookbook.* We also did ones based on *The Young and the Restless* and *The Beverly Hillbillies.*" Amy Lyles Wilson, now a theologian and a columnist for a Nashville magazine, was the Rutledge Hill editor asked to write the text—which involved reading the scripts sent over by Warner Bros. to find story arcs that could translate into menu items. (Ross being dumped by his pregnant lesbian wife = a chapter on comfort foods.) Wilson doesn't remember much about the project, other than the process being "a delight"; to her, it was just an assignment. But Curtis recalls that it was a bona fide best-seller; that it inspired two moments of levity on latenight talk shows (Leno monologued about it on one, and David Schwimmer dissed it on another); and that he himself used it for years ("The pepper jack crackers and the cherry tomatoes marinated in pepper vodka are great for parties."). "Some of the food was from the show," Curtis told me. "After all, Monica was a chef. And the rest Jack Bishop came up with." Bishop, who developed the recipes, has all but scrubbed his involvement with the book from his bio—which reveals that he helped launch *Cooks Illustrated* and set the tasting protocols for America's Test Kitchen, the venerable lab in which food scientists work toward a more perfect pancake and the like. In other words, Bishop is legit, and it would seem that he believes *Cooking with Friends* is not.

It's a shame Bishop doesn't embrace *CWF* in his CV. He ought to claim it proudly. Whatever lameness or cynicism may be inherent in its packaging, it's a worthy cookbook, as evidenced by many incredulous Amazon.com reviews ("My wife and I still make the macaroni and cheese . . . it's just the perfect recipe for some reason"; "The recipes are more complex and refined than you would expect."). This cookbook *should* have sucked, because it didn't need to be good—all it needed to do was exist, to be visible in various B. Dalton outlets in various malls that winter, to sell enough to cover its production costs. What it's done instead is sit on an improbable number of bookshelves for sixteen years, doing its part to bring people sustenance and joy.

Maybe that sounds overblown. But how often does a cleverly timed piece of merchandising really last, and really mean something to someone? These things are born to die, created only to be discarded as tastes evolve. Yet this artifact of the mid-nineties remains, and even, in the case of a half dozen recipes, transcends. (Despite the name, I'm especially devoted to the Monkey Lovin' Mocha Mouthfuls, the recipe for which appears here.) If, in our throwaway culture, that doesn't move you, I don't know what would.

There's a parallel fickleness in the food world—we eager eaters jump wholeheartedly onto the bandwagon du jour, and then claim to tire of our pastel-colored iced cupcakes and braised pork belly and authentic ramen once the *new* new thing arrives. But we're not actually tired of cupcakes and bacon and noodles. (If you are, I suggest you undergo medical testing.) We're leaving behind the fad, not the food. Your mouth is a fundamentally stable environment: you will always love to eat the things you love to eat. It's not 1991 anymore, but that doesn't mean I don't still like sundried-tomato pesto. And I'm no longer ten years old—I've eaten all kinds of crazy, wonderful things in the twenty years since I was—but that doesn't mean I don't still love those simple, homey stuffed peppers. When it comes to food, what matters, what *lasts*, is the good, middle-of-the-road stuff like that found in *Cooking with Friends*. That's the stuff people crave. I've never thought to myself, *I could go for some seawater gelée*, but I've sure as hell wished I could come home to a platter of Mrs. Tribbiani's Roast Chicken.

Before that Christmas morning, my preoccupation with food and cooking had been a solitary one, explored while holed up in my bedroom, making lists of restaurants to visit and poring over Martha Stewart's collected recipes, but more than that, it had been wrongheaded in its estimation of what constitutes worthy cuisine. I thought good food had to be complex and intimidating, but the *Friends* cookbook widened my perspective: it showed me that eating well is mostly about simplicity, about approachability and inclusion.

And with its focus on, well, friendship, the book makes it plain that cooking is not solitary at all. Food is about enjoying the company of those you care about—those who'll be there for you, because you're there for them, too.

After I spoke to Amy Lyles Wilson and Bryan Curtis, and after I learned that Jack Bishop is a respected food professional who evidently needed some extra pocket money in 1994, and after I took a quick glance at the book and was reminded that Matt LeBlanc used to be a Levi's model and that Matthew Perry's father famously starred in a series of Old Spice commercials, a question occurred to me. So I gave my Aunt Karen a call. "Oh, yes, of course I watched *Friends*," she said. "I loved it. I still do. I never cared for Monica, though—she was just too fussy."

Monkey Lovin' Mocha Mouthfuls

(adapted from *Cooking with Friends*)

4 tablespoons unsalted butter
2 ounces semisweet chocolate (I use Scharffen Berger, and I double it to 4 ounces)
1/3 cup sugar (I always substitute brown sugar—in this and in all desserts)
1 large egg
1 tablespoon coffee liqueur, such as Kahlua (though a tablespoon of brewed espresso does just fine in a pinch)
1 teaspoon instant espresso powder (though I like to use actual coffee grounds, for the texture—which may be an acquired taste)
1/3 cup flour
1/3 cup chopped walnuts, plus 12 walnut halves
(The recipe doesn't call for it, but I add a ½ teaspoon of kosher salt and a teaspoon of vanilla extract.)

Preheat the oven to 350. Generously grease a twelve-cup mini-muffin tin and set it aside. (If you only have a regular muffin tin, it's fine—just let the cupcakes bake a little longer, until a knife stuck into the center emerges clean.)

Melt the butter and chocolate together in a double boiler (or, like me, in the microwave), stirring until smooth. Set mixture aside to cool slightly. Stir in the sugar until smooth. Whisk in the egg, liqueur, and espresso powder. Fold in the flour and chopped walnuts.

Spoon the batter into the prepared tin, filling cups about three-quarters full. Place a walnut half in the center of each cup. Bake about twenty minutes. Let the cupcakes cool in the tin for five minutes, then turn them out onto a wire rack to cool completely.

Note: If cupcakes without frosting make no sense to you, (a) I understand, and (b) feel free to make use of those tubs of frosting at the grocery store. I always do.

The Swedish Chef

By Joy Manning

From *TableMatters.com*

As a recipe editor (Tasting Table, *Prevention*, *Cooking Light*) and author of her own cookbook (*Almost Meatless*, 2009), Joy Manning was intrigued by the buzz surrounding Magnus Nilsson's *Fäviken* cookbook. How could recipes from a locavore restaurant in rural Sweden possibly translate to her Philly-area kitchen?

When it comes to cookbooks, I am typically willing to do whatever the writer asks of me. Order obscure ingredients online and pay more for shipping than the product? I've done it. Visit seven specialty and international markets to make a specific pan-Asian noodle dish? No problem. Start a dinner three days in advance to allow gels to set and flavors to meld? I am ready, willing, able.

So when I got my oven mitts on *Fäviken*, a new cookbook by acclaimed Swedish chef Magnus Nilsson, I looked forward with pleasure to the rigors of what I had heard was an ambitious, challenging cookbook.

Before glancing at any of the recipes, I read the long introduction by Bill Buford, author of one of my favorite culinary memoirs, *Heat*. He dedicates numerous paragraphs to describing the stark remoteness of Nilsson's restaurant (also named Fäviken). According to Buford, a visit there requires employing the services of the region's single cab driver. He tells the restaurant's origin story, explaining how difficult it was for Nilsson to hire anyone to work at his new restaurant due to its isolated location in the northern part of snowy Sweden. Though Nilsson's ambitious daily hunting and foraging is reverently described, I was no less confident I could cook from this book.

Next comes a foreword by food writer Mattias Kroon. In it, he describes an Alice Waters–like dedication to the local and the seasonal. To my American sensibilities, this is hardly a novel approach to cooking. I've become so inured to this manifesto, in fact, that I can scarcely suppress an eye roll when I hear it in restaurants—mostly because, in reality, few places actually cook according to this code. One look at a restaurant kitchen's spice rack or the olive oil likely to be served with bread will reveal sins against the gospel of local.

But according to Kroon, and as was evident when I moved onto the recipes, Nilsson has conscribed the scope of his culinary creativity to only those foods he can coax from the miserly arctic landscape that surrounds him. His cooking must be like a haiku, where limitations and restrictions force a lean poetry into existence that couldn't have been conjured any other way. With mere weeks as a growing season and a severely limited range of things that will grow in the first place, Nilsson must rely on a range of preservation techniques and genius twists to keep his food interesting through the long, dark winter where he lives and cooks.

That said, Nilsson's restaurant is situated on a large piece of unspoiled wilderness where he forages and hunts regularly. He is near enough to the water that he gets daily deliveries of just-plucked-from-the-sea-bed scallops and other fish.

I, on the other hand, live on a tiny scrap of concrete in the middle of asphalt-bound Philadelphia. I have not even a window box or container garden at my disposal. In the foreword, Kroon comes out and says that the type of food made at Fäviken simply doesn't travel. I wondered if that were the case, why anyone would go to the trouble to write a cookbook about it.

Page 25 had a somewhat reassuring headline: How To Use The Recipes. (By now, I was having considerable doubts I could even comment on a book it seemed impossible to cook from.) In this section, we learn that:

1. The recipes are vague and confusing—but it's OK, they're meant to be that way.
2. The instructions shouldn't be taken literally because they are just suggestions to help the reader understand where good cooking really comes from—intuition and passion.

3. We should not even try to replicate the recipes because we are not from northern Sweden. Northern Sweden is the unlisted yet most crucial ingredient in every recipe in the book.
4. We should be inspired by the approach the recipes exemplify and actually create our own recipes from our own local ingredients.
5. "If it tastes good, it is right." This is obviously my favorite line in the book.

Unhelpfully, this section concludes with two famous last words: "Good luck!"

Still, I was determined to find a recipe from this book I could, in spite of being warned to the contrary, actually recreate.

Some dishes looked like candidates at first glance: Beef marrow and heart with grated turnip and turnip leaves, for example. Upon closer examination of the ingredients list, what I needed was not merely a turnip, or even a local turnip, but a turnip "that has been stored in the cellar with its little yellow leaves that have started sprouting towards the end of winter."

Even if I possessed such a turnip, I don't think that my rowhome basement, complete with its bug graveyard and fine toxic coating of dryer lint, would be an appropriate place to store it. And even if it were, I've still got months to go before the end of winter and this story's deadline looming.

I was drawn to the rackfish and sour cream recipe and could reasonably access the necessary ingredients, but I don't have the pH testing kit I'd need to "control the pH level so that it drops quickly to below 4.46." Even if I did, there are no instructions given regarding how to manipulate a pH level. How fast, in minutes or hours, is "quickly"? Regardless, I didn't have the six months minimum I'd need for this preparation to "mature."

Other impossible-to-procure ingredients include:

- The burnt-out trunk of a spruce tree
- "good, clean" moss
- 2 handfuls old autumn leaves from last year
- 1 lavender petal from last summer

After combing *Fäviken* cover to cover multiple times, I had to face facts. There was almost nothing in this cookbook that I could really cook. I zeroed in on a recipe for "Douglas' Shortbread Biscuits," which does call for homemade jam. I actually don't make jam, but I have a jar a friend made and decided to proceed with that.

Unfortunately, though I followed the instructions to the letter, the recipe just didn't work. Crumbly and dry, the dough was impossible to roll into the spheres depicted. I mounded them up in little craggy hills only to watch it collapse into a mound of gravel-like crumbs when I tried, as instructed, to make an indentation with my finger for the jam. Ultimately I pressed all the loose crumbs into a small baking sheet in a single, jam-dotted layer and hoped for the best.

What I decided to do next was follow Nilsson's instructions for using his book. I could take inspiration from his dedication to making a truly local cuisine from a pretty stingy environment. Given the cold and the dark and the abbreviated growing season, he is more or less wringing blood from a stone. It makes what Alice Waters does, from her agricultural Eden of a home base in California, look easy.

If Nilsson can forge a local cuisine from so little, surely I can consciously lay off the olive oil, lemons, and avocados that often shape my home cooking–at least for this one meal.

I would like to tell you I foraged for mushrooms in the hills of nearby Kennett Square, Pennsylvania, the mushroom capital of the US, or that I donned my hunting gear and shot a deer for a cauldron of venison stew. A more rugged soul might take just that inspiration from *Fäviken* and its chef, frequently seen in photographs swaddled in a furry pelt of something he probably recently shot and ate.

My way of interpreting the recipes was to visit a food vendor that sells only regional, environmentally friendly ingredients. I chose what appealed to me (chicken sausage, shiny red cabbage, potatoes, butter), added nothing far-flung from my pantry, and marveled at my luck. Even in December, at least in Pennsylvania, we have a feast of local ingredients at our fingertips.

Though this main course appears nowhere in the *Fäviken* cookbook, my dinner was more in its spirit than the shortbread cookies, which looked like a crumbly mess but tasted good. So, according to Nilsson at least, they were right after all.

The Gingerbread Cookie Reclamation Project

By Tim Carman

From *The Washington Post*

Intrepid food reporter Tim Carman scours DC for cheap eats in his The $20 Diner column; formerly at *Washington City Paper*, he won a James Beard Award for his Young & Hungry column. But sometimes the food you want most isn't sold in even the most authentic neighborhood restaurant.

The gingerbread cookies would arrive the moment my grandparents pulled into our narrow driveway on 123rd Street in Omaha for their much-anticipated Christmas visit. The cookie tins, one a repurposed Saltine cracker container, were usually tossed in the trunk, as if they were hostages. My older sister and I would rush the vehicle, perhaps pausing long enough to hug our grandparents, and begin our annual campaign to survive on the sweets of the holiday season.

So remembers my older sis, who more than 20 years ago started calling herself Deborah, as in Deborah Kellogg, her married name. As a boy, I always knew her as Debbie, or sometimes just Deb, an informal, diminutive name that belied her place in the family hierarchy. She was the bossy first child. I was the quiet second one.

Regardless of how I viewed Deborah when we were kids—artistic, culturally aware, soul-sucking Medusa—she became, as so many firstborn do, the responsible one as an adult. She checks on and cares for ailing relatives and friends. She sends cards and gifts on birthdays. She knows the family history better than anyone else in the clan.

Deborah has also become, via sheer indifference from the rest of us, the custodian of the family's gingerbread cookie recipe. In this regard, and in this regard only, she is more Betty Draper than Betty Crocker, failing to notice when the recipe had wandered far away from home.

How else do you explain a nearly 35-year span in which the family gingerbread cookie had not one speck of—wait for it, *waaaaait* for it—ginger? For more than three decades, Deborah has baked these cookies in all manner of shapes, each without the namesake ingredient, and passed them out to co-workers, family members and "Mommy & Me friends, which is a lot of people," she tells me over the phone from Los Angeles, where she lives with her husband, Mark, and their son, Bryant.

And no one noticed the missing ginger, least of all Deborah herself. "I know," my sister says now. "It's embarrassing!"

She reminds me that she sent the offending cookies to me once or twice, too. "Did you ever question if they were gingerbread cookies?" she asks, the accusation ensnaring me like sticky cobwebs in the back yard.

Of course I didn't. Part of that has to do with a kind of culinary habituation: Once you eat something for so many years, you pay less attention to its flavors and textures, gobbling it down mindlessly, your brain automatically filling in the missing details. I think that is particularly true with our family's gingerbread cookies. It was a distinctly homely thing in the first place: a thick, dry beast slathered in pink icing (yes, pink) and always in desperate need of dunking in milk. I still loved it, with every molecule in my body, like only a cookie-addicted boy could. It always reminded me of Monna Kuykendall, my maternal grandmother, and her warmth, generosity and (for some unexplained reason) souvenir spoon collection.

Anyway, about two years ago, as the gingerbread story unfolds, Deborah was visiting relatives when she realized the horrifying truth about her ginger-less gingerbread cookies. True to her first-born, bossy-sister personality, she wasted little time regretting her 35 years of spice-free Christmas cookies. Instead, she conducted an FBI-like investigation to track down the origins of the family recipe. By the time she was done, she had collected five gingerbread cookie recipes, spanning four generations, and forwarded them all to me.

Which launched my own attempt to research the recipe that

produces a cookie everyone in the family loves to eat, but few love to make. After spending almost an entire weekend reviewing recipes, and baking and baking some more, I came to one incontrovertible conclusion: My family is full of lousy copyists. Every generation made errors in copying the recipe from the preceding generation, sometimes omitting ingredients (such as ginger or a full cup of sugar), sometimes transposing the amounts needed, sometimes neglecting directions altogether. It was a game of telephone, home baker-style, and the message had become so scrambled that it was like Bill the Cat translating the words "I love you!" into "Eck oop thhhttpd!"

The original recipe is attributed to my maternal great-grandmother, Stella Miller, whom everyone called Mimi (pronounced "Mimm-me," not MeMe). Mimi Miller was born in the late 19th century in Ohio and was known among the family as an excellent baker, remembers my mother. Around the holidays, Mimi would make bourbon balls, Russian tea cakes and, of course, "ginger cookies." Her moist, russet-colored gingerbread cookies were based on a beautifully minimalist recipe, one that calls for a modest amount of flavoring agents, like molasses and cinnamon, another form of Midwestern self-denial. Most important, though, the recipe did not call for a set amount of flour. Instead, the directions just said to "alternate buttermilk + flour till a soft dough to roll."

In the span of one short generation, however, Mimi Miller's flowing, open-ended recipe had hardened into a set rule over the amount of flour. In her own handwritten recipe for Ginger Cookies, Monna Kuykendall, my grandmother, directed all bakers to sift the dry ingredients "with about 8 cups flour, enough to roll out to cut." My mother, Kay Billingsley, and my older sister dutifully followed the eight-cup directive in their own recipes, even as they omitted, ignored or changed other steps and ingredients. (My mom's icing, for instance, called for blending butter, not whipping three reserved egg whites, which she arbitrarily decided belonged in the cookie dough instead.)

Let me tell you something about trying to incorporate eight cups of flour into this dough: After a certain point, it's like trying to roll out a hardened lump of potting clay with a toothpick. I suddenly realized why my family hated making these cookies. This was weight training, not baking. The fascinating part about this blizzard of flour is that the resulting gingerbread cookies are still delicious when topped with icing, which helps sweeten the slightly bitter, molasses-rich dough that's short one whole cup of sugar compared with the original cookies. My main problem with these flour hogs is that they turn to rocks within 48 hours.

This recipe mutation, I realized, needed to stop before Mimi Miller's original gingerbread cookies ultimately morphed into frosted paperweights. The proper course of action, it seemed, was to go back to the source recipe, as an homage to my great-grandmother, the baker, the one who injected flavor and sweetness into the holidays through many generations. I followed her recipe exactly, save for one thing: I ditched the pink icing, which, according to family lore, became a tradition when there wasn't enough red food coloring on hand.

The time had come to correct this longstanding early-20th-century (and probably apocryphal) pantry deficit. Could we not spare a few more drops of food coloring? Mimi Miller's legacy, after all, deserved to be preserved in deep, vibrant shades of red and green. I mentioned this to Deborah, and she wholeheartedly agreed. She even asked me to bring some gingerbread cookies to our younger sister's wedding later this month. They will be the gift of something old.

Mimi Miller's Long-Lost Gingerbread Cookies

Before it finally comes together at the end, this is one sticky dough. Accordingly, it's better to use a hand mixer; the dough's sticky stage tends to gum up an electric mixer.
MAKE AHEAD: The dough needs to be refrigerated for at least an hour before it is rolled out and baked.

Makes 60 cookies

For the Cookies

1 ½ cups solid vegetable shortening
1 cup granulated sugar
1 cup packed light brown sugar
1 cup molasses
1 large egg, plus 3 large egg yolks

6 cups flour, plus more for the work surface
2 tablespoons ground ginger
1 tablespoon ground cinnamon
2 teaspoons salt
1 cup buttermilk
1 tablespoon baking soda

For the Icing

3 large egg whites
1 teaspoon vanilla extract
3 cups confectioners' sugar
Green and red food coloring (optional)

For the cookies: Use a hand-held electric mixer to beat the shortening and sugars together in a large mixing bowl. Add the molasses, the egg and the egg yolks, and beat until combined.

Sift the flour, ginger, cinnamon and salt into a separate large bowl. Pour the buttermilk into a large measuring cup or glass and stir in the baking soda to dissolve it.

Add about one-quarter of the dry ingredients and about one-third of the buttermilk mixture to the shortening-egg mixture, and beat to incorporate. Repeat two more times, adding one-quarter of the dry ingredients and one-third of the buttermilk each time and making sure they are incorporated.

Dust a work surface with flour and turn out the dough out onto the surface. Using your hands, blend in the remaining flour by kneading it into the dough. The dough should be soft and a little tacky, but not overly sticky. Form the dough into 2 disks, wrap with plastic wrap and refrigerate for at least 1 hour.

Preheat the oven to 375 degrees. Dust a work surface with flour. Linc a baking shcct with parchment paper.

Work with one disk of dough at a time. Use a rolling pin to roll out the dough on the work surface to a thickness of ¼ inch. Cut out individual cookies as desired, transferring them to the prepared baking sheet. Bake for 8 to 10 minutes or until the cookies just begin to firm up. Transfer them to a wire rack to cool. Repeat to use all of the dough, mixing the scraps together, re-rolling and cutting them into shapes.

For the icing: Beat the egg whites in the bowl of a stand mixer or hand-held mixer until the whites form stiff peaks. Beat in the confectioners' sugar and vanilla extract until the mixture is creamy. If desired, add drops of red or green food coloring to create your desired hue.

When the baked cookies have cooled, use a dull knife or offset spatula to paint the top of each one with a layer of icing.

Hortotiropita and The Five Stages of Restaurant Grief

By Michael Procopio

From *FoodForTheThoughtless.com*

Michael Procopio has knocked around the San Francisco food scene for years, holding many jobs, none of them too distinguished. (He still waits tables.) In his irregular—and irreverent—blog Food for the Thoughtless, he invites us into his cranky gourmet life—like the effort to resurrect a "lost" menu item.

Sometimes, there are things a person takes for granted, thanks to their close proximity or easy availability: a spouse, a friend, a favorite market, a booty call.

When one of them packs up and leaves town, he or she realizes the great thing that was always at hand is now out of reach, only to be replaced by an un-healable abscess of sorrow. Or a substitute, which will be constantly compared to the original, for better or for worse.

Now you can understand my state of mind when, earlier this year, I suffered my own, devastating loss–the *spanakotiropita*, served at my restaurant since the day it first opened, vanished into phyllo-thin air.

Spanakotiropita (Greek spinach and cheese pies) aren't especially glamorous by nature. They weren't exactly the show-stopping feature on our menu, but it was comforting to know they were always there like a fresh box of Kleenex or a shut-in roommate who knows the Heimlich maneuver. They were homey, a little homely, and entirely delicious, no matter what Olympia Dukakis says about them.

I was horrified by their disappearance and mortified by the all-cheese *tiropitakia* which replaced them.

"But *why* did the *spanakotiropita* have to go?" I asked our chef, as if I were a bewildered child asking his mommy why daddy left with that big suitcase or why on earth she was burying a favorite pet hamster behind the rose garden.

"Oh, just trying something new," he said.

Just trying something new. I wondered to myself if this was the culinary version of a midlife crisis, like getting rid of a dependable car with great gas mileage and the always-there-for-you wife who put you through grad school and replacing them with a 2-seater sports car and a blond with big tits to put out inside of it.

There was nothing I could do but accept this answer from an otherwise reasonable man. But it would be a cold day in restaurant hell before I would ever accept this wholesale abandonment of an old favorite for a new item, no matter how big its tits were.

I found myself flying through Kübler and Ross's *Five Stages of Grief*:

1. **Denial**: I refuse to believe that anything of this horrible magnitude could ever befall my beloved restaurant.
2. **Anger**: I want to stab these new pies with a steak knife.
3. **Bargaining**: Perhaps if I get enough restaurant guests to sign a petition, the old pies will come back. Or, just maybe, if I prayed hard enough, they would return.*
4. **Depression:** I cannot will these new pies to taste anything like the old ones and therefore am considering suicide.
5. **Acceptance:** I never made it that far.

I was grateful that I was able to process all of this terrible grief within the span of a few days. And when I recovered, I came to a few important realizations:

1. I am a big boy. I can handle this sort of trauma like a champ.
2. I am an able cook and recipe developer. I should make my own damned *spanakotiropita* if I can't handle the fact that they aren't going to be made available to me by my restaurant and the small army of prep cooks therein.

*The *spanakotiropita* did, in fact, return to our restaurant menu as I hoped and prayed they would. It's almost enough to make one believe in the power of prayer.

3. If I make my own, I can put whatever I like into them and make them whatever shape I want them to be. I can be the master of my own Greek pie destiny.

And with that realization came a great relief. And, I think, a great recipe.

Hortotiropita or, in American English, Greens and Cheese Phyllo Pies

The great thing about phyllo pies is that you can fill them with anything the voices in your own head tell you to. Go ahead and be inspired: lamb, greens, lemon curd, cement, whatever. Listen to your voices.

You can also shape them however you like. In this case I have abandoned the folded-flag look of traditional pies and replaced it with the shape of my favorite Greek dessert, *galaktoboureko,* or, in Chinese terms, an egg roll.

This recipe, which is suited to my particular tastes and needs, is merely a guideline. All that matters is that you love the taste of your own filling. Interpret that last sentence however you wish.

Makes about a dozen pastries.

3 bunches chard
1 bunch mustard greens
2 bunches of beet greens, ripped from six large golden beets
2 leeks, sliced into manageable, but not tiny bits
2 bunches of scallions, sliced the same way as the leeks
3 tablespoons of butter for sautéing the leeks and scallions
¼ teaspoon of salt
½ teaspoon ground black pepper
1 tablespoon Aleppo pepper
10 ounces Greek feta, crumbled.
1 cup grated Parmesan
4 Tablespoons finely chopped dill.
1 package of phyllo dough
12 tablespoons of melted butter with which to brush the phyllo sheets.

For Garnish (which is purely optional, as is pretty much everything else)
3 teaspoons of sesame seeds
1 teaspoon fennel seed

1. Clean your greens, remove their stocks and stems, and roughly chop. Set aside.

2. Toss 3 tablespoons of butter into the bottom of a large stockpot or a very large sauté pan and melt over medium heat. Add the leeks and scallions, moving them about the bottom of the cooking vessel until they are soft and vaguely translucent. The idea is not to brown them, but rather to weaken their resolve. Add the chopped greens a handful or two at a time, stirring them about with tongs or a large wooden spoon to wilt them/coat them with the butter and warm the leeks and scallions. Repeat this action until all the greens have found their way in. Cover and cook on a medium-low flame, stirring and tossing occasionally until all the leaves are wilted. The contents of the pot will have reduced by about $^2/_3$ their original volume (about 7 to 8 minutes). I hope you do not find this at all alarming.

Do not overcook. Nothing horrifying will happen if they do, it's just that I want you to be mindful of the fact that the greens will be cooked further when eventually wrapped in phyllo and shoved into a hot oven.

Empty the hot, flabby greens into a colander which, if you are wise, will be strategically placed into your sink. Drain well, squeeze as much liquid out of them as possible without straining yourself or traumatizing the steaming vegetation. If you are the type of person who enjoys such things, reserve the greens, sweat/liquid/unwanted moisture, let cool, and drink.

Spread the strangled greens into a large casserole dish and let cool to room temperature. You may also transfer the greens to a large bowl, but they will take much longer to cool if you choose to do so.

3. When the greens have sufficiently cooled, add the salt, pepper, Aleppo pepper, feta, Parmesan, and dill. Combine well.

At this point, I prefer to transfer the mixture to a smaller vessel, cover it tightly, and refrigerate it until I am ready to use it. Making this a day in advance of baking the pastries is a very good thing. The flavors are more prone to mingle that way.

4. About an hour before you wish to assemble your *hortotiropita* heat your oven to 450°F and place a rack to the upper third of the oven. Remove both the phyllo and the filling mixture from the refrigerator and let them warm up to the idea of their impending intimacy (room temperature). During this time, you may also wish to melt the butter. (Some people insist upon using only clarified butter for brushing onto their phyllo. I say "bravo" to them, but I find it an unnecessary waste of time. I can think of so many other ways of squandering whatever time I have left on this planet. Very few of them have anything to do with melting butter.)

5. Make certain you have a large enough work surface to accommodate a) your unfolded phyllo, b) a cutting board or prep space wide and long enough to give the phyllo you are working with enough room to manuever, c) a half-sheet pan **lined with foil or parchment** (which will comfortably hold twelve pastries), and d) a place for your bowl of filling and melted butter, respectively.

6. Place a clean kitchen towel over the surface of the space where you would like your phyllo unfurled. Carefully unpackage said Greek pastry sheets and lay them flat over the towel with a combination of care and confidence. Lay a second clean towel over the phyllo sheets to prevent them from drying out. Which happens much sooner than one might think it would. I find that giving the top towel a very light mist of water from a spray bottle helps. However, I do not recommend over-moistening, because that would be extremely unfortunate for both the phyllo and the person attempting to manipulate the phyllo. Rather, pretend you are about to iron out a subtle wrinkle from this top towel. A few, short mists. If you are unfamiliar with the subtleties of ironing, you may wish to skip this step and just work as quickly as possible.

7. To assemble the pies, place one sheet of phyllo onto your work space and brush with butter from the center and work your brushstrokes to the outside edges. Place 85 grams of fill-

ing (yours do not have to be 85 grams, but I do recommend weighing out your filling to whatever amount pleases you to get uniform results) in the left-hand center of the pastry sheet, about 2 inches away from the edge.

Fold the bottom of the sheet up to the center, fold the top down to the center until the length of your pastry is the one you desire. Mine happens to be the approximate length of my iPhone. Give a light brushing of butter to the newly exposed surface. Roll the pastry over until you have reached the end. Place flap-side down onto the awaiting sheet pan. Repeat until you have used up all of your filling.

8. **Take the tip of a small knife and pierce each pie to its foundation five times.** I cannot stress how important having steam vents is. I took a batch of these to a party this summer, became distracted by cocktail-wielding friends, and forgot all about piercing. Most of them exploded. However, they were still delicious.

9. Brush the tops of your pies with more butter and then pop into the oven to bake for 8 minutes. After 8 minutes have elapsed, rotate the sheet pan, sprinkle the pies with the sesame and fennel seeds, then return to the oven for about 5 more minutes or until the pastry is golden brown. Remove from the oven and let cool for a few minutes because burning-hot cheese is an unpleasant sensation to one's mouth. Unless, of course, one is mentally prepared for it, as in the case of ***saganaki***.

Serve warm with a beer, some friends, a little ouzo. Whatever you wish to serve them with, just be certain one of those things is a napkin–these are flaky little bastards.

Lobster Lessons

By Aleksandra Crapanzano

From *The Cassoulet Saved Our Marriage: True Tales of Food, Family, and How We Learn to Eat*

Screenwriter and food essayist Aleksandra Crapanzano comes by her passion for cooking honestly, having grown up in a gourmet-loving household in Paris and New York. Imagine then her frustration, facing a beach house sojourn with a quirky in-law mired in a serious food rut.

Rituals are at once burdens and gifts; this is what makes them worth doing, and having, and keeping. It was a remarkable old woman who taught me this lesson—and how, along the way, not to cook a lobster—and I will never forget it.

John and I had been together a year. I had met his parents and he'd met mine. We had moved in together, traveled together, eaten great meals together, but we had not yet settled into (how could we have?) any enduring rituals. Then when summer arrived, it was time to get serious. Serious, for John, meant introducing me to a tiny beach cottage on the east coast of Nantucket, where he'd spent at least a part of every summer of his life; serious meant our spending a few weeks there with his permanent Other Woman, his great-aunt Margaret, whose cottage it was.

Eighty-two years old and a legend in children's book publishing, Margaret, John had warned me, was a creature of habit. To be precise, dietary habit. I'd already heard tales of her spartan daily regimen, which consisted largely of grapefruit (three), skim milk (two tall glasses), and a tuna-fish sandwich. Dinner was, without variation and without fail, a cold chicken leg (boiled), two red potatoes (also boiled), and a pile of grayish green beans (ditto). I was twenty-one that summer, already something of a food snob, and spartan wasn't really in my repertoire.

The first sign of a new world order came on the day we were supposed to pick Margaret up at the ferry terminal. John, who had never before shown the least interest in cooking, suddenly declared, in the voice of an anxious sergeant, that he knew what his aunt liked to eat and how she liked to eat it—and that while we were all cohabiting, he would take charge of the meals, if that was all right with me. I watched in horror as he filled an entire shopping cart at the A&P with water-packed tuna and low-fat mayonnaise. When I reached for a head of garlic, he simply shook his head in dismay, sensing perhaps the inevitable clash of palates in two of the women he loved best. But it was the margarine that almost brought our relationship to an early end. It would be months before we again crossed the threshold of a supermarket together.

From that first dinner with Margaret in her cottage, I remember her smiling at me as the three of us clinked glasses over the table, making me feel wonderfully welcome. But the food itself? Let's just say that, as with any real trauma, the details are buried deep in my psyche.

The following day, I walked up from the beach to find John waiting for me in Margaret's cherry-red 1967 Buick convertible. "Let's go get the lobsters," he called out over the noisy engine. This was promising. I hopped in. Lobsters, corn on the cob, and baked potatoes: It would be messy and buttery and fun. That evening, I was digging out an old T-shirt, knowing I'd be sprayed and stained by dinner's end, when I looked up and caught sight of John through the window. He was stumbling up from the ocean, through the beach grass, weighted down by an enormous black lobster pot, the water sloshing out by the gallon and running down his legs. As he came up the porch steps, I asked him what he was doing. "If you want your lobsters to taste of the ocean, you have to cook them in ocean water," he explained. Margaret, I learned, had been cooking lobsters this way all her life, as had her parents. It was hard to think of refuting the idea, even when John described the hours and boxes of Brillo it would take to scrub the pot clean.

The smell of boiling brine brought me into the kitchen, where I found Margaret and John standing at the stove. John was holding the lid down on the steaming pot so the lobsters, despite their desperate tail-banging, couldn't escape. Margaret had her hand on top of his and was pressing down with her frail fingers. Years ago, when John was a boy, it would have been Margaret's strength that kept the lid in place. Roles had reversed, but they were still a team. Yet something was terribly wrong. The minutes were ticking by, and the lobsters were still boiling away in the pot. I waited and waited, biting my tongue. After a full twenty-three minutes—not a second more nor less by the stovetop timer—Margaret gave the word and John removed the ruined creatures with a long pair of tongs.

As I silently mourned the soggy ruins on my plate, Margaret washed hers down with plenty of white wine and began telling marvelous stories. She'd been coming to Nantucket since the 1920s and told of riding her bicycle as a girl to fetch ice for her mother's icebox, five miles each way. On sunny days, the ice would start to melt and drip from the basket down her legs and between her toes. She told of the winter when the kitchen—an old farmer's shed—had been drawn by sled all the way across a frozen Sesachacha Pond and attached to the cottage. She told of volunteering in London during the Blitz, when food was rationed, and of the magical day a friend brought a dozen fresh eggs to her as a rare gift. So rare that all her friends and neighbors showed up for a spontaneous "fresh eggs party." As Margaret scrambled them over a makeshift stove, an air-raid siren wailed, but no one left to take shelter. Not before savoring a taste of peace. Not before remembering a better time.

Now, more than fifty years later, at the end of our dinner, Margaret dabbed her lips dry, set down her checkered napkin, and heartily proclaimed: "These lobsters are the best I've ever had." Cheeks rosy from the sun, a glass of wine in hand, her merry blue eyes full of wonder, she seemed impossibly young—and I was smitten.

The thought of those scrambled eggs kept me awake that night. For fifty years, Margaret had held their taste in her memory. Clearly she had an appetite for something beyond her boiled regimen. I decided to feed that hunger and, the very next day, took over the kitchen.

If my plan was to work, I reasoned, I needed to find inspiration, rather than dread, in Margaret's usual fare of milk, tuna, and a narrow range of boiled things. That first night, I simmered a loin of pork in milk with a few sage leaves, a little lemon zest, and a hidden clove of garlic: A dish so comforting and mild, it tasted of childhood. Margaret was transfixed by the golden curdles of milk in the sauce and seemed to suspect me of alchemy. I said nothing to dissuade her of this lovely hypothesis. *Vitello tonnato* for lunch the next day satisfied her need for her daily ration of tuna and begged for a bottle of rosé and a sleepy afternoon. Vacation had finally begun. *Boeuf a la ficelle* had us discussing the health virtues of boiling, and John watched in disbelief as Margaret took, with an enthusiasm bordering on compulsion, to the cornichons I'd set out.

Dinner by dinner, I moved slowly through the classics, rewriting the parameters of Margaret's diet. And while it was sometimes a burden to cook for her, it was also a joy. She responded to good food with an appetite some eighty years in the making but still girlish in its pleasure. I had, it seemed, opened a Pandora's box of tastes.

The following summer, an actual box arrived from Margaret's office the day before her arrival—this one sent via FedEx and containing dozens of recipes that Margaret had clipped from newspapers and magazines throughout the winter months. A short note was attached, in which she expressed her hope that I'd want to take a crack at all of them. With no fancy appliances, no gadgets, a single sharp knife, and a colander with only one remaining leg, I cooked every single dish. It was the stuff of fantasy—asparagus flan and summer pudding, oyster chowder and strawberry soup. Margaret kept religious track of them all, noting the ones she particularly liked and filing them away for future summers. It never occurred to her that she might take a recipe home to New York and try it over the winter. Habits might be broken on holiday, but Labor Day returned life to its proper austerity. Still, the thought of Margaret clipping away—dreaming, really—through the long, cold months conjured the irrepressible hope of a love affair.

The years went by and Margaret's age finally took its long-delayed toll. There was the first summer she could no longer walk the fifty feet to the beach. She'd sit on the porch steps staring at that small, insurmountable distance. And then the summer when her hands were no longer strong enough to crack a lobster shell. John tenderly took the lobster from her, cracked it, and gave it back, continuing the conversation all the while. At the end of dinner, with undiminished fervor, she declared it the best lobster she'd had yet. By then, I'd learned that she graced every lobster dinner with those same words.

Margaret's impatience with her weakening body inevitably turned outward. At five o'clock sharp, she would stomp her cane and call out from the porch: "It's time for a drink!" John and I would scurry, leaving computers, work, sentences half-written–John to get white wine from the fridge, me to get the requisite peanuts. We were older, our obligations had multiplied, summers no longer stretched into fall. Our own frustrations occasionally began to simmer.

One night in particular has stayed with me. Margaret had just arrived, and we were to have our annual lobster feast. It had taken me ten years to scale the boiling time down to a palatable twelve or thirteen minutes, and I'd permanently replaced the dreaded margarine with actual butter. But change is not always a friend. John was in the throes of finishing a new novel and had been at his desk, writing, a solid ten hours by the time he broke for the day. Showered, eager for a glass of wine, he'd already put on fresh khakis, uncorked a good bottle, and settled into the Kennedy Rocker when Margaret appeared with the lobster pot.

The wind was up and we could all hear the ocean roaring on the beach. John asked if this once we might use salted tap water. Margaret's response was a simple enough "No," but the indignation in her voice was unmistakable. John was silent–and as angry as I'd ever seen him. "It just won't do," added Margaret, impatiently tapping her cane on the floor. But John was already rolling up his pants to perform his time-honored chore.

The water was freezing and the sky steel-gray that evening. Margaret sat down on the porch steps and watched John disappear over the dune. I observed her from a few feet away. Far from victorious, she seemed to be questioning herself, wondering, no doubt, if time had made her ways too fixed, irrelevant. I took a seat next to her. Stupidly, I tried to tell her that she was right, even Jasper White, the great New England chef, called for cooking lobsters in ocean water. But that was hardly the point. It was, of course, the ritual, in all its effort, that mattered. It set the meal squarely in her history, some ninety years of it by then, and set it apart from other days and other meals.

John came up the porch steps, bent over his burden. Margaret, surprising us mightily, conceded that next time we might try tap water, but John shook his head. It wouldn't be the same. And seeing him standing there, soaking wet but smiling, his arms trembling under the weight of the huge lobster pot filled with fresh seawater from the Atlantic Ocean, I couldn't help but agree. At the end of dinner, Margaret, true to herself, rose to the occasion—she declared her lobster the very best she'd ever eaten.

This summer Margaret will be ninety-seven. She'll come to Nantucket with a caretaker, an oxygen tank, and a wheelchair. Her short-term memory is under assault, but the past she remembers with intense feeling. Traditions are more important to her than ever. They connect our family. John and I now have a little boy and a large dog. When it's time to collect the ocean water, I imagine I'll give our son a bucket and Margaret and I will watch him traipse after his father, learning the way we have always cooked lobsters.

Pork Cooked in Milk

This is a tasty dish but not a pretty one. Garnish as you see fit with additional lemon zest and sage leaves. Serve with egg noodles or rice.

Serves 6

3 pounds pork loin, tied by butcher
2 teaspoons ground sage
2 teaspoons sea salt, preferably Maldon
Freshly ground pepper
1 tablespoon grapeseed or olive oil
6 sprigs of fresh sage
1 to 5 cloves garlic
2 cups heavy cream
1 cup full-fat organic milk
Grated zest of 1 lemon

Rub the ground sage, salt and pepper into the pork loin and

leave to absorb the flavors overnight in the fridge in a large zip-top bag, with the air squeezed out.

Heat a large oval Dutch oven over medium-high heat for 1 minute. Add the oil and tilt the pot so that the oil forms a thin layer over the bottom. Heat another minute, then add the pork, fat side down, and brown. This should take about 20 minutes, estimating about 4 to 5 minutes per side and ends. When the pork is crusted in a rich gold, remove it. Discard the fat from the pot.

Return the pot to the heat and add the fresh sage, garlic, cream, milk and lemon zest. Bring to a simmer. Return the pork to the pot and return to a simmer. Partially cover and cook until the pork reaches 145°F. This should take about an hour and 15 minutes.

Resist the urge to touch the pork while it's cooking. As I mentioned, this is not a pretty dish. The milk curdles, but once those curdles thicken, they turn to a blissful custard. If the curdles have not thickened to your liking by the time the pork has cooked, simply remove the pork and continue cooking the liquid.

Serve with custard in a gravy boat.

A Bountiful Shore: Celebrating Thanksgiving on the Chesapeake Bay

By Bernard L. Herman

From *Saveur*

Family traditions cling fast to Thanksgiving feasts. As an American Studies professor at the University of North Carolina, Bernard L. Herman can be forgiven for obsessing a bit about the Chesapeake Bay *terroir* of his family's time-honored Thanksgiving dinner menu.

Just before dawn on Thanksgiving morning, I pull on my waders, grab a basket, and splash my way to the oyster cages that lie a hundred or so yards from our house on the banks of Westerhouse Creek, not far from the shore of Chesapeake Bay. Light from the kitchen windows flickers across the water. The first winter jellyfish pulse in the flowing tide. Hauling one of the cages onto the lip of a sandbar, I brush away seaweed, unhook the lid, and peer at the oysters inside. Silvery grass shrimp somersault across the shells. Mud crabs skitter to the cage's bottom. A drowsy oyster toad squirms in a corner. Into my basket, I toss big handfuls of oysters—a favorite delicacy at the Thanksgiving meal my family hosts every year on Virginia's Eastern Shore, the long, narrow peninsula that forms the eastern boundary of the lower Chesapeake Bay.

I have loved this place since I was a child growing up here in the 1950s. Even after I moved away, I stayed connected to the Eastern Shore. Over the years, I looked for ways to return to the place, visiting often, and writing academic papers on the peninsula's food and folk traditions, old and new—from the annual October snapping-turtle feast to the everyday life of the Eastern Shore's early settlers and native communities. About ten years ago my wife, Becky, and I bought a second home here, a 1720s brick house south of the village of Bayford, about 20 miles from the peninsula's southern tip. It has become my family's favorite place to spend Thanksgiving.

The company isn't huge by holiday standards: This year it's just me and Becky; my mother, Lucy; my sister, Fredrika (who goes by "Freddie"), and her husband, Paul; their daughter, Jessica, and her six-year-old son, Peter; and our daughter, Lania, who's brought her friend Samantha, whom everyone calls Sam. As for the meal, it tends to be a bit over the top. For me, it's a coming together of all my favorite Eastern Shore traditions, and a celebration of the local foods that have fed the people of this peninsula for generations—all of it combined with the favorite holiday dishes of the rest of my family.

The Eastern Shore is 70 miles of sandy, fertile land abutting the country's best clamming and oyster-growing waters. The climate is Mediterranean, and home gardens here yield figs, peaches, and even pomegranates. No matter what time of year it is, when I'm on the Eastern Shore, I always seem to be thinking about provisioning our Thanksgiving meal. Becky and I start our preparations early, in July and August, when we and our friends put up fruit preserves, and savory pickles made from the tomatoes and okra that the area produces so abundantly.

Throughout the fall, our neighbors who hunt and fish make their contributions, too, though what gets to the table depends on luck and weather. Our neighbor Jon Moore presents us with six venison roasts, and another friend, ace oyster grower Tom Gallivan, drops off a 25-pound bluefish. I rub the venison in black pepper and cayenne, and cure it in the smoker in our backyard, then fillet and smoke the bluefish, before storing both away until November.

As the holiday draws near, our preparations intensify, peaking two days before Thanksgiving, when I embark on the annual "big loop," an epic, daylong drive to visit purveyor friends along the shore. It's my version of the Thanksgiving harvest. The trip ranges from one end of Northampton County to the other, along back roads bracketed by creek and marsh, field and woodland.

This year, Sam accompanies me. Our first stop is Pickett's Harbor Farms, at the southern tip of the peninsula, where W. T. and Tammie Nottingham live on land W. T.'s family has farmed for generations.

They grow heirloom sweet potatoes, including a variety called Hayman that is virtually unique to this area and prized for its dense white flesh and intense sweetness. We pick up a couple dozen of them, plus a medley of other kinds for cooking into casseroles. Next, we drive north to visit James Elliott, the co-owner of A. & J.'s Fresh Meat Market, in the little railroad town of Cheriton. A. & J.'s is where we get our turkey, always naturally raised. James also makes a sage pork sausage that really sings. This year I buy some for our hominy and oyster stuffing, and, as I do every year, I ask him what goes into the sausage. He gives me the same wry answer he always does: "That is something I'm not telling."

After that, we head to JC Walker Brothers Inc. clam house in Willis Wharf. "These just came off the grounds this morning," Hank Arnold, the owner, says as he hands me a 250-count bag of littlenecks. Finally, before heading home, we make a return visit to Tom Gallivan, our oysterman friend, who owns Shooting Point Oyster Company in Bayford, to retrieve two mesh bags of Shooting Point and Nassawadox Salt oysters, to supplement the haul from my own oyster cages.

The next day, Wednesday, preparations really shift into high gear. While I brown the sage sausage in a cast-iron skillet for the stuffing, Becky makes a couple of sweet potato casseroles and a pumpkin cheesecake. I turn next to the smoked bluefish, making a creamy, brandy-spiked pâté. Finally, Lania and Sam prepare an old family standby, juicing lemons and chopping oranges and apples for a cranberry relish that's based on a recipe my mother, a retired elementary school teacher, coaxed from a lunchroom cook in the 1960s. Once our two refrigerators are full, Becky and I tidy the kitchen and turn in for the night.

On Thanksgiving Day, by seven o'clock, I've returned from my oyster beds with a hundred or so Westerhouse Pinks, as I like to call the mollusks native to our creek. I take them over to an old workbench, which will serve as an outdoor buffet table that we've set up in the yard. I lay out a couple dozen of my oysters on ice-filled wooden trays, alongside the ones from Tom Gallivan, then light the propane burner on the pot steamer that I'll be using to steam the littlenecks. Sam and Lania bring out some pickled okra and pickled figs, the bluefish pâté, and the cured, smoked venison, sliced paper-thin and served with rounds of crusty bread and coarse brown mustard. At our home, the eating on Thanksgiving starts outdoors, and it starts early.

By ten o'clock, almost everyone has arrived, and the festivities officially commence. In the middle of the yard stands a towering pyre of branches, driftwood, and old stumps, fuel for the bonfire that we always light on Thanksgiving morning and keep burning into the night. This year, Sam does the honors, touching a match to the pile. Flames erupt high in the air, and everyone cheers.

The bonfire lit, it's time to shuck the first oysters. I pop open one of my Westerhouse Pinks; it's fat and sweet. Then I taste a Shooting Point Salt, which has a briny, mineral tang. My brother-in-law, Paul, the family's Thanksgiving sommelier, shows up with a case of domestic bottles from his cellar. For the oysters, we open a chardonnay crafted by Chatham Vineyards just up the road.

As morning turns to afternoon, guests beat a path between the roaring bonfire and the steamy warmth of the kitchen. The turkey—stuffed with the sage sausage and hominy, rubbed with olive oil, and seasoned with fresh parsley, salt, and black pepper—has been roasting for a couple of hours already, and it's filling the room with its aroma. Various family members pursue culinary tasks under Becky's gentle direction. Freddie and Jessica plate creamed spinach and a layered vegetable terrine. Becky pulls a pan of roasted oysters from the oven and sets them out with one relish of pickled green tomatoes and another of horseradish, beets, and cranberries. The cooks snatch the oysters right off the baking tray, and in minutes, they're gone. Just before dinner is served, Becky improvises a last-minute dessert of roasted pears stuffed with minced pear, almonds, dried currants, and raisins.

Finally, by midafternoon, all the dishes are ready, arrayed on our kitchen table. In the dining room, my late father's huge, three-by-eight-foot writing desk has been put into service as our dinner table. I head outside to throw a few more branches on the fire and then come in to grab a plate along with everyone else. It is a sumptuous spread: the freshly carved turkey; a platter of thin-sliced aged country ham; the baked Hayman sweet potatoes, incomparably luscious; the Brussels sprouts and rosemary potatoes; plus the pumpkin cheesecake, an apple pie, a boozy rum Bundt cake, and Becky's sugar-glazed roasted pears, which are destined to become a regular addition to the holiday menu. There is no order to serving. Everyone just descends on a favorite dish.

At last, seated, glasses raised, we toast the day, and then we toast the cooks. Becky, looking tired and elated at the same time, clinks her glass with Lania's and says, "Aren't we lucky?" In no time, guests are heading back into the kitchen for seconds. Before dessert, I read aloud from *The Sot-Weed Factor*, John Barth's great novel, written in 1960, about life in the Chesapeake Bay country of the late 1600s. I select a passage that describes an imagined eating contest between the English explorers and the Ahatchwhoop Indians to choose a king:

> [T]he rest watch'd in astonishment, the two gluttons match'd dish for dish, and herewith is the summe of what they eat: Of keskowghnoughmass, the yellowe-belly'd sunne-fish, tenne apiece. Of copatone, the sturgeon, one apiece. Of pummahumpnoughmass, fry'd star-fish, three apiece. Of pawpeconoughmass, pype-fishes, four apiece . . . "

After a few more lines I break down laughing. By the time the dessert wine and the grappa come out, we're starting to feel like the culinary combatants in Barth's book.

Once night falls, most of the rest of the family departs. The kitchen is a wreck, but it can wait. It's growing chilly, and Becky, Lania, Sam, and I return to the dying bonfire with glasses of wine. "That was a great Thanksgiving," I say to Becky. "Let's talk about next year."

"Let's not," she replies. "We've had enough fun for one day."

But I can't help thinking about next Thanksgiving's big loop, about what we'll cook and eat. Down by the creek the night herons are calling to each other raucously, and I can hear the rasp of the breeze in the marsh grasses. It is the soundscape of the Eastern Shore.

To Be a Chef

Empire of the Burning Tongue

By John Swansburg

From *New York Magazine*

Being editorial director of the digital magazine Slate should keep John Swansburg too busy to take other gigs–but the opportunity to profile hot-chef-of-the-moment Danny Bowien for *New York Magazine* was evidently too good to pass up.

The sun is setting, shrouding the Lower East Side in a soft evening light, but the hair and nail salon directly above Mission Chinese Food casts an unflattering glow across the stretch of pavement where a gaggle of would-be diners bides their time. As usual, the wait is over two hours. Among the crowd outside 154 Orchard Street is a pair of middle-aged guys in loafers, hemmed jeans, and pressed button-downs who are leaning on a Cadillac Escalade like they own it. But most patrons are younger and have come here on foot, with time if not money to burn. Perched on a planter that provides the only seating is a fellow with a cotton kimono, complicated piercings, and a leg cast–the result, one feels safe assuming, of a fixed-gear bicycle incident. A young couple strolls up and stares quizzically at Mission's forbidding exterior, a plate-glass window stenciled with some untranslated Chinese characters. "I thought it was, like, a restaurant," the guy says to the girl. He's not the first to be confused. The face Mission presents to the street is not that of the hot spot it is, but rather one of an iffy purveyor of spare ribs and duck sauce.

Six steps below sidewalk level is the small foyer that functions as Mission's takeout counter, waiting area, and storage for stray 30-pound boxes of dry chile peppers. A second group of customers clogs this room, huddled around a Rubbermaid garbage can holding a sweating keg of Narragansett. The beer is free, but the city of New York says you can't drink it on the sidewalk, and there's space for only a handful of people to sip from the Dixie cups Mission hands out. It's a self-selecting crowd: The heat emanating from the adjacent kitchen and the hip-hop throbbing from the house speakers give the waiting area the comfort level of a down-market discotheque. Getting to the beer is arduous enough that on many nights the restaurant won't kick a single keg.

Above the gratis beer hangs the kind of backlit menu board more typically found in ethnic restaurants where non-native speakers are encouraged to order by number. For the first four months Mission was in business, under that display hung a piece of tinfoil on which someone had scrawled "Please Wait 2 Be Seated" in Sharpie, as if management hadn't anticipated the demand for tables and had to hastily fashion a sign to keep people from wandering into the packed dining room. But that could hardly have been the case. Though much about the restaurant feels improvised, it arrived in New York this spring from San Francisco surfing a sustained wave of hype. The original Mission Chinese opened in that city's Mission district in 2010, as a pop-up restaurant nestled inside an existing Chinese establishment: Lung Shan, an unloved hole in the wall. But its take on Sichuan cooking—with dishes like thrice-cooked bacon and an Islamic lamb hot pot—quickly won praise from various deans of American food writing, Mark Bittman, Anthony Bourdain, and Alan Richman among them. Soon, Danny Bowien, Mission's chef, was showing America how to prepare hand-pulled noodles on the *Martha Stewart Show* and scouting for a New York location.

He settled on the first space he saw. Six months later, the restaurant he opened in its inhospitable confines is still reliably thronged, somehow simultaneously a must-visit for finance types, freelance types, chowhounds, and food critics emeriti. ("Finally made it to NYC's Mission Chinese," Frank Bruni tweeted a couple of weeks ago. "Better even than I'd heard. Wow.") A profile of Bowien in the December issue of *GQ* mentions the chef in the same breath as Mario Batali and Jean-Georges Vongerichten. Like those impresarios, Bowien is eager to expand, and there are plans for an offshoot in Brooklyn, Paris, or that culinary capital Oklahoma City, where he grew up. Last week, he floated the idea of a Mission Burrito on Facebook. "WTF when?!" replied one fan, presumably already packing a tote bag for her first visit.

"It was kind of a joke," Bowien says. "But New York does need to eat good burritos. It's something I've been messing around with." He stresses that any new locations or ventures remain tentative. "We have a couple of awesome leads, but I can't say which one's next because we're still deciding. We're a tiny company. It's just, like, me. And a couple of other people." But if Bowien can seem to be flying somewhat by the seat of his slim-fit pants in his nascent empire building, there's nothing coincidental about his success. He and his restaurant arrived at a moment when some New Yorkers seem to be tiring of knee-jerk locavorism and all things rough-hewn, of places that rely on now-shopworn culinary and stylistic cues to announce that they are fashionable dining establishments. Mission, by contrast, adheres to no discernible set of rules and has to be experienced to fully appreciate its complicated appeal. But before you experience it, you have to wait. The wait is part of the experience, too.

Most nights, the woman with all the power is Anna. She's the keeper of the clipboard, taking names and informing customers how long they can expect to cool their heels. A different kind of establishment, arriving in New York with high expectations and a mere 41 seats to offer, would have hired a seasoned professional to work the door. Anna is a sixth-year undergraduate at NYU who had never worked in a restaurant. Early on, she was quoting patrons waits of three, four, even five hours, not realizing that very few people would wait that long for a table, no matter how many times Mission was cooking its bacon. Nowadays, when the line stretches into a third hour, she politely turns customers away. Her estimates have grown more accurate, though there are still nights when the margin of error is plus or minus 30 minutes. She's happy to call your cell when your table is ready. But don't wander too far.

One night I get the call while sipping a pint of Hitachino at Blue Ribbon Sushi Izakaya, a block north on Orchard but a world away from Mission Chinese. (It's well-appointed, sprawling, and empty.) My party hustles back to the restaurant, and Anna leads us to our table. The dining room is separated from the restaurant's entrance by a narrow corridor where a long rectangular window opens onto the cramped kitchen. More often than not, if you look through this window as you pass by, you'll see a skinny guy wearing his shaggy, blond-streaked mane loosely collected under a baseball cap. This is Bowien, perhaps the world's least likely celebrity chef.

Bowien didn't train at a renowned culinary school—he signed up, then dropped out—or apprentice himself to a master. He cut his teeth working the line in kitchens in New York and San Francisco, aspiring to be a cook, not a chef, and certainly not an impresario; his goal was just to work somewhere like Momofuku, not open a worthy rival. As he's fond of noting, he'd never cooked Chinese food before launching Mission Chinese in San Francisco and had never opened a proper restaurant before Mission New York. He's not even Chinese: He's Korean, raised by adoptive parents in Oklahoma, where he fell in love with food watching cooking shows with his mother. He started off calling his cooking "Americanized Oriental food," though he now prefers the term "weird Chinese." He never considered attempting authentic Chinese cuisine; when a restaurant sells itself that way but doesn't live up to the billing, he believes, "people will tear you apart." Instead, Bowien takes classic Sichuan dishes and runs roughshod over the traditional preparation. They don't eat kung pao pastrami in Chengdu.

One way to introduce yourself to Bowien without sticking out a two-hour wait is to watch a video produced by *Vice* as part of the magazine's "Munchies" series. It depicts Bowien and several chef friends getting drunk on cheap beer, then gruesomely slaughtering live crabs for a stew. It's a minor miracle no one loses a finger. "I don't even remember cooking anything last night," he says to the camera the next day.

"I can't even tell what's going on in my mouth right now," says my dining companion, a law professor whose dream meal is a double order of crab rangoon. He's been dipping into the mapo tofu, one of Mission's signature dishes, which conjures sensations of heat but also an anesthetizing numbness. Having been victimized previously by the dish, I've been sampling it judiciously, fishing out the soft cubes of bean curd and letting the chili oil drain off before eating them. Soon arrives a plate of chicken wings sitting atop a nest of hot peppers and crispy tripe. I dive in and, feeling lucky, take a bite of one of the peppers. Cruelly, it doesn't reveal its full force immediately, leading me to take another foolhardy nibble. When the spice does hit, no amount of beer or rice will calm its fury. Later, seemingly safe at home, the pepper will torment my innards and power feverish, hallucinatory dreams. ("Sichuan peppercorns," *GQ*'s Brett Martin astutely observed, "are essentially drugs.")

Not every dish on the menu is quite so devastating to the palette or GI tract, but many of the most popular entrées, the ones most eagerly discussed around the keg, have ominous double-flame icons next to them on Mission's laminated menus. At Pok Pok, when you order Andy Ricker's signature wings, your server will ask you how spicy you'd like them. "Not spicy" is an option. At Mission Chinese, tamping down a dish's intended heat is not encouraged. And while the fiery items are always fiery, the kitchen can be terrifyingly inconsistent. Sometimes the thrice-cooked bacon is very spicy. Sometimes it's untenable.

At first, I experienced the mind-altering heat merely as an all-out assault on my palate. But over the course of my visits, I came to realize that the spiciness is very much part of Mission's popularity, even for those diners who lack an iron-plated esophagus. It presents a challenge, one that lends a trip to Mission a sense of adventure. Waiting by the keg or outside on Orchard, it's not uncommon to overhear a repeat customer recounting his conversion experience with missionary zeal to a group of novices. Once inside the dining room, the spiciness inspires a feeling of camaraderie. Just how molten are the Mongolian long beans? A fellow diner with a sweaty nose and an opinion on the matter is rarely but a few feet away.

But Scoville units aside, the food is also good, and that obviously matters. Over the course of several months, I had five meals at Mission with seven different companions, and no one ever left disappointed. (One friend, stuffed to the gills and handed a takeout box heaping with leftover wings, texted a neighbor and arranged a late-night doggie-bag drop.) But it's not merely a matter of being good. St. Anselm, the Williamsburg steakhouse, is good. It's very good. And like Mission, it's small, inevitably packed, and favored by the footloose. But while its size, clientele, and antebellum-lumberjack aesthetic (mounted saws, torn flags) set St. Anselm apart from the city's grand steakhouses of old, its menu isn't all that different from what you'll find around the corner at Peter Luger: meat, potatoes, creamed spinach. At Perla, Gabriel Stulman's newest West Village outpost, you can order some highfalutin junk food—a PB&J made with foie gras, a bowl of painstakingly seasoned potato chips—to nosh on during your server's presentation on the provenance of the lamb chop . . . which, noble as the farmer who slaughtered it may have been, is still a lamb chop. Bowien's "weird Chinese" may not be authentically Chinese, but it is authentically weird. The "catfish à la Sichuan" that used to be on the menu was actually seasoned à la Baltimore, with Old Bay. The braised pig tails are marinated in smoked Coca-Cola.

The sense of adventure is further fostered by the space itself. The design playbook for new restaurants has yielded familiar aesthetic tics: Edison bulbs, Mason jars, Edison bulbs in Mason jars. Maybe some flea market bric-a-brac to telegraph the establishment's obligatory lack of pretension. Maybe a chalkboard listing tonight's selection of locally pickled cocktail onions, or some other detail worthy of a *Portlandia* sketch. At Mission, one wall bears a Technicolor Chinese painting depicting Communist leaders on horseback; another has a vintage Michael Jordan poster taped up with all the ceremony of a dorm-room adornment. Nearby hangs a giant wall calendar on which Bowien scrawls his upcoming commitments for all the world to see, less out of a belief in radical transparency than practicality: He can see it from the kitchen. At a time when so many restaurants look like they're trying too hard, Bowien's place distinguishes itself by appearing to barely try at all.

Another thing that makes Mission feel different are the prices. A single dish at Red Farm, the cleaner, brighter Chinese fusion restaurant on Hudson Street, can run you upwards of $25. At Mission, you can eat like a Qing Dynasty decadent for about the same amount. Indeed, overindulging is part of the experience: You wait two hours, you get very hungry, you get a little drunk, you order more than you can possibly eat, you find yourself pleasantly surprised at how cheap it all was. Then you bring the leftovers to a neighbor, who now owes you a favor.

One Tuesday morning, I make my way to Mission Chinese to meet Bowien. The place seems deserted. After knocking a few times, I try the front door, find it unlocked, and let myself in. Making my way toward the dining room, I run into Bowien as he's heading into the kitchen. He introduces himself, then apologizes—he needs a few minutes. One of his cooks has called in sick. He needs to do some prep work before he can sit down to talk.

Bowien emerges from the kitchen about ten minutes later. He wears a faded T-shirt, short-shorts (a warm-weather Bowien trademark), and black oxfords with black socks pulled up over his calves. He'd look like a corporate attorney who has somehow misplaced his pants but for his copious tattoos, his clear-plastic-frame glasses, and that haphazardly bleached hair, which instead give him the look of an itinerant barista. He carries himself with an appealing diffidence, not the cocksure strut you might expect of a guy who's rocketed to the top of the New York restaurant world. "I don't get it sometimes," he told me. "We're just trying our hardest to make things good. But I feel like we are overrated in a lot of senses. I think that the food is delicious. But are we doing it better than 99 percent of the other restaurants out there? I don't think so."

He may look the part of the unassuming hipster, but as has been noted in the growing body of Bowien hagiography, he has a formidable work ethic, putting in 96-hour weeks. Seeing him on the job is also part of the Mission experience. Whenever he emerges onto Orchard Street, as he often does over the course of a night—to make a call on his iPhone, to run down the block to grab a bag of beef jerky for a mid-shift snack—a ripple of excitement passes through the huddled table-seekers. There's nothing new, of course, about a rock-star chef leveraging his celebrity to keep his restaurant packed. But this is a different kind of act.

Talking with Bowien, it's easy to see how he's become a hero to the young people who make up what Adam Platt, in his Mission review, dubbed the No-Reservations Generation. He is driven without being a striver, ambitious without being careerist. And he's more interested in the craft of cooking than the showmanship of being a chef. "I spent so many years just trying to flex as a cook and say I'm going to be the baddest line cook ever, have the sharpest knife," he says. In 2008, when he was cooking Italian dishes at San Francisco's Farina, he took his knives to Genoa, where he competed in the World Pesto Championship—and won. Then he grew restless and decided to start a pop-up Chinese place, for no other reason than Chinese was the food he most liked to eat on his days off. (And because he didn't like that his friends couldn't afford to eat at the fancier places he'd been cooking.) Barely two years later, Pete Wells would be raving about Mission Chinese in the *Times*: "Mr. Bowien does to Chinese food what Led Zeppelin did to the blues." But it might be more apt to say that Bowien has done to cooking what Pavement did to rock: He showed you could be a virtuoso with the mien of a slacker.

Mission Chinese opened before securing a liquor license, so for the time being it's just beer, sake, and a few house cocktails made with *soju*. Torrey Bell-Edwards, one of Mission's bartenders, confirms that two of the cocktails—the One-Eyed Jack and the Great Northern—are named for fictional establishments from David Lynch's *Twin Peaks*, a Bowien obsession (and a canonical work for members of the No-Reservations Generation). "We're working on a new one," he says. "A variation on the Arnold Palmer called the Laura Palmer." The theme continues in the bathroom, where Bowien has jury-rigged an iPod to loop Angelo Badalamenti's instrumental theme for the show and a framed portrait of Palmer hangs above the toilet. Since the restaurant opened, the Palmer picture has twice been stolen. The piece has no intrinsic value—it's a jpeg from the web, blown up and printed out—but apparently some of Bowien's fans want a souvenir.

Bell-Edwards surveys the dining room from under a San Francisco Giants fitted hat. I ask him if he followed Bowien from California, as many Mission staffers have. He did, though he didn't work at the original location—he got to know Bowien by serving him drinks at the Elbow Room, a San Francisco bar. Politely, I ask him if he thinks it at all strange that Bowien would bring in a bartender all the way from California, despite having never worked with him. "He'd rather trust you and like you than worry about your pedigree," he says. Anna, the hostess with no restaurant experience, is a friend of a Bowien friend. Aubrey Hustead, the assistant general manager (whom regulars will recognize as the baby-faced guy wearing the Adidas headband), had worked at San Francisco outfits run by Bowien associates, but at 27 he's hardly what you'd call an industry veteran. That Hustead and Bell-Edwards, as well as several of the wait staff, would return the chef's trust and move across the country to take a job with a guy opening his first real restaurant testifies to the power of Bowien's off-handed charm.

One day I visit with Bowien shortly before the lunch-hour rush. His staff buzzes around us, pulling down chairs from the dining room rafters, where they're stored for the night—one of many work-arounds required to make this tiny space viable. "I went to Noma recently," Bowien tells me. "There was this sense that everyone there was just pushing toward this common goal. The servers—everyone. Everyone was going to bat and trying to make something honest and good. That's what resonates." Mission could hardly be more different than René Redzepi's spare, pricey Copenhagen mecca. But both embody their founders' singular ideas of what a restaurant should be. Mission's food reflects Bowien's adventurous, irreverent tastes, and consequently some of it is going to toast your taste buds. The wait staff look like they were rounded up at a Hayes Valley bus stop and are prone to bringing you a bowl of rice porridge you didn't order and forgetting the sizzling cumin lamb that you did. But they're always in motion and unfailingly friendly—"Be nice" is another core tenet of Bowien's belief system (and another rationale for importing people from California). Mission's ambience, too, is pure Bowien, from the soundtrack (golden era hip-hop, metal) to the keg ("If people are going to stand here and wait, let them drink free beer") to that vintage Jordan poster ("I wanted that poster when I was a kid and never got it"). The place isn't for everyone, but it's authentically its own, and that speaks to a clientele that's learned to sniff out (thrift-) store-bought, hand-churned idiosyncrasy.

There's a risk that as Bowien branches out, it will be harder to imbue each new place with his philosophy. (Also, you can't fly back from Paris to man a wok every time a cook calls in sick.) This is a risk that any entrepreneurial chef would face, but it's an especially acute one when your formula is a lack thereof, that exciting sense that you and your crew are making it all up as you go along. Bowien, though, seems constitutionally ill-suited for stasis. I arrived for an early dinner one night to find him sitting at one of the tables in the dining room, ear buds on his ears, working on changes to a menu that a long line of people were waiting outside to sample. Bowien explained that the tinkering is as much about keeping his staff happy as anything else. "I have to keep all these cooks motivated back there," he said. "Cooks get very weary after a while. They want to make this food and next thing you know they want to make regional Italian food, so they go to another restaurant." At Mission, the cook in charge is more restless than most.

The King of the Food Trucks Hits Hawaii

By Jonathan Gold

From *Food & Wine*

Los Angeles Times restaurant critic Jonathan Gold was an aficionado of food trucks long before the rest of America caught on, singing their praises in his Counter Intelligence column for *LA Weekly* magazine, and along the way earning a Pulitzer Prize—the first ever for a food writer.

Honolulu is littered with fancy restaurants, where dishes like sea urchin-garnished jumbo shrimp are a fixture on 12-course tasting menus. It also has its share of breathtakingly expensive sushi spots. Those are not the kind of places that appeal to chef Roy Choi.

As I sit with Choi over dinner in a Waikiki *tonkatsu* parlor, contemplating a $30 sliver of Japanese fried pork, we are talking about Spam *musubi:* rectangular bricks of vinegared rice stuffed with pink, glistening slabs of the lunch meat, then wrapped in seaweed. Spam *musubi* is a crucial totem of what Hawaiians call "local food," the shotgun marriage of Polynesian ingredients, Asian flavors and American specialties that you find at drive-ins, bowling-alley coffee shops, lunch trucks, mall food courts—pretty much anywhere the regulars tend to outnumber the tourists. Spam *musubi* is quintessential gas-station food—you see it in a cooler in the back, near the Red Bull and the Coors Lite.

I think we should try the *musubi* at He'eia Pier General Store & Deli, which was just reopened and has been getting good notices for its reinvented lunch specials made with organic, island-grown ingredients, or at least at Iyasume, where *musubi* is the specialty of the house. Choi thinks we need to go down the street to a 7-Eleven. I'm not sure I agree with him, but I admire his style.

Even if you think you know everything about chef culture, Choi is that *other* guy—his gaze intense, his Lakers cap skewed, his sartorial style somewhere between skate-punk, Koreatown dandy and East L.A. *veterano*. Born in Korea, he grew up shuttling among Los Angeles neighborhoods with his scholarly dad and restaurateur mom, who always managed to prepare multicourse Korean breakfasts no matter how many hours she worked. He was the speaker of his class at the Culinary Institute of America in Hyde Park, New York, and spent a decade as an executive chef at grand hotels.

Choi first came to prominence when he left the mainstream food world to start Kogi, the Korean taco truck that not only jump-started the national food-truck craze but also the rush to elevated street food. He logged time at Le Bernardin, but he cooks like a dude as obsessed with carne asada picnics as he is with his mother's kimchi. Instead of expanding his Kogi franchise, he's opened a series of inspired places: the rice-bowl spot Chego, the Hawaii-inspired A-Frame and the small-plates-style restaurant Sunny Spot, loosely based on Jamaican roadside dives. He has an intimate knowledge of Koreatown in Los Angeles, and he was an *F&W* Best New Chef in 2010, but his favorite destination is neither Paris nor Korea but Hawaii, which he first got to know as an adolescent dumped off for a summer at an aunt's house in Honolulu. He has visited almost every year of his adult life. It's where Choi feels at home, and where he finds inspiration for everything from his restaurants to his upcoming book, *Spaghetti Junction: Riding Shotgun with an L.A. Chef*. "I translate Hawaii as a place where people make sure I'm having a great time, eating terrific food, without any expectation of anything in return," Choi told me. "It's a place for people to be happy. It sounds corny, but in Hawaii, it's not; it's uncorny."

Honolulu is a multiethnic city where currently fashionable things, like Asian-inflected European cooking, are as likely to show up in a construction worker's lunch box as in a tourist's four-star dinner. Supermarket staples like chuck steak, flown in from the mainland, cost almost as much as great local tuna. And the line dividing canned lunch meat from spectacular local shellfish is occasionally finer than one might wish.

In the Honolulu calculus that splits food into what is eaten with a plastic fork and everything else, it is clear which side of the plate-lunch divide Choi stands on. Deprive him of *malasadas*, shave ice or *laulau* (taro-wrapped pork), and he is an unhappy chef indeed.

So the next morning finds us in a rented car, creeping through morning traffic, on our way to the first of three breakfasts: the beginning of a hundred-thousand-calorie journey around Oahu that will fuel Choi for the rest of the year.

We pull into the parking lot of Leonard's, a cramped bakery that's the home of Hawaii's best-known *malasadas*: slightly sweetened beignets, best eaten scorchingly hot, dusted with granulated sugar. The line inside is endless, snaking back on itself, slowed by customers who take forever to decide among the hundreds of pastries in the long glass bakery cases, even though they inevitably end up with *malasadas*.

"The karma's coming back to me," says Choi, whose trucks generally inspire even longer waits.

We eat leaning against the wall outside. A bus full of Japanese tourists pulls into the lot. Each of them takes pictures of the vintage neon. Tour guides distribute *malasadas*, one each, daintily folded in napkins. The Japanese do not look thrilled.

We double back to the Rainbow Drive-In, draped with banners proclaiming its 50th anniversary. It's a fast-food place with outdoor tables and a cantilevered shade—a famous center of "local food." We order far too much: a teriyaki plate, chili rice and something called long rice, which is thin, slippery glass noodles cooked in chicken broth. We also try the local-food specialty *loco moco*: an enormous plateau of rice topped with a well-done hamburger patty, drenched in a viscous, dark-brown goo and topped with a fried egg.

"This isn't delicious," says Choi. "Or, rather, this is a different kind of delicious. When you come out of the ocean after surfing all day, *loco moco* is the best thing you ever tasted."

We stand in another line at Helena's Hawaiian Food, often said to serve the best plate lunches in Honolulu, where Choi is treated like a movie star by a California newscaster who frequents Kogi and

I am drawn into an argument about the best hand-pulled noodles in the San Gabriel Valley. In the world of plate lunches, Helena's is stunning: a profoundly smoky version of the traditional luau dish *pipikaula,* made from short ribs that have been dried on racks in the kitchen; fried butterfish collar; tripe stew with homemade chile pepper water; squid cooked down with taro leaves; and *lomi* salmon, which is like a mild salsa with cubed fish tossed in with the tomatoes. For dessert, there are jiggly cubes of *haupia* pudding, made with coconut cream. We are happy, and we are full.

But five minutes later, we are at the Shimazu Store, a battered storefront a mile or so down the street, for the first of many cracks at Hawaii's famous shave ice, a kind of giant, fluffy snow cone flavored with homemade syrup that seems to be an obsession of Choi's: guava, *lilikoi* (passion fruit), lychee, milky green tea, durian. Shave ice is always found in a storefront a little out of the way, and it's always served in portions far too big for one person to get through before the ice collapses over your hand with a splash. The pavement for blocks around each store is stained with dead shave ice and weeping children. I finally talk Choi into going back to the hotel for a nap.

Dinner that night is at Side Street Inn, a 20-year-old bar in an alley. Side Street is kind of a prototype of the modern *izakaya* that has been popping up in large American cities for the last couple of years, an aggressively multicultural house of big eats that just happen to be served on shared platters, lubricated by oceans of beer. Choi has been coming here for years. We are greeted effusively by owner-chef Colin Nishida.

"People keep asking me for my pork chop recipe," he says. "It is very short—garlic salt, flour and cornstarch, that's it."

"I thought I tasted Lawry's salt," says Choi.

"Nah, although I love the stuff."

"No egg wash?"

"Why the hell would I do that?"

Ninety minutes later, we've gone through enormous platters of Japanese fried chicken, kimchi fried rice and sweet-sticky baby back ribs with a thick hoisin glaze that Choi adores. He has also come to agree with Nishida about the crunchy fried pork chops: Why the hell would he use egg wash?

Outside of Honolulu, which resembles a typical midsize American city in a lot of ways, Oahu is a not-immense place where the great American road trip quickly runs out of road. Among other things, I wanted to taste the definitive version of a local specialty, *huli huli* chicken. I found it within an hour of leaving the hotel, in the parking lot of a Malama Market, where Ray's Kiawe Broiled Chicken truck sets up on Saturday and Sunday afternoons. I had imagined a guy cooking out of a van, but the grill was as long as a semitrailer, shaded by a dented tin roof, heaped with fuming kiawe charcoal over which spun 30 to 40 chickens threaded onto special rotating spits. Choi finds Dino, the owner's son; he tells us the chickens go from raw to cooked in just 25 minutes. But he has to keep a lot going at once in case a tour bus drops by, an event that's both lucrative and unpredictable.

Down the street, Matsumoto Shave Ice—home of the most famous version in the world—is totally set up for the tourist trade, an old grocery channeled for the sale of dripping ice cones and T-shirts. Choi is recognized by a Kogi fan from Oakland, a young Filipina in the area for a friend's wedding, who pumps us for information on restaurants both in Honolulu and back in California. The rainbow shave ice, we all agree, is grainy and second-rate.

We continue driving around the island, stopping to admire the beach at Banzai Pipeline, familiar from a thousand televised surf competitions but as flat as a pond at this time of year. We fly past a gaudily painted truck promising Korean tacos and end up at Giovanni's, beyond the local shrimp farms, a heavily graffitied truck that doesn't look as if it has ever moved from this spot. It's outfitted with a huge dining area shaded by a metal roof. Giovanni's is famous for its garlic shrimp, and the scent of chopped garlic surrounds the truck like a cloud. The menu, such as it is, is painted on a surfboard, but there's no reason to get anything but as many garlic shrimp as you can hold; firm, sweet and swimming in scented oil.

I make Choi drive back to Shogunai Tacos, the Asian truck we'd seen earlier. The Japanese taco, wrapped in a flour tortilla, isn't completely horrible—the fistful of braised pork and crumbles of nori make it taste a bit like *yakisoba*, rendered in taco form—but the Korean taco is dreadful, seasoned with rank kimchi and clumps of orange cheese. Choi's face contorts.

"You're kind of responsible for this, dude," I say.

"I probably am," he says. "And I'm not sure what to think."

Fish and Game

By Peter Barrett

From *Edible Manhattan*

Having himself ditched Brooklyn for a rural life in the Hudson Valley, painter and food writer Peter Barrett (acookblog.com) had special insight into why Manhattan chef Zak Pelaccio of Fatty Crab fame might choose to reinvent himself in a locavore's haven upstate.

Zak Pelaccio looks like someone you might see at a Phish concert: stocky, convivial, with a scruffy red beard and unruly curls spilling out from under a multicolored knit beanie. But that appearance belies extraordinary creative talent, the ability to speak in long, eloquent sentences, and a 10-year history of being well ahead of the culinary curve. He was cooking farm-to-table food before that was a thing, doing pan-Asian mashups with pork belly before David Chang popularized it and going deep with the complex, soulful funk of fermentation before any of those flavors made it into the mainstream.

Pelaccio, 39, gained real renown for cooking unpretentious Malaysian-influenced food back in 2005 when he opened Fatty Crab in the West Village. Not long after, he added Fatty 'Cue in Brooklyn, plus a Fatty Crab on the Upper West Side and another in the Virgin Islands. But as time passed, Pelaccio recognized that he required a greater level of independence: "There wasn't enough of me in there, ultimately," he says, noting that it took some soul-searching to resist the allure of becoming a celebrity chef. "Now I'm just a partner and occasional collaborator."

At the end of 2011, Pelaccio and his partner of seven years, Jori

Jayne Emde, moved upstate to a post-and-beam barn they renovated on property in Chatham that his parents bought in 2005. The move brought him closer to the farms he'd long worked with, and inspired his new restaurant venture, Fish & Game, slated to open in the town of Hudson just about the moment you read this.

Pelaccio's exotic preparations have always featured locally grown ingredients, but Fish & Game is more place-based than ever. A laminated map of the region, about five feet square, hangs on a wall outside the kitchen. A star in the middle marks Hudson, and there's a circle drawn around it: the 40-mile radius from within which almost all the food will be sourced.

"We're retraining ourselves to do very simple and exclusively product-driven, nose-to-tail food and create a regional cuisine," he says. "We're still going to buy citrus, and other things, but whatever we can get from this area we're going to use," he continues, eagerly poring over the map. "Without being preachy or full of ourselves about how it should be done, we're just doing it."

Off the Menu

Pelaccio's been sourcing from local farmers for a decade and now that he's their neighbor, he's been busy lining up agreements with Hudson Valley growers to grow ingredients for what he calls "very good home cooking," depending on what comes in the kitchen door each day. "It's a kind of improvising, free-associating based on the available ingredients and our experiences."

Diners have the choice of a short meal or a long one but there is no printed menu. Some dishes are large enough to share, and others are the size of little treats. And different tables will get different cuts of the same animal; since each pig has only one heart, only a few people a week might see strips of such a delicacy, quickly grilled and served with a sweet and sour sauce reminiscent of a dish that Pelaccio remembers fondly from Bangkok.

"Anybody who says they're cooking this way but they're doing 150 covers and everyone gets [pork] belly, they're full of shit," says Pelaccio. "It cannot happen. You might get some neck, and the next table might get shoulder. They may be prepared similarly, with the same accoutrements, or sauce, but the cut will be different." To diners who only like lamb rack or center-cut salmon fillet, he suggests, "Get over it."

As the crew breaks down a lamb from Wil-Hi Farms in nearby Tivoli, they treat each piece differently to see which preparations stand out. Each cut gets a distinct seasoning and then is vacuum-bagged and cooked *sous vide*. A rack of lamb ribs gets slathered in cooked rice spiked with coriander and chili and then is left to sit out at room temperature for a week to ferment before its final preparation.

Emde, 33, is slim, blonde and energetic, with a quick and contagious smile. "We met at Five Ninth," Emde remembers, referring to the Meatpacking District restaurant that preceded Fatty Crab, where Pelaccio was the chef. "He hit on me," she laughs. "It was awful."

That loving mockery is a hallmark of their longstanding relationship, and it extends to the whole group; these people clearly enjoy working together, and despite construction delays, spirits remain high. The mix of jokey familiarity and serious collaboration makes for an enviable work environment.

Ragging on Emde for using pricey Gegenbauer tomato vinegar to make a *gastrique*, a sweet and sour vinegar-based sauce, Pelaccio quips, "If you hadn't used it all, it would be really nice on the lamb."

"There's a little bit left," Emde, who functions as the "co-executive chef" but doesn't pay much mind to the title, playfully retorts. "You're an asshole. It made the best gastrique."

"A 60-dollar gastriquc," puts in chef de cuisine Kevin Pomplun.

"The gastrique would be great with lamb shoulder," Pelaccio concludes. All nod in agreement, and segue into a discussion of the best way to pickle lamb shanks.

While the cooking is clearly enjoyable, Emde acknowledges the tedious nature of much of the other work. "The reality shows don't give any idea. We spend so much time on the computer, on the phone." Indeed, general manager Scott Brenner and bar director Kat Dunn did not move from in front of their laptops all day until it was time for Dunn to work on a cocktail recipe. The first stab at a garnish, a slice of charred lemon hanging limply off the edge of the glass like soggy calamari, is not well received.

A long discussion ensues about how best to capture the flavor of burnt citrus, and the tradeoff between aesthetics and flavor. Pelaccio is insistent about the order of steps: "Char the zest, then steep the juice in it. If not for this, then for something else. We need to try everything, to establish a vocabulary."

Dunn says that, like the food, all of the cocktails are rigorously analyzed so the technique is flawless and consistently repeatable. "We ended up macerating the tequila sous vide with [citrus segments] and zest for 90 minutes at 160 degrees, which gave the best flavor. With every step, they ask 'How did you do it? Is there any other way to get a better result?' We tried each one six different ways, to see." She makes another, and Pelaccio says, "This one doesn't pop like the first one. Learning why is the most important thing."

Laying the Foundation

Fish & Game is named for the road where Patrick Milling Smith, Pelaccio and Emde's business partner (and producer of the Broadway version of *Once*), has his upstate home. "It seems fitting," says Emde, of the meaty cuisine.

The kitchen staff set up shop while Fish & Game was still a construction site, separated from the rest of the restaurant by zippered walls of construction plastic that shielded the dust (but not the cacophony of the construction, which fought with the music and the constant roar of the vent hood over the grill). The team originally planned for a 2012 fall opening, but construction delays pushed it into May; the kitchen has been built where there was once a driveway, behind the building, and excavation revealed the need for a foundation and steel supports that were not planned for. Pelaccio and Emde took the delays in stride; payroll still had to be met, but they were happy to be in the kitchen.

"We're anxious, but it's nice to be in here finally," Emde said back in February, patting the counter. A week later, they had to move out again; workers were spraying foam insulation, and the team had to decamp back to their home kitchens for a few days.

Running down the middle of the kitchen is a 16-foot-long island topped with a three-inch-thick rock maple butcher block. Overhead, mid-century light fixtures made of perforated yellow-painted metal bought at a vintage store in Philadelphia shine down on the work surface.

One corner is occupied by a large wood-fired oven built of recycled brick, with an adjustable grill grate alongside that raises and lowers with a big steel wheel on the side. Most food spends some time in or on the fire before it sees a plate. Besides the different meat cuts, the team did extensive sous-vide time and temperature tests for all sorts of vegetables so they can cook them ahead of time and then finish them in the wood oven for service, yielding a perfect balance between fire-roasted and al dente.

One of the first things they did upon arriving in the space was to unpack the rotary evaporator, a vacuum still that allows for creating intensely concentrated essences out of almost anything. In a vacuum, liquids boil below normal temperatures—even well below 200 degrees, depending on the pressure—so flavors can be released by gentle heating. Both the distilled extracts and the remaining reductions can be used, depending on the original product.

Early trials at the Fish & Game test kitchen included some of Emde's hard cider and ginger wine, and Old Overholt Rye, a venerable American whiskey. The rye reduction is for marinating livers for pâté: "You can get the flavor without the alcohol, which cooks it," Pelaccio explains. And while the cider did not excite, the ginger reduction made Emde shout in delight. The alcohol, boiled off and condensed in another vessel, was less interesting, but seemed well suited to becoming vinegar. Next up for extraction were borage and geranium leaves, grown by Old Field Farm in Greene County, one of several farms currently growing crops for the restaurant.

The day before, the group took apart a pig from Pigasso Farm in Copake, and they're treating each primal cut differently, exploring possibilities as they did with the lamb. One leg is cured for prosciutto: packed into salt in a plastic tub and lugged to the walk-in. The belly is cured for bacon, some ribs get rubbed and scored and put on the grill—low at first, fat down, then higher up, fat facing up so they baste slowly in the drippings. They stay on there all day. A small chop is quickly cooked in some rendered fat in the wood oven, and the result is as eloquent an argument for pastured meat as anyone could wish for.

The nose-to-tail ethos is visible all over the kitchen: pots of pork fat rendering, the pig skin simmering in water before being dehydrated and then deep fried. Bones, raw or roasted, make stock.

Finishing Touches

Pelaccio's relationship to food is instinctive and sensual. His book, published last year, is titled *Eat with Your Hands* (Ecco), and with good reason. Besides eating with them, he uses them constantly to cook: pushing lamb into a pan to brown the surface, turning ribs on the grill, snatching morsels from the pot of beans and ribs. He also hands food to people regularly to taste, always with a warm generous smile.

The clearest illustration of his touch came with a lamb shoulder. Rubbed lightly with salt and pepper, he browned it well in a large iron Staub Dutch oven, poured off the fat and threw in an onion, unpeeled and halved, a bisected head of garlic, carrot, celery and a few whole red chilies. Lidded, this went in the oven for hours—"at least four," he offers—and sat for a while next to the stove while various processes were discussed, decided and implemented. At one point he reached over and lowered the heat and afterward remarked, "That's the sort of thing you can't teach. I don't know why I did it just then, but I knew it needed it." Meltingly tender, deeply flavored and ostensibly easy, it was the center of the "family meal," a.k.a. staff dinner, that evening.

The following week, a different shoulder treatment—cooked sous vide and then finished in the wood oven, slick and tender and intensely fragrant with herbs—gets dunked in a fondue that chef Pomplun whipped up: heavy cream, grated sheep cheese and a glug of sherry. The rich, tangy sauce doubled down on the comfort food texture while offering a sharp, nutty counterpoint that amplified the meat flavors to extraordinary effect. The fermented lamb ribs, now a week old, come out of the combi oven, where they have steamed for hours, and get finished on the grill. A few go in the oven to see if it makes a difference. They're seriously funky, almost cheesy, but not quite complete.

Pelaccio whisks a bit of lemon juice and oil into the steaming juices, dunks in a rib, and the meat is suddenly in sharp, delectable focus: finished.

"I would probably just serve a few of these on a plate with the vinaigrette and some herbs," he says, when asked about presentation. A deceptively simple dish, since by the time the ribs reach the diner they will have undergone fermentation and two or three cooking methods.

The plates for Fish & Game were thrown by a friend in Amagansett, in food-flattering white and off-white. "They have energy to them; they're very cool," says Pelaccio. Until the flatware was delivered, the kitchen staff ate with their hands.

As winter softens into spring, more vegetables arrive, both as overwintered roots and new sprouts, and the kitchen staff is visibly thrilled. A few weeks before opening, Emde is at work making "abacus beads," sticky dumplings that look like fat orechiette, but out of fresh-dug parsnips instead of the traditional taro root. A delivery of baby greens from Common Hands Farm comes in–mizuna, radishes and a spicy mix–and she eagerly tastes them, grabbing more to toss with the beads and the ground pork sizzling on the flat top. Chef Pomplun is working on a milk-poached salsify dish, finished in the wood oven, with brown butter and hazelnuts and a generous strewing of sunflower sprouts and red-veined sorrel. A loaf of his brioche, a golden cloud of butter and egg with just enough flour to give it shape, sits on the end of the counter with a knife nearby, steadily getting shorter as the day lengthens.

Emde also makes leeks, roasted in the hot ashes at the edge of the fire, then peeled and dressed with anchovy vinaigrette and salt-cured egg yolks shaved thin like bottarga. Pelaccio bangs out a spontaneous combination of olive oil cake, candied carrots, and fresh cheese that tastes at once ancient and modern: simple flavors, but straddling the sweet/savory line in a contemporary fashion. While some dishes, like the salsify, are firmly codified, it's still only temporary; all the combinations are subject to change as the seasons progress and the ingredients shift. That adaptability is the governing principle of the place.

The dynamic here seems like a band rehearsing for a gig; Pelaccio is the clear leader, but everyone's input is expected, even encouraged.

"In the past, I would collaborate, but mostly I had ideas and people executed them. Now I sort of hang back; I want them to stretch their legs and find their own voices. Jori and I have been cooking together for years, and a lot of what I was doing came from her." Emde is a prodigious preserver; jars of vivid vegetable pickles line shelves over the counter, vinegar ferments in carboys on the floor, and homemade Cynar ages in oak barrels under a table. The couple tends a large garden in Chatham where they grow food for themselves and the restaurant, and they plan to expand it. Fermentation in all its forms will be an ongoing process, and the various preserved foods will find their way into many dishes. The large I-beam over the opening into the dining room serves as a shelf for quickly multiplying jars of condiments.

Reflecting on their decision to try a new, highly personal approach to cooking, a hybrid of high-end refinement and down-home accessibility, Pelaccio returns to the reason he opted out of the franchise model.

"Good cooking takes time, it takes love and attention. A lot of the restaurant business is not like that. But you are in a service industry, and your job is to make people happy."

Emde comes over; she wants to make a vitello tonnato–type thing but with lamb belly and anchovy, using her homemade Worcestershire sauce. Everyone weighs in with possible permutations, ideas fly. Pelaccio pauses. "Fuck it—let's just cook Asian food." Emde responds: "You'd make everybody happy."

Pelaccio smiles. "Yeah, except the people in this room."

His Saving Grace

By Kevin Pang

From *The Chicago Tribune*

Trib features reporter Kevin Pang usually deploys his wicked wit writing about pop culture, comedy, and the cheap-eats end of food. After a notable 2011 story of a bad-boy chef going off the rails, however, Pang dug in to profile another chef, whose quest for redemption might have a happier ending.

It was the most important night of his career. Curtis Duffy hovered over plates inside the gleaming white kitchen of his new restaurant, Grace. Head down, with the poker face that was the 37-year-old's default demeanor, he arranged long celery curls, ricotta and fried sunchokes into a three-dimensional wreath resembling the architecture of Antoni Gaudi.

The lock on the glass front door was unbolted, and the first customers walked through.

Finally. The restaurant was supposed to have opened in March. It was now December. The equipment that arrived broken, the delays, the cost overruns—all of it had turned many of his nights sleepless. But so did the pressures of high expectations. Curtis had worked his way up through the finest restaurants in Chicago—Charlie Trotter's, Trio, Alinea—and earned four-star reviews under his name at Avenues in The Peninsula hotel on the Magnificent Mile. But this restaurant, Grace, was his.

What would customers think? How would food critics react? What if the restaurant was a failure? The hypotheticals lingered, but on this December night, the what-ifs became secondary.

He was mostly anxious about the 9:30 p.m. reservation.

It was booked for Ruth Snider. In many respects, she was the woman who had saved Curtis. She steered him at a time his life felt aimless, back when he stole from supermarkets and bullied kids in his neighborhood. She kept an eye on him during his travails, through family turmoil . . . before and after the murder. They cried on the phone with each other.

This is a story of the small-town kid who proved himself in the big city. Of connections forged and lost on the path to becoming the best—no matter the cost. Of closing your eyes and hoping your problems disappear.

It's a story of a chef, and what cooking gave him and what it took away.

Mostly it's a story about family.

While the glitterati and food critics in attendance on opening night snapped pictures of the food on their tables, Curtis Duffy focused on Snider, the middle school teacher who—in a way she's too modest to take credit for—helped make Grace possible.

Curtis could've booked her reservation at an earlier time. But he chose 9:30 p.m., the last table of the night, when they could have the whole restaurant to themselves. There was something he had to tell her.

Runaway

Running away was the easy solution. Curtis did so every few months from his Colorado home, over the injustices imposed on a 10-year-old boy: getting grounded, or having toys taken away. One day, Curtis announced he was leaving the family—this time, *forever*. But Jan Duffy called her son's bluff.

"Let me help you pack," she said. "We'll go to the supermarket and pick up some food for you."

He stewed in the front seat of his mom's car, and got as far as the supermarket parking lot. It ended with a contrite Curtis in his mother's embrace. She turned the car around. Looking back, the message stung. You can never really run away. Some problems will always follow you, even when you're old enough to have children of your own. Even then, there is no running away from what you are.

A couple of years later, in 1987, when Curtis was 12, his father, Robert "Bear" Duffy, gathered his wife and three kids for a family meeting. "We're moving to Ohio," Bear said. No warning, no time to reason or argue. The Duffys would leave Colorado Springs in two weeks.

In Colorado, Curtis had his skateboard, his friends, his own bedroom, a big backyard to run around. Why leave?

Bear, a Vietnam War veteran given his nickname by his biker friends, pulled in decent money at his father-in-law's tire retreading company. He'd been under the impression the business would go to him when his father-in-law retired. Instead, the company was sold to someone else. Bear was devastated, family members said. They believed Bear saw a convenient escape: Move closer to his family near Columbus. And so his decision was final. There was no talking Bear out of anything.

What had been a steady job in Colorado Springs became a string of odd jobs in Johnstown, Ohio, 30 minutes outside Columbus: a lawn mower repair shop, a tattoo parlor, whatever garage that would spare a few dollars for him. At one point, he was even an officer in the town's small police force. Jan found steady work at a supermarket. Still, the Duffys went from a five-bedroom house in Colorado to a two-bedroom apartment in Johnstown. There weren't enough beds for Curtis to claim one, so for a while he slept on the floor of a walk-in closet.

Curtis felt trapped in a small town, wearing out the tape on his speed-metal cassettes, prone to bursts of rage. He and his older brother, Robert Jr., went out looking for fights.

"My brother and I weren't the easiest kids," Curtis said. "We were bored out of our minds."

(Attempts to reach Robert Jr. for this story were unsuccessful.)

Around Johnstown, everyone knew Robert Jr. as "Tig," short for tiger, all paunch and brawn. Curtis was "Bones," tall, lean, a tough shell. The Duffy boys made an intimidating tag team. They used fists, hammers, even their skulls as weapons, Curtis said: One time he pummeled a kid's face so badly the boy was later fitted with braces.

Curtis got an after-school job stocking shelves at the local Kroger supermarket and quickly hatched a scheme for more money: He stashed a case—dozens of cartons—of Marlboro cigarettes in a garbage can and planned to retrieve it after-hours, then sell the cigarettes to friends. An inventory check revealed the missing case, which was easily traced back to one Curtis Lee Duffy. Stealing that many cigarettes was considered a felony, but the store manager decided against pressing charges. If Curtis' uncle weren't also a cop who turned a blind eye at his nephew's indiscretions, Curtis surely would have landed in jail.

School? If he felt motivated, Curtis said, he'd work for a C. The thought of home economics class was even less palatable, especially when it was mandatory for all sixth-graders. There Curtis sat, choosing a table as far back as possible in Room 12 of Adams Middle School.

And that is where the switch flipped for him, the filament glowed and the bulb flickered on. All it took was a word: Something something . . . yada yada . . . *pizza*.

His teacher, Ruth Snider, knew what to say to middle school boys who thought only girls cooked or sewed. It was an attitude she had seen in many other adolescent boys with machismo to burn.

In her first lesson, Snider promised the officially sanctioned food of 12-year-olds.

By the end of that 45-minute class, Curtis had punched out circles of Pillsbury biscuit dough, slathered on spaghetti sauce, slapped on discs of pepperoni and covered it all with cheese. Cooking provided something lacking in Curtis, he'd later realize: a sense of ownership and control, an illustration of cause and effect. Get your hands in the dough, give a damn about something, and watch results bubbling from the oven 12 minutes later.

Snider witnessed the transformation. In Curtis she saw a boy who put on a hard exterior but behind it was sullen and painfully shy, a student still adjusting from being uprooted. He was all nervous tics, fingers constantly inside his mouth, nails emerging chewed down, arms crossed in a defensive posture. But with every fruit kabob skewered and every cinnamon roll baked, Snider watched his veneer crack, slowly, then in large pieces, until the boy felt safe in the classroom kitchen. Now Curtis actually *looked forward* to coming to school.

"He saw adults as the enemy, not sure who to trust on the outside," Snider said. "I know he trusted me."

On the first day of seventh grade, with home economics no longer mandatory, Curtis walked into Room 12 on his own. And in eighth grade, he took Snider's class a third straight year.

Snider had seen thousands of kids pass through her classroom since she'd begun teaching in 1973. Most she never heard from again. But Curtis . . . something about the sadness in his brown eyes. She knew his history. She knew others around town whispered about his family. In Johnstown, population 3,200, gossip traveled with the wind. Even after Curtis left her classroom, she vowed to keep tabs on him.

His cooking fuse lit, Curtis begged for a job at a local diner called Ohio Restaurant #2, the greasy spoon on Main Street people in town called "The Greeks." The boy was now 14. After baseball and wrestling practice, Curtis went there and washed dishes for four hours, and was paid $15 cash.

Menial tasks became a game to him, and a game was something into which he could channel his angst. He'd rush through washing dishes for the chance to prep food for the next day's service. Even in peeling boiled potatoes, Curtis sought to remove the skin in a single unbroken coil, mesmerized by the challenge. Submitting himself to the kitchen diverted him—from fighting out of boredom, from stealing for the thrill. From listening to his parents' latest screaming match.

Bear and Jan fought with increasing regularity; she'd discovered he was cheating on her. And money, too, was always an issue. Bear was a bear of a man, with tattoos for sleeves and an intimidating chest-length beard to go with his shoulder-length hair. He had been a Golden Gloves boxer in his youth, and now when rage seeped to the surface, he had no problems getting physical with his wife. In 1989 he pleaded no contest to domestic violence charges and was ordered to undergo alcohol and family counseling after he punched Jan in the chest and mouth. Jan wouldn't retreat—Trisha Duffy, Curtis' younger sister, remembers her mom punching back. The family's splintering seemed irreparable.

Curtis, meanwhile, kept running away to the kitchen.

His high school cooking teacher, Kathy Zay, connected him with her restaurant-industry contacts. Curtis took a job at a country club in New Albany, an affluent Columbus suburb, that altered his concept of food. It wasn't just that wealthier patrons dined on fancier food; rather, it was the idea of cooking as a form of self-expression. Bear was a tattoo artist, and Curtis believed his father had passed down an artistic gene.

At New Albany Country Club, Curtis' job title was dishwasher, but he also learned the one skill every chef must master to succeed: how to properly hold a knife. The key was finding that center of balance—or else you risked hurting yourself.

From one kitchen to the next, each more prestigious than the last, Curtis' bosses entrusted him with more responsibilities. Yet even as he found a job at age 16 cooking at greater Columbus' most exclusive golf club—Muirfield Village in Dublin, Ohio, its 18-hole course designed by Jack Nicklaus—not once did his parents dine where he worked. It was as if Curtis led two lives separated by 25 miles: one catering to the rich, where a set of golf clubs costs more than several months' rent, and the other, where fast-food clerk was a career choice for some neighborhood friends. He chose to live in the former.

He was devastated that Trisha, then 15, got pregnant. Rather than confront the news, Curtis stopped talking to her. Focus hard enough on cooking, he thought, and maybe you can block out everything else.

Amid the tumult, came one happy moment: the first time he cooked for his parents. For those few hours, the blame game between Bear and Jan ceased. Curtis, having watched a line cook at Muirfield Village prepare penne alla arrabiata hundreds of times, improvised at home with tomatoes, garlic, black olives and red chilies. He approximated, tasted, tweaked and tried again. It made so much sense to him. This was cooking: a subjective, intuitive art with no right or wrong way. That night his parents found common ground: They were astounded by their son's cooking.

"It was the first time I cooked something I was proud of . . . " Curtis said, pausing, "and the only time my parents ate something I made."

Any residual goodwill from the homemade dinner quickly disappeared. The fighting between Jan and Bear intensified, and so too did Curtis' focus. He moved into an apartment with his best friend and wrestling partner, Tony Kuehner. When he wasn't cooking at the country club, he entered culinary competitions through his vocational high school and smoked the field. In a competition staged by the Family, Career and Community Leaders of America in 1994, he carved a floral centerpiece from cantaloupes, pineapple and honeydew in 25 minutes and took first place in his category in the state.

Around the same time, in spring 1994, the fighting finally broke Jan Duffy down. She had had enough. By then, Bear and Jan were living in St. Louisville, a 30-minute, country-road drive from Johnstown. She moved out, filed for divorce and took Trisha with her to an apartment back in Johnstown.

Curtis, Trisha and court documents paint a picture of a man desperate to win his wife back in the months that followed. Thinking that getting in shape would show his commitment, Bear took to the gym and in four months shed nearly 100 pounds. He tried sleeping pills and an antidepressant; he thought they would stifle the rage. When that didn't have the desired effect, he quit cold turkey, but cutting off the medication so suddenly did more harm than good.

Paranoia consumed him. Bear found out Jan's boss at the supermarket was hitting on her. So he showed up at her workplace unannounced. Although he had left the police department years ago, Bear used his old equipment to tap her phone.

On April 29, 1994, Jan Duffy filed a civil protection order—one step up from a restraining order—in the Licking County (Ohio) Common Pleas Court. It barred Bear from contacting Jan by phone, or entering her home or place of employment. The order also called for Bear to turn in all his guns to the sheriff's department. WBNS-TV, a local news station in Columbus, reported that in a July 21 court hearing, Bear told the judge he "would never hurt his wife."

On Monday, Sept. 12, 1994, the day of the Duffys' 18th wedding anniversary, Bear tried saving his shambling marriage one last time. He showed up at Jan's apartment door unannounced at 6 a.m. with a card and a rose. He pleaded. A family friend would later tell *The Advocate* newspaper of Newark, Ohio, that Bear said to Jan: "Till death do us part, baby." But Jan said it was over.

Trisha was awakened by the screech of her father's car peeling away.

That morning in central Ohio was warm for September. The top local story splashed across the front page of the newspaper: "New City Engineer To Update Computers."

Thirty-seven-year-old Jan Marlene Duffy left for work at the supermarket.

Seventeen-year-old Trisha Ann Duffy readied for Mrs. Sommers' English class at Johnstown High School.

Twenty-year-old Robert Burne "Tig" Duffy planned on stopping by his father's house.

Nineteen-year-old Curtis Lee Duffy studied in his apartment on his day off from work.

Thirty-nine-year-old Robert Earl "Bear" Duffy switched to Plan B.

September 12, 1994

At 12:15 p.m., Jan and a co-worker crossed the parking lot from Kroger, where they worked, to a McDonald's for lunch. In the back lot, Bear waited inside a two-door brown sedan.

He pulled up next to them, brandishing a carbine rifle. He told the co-worker to run away. He threatened to shoot his wife if she didn't get in the car.

Curtis had a day off from cooking at Muirfield Village Golf Club, so he studied for his Columbus State Community College culinary classes. He and his brother had made plans to visit their father that day, but Curtis had so much homework he decided to stay home instead. He would study until his girlfriend Nikki Davis, a senior at Johnstown High, came to visit after school.

Nikki and Trisha were sitting in the same English class when Trisha was summoned to the principal's office, where a police officer and Jan's supermarket co-worker waited for her. The co-worker, still shellshocked, explained what had happened. The officer said Trisha had to come with him now.

Bear's car hurtled east toward St. Louisville, 18 miles away, to the home where he and Jan had lived until she'd moved out months earlier with Trisha. He'd already disengaged the locks and removed the door handles.

When they arrived, he made Jan call her mother in Colorado and relay a message: Don't get the cops involved. Jan's mother called the Licking County Sheriff's Department anyway, and soon sirens converged at 8146 Horns Hill Road.

Nikki rushed over to Curtis' apartment and asked if he had heard what was going on. He hadn't. Not long afterward, police knocked on the door. "We have to go now," the officer told Curtis.

By the time police arrived at Horns Hill Road, Bear's sister Penny Duffy was already pacing in front of the house with an envelope of handwritten notes that Bear had dropped off at her workplace after leaving Jan's apartment. Penny hoped to reason with him through the window.

Two hours passed. Bear kept telling officers he was giving himself up.

Four hours. Bear told his sister Penny there was no way he was going to prison like their father. "You know what they do to ex-cops in there?" Bear said.

Six hours. Bear prayed with Penny and reminisced about their childhood.

Eight hours. He said, "There's no way out of this."

The chronology of what happened next differs between police and an eyewitness. According to a sheriff's narrative of the incident, at 10:45 p.m. the sheriff's department heard a gunshot, at which point a half-dozen officers stormed into the house with battering rams and flash-bang grenades.

But Penny didn't believe it was a gunshot that triggered the raid. She said it was Bear unlocking the deadbolt from the master bedroom to the backyard and the audio surveillance unit picking up an amplified noise—what police thought was a bang. She said that was when they went in and Bear panicked, firing his gun.

This much was clear: He shot Jan once through the chest. He placed her on the water bed, lay next to his wife and fired a single bullet that pierced his heart and right lung. Water slowly drained from the mattress.

He was dead. Jan, though, had a faint pulse when paramedics rushed her to an ambulance.

Curtis was several houses away and under police protection when he heard the tear gas shells fired into the house. In the noise and confusion, Curtis recalled, an hour passed before he received any information about his mother. He thought he heard that she was being treated at nearby Licking Memorial Hospital. He pleaded with his girlfriend's family for a ride.

"I need to see my mom."

"I'm sorry, Curt," his girlfriend's mother told him. "She died at the hospital."

Days bled into nights. Sleep proved impossible. The next thing Curtis knew, he was standing at his father's funeral in Newark, Ohio. Many of Bear's biker friends showed up. No one from Jan's family attended.

Ruth Snider, the home economics teacher who inspired Curtis to cook, was there too. She noticed the thick, dark rings under Curtis' eyes. "He looked like he was in a dream state," Snider said. "Curtis hadn't grasped the severity of it yet."

She handed him a letter she had written, telling him: "You are not alone."

Jan's family wanted a separate funeral for her in Colorado. Curtis and his two siblings didn't have money for plane tickets, so they said goodbye in an impromptu gathering at a funeral home in Ohio.

There wasn't even a coffin—Jan Duffy's body lay on a gurney beneath a white sheet. Curtis' sister, Trisha, reached out and touched her mother's cold skin. "She has goose bumps!" Trisha said aloud. Curtis stood catatonic. He lifted the sheet and saw the bruises, the gunshot wound in the chest. And then his mother's body was wheeled away and taken to an airport. Some weeks later, a relative mailed Curtis photos from his mother's funeral.

What Curtis remembers most about that time was the morning after his parents died. He, his brother and his best friend went back to Bear's house to collect his father's belongings.

The remnants of tear gas burned his eyes. He navigated around glass shards from blown-out windows, a T-shirt shielding his nose and mouth.

In one room, Curtis found a blue spiral-bound notebook. He recognized the cursive on the page immediately from the distinctive, swooping "G's." For such a rugged man, Bear's handwriting was all soft curves, elegant and graceful.

The notebook contained letters Bear had written to family members. It was dated six months earlier. Bear had addressed a page each to his daughter, Trisha, his son Robert Jr., his wife, Jan—before she had filed for divorce. But no words followed for them.

The only person Bear wrote a full letter to was Curtis—two pages, single-spaced. The message Bear left behind was prescient, as if warning exactly how Curtis' future would unfold.

> Curt,
> This is dad . . .

> Slowly Curtis re-entered the world, and he seized upon the one stable thing in his life: the kitchen. When he'd first started cooking five years earlier, the kitchen was a place to run away to from the fighting at home, a place that kept him from bullying neighborhood kids.

Now his parents were dead. Every hour focused on cooking was another hour not dealing with his confusion and anger. He dreaded the end of the shift. While other chefs at Muirfield Village Golf Club went out for drinks afterward, Curtis stayed in the head chef's office and dived into the cookbooks. One of those, a new addition to the library, caught Curtis' eye: an oversize burgundy-colored volume by a Chicago chef named Charlie Trotter. That name would stay with him.

In the moments he surfaced for air, Curtis took off in his Jeep with no particular destination, drowning out the whys with the radio's machine-gun guitar riffs and crashing cymbals.

Like his father, Curtis had an idea for a convenient escape. He could leave Johnstown, make the 20-hour car ride back to Colorado. He told best friend Tony Kuehner, "Let's go." They had one chance to change everything.

When they arrived, Curtis and Tony visited the mausoleum in Colorado Springs where Jan was interred.

Years earlier, Jan had sat Curtis down on the living room floor. She had something important to tell him. His real mother left Bear, Robert Jr. and Curtis when he was 6 months old. You're not my biological son, Jan said, but I love you all the same. Curtis cried all night—not out of anger or betrayal, but for fear of never seeing her again. Jan assured her son: I will always be there.

The best friends also went in search of Bear's ashes, which had been sent to Colorado. Curtis was told his father's ashes were scattered on

Pikes Peak, beneath a pine with a wooden cross on it, and they drove up the mountain looking for it. Curtis stared at the photograph of the tree from all angles, then scanned the snow-blanketed tableau. They never found it.

"I was looking for that reconnection," Curtis said, "to have that quiet moment and reflect and say a few words."

After coming down from the mountain, Curtis and Tony were dining at a pizza parlor when the Harry Chapin song "Cat's in the Cradle" started playing.

> When you comin' home, son, I don't know when,
> But we'll get together then, dad,
> You know we'll have a good time then.

It was a song Bear and Curtis had listened to together. Curtis broke down. This was the man who had killed his mother.

In the end, running away to Colorado didn't provide solace. The kitchen jobs paid poorly, and Tony wasn't thrilled with washing dishes. A standing offer from Muirfield Village Golf Club, however, remained. Any time Curtis wanted to come back, there was a job waiting for him. After four months, he and Tony loaded their cars and headed back to Ohio.

His home economics teacher, Ruth Snider, was there for him. The two spoke on the phone often, and in each conversation they let their guards drop lower. "Every time I iron my jacket or sew a button, it reminds me of you," Curtis told her. Eventually, he felt safe enough to cry when they talked. The subjects of conversations were irrelevant; it mattered to him that she listened.

Meanwhile, there was someone at work. He'd been eyeing the server with the flowing brown hair. Curtis learned her name: Kim Becker. She could sing opera and play the violin. After he'd stockpiled enough nerve to make conversation, he said, "You know, maybe one day I'll become the lead singer of a band."

"Sure," he said she told him, "as long as I can give you singing lessons."

Others at Muirfield Village recognized the signs of a blossoming romance. A co-worker organized a dinner at his home and invited Curtis and Kim. The evening felt effortless. They laughed together over great food and pours of wine. His hunch grew over weeks and months, and when it passed the point of certainty, Curtis whispered to a fellow cook, "I'm going to marry that girl one day." Three years later, halfway up Pikes Peak next to a fallen tree, Curtis got down on one knee and asked Kim to make it official. (Attempts to reach her for this story were unsuccessful.)

Gradually, Curtis' ties with his Johnstown past faded away. More time passed between phone calls to Trisha and his brother, Robert Jr., until they barely spoke at all. Curtis was making $80,000 a year at age 24 as chef de cuisine at Tartan Fields Golf Club in Dublin, Ohio. But he equated small-town life with small-town ambitions. The good pay meant nothing if the challenge wasn't there.

"If my priorities stayed in that town, that's where I would be. But I've always wanted something greater than that place."

Remembering the burgundy cookbook at Muirfield Village, he drove to Charlie Trotter's restaurant in Chicago to volunteer his services for a few weeks. He returned to Ohio humbled. Curtis thought the recipes described in the cookbook were conceptual dishes meant to inspire and provoke. Trotter was actually *serving* those dishes to guests nightly. He had to move to Chicago.

In January 2000, Curtis spent his "Goodbye, Columbus" dinner with—who else?—Ruth Snider. They dined on steaks and offered the obligatory farewell sentiments: Let's keep in touch. . . . Call any time. . . . Don't be a stranger. But at some point during the night, the words "I love you" tumbled out for the first time, him to her, her back in response, natural as an exhale, and it solidified what they knew to be true. Curtis was the son Ruth had never had, and Ruth the mother Curtis had now.

Ascent

Sure, workdays at Charlie Trotter's lasted 14 hours, six days a week, the paycheck was a pittance, and he was fulfilling someone else's grand culinary vision. But Curtis was surrounded by like-minded kitchen grunts, uncompromising in their collective desire to become the best. Not the best in Chicago, but *the best*, full stop. Entry-level cooks traded an $18,000-a-year salary for Trotter's name on their resumes.

In 2003, Curtis went for a meal at the since-closed Evanston restaurant Trio, where a young chef named Grant Achatz—just 15 months Curtis' senior—was making noise with his avant-garde interpretation of fine dining. Achatz remembered that night: This cook from Trotter's kitchen was dining with him, and whenever someone from a competing restaurant visited, he made sure to serve a meal that said, in no uncertain terms: *You're not employed at the best restaurant in town.*

After that dinner, Curtis was sold. On a day off from Trotter's, he spent time in Trio's kitchen as a tryout. After seeing Curtis in his kitchen, Achatz told him:

"You don't need to work here. You should be doing your own thing."

"But I want to work for you," Curtis said.

"Well, I can only pay you $16,000 a year."

"Fine."

At Trio, Curtis ascended from the cold foods station to head pastry chef, becoming one of Achatz's top deputies. The two spoke a common language without uttering a word. Both were quiet figures amid the noise of the kitchen, and when they did converse, it was about the new cuisine emerging from Spain, or the burgeoning usage of laboratory science as a cooking technique. It was a workplace where "No" was no match for "Sure, let's try it."

When Achatz left Trio to open Alinea in 2005—a restaurant that *Gourmet* magazine would soon deem the best in America—he tapped Curtis as chef de cuisine, his right-hand man.

Curtis' career took on the momentum of a wheel rolling downhill. Faster. Better. More. To lead such an ambitious kitchen, 90-hour workweeks became the norm. Nights, holidays and weekends took Curtis away from home. He'd return from work to find his wife already asleep for hours. Many nights, fear kept him awake: fear of failure, fear of slowing his forward momentum, fear of being second-best.

Then, midflight in his meteoric rise: Kim was expecting their first child. He wished for a son to play baseball with and ride motorcycles together, as Curtis had with his father. But the Duffys were bestowed a daughter, Ava Leigh, and when she clutched her father's pinky finger in the hospital room, Curtis' eyes welled up. Everything would be for her. And when daughter Eden arrived three years after Ava, Curtis felt whole in a way he hadn't since his Colorado childhood.

His family was intact. He thought back to his Johnstown years: My daughters will not sleep on the floor of a closet.

Curtis left Alinea after three years to make a name for himself. His goal of becoming one of the best chefs in the country was, he said, as much about personal validation as providing his family financial security. Curtis took on the top position at Avenues, a restaurant in The Peninsula hotel on Michigan Avenue where dinner for two cost $700.

Finally, he could showcase his food, and his good name would rise and fall with the restaurant's successes and failures. He assembled a team that had to jell quickly in the tight confines of Avenues' kitchen, and members of the Avenues family spent more time together than with their actual families.

On the day the Chicago Michelin Guide was unveiled in 2010, the Avenues team gathered in a suite at The Peninsula. Curtis knew the restaurant was receiving prestigious stars in the international guidebook; the question was how many. The call came to Curtis' cellphone, and a man speaking in a French accent congratulated Avenues on winning two Michelin stars. Only two other restaurants in the city received that honor—one of which was Charlie Trotter's. Alinea and L20 received the highest rating that year, three stars. In the hotel suite, the Avenues staff burst into applause and champagne overflowed.

"I must forge ahead," Curtis told himself. "I want that third Michelin star."

He had always worked for someone else. He needed to become his own boss. This was the moment he'd worked for all his life: to become chef and owner of his own restaurant.

Work harder. Push further. Stay that extra hour.

"What about us?" he said his wife asked him. "Nothing's ever good enough. It's always more and more and more. A second restaurant. A cookbook. When will it be about our family? I can't . . . "

Kim had moved to Chicago not knowing anyone who lived here, he said. She'd made that sacrifice for her husband's career. At last, Curtis saw his selfishness.

"You try to look for that balance in your day-to-day life. (You say) 'I hope and pray that when I get to that point, people will still want to be around me,'" Curtis said.

When he was a teenager, Curtis learned that the key to properly holding a knife was finding the point of balance. At that age, he didn't realize it would become a metaphor.

The kitchen was a place to run away from the chaos of his original family, and it had driven him to pursue a goal. That pursuit ultimately cost him another family—and his 11-year marriage.

"Opening my own restaurant is supposed to be the greatest moment of my career," Curtis said. "And it's happening at the worst moment of my personal life."

It took many years to arrive at a place of forgiveness, but Curtis has found that place with his father, insomuch as anyone could with someone who killed his mother. Still, moments of hatred toward his dad surfaced—Bear, for instance, got in his goodbyes without giving Jan the same opportunity. Curtis thought: What a selfish act. But the anger subsides, because love for his parents never goes away.

Once in a while, in his garden apartment a few blocks west of where Kim and their daughters live, Curtis revisits the blue spiral-bound notebook he found at his father's house the morning after his parents died.

Bear addressed each page to a different member of his family. But there was nothing written on them, except for one. The only letter Bear wrote in the notebook was to Curtis.

> 3/1/1994
>
> Curt,
>
> This is dad. I'm telling you from my heart that you're a very special young man and I wish I could tell you how proud of you I am . . . You'll be a great chef, no doubt in my mind, you'll be one of the best in the world some day . . .
>
> Your life is just beginning. Try to do all the right things in it. Make sure if you ever get married and have children, that you show them and your wife all the love in the world. Always take time to be with them and show them love. Your wife should be shown the most love of all. Always take the time to talk to her and hear what she has to say because she'll be the most important person in your life . . .
>
> I ask you, Curt, to look back and see how many wrong

things you have seen me do, and please don't walk in my footsteps because you'll be in a world of pain, hate, and sure won't be loved and won't be able to show love. So please be a better person than I was. I know you can . . .

Remember I love you, son, and always will.

My love,
Your dad

Tomorrow

When Curtis was still at Avenues, he became a name in the city, and diners started asking for autographs. He pondered what to write. Eventually he signed all menus this way: "It's all about grace."

The word "grace" rolled off his tongue, effortless and soft. He saw it defined in his cooking style—elegant, delicate, the rock 'n' roll celebrity TV chef-antithesis. Curtis favored light over heavy in his food, seldom using butter or cream. At Avenues, half his menu was vegetarian.

"Grace" was also something he found working behind the hot stove. The significance didn't escape Curtis. The word resonated so much he named his younger daughter Eden Grace.

"If I ever owned a restaurant," he told himself, "it will be called Grace."

His wine director at Avenues, Michael Muser, was a man with the opposite personality: boisterous, ebullient, not above pulling practical jokes on strangers. But the two became fast friends over a shared love of motorcycles, cigars and fine wine, and they decided to become business partners.

The two found an Avenues regular—a real estate man named Mike Olszewski—who agreed to help bankroll their dream: to operate the best restaurant in the country, uttered in the same breath as heavyweights The French Laundry and Alinea. They began by leasing an old frame shop in the West Loop, near restaurant neighbors Girl & The Goat, Next and Blackbird.

When Curtis announced he was leaving Avenues in July 2011, he set a goal of opening by the following March. But building a restaurant proved different from composing a menu.

If he planned to charge $250 a person for dinner, then every detail had to be thought out. And every detail strained the budget. An Internet router. Paper clips. Light fixtures in the bathroom. They thought about getting trays on the table that would accommodate a diner's cellphone.

If there were disagreements among the three partners, they typically fell along this line: "Do we buy the best version of what we need, or should we be cost efficient?" Muser, for instance, wanted horseshoe-shaped white leather chairs in the dining room that cost $2,300 each. Curtis told him he was crazy. Eventually they decided those chairs were the most comfortable, and they talked the dealer down to a discounted price of $1,000 each.

Curtis' cooking was the sort of intricately plated food to be consumed in six bites or fewer–just enough before the palate, mentally, becomes numb to the same flavor. "You want diners to say, 'I wish I had one more piece of Wagyu beef, one more piece of salmon," Curtis said. "You want them to not have *just enough* of a dish; you want them to crave for one more bite."

So the plateware, Curtis decided, should act as more than serving vessels and actually enhance the taste of a dish, even if just in the mind. A chestnut puree's creamy texture might be accentuated, he reasoned, if it was served in a bowl with no edges. He ordered curved bowls from France that resembled overinflated inner tubes.

Another idea was serving a dish inside an edible tube made of flavored ice; the diner would crack the tube with the side of a spoon to reveal what was inside. Curtis visited the Chicago School of Mold Making in Oak Park to collaborate on a custom silicone canister that could freeze water into a tube in 45 minutes.

The plates alone cost more than $60,000. An all-granite-countertop kitchen equipped with the ovens and fridges needed would cost $500,000 more. In all, the partners said, to build Grace from an empty concrete shell cost $2.5 million.

As at Avenues, Curtis planned two menus of 10 courses each, one meat-based, the other mostly vegetarian. Labeling his cooking as a specific cuisine is futile–"progressive American," if one prefers pithiness, though obscure ingredients such as *sudachi* (a green citrus fruit from Japan) or Queensland blue squash are centerpieces of dishes. When Curtis brainstorms dish concepts, it's a free-form exercise with pen and paper. After many years, he's developed a "mind's palate"–Curtis could name three disparate flavors and, in his head, know exactly how they'd taste together. In his sketch pad,

Curtis would jot down a main ingredient to anchor a dish. Then he'd scribble off supporting ingredients that might pair well, or, if it's the effect he's seeking, clash in a palatable manner. His notebook is like a casting director's clipboard: a long list of candidates, whittled down to achieve on-plate chemistry.

While Curtis and his culinary team focused on food, every passing day at the Randolph Street space brought a new set of problems. Sheets of glass arrived cracked. The kitchen ventilation hood came in the wrong size. Construction crews checked out by 3 p.m. most days. No surprise, Curtis and his partners blew past the proposed March opening date, and delays would push it back to April, then June, then August. September came, and the kitchen wasn't even installed.

Then October. And November.

Curtis' frustration was visible. He'd lifted weights at 4 a.m. every morning—now he didn't have time for it and began gaining weight. Hairs above his ears turned gray in greater numbers.

But slowly, surely, exasperatingly, the blond-wood millwork walls and frosted windows and glass pendant lamps were put up, 64 white leather chairs were placed in the dining room, and by December, Grace restaurant went from figment in Curtis' mind to reality.

Industry friends were invited in for a series of three practice dinners. Even these test runs required 14-hour workdays. By the end of practice night No. 3, the waitstaff walked with chin up and upright posture. They had passed all the written tests on ingredients, wine pairings and related allergies. Cooks, meanwhile, achieved their goal of five minutes between an empty plate taken away and arrival of the next course. Behind the glass-enclosed kitchen, dinner service was an exacting, choreographed dance invisible to customers.

On Dec. 11, Grace opened its door to the public at last. Curtis got his usual three hours of sleep. If he was excited, there was no outward sign of it—long ago he had learned to keep his head down and focus on the task.

He knew Kim and their daughters would not attend. They had prior commitments, he said. He wished it weren't so.

"I wanted them to walk through the door before anybody else."

But there was one other person he wanted on hand for the first night of service.

A taxi pulled in front of 652 W. Randolph St., and Ruth Snider emerged in a red coat and shimmering black gown along with her daughter Lauren.

They had arrived for their 9:30 p.m. reservation.

It had been three years since Curtis and Snider had last seen each other, and when they met in the restaurant's front lobby,

They'd first met when Curtis was 12, when he and his older brother had beaten up neighborhood kids for fun. And she stayed with him through all that followed–his parents' deaths, his dash out to Colorado, the christening of his daughters, the pending divorce. Snider was there the moment Curtis fell in love with cooking, and now she was here on opening night.

Snider and her daughter sat at the table closest to the kitchen window and watched as Curtis plated each dish for them. He instructed his cooks that no one else would prepare Table 11's dinner.

Snider watched Curtis float through the kitchen–the same quiet sixth-grader who'd made Pillsbury biscuit pizzas in home economics class–now 37, bringing out an ice cylinder made from ginger water, with kampachi fish, golden trout roe, pomelo segments and Thai basil intricately embedded inside the frozen tube. She said afterward that it was the best meal of her life.

As the last dessert plate was cleared, Curtis sat at her table. He was no longer the reticent boy.

"You've given me something more than any amount of money can give . . . unconditional love and values of life," he told her. "I could never repay you. But the ability to be able to give back to you what I do . . . cook for you . . . means more than anything."

The roads were empty by the time Curtis drove back to his Lincoln Square apartment at the end of the night.

"It's been a good day," he said.

The clock on his phone read 3 a.m.

Some things don't ever change. This was his life now, but the chef only knew one way. Tomorrow had already arrived.

By 7 a.m. Curtis Duffy was buttoning up his chef's jacket once more, back at his restaurant, back at Grace.

Spin the Globe

By Francis Lam

From *AFAR*

Like a master of all food media, Francis Lam has proven his culinary chops in print (*Gourmet*, *The New York Times*), digital media (Salon, Gilt Taste), TV (*Food(ography)*, *Top Chef*), and now books (editor-at-large at Clarkson Potter). One thing he never forgets: Cooking stories are always stories about people.

When I'm traveling, what matters—what really matters—isn't that the food be the fanciest or even the best, but that it tells you that you can be nowhere else but here. Those meals have their own deliciousness: Nothing locks in the memory of a place like a taste of something real, a taste that connects me to the person who made it.

That's the kind of eating I was hoping for when I emailed a Trinidadian for restaurant tips on nearby St. Vincent. Like every Trini I know, this friend is fireworks-proud of his people's food—its mix of indigenous, East Indian, African, European, and Chinese flavors. But it turned out that pride stretches only so far into the rest of the Caribbean.

"St. Vincent's just a big rock," he scoffed, probably while munching on a life-changing curry-stuffed roti. But his wife, sweetly annoyed, told me to go prove him wrong. I was headed to the Caribbean on short notice, and so her command became my mission. It pursued me through my flight from New York, prodded me out of my hotel, into the streets of St. Vincent's tiny capital, Kingstown, and up to the national tourist services office.

There, I asked about local specialties, and a delightful young brochure-slinger named Whitney whipped out a notepad and started on a playlist of old-school Vincentian culinary hits: breadfruit with jackfish; dried blackfish; and salt fish with "bakes"—buns that are, charmingly, fried, not baked.

But then she said, "Well, honestly, I prefer KFC." Tapping her pencil, she waited for a fourth iconic dish to occur to her before she basically gave up, adding "banana." Which actually was a great tip.

Back outside, at a proudly arranged table of peanuts, rice, and fruit on the street, I bought tiny bananas that tasted—I swear—like cloves and cooked pineapple melted into cream.

I hit some lucky strikes my first couple days. At a restaurant on the way back from hiking the magnificent volcano La Soufrière, my guide steered me to camouflage-colored callaloo, an earthy stew of greens, goat, and smoky charred breadfruit (think plantain flavor in a potato's body). And back in Kingstown, out of the back of a car, I bought a great bake with salt fish.

As I ate it—first chewy and sweet, then chewy and salty—I watched the rolling parties that are, technically, mass transit on St. Vincent. Vans painted with names like SWAGGA, Street Styla, and the Hard Knock Champion Squad blazed past coconut carts and buildings painted Caribbean blues, pinks, oranges, and yellows. Dancehall blared from their windows, the music shredding the cheap speakers: banging, hard and furious. Fare collectors, more like hype men, whipped open their doors and called out, "Where you gon' to?" before getting back to the party inside.

On my third night, I happened upon a restaurant called Aggie's. It looked more like a house than a business, an impression supported by the fact that the two staff—the only people there—seemed unsure of what to do when I arrived. The man just disappeared inside. The woman said, "We have beef, pork, fish, and conch."

I stared dumbly, until she elaborated on how she could cook them; I asked for the conch in souse, because I had no idea what souse was.

I sat on the porch to watch the daylight sink into the hills. In the kitchen, I could see the woman cutting vegetables in her hand, like home cooks do. When she came out, she brought a bowl of broth with the sea taste of conch, brightened with cucumbers doused in lime and candy-sweet onions. It was the cleanest, most refreshing soup; it tasted the way you want life to be on a sunny island.

Afterward, we talked at length about conch, unconstrained by other customers. The woman said this was Miss Aggie's place, but that she, Eloise, was the second cook and supervised the younger ladies during the day. Eloise is tall and round, with a kind face and rough hands. I liked her instantly. We shook hands as I said goodbye, and she held onto mine for a moment longer than I expected as she told me her brother and I shared the same name.

The next night I returned, again to an empty restaurant. "I had to have more of your cooking," I said to Eloise, and she smiled with just a hint of a flirt.

After another lovely dinner—whelks in silky Creole sauce—Eloise asked to have a picture taken with me. I promised to print it out and bring it back to her, and, emboldened, I asked if I could go into her kitchen and learn to cook with her. I wanted to see her hands in motion, to see how she cooks such wonderful food for, apparently, nobody. She looked unsure, shying from the idea, until she eventually said yes.

I came back the next morning to a bustling kitchen with half a dozen women bumping about. Eloise wasn't there yet, but I poked my head in and spouted the cheesy comment, "That curry smells terrific!"

A broad woman with a no-bullshit air looked up.

"That's sugar, for stew pork," she said. It's not a curry, in other words. She shook the pot, the bubbling caramel dancing on oil, then dumped in a massive bowl of meat, sending a flurry of bay leaves into the air. This was Miss Aggie.

She hustled, giving commands that were direct, short, and sometimes expressed with an urgency that sounded like exasperation. But she welcomed me in and set me to work.

As I scrubbed green bananas and introduced myself to the other women in the kitchen, Miss Aggie found moments in between cooking and hectoring her cooks to talk with me about Chinese food, her distaste for big cities, and visiting her husband in Boston, where he lives.

I asked Miss Aggie how she started the restaurant. "I always wanted to be a schoolteacher," she said, "but I got pregnant along the way." She spoke frankly during our short chats; it felt generous of her. When she left to set up the dining room, however, the other women seemed to breathe a little easier, all except for Shackie. A young, lean woman with sleek dark skin, Shackie moved with intense focus; she cooked like she meant it.

Finally Eloise arrived, her round face curled in a smile, and I gave her a hug. Miss Aggie called to her to fry some fish, and Eloise chatted with me as she first finished up a dough Aggie had started for bakes. Shackie walked up and talked to Eloise in dialect, their words sparring in jagged, teasing rhythm, until Eloise said to me, "Say no, Francis, just say no." I looked at her, confused.

"She says she's going to steal you from me," Eloise said, and Shackie slipped away, cackling, as Miss Aggie came back in to announce that customers were arriving. Lunchtime proved to be much busier than dinners. "The fish!" Miss Aggie barked. "Eloise!" Things got frantic. Pots got stacked on pots, tilting precariously.

Eloise showed me how to roll the bake dough into round buns and fry them while she tried to get the fish going. She shifted beat-up pans on the stove, settling on one buckled beyond recognition and another that had long ago lost its handle. Guests were coming in, calling for rice, bakes, fish. Miss Aggie blasted through the kitchen again, grumbling something at Eloise, and Eloise shifted her body, blocking from Aggie's urgent demands. I kept making bakes, trying to ignore the fact that Eloise's face was pinching up, turning red. After a few more bakes, she handed her tongs to Shackie and left.

I found her a few minutes later on the porch, waiting for a taxi to take her home. I poured her some water, and she said something about not feeling well. I poured again. She seemed less ill than flustered.

As the cab arrived, Eloise asked for my number. I said I was leaving the next day, and she told me to take care. I went back into the kitchen.

The fish all done, I asked Shackie how long she's been cooking. "Why, I look like a professional?" she asked. Just a few months, it turns out, but she added, "Miss Aggie, she rough and tings, but it harder for you if she soft. This way you learn." Sweat on her brow, fish in her pan, she looked proud of her work.

"OK, you've helped enough. I hope you learned something," Miss Aggie said to me. "Sit down, have some lunch," she invited.

I had one of my bakes, some green beans, and Miss Aggie's stew pork, the one she was caramelizing sugar for when I arrived. It was salty, fatty, bitter, sweet–delicious and complicated.

I ate slowly, taking in the room and the sounds coming from the kitchen, and I thought about what I would tell my Trini friend about life on this rock.

To Serve and Obey

By Karen Barichievy

From *Fire and Knives*

Armed with culinary school qualifications, freelance writer Karen Barichievy began working as a private chef in the Scottish Borders. Perhaps she shouldn't have been surprised to find that the life of a 21st-century spatula-for-hire wasn't anything like *Downton Abbey*.

Even in late August there is a bite to the morning air here.

I hurry towards the dark bulk of the house, down the moss-covered stairs to the basement door. Open it quietly—wouldn't want anyone else to stir.

I turn on Radio 3, reminding myself to turn it right down before breakfast. And to open the windows, because He doesn't like it too warm in here. But for now it's cold, and I shelter by the AGA, pulling on chef's whites and apron. I slosh the kettle half full for speed and flick it on. Reaching for the biggest mug I can find, a bucket, really, I tip in three heaped tablespoons of Nescafé. The craving for sleep is still tugging at the corners of me, and I pop two ProPlus tablets in my mouth, chasing them down with the coffee. The first mug of the day is unequalled. Comforting, reviving, just the faint bite of caffeine as I swallow. There'll be many more today, perhaps twelve, even fifteen, but they will be glugged only for their impact. None will match this one.

I open the dishwasher, and check if it worked properly. Not really, the bloody thing. So I pile half of its contents into the sink to hand-wash them later. Extracting the cutlery, I check the breakfast table, set in the small hours when my brain was sluggish. Knives and forks for cooked, knives for toast, spoons for cereal and fruit, teaspoons for coffee. Mugs, cups, napkins, butter dish, salt pepper. Malt vinegar in case He wants kippers, brown sauce in case He wants a bacon sandwich instead. Jams, marmalade, honey, Marmite, peanut butter. Cereal—one gluten-free, one sugar-free. What have I forgotten? Something, I know it. It'll come to me.

To the pantry next, where excavation begins in fridge one. Milk, orange juice, apple juice, yoghurt, blueberries, strawberries, raspberries, blackberries, mango, pineapple, passionfruit, grapefruit—pink and white.

Arms overflowing, I carry them through to the kitchen. Then back to the pantry to fridge two. Bacon, sausages, black pudding, kippers, tomatoes, mushrooms. Eggs from the windowsill. Another loaf of bread. Ferry it all back to the kitchen. Two pans on the electric cooker—one for kippers, one for poached eggs. Half the boiled kettle in each and set them to simmer. If He asks for either, he wants them produced as close to instant as I can make them. Two more pans on the side for mushrooms and tomatoes. Is it worth taking out another in case of fried bread? Probably not.

I may as well start with fruit prep. Checking over the berries for mould, bits of stalk and hardy bugs that have survived their journey from the finest greengrocer in London. The blackberries are mouth-puckering. I get to work on them with a few drops of lemon, a cascade of icing sugar. A dollop of tayberry jam in a saucer, microwaved for 20 seconds. Dribble the molten red liquid over the berries. Turn them gently, because I don't want a scarlet mush. Taste. More lemon juice. Stir again. Check. The balance of sweet and acid, of fruit and freshness. A little lemon zest, probably three or four strokes on the Microplane. Stir again, scrape in the last of the warm jam. Arrange so that the plate is a jumble of deep, gleaming colour on the table. Next.

Pineapple, sliced thick enough to hold its shape, but not to be a boulder in the mouth. No brown speckles from the peel, no fibrous core. Mango, score each way, turn the skin inside out, slice off the perfect cubes. I check that none of the stone has been caught in the flesh. Passionfruit—four should do it. Two go in as seeds and pulp, the other two through a sieve. Pushing and forcing at the seeds, gleaning more yellow pulp. Scrape the bottom of the sieve. This is taking too long, but there can be no crunching on seeds to spoil the perfect mouthful of tropical flavours. Push, scrape, push, scrape. I check beneath the sieve, scrape the last of the pulp, and stir it into the fruit. Lime juice, one should do, lime zest, lots this time. Microplane again. Stir, taste, a little icing sugar. Stir again. On the table. Next.

Three oven trays, lined with baking parchment, on which I lay out sausages, bacon and black pudding. Sausages first, in the top oven of the AGA. Set the timer for ten minutes. Back to the larder. My brain snags, what did I come in here for? Ah yes, I remember: fillings for the picnic rolls.

A plate of sliced roast chicken awaits in fridge two there's a bunch of tarragon in fridge one. I snatch some butter and a bowl of thick yellow mayonnaise, made from some decent eggs I found on a farm coming south. Two bags of brown baps on the windowsill. Unload them all in the kitchen. It's soup next. Fridge two, at the bottom, lurking in a Le Creuset big enough to hold a suckling pig. I have to kneel and grip it with both hands to lift it. The thought of dropping it steels my arms, and I heave it next door, onto the slow side of the AGA top.

The timer dings. Sausages. They're browned on top, so I give them a turn for a final ten minutes. The black pudding had better go in too. Timer on again. Back to the fruit. Grapefruit now. His favorite–I've noticed He likes the white more than the pink. When I segment grapefruit, I am back at Leiths in the teaching kitchen, with Claire at my shoulder. She is saying nothing, the faintest frown puckering her brow. A look in her eyes that is half surprise, half disappointment. How can a student be so cackhanded, she wonders, as I hack at her perfect fruit, creating only deformed balls of mush. Until I went home one weekend and bought twenty oranges and a dozen grapefruit and found somewhere a measure of dexterity.

I burrow around in the drawer for my fruit knife. It has a serrated edge and is sharp enough to draw blood with merely a whisper of pressure. Slice off the top and bottom of the fruit, just enough to reveal the tips of the segments. Then cutting off the peel, following the downward curve of the fruit, taking away the pith, but not pillaging the segments. The fruit must maintain its shape, Claire would say, no mutilated blocks. Round until I've come full circle. Then tidying away the remaining traces of pith. There must be no white except the faintest trace of veins between the segments. The trimmed fruit is a perfect pink orb.

My hands are dripping juice, and I check the clock. Faster, faster. I saw gently on either side of the segment, leaving the membrane behind and extracting a perfect sliver of fruit. Then the next one alongside. Watch for pips. Now the white grapefruit. There is a pile of fruit peelings spilling into the sink by the time I'm finished. Wash hands, clear the mess, wipe the rim of the grapefruit bowl, stir the grapefruit into an even salad of pink and white. As if anyone would notice but me. On the table. Next.

Give the soup a stir, check it's not catching on the bottom. Haul out the sausages–there's probably a minute left on the timer, but they're caramelised and look well enough. That reminds me, hot plates, hot platters to go in the warming oven of the AGA. How many will eat hot? Perhaps eight, maybe ten. I turn the black pudding, time for the bacon to go in too. Top rack of the top oven, submit it to brief, brutal heat and watch it like a hawk. Set the timer for two minutes.

Tomatoes next. A glug of sunflower oil in the pan, better start on the hot plate of the AGA, because the soup is still hogging the cooler one. Slice the tomatoes in half, sprinkle with coarse sea salt and a grind of pepper. On the burner, go. The mushrooms are next. I pick through them, brush them free of earth and muck, dock their tails, and quarter them. Cooking space is getting more complicated now. The soup gets shifted onto the warming plate. A cast iron frying pan takes its place, and I cut off a third of a pack of butter and a splash of oil, and wait for it to melt and fizz. When the butter is spitting, the mushrooms are in, with more sea salt and pepper. The timer is demanding my attention for the bacon. It's not quite there. Another thirty seconds will take it to the razor's edge between crisp and burnt. I'd better wait–if I walk away it will char, and I'll have to start again. Hunker down by the AGA, gulping my tepid coffee, listening to the bacon hissing inside. Ten, nine, eight . . . I force myself to be patient.

Bacon in the warmer, sausages in the warmer, black pudding in the final stages. The tomatoes are cooking too fast, so I turn them and move them to the slow plate. They'll have to share with the mushrooms. Five minutes until I need to nurse them again.

Time to start the baps. They'll be down before I can fill them, but I can get the chicken close to edible. I choose my desert island knife, a 10-inch Wusthof, an extension of my hand, reassuringly heavy enough to crush and chop, wide enough to scoop into a pan. I start with the tarragon, stripping it from the stalks, and chop it coarsely. I want it well disciplined, there'll be no throat-catching fronds of herbs here. Then a handful of chicken, cutting it down from slices to cubes. I check for skin—He hates that—and any tiny bits of gristle or bone. At least three dollops of the mayonnaise, the tarragon, and some pepper. I collar a stray half lemon and squeeze that in. Stir it up to a yellow and green mulch and taste. Good, but I need more tarragon. It isn't holding its own against the mayonnaise. Perhaps it's Russian rather than French tarragon. The latter is a weaker, more insipid cousin to the Gallic version. But this isn't London, there is no stocked-to-bursting greengrocer around the corner. It's make do or go without. I give up and chop the rest of the tarragon. Damn, I'd been hoping to hold some back for Béarnaise for tomorrow night. I shall have to find some more somewhere, or raid some unsuspecting garden. I give the mixture a stir, taste, add more pepper, a few grains of salt, the last of the lemon. It's better now—sharp yet creamy, brightened with the tarragon, a decent contrast to crusty brown bread.

The floorboards upstairs are creaking. Someone's early. It'll be Him, I should think. The BlackBerry will have sprung to life in the pre-dawn and not ceased since. I open the windows, knowing He'll be down for tea in a minute. I get the teapot warmed, and the cafetière—I knew I'd forgotten something. His footsteps are quiet on the carpeted stairs that lead to the kitchen, but his breathing is familiar. I turn down the radio and check the tomatoes, now soft on both sides, with caramelised tops. There's a slot for them in the warming oven and I cram them in, then taste the mushrooms. They're not yet a deep crisp-edged gold, so I encourage them with another wedge of butter and two minutes more on the AGA.

I load the toaster with four slices of bread, ready to go. The toast racks perch on plates, awaiting their burden.

"Good morning." He's come in so quietly I missed him. For a furtive second I check the kitchen. Mess under control, windows open, radio low, kettle boiled, teapot warmed.

"Hi." He is curt to the point of offhand in the mornings. Best to speak when you're spoken to.

He glances at the mushrooms and the fruit on the table. Then picks a few grapes from the fruit bowl on the dresser and crams them into his mouth.

"Is anyone else down?" Rhetorical question. I say nothing, concentrate on finishing the mushrooms.

"Do I have time to get the papers?" Another rhetorical question. He makes the rules.

"Absolutely, shall I get your tea on so it's ready when you're back?"

He's already left the kitchen, heading for the back door. "Yes, thanks," he calls without turning around.

He'll be no more than five minutes. He's left his BlackBerry by the fruit bowl, and it is already buzzing and pinging. I wonder if I should run out to him with it. But he does nothing accidentally. He will have wanted to be rid of it for a moment.

I should have asked if he was for kipper or poached eggs and bacon. That way they could've been ready for his return too. Damn. More creaking upstairs. Someone else is up. I fill the teapot, re-boil the kettle, and load up the cafetière with coffee. It might be worth splitting and buttering the baps.

The bread knife is in my hand when I hear a heavy tramp down the stairs. Forget it. It will be better to focus on the here and now. It's one of the guests, following the decreed time for breakfast, eager to avoid His wrath. None of His sons will, of course, but guests know better than to delay departure for the river.

Tea on the table, coffee made. Two or three of them have shuffled into the kitchen, warming themselves in front of the AGA. Wondering why the windows are open, but they know better than to ask. He returns with the papers, and the room shifts towards Him as He sits down at the top chair, reaches for the teapot, pours, stirs. Then straight for the grapefruit. He'll eat it in less than a minute.

"Kippers or poached egg?" I ask, catching His eye.

"Kippers. I'm trying to be healthy. Thanks." The others are helping themselves to fruit, pouring coffee, waiting for Him to lead the conversation.

He ignores them and flicks through the papers.

"Would anyone else like a kipper?"

"Yes please," that's one.

"Can I have poached eggs, please?"

"Just some toast for me, thanks," says the third, trying to be easy.

I crack an egg, stir the simmering water in the saucepan to create a whirlpool, and drop it in, let it swirl into shape, then add the other. Keep the temperature low, no bubbles. Toast in and go. Kippers will be ready to turn soon. Two more guests are down, one still pulling on his jumper. The other is on his phone checking the fishing conditions.

"I think we're going to need more tea," He says, pouring the last of it into His mug.

Kettle filled and on, teapot retrieved, rinsed and bags in.

"What can I get you chaps for breakfast?" I ask as I put the platters of sausage, bacon, black pudding, tomatoes and mushrooms on the table.

They slaver obediently over the bacon, and then one asks: "Any chance of some porridge?"

The first batch of toast is done, very done. Not quite burnt, but too close for comfort. In the rack on the table. Second batch on. The poached eggs are soft to the touch. I lift them out with a slotted spoon, dab them dry with kitchen roll, then slide them onto a warm plate. The guest is munching the last of his fruit as I take them over. Hurry, this plate is burning my hand to the bone. He sees me, swallows the last, and I clear and serve in one.

How did I forget about porridge? Into the pantry, snatch the oats. We may be in Scotland, but there'll be no water and salt in this porridge. Rather 80 percent milk, 20 percent double cream. On the AGA top: it should be the cooler plate, but this is urgent. So it's the hot plate, and live dangerously. If I ignore it for even a minute it'll be burning on the bottom.

He would usually be asking for his kipper by now, but He's been momentarily distracted by the *Racing Post.* The fish is done, certainly. Remove, pat dry, onto a warm plate. He clears a space for me to put it in front of him. I bring over the vinegar. There is toast to hand. He'll be content for a minute or two.

The second batch of toast is ready, and the guests are into the hot food, shoveling on bacon and tomatoes. Another one is down, and he'd like fried eggs please. Soft, but not too soft. Someone asks for ketchup. How could I have forgotten that? I dart into the pantry, fridge one, inside door at the bottom.

His phone rings, an invasive trill. Anyone else would apologise and take it upstairs. He answers around a mouthful of toast, not moving an inch.

"Yes, how's it going there?" He asks, chewing and reaching for another slice of toast. He'll be wanting marmalade with that one. It's at the far end of the table; I divert my attention from the fried eggs and porridge to take it over to him. He raises his eyebrows in acknowledgment.

Fried eggs are good to go. There's no point flipping them, American diner style–better to use enough hot oil to spoon it over them until the yolks turn from gold to a pale yellow-pink, just enough so they're warm and runny. Leiths would insist that the white remain perfect, with no crisp edges, but in the real world seriously hot oil ensures the faintest crisp frill at the edges, and no one likes a flabby white. On the plate, and served. The porridge has thickened and swelled, a little stirring and it will be ready. Perhaps a final dash of cream at the end.

He's getting faintly agitated with the caller. "Well, what can we do then?" I can hear a voice rising to placate Him.

"Fine, do it." There's a pause, while the caller is trying to cram in explanations or pacifications. That's a mistake. Keep it brief, rational, to the point. No fuss, no drama.

"Yes, four, if that's what it takes." Another pause, He sighs, takes a large bite of marmalade toast, lets the caller gabble on. "The vet OK with that?"

"No, I'm happy," he says after a moment, and without preamble hangs up.

There is an expectant silence from the well-trained guests.

As I serve the porridge, satisfied that its texture is correct, with a bowl of brown sugar alongside, He announces: "I've just bought a horse."

Before anyone can say anything, there is a muffled call from upstairs. "Dad, what did you do with my waders?"

He ignores it. "Outbid the Saudis. Four million."

"Did you see it before you came up then?" asks someone.

"No, but the trainer did. So we'll see how it goes."

"Dad, I said what happened to my waders?" His son stomps into the kitchen, hair in disarray, shirt hanging out.

"I've got no idea. Ask your mother. You're late. We're leaving in ten minutes."

Ten minutes for breakfast stragglers, for filling the rolls. Putting the soup into flasks, slicing some cake. Filling coolboxes. That reminds me.

"What drinks would you like today?"

He thinks for a moment. "Let's take it easy today. Three Krug and a couple of rosé. And lots of water."

I dart into the pantry for the coolboxes and he calls after me. "And fruit . . . can we make sure there's plenty of fruit."

"Of course, no problem." He reminds me to pack fruit every morning. And water. Just in case it slips my mind.

"And have we got enough ice packs?" Rhetorical question, really, but I call out my assurances.

Two flasks, check the soup is piping hot. This is pea, mint and chorizo–not His favourite, way too metropolitan for him, I know this. But He'll like tomorrow's one.

I split the baps, butter them in a moment and pile in the chicken. As long as the second wave of guests doesn't come down for breakfast for a few minutes all will be fine. I slice up most of a banana and chocolate loaf, put together a bag of fruit, then add half a dozen chocolate bars. The Krug went into the fridge last night, but I cover the bottles well with ice packs, load the food on top and then quickly make a cafetière of coffee for the final flask.

What else? Corkscrew? Check. Kitchen roll? Check. Spoons for soup. Better wash some. A final inspection of the champagne glasses–He likes them gleaming. A large bag of crisps, and that–surely–must be it. I'm plundering fridge two for soft drinks when I spot the pork pie. They'll go mad without that, not to mention that it took me a morning to make. A few wedges to keep the wolf from the door, well wrapped, and slotted into the final nook in the coolbox.

"Ready?" He asks, and it is of course a rhetorical question.

"Absolutely," I reply, filling the final flask with coffee.

A few moments later the picnic is hauled out of the kitchen and I survey the debris from the first wave of breakfast.

This Is Tossing

By Chris Wiewora

From *Make*

Currently pursuing an MFA at the University of Iowa writers' program, Chris Wiewiora has published fiction, nonfiction, and interviews in *The Good Men Project*, *Bull: Men's Fiction*, and the Chicago-based literary magazine *Make*. Even a job at a pizzeria provides fodder for his literary vision.

It's 10AM. An hour before Lazy Moon Pizzeria opens. You have an hour—this hour—to toss. You're supposed to have 11 pies by 11AM. One hour.

You have always failed to have 11 by 11. Sometimes you fail because you went to bed after midnight or didn't have a bowl of cereal in the morning or you tear a pie and then you're already down one and you don't believe you can ever be anywhere near perfect. On those days, the store manager comes over and inspects your not-yet-full pie rack and shakes his head. More often, you fail because the manager didn't turn on the doughpress, so you have to wait for it to warm up; or he didn't pull a tray of dough from the fridge, so all the doughballs are still frozen; or one of the two ovens wasn't turned on, so you'll be slower without being able to cook two pies at once. On those days you shake your head and maybe swear a bit, cursing the situation more than the manager, because you already feel like a failure before you've even started. Either way, this everyday failure to meet a near impossible expectation weighs down on you. If you could do 11 by 11—just once—you feel like you would truly be a professional, albeit a professional pizza tosser, and it would prove that what you do in this restaurant matters.

But instead of focusing on all that, focus on what you can do: try to go to bed early the night before, in the morning eat a bowl of cereal with your coffee, and on the way to work take it easy, drive nice and easy—not slow or fast, but easy—because 11 by 11 is hard, almost impossible, and you don't need to think about that when you open the door to the restaurant's *err-err* electronic buzzer.

And today when you walk in, in between the *err-err*, the music blasting through the restaurant's sound system is good; some simple drum beats, a bass line thumping in your throat, and guitar riffs with a hook. Bluesy rock 'n' roll. You bounce your foot as you put on your apron and clock in a few minutes early.

You wash your hands humming the Happy Birthday song to yourself. It's not your birthday, or anyone's birthday that you know of, but you're supposed to wash your hands for approximately 20 seconds. There's a laminated paper above all the hand-washing sinks that says to sing the ABCs, but you don't want to feel like some kid who doesn't know how to do his job.

Today, and all days that you toss, you're tucked behind the counter by the door, where you will welcome customers when they come in. But for now you should focus on tossing. You take a look at the clock. It blinks 9:59AM. You have an hour.

You check that the doughpress is on; it ticks like a coffeemaker's hotplate. The temperature knob is set right. And (yes!) there's a tray of dough already out. You're ready. Here goes.

The dough has risen a little, each bag forming a sliced-off cone, a plateau. You take the spray bottle of extra virgin olive oil and squirt twice on a hubcap-size round plate that you call the swivel plate because it's set on a swivel arm attached to the dough press. You spread the oil on the swivel plate with your bare hands, glossing the surface as well as your skin.

You pick up a bag of dough, feeling its weight settle in your palm. You know it's at least three point five pounds, no more than three point seven five. And out of the plastic, the dough feels like condensed flesh, like a too-heavy breast. You can't help that that's what you think of when you take the mound of dough in your hands and place it nippleside up on the swivel plate.

You push the cone down into itself to form a thick circle. You keep pushing with the palm of your hand around and around the circle to even it out, so the circle of dough will fit in the space the swivel plate will swivel under. Above is a heated plate that will come down and sandwich the dough.

You swivel the swivel plate, lining it up with the hotplate, and take hold of a lever in front of you and pull down with both hands. You don't press down so hard that the dough spills out of the circumference, but also not so lightly that the dough only warms on the outside while the core is still cold. You count six "Mississippi's" as the dough flattens and warms and expands into a bigger and bigger and bigger and bigger and bigger and bigger circle.

You pull up the handle, swivel out that swivel plate, take the edge of the dough in your hand, flip it over like a pancake, swivel the swivel plate back into its space and pull down on the handle, letting the hotplate press down again. You repeat until the fourth flip, when you *really* press down, spilling the dough out the sides. You lift up the handle and again swivel out the swivel plate, but now you lift the dough up and off the swivel plate altogether, placing it onto a tray called a sheetpan.

This circle of dough is called a patout, because before the dough-press–and you can imagine how hard it was to do this–tossers would have to physically push down on the cold dough and shape it with force. No more than six patouts stack each tray, because more than that squishes them with their own weight. When you have filled two trays they go one above the other on a rack-cart that you wheel under a stainless steel counter.

At the counter, you burrito-roll each patout off the tray and unfurl it. There are two plastic containers: one with bright yellow grains like sand (but it's cornmeal), and another filled with fluffy flour. For now, it's only flour you need. You take a handful and spread it on the stainless steel counter, powdering the olive-oil-slick dough. Along the edge of the floured patout, you press into the dough with your fingers in a 180-degree arc, forming a crust on half of one side and then the other. And so, one by one, your stack of patouts is floured up.

Behind you is the pie rack where large wooden paddles called peels rest after they've pulled pies out of the oven to cool. On top of the pie rack is a square peel without a handle. Next to the floury counter is another counter where this particular peel goes. On it, you will sprinkle—just sprinkle—a little bit of cornmeal so that when the big thirty-inch "skin" of the pie is laid on top and the sauce is ladled onto the skin—when that is all done you can easily shake the pie off the peel, leaving it in the oven to bake.

Now, you set your stance. Lower body: legs under your shoulders and knees bent, with your weight up on your forefoot, your heels hardly touching the linoleum floor. Upper body: torso taut but elastic, because you know that you will be twisting back and forth. Then with your hands straight out, fingers together like you're about to go swimming and thumbs tucked in so they don't pierce the dough, you're ready.

You lightly pinch the first patout. The flour makes taking the patout off the stack feel like a silky turn of a page. You lay the patout over your other hand and, it's odd, but initially you slap the dough back and forth with your hands. It begins in your wrists, the dough not only slapping but also rotating between your palms in a figure eight, an infinity symbol, an hourglass.

If someone looked closely they would see that in front of your chest, your right middle finger briefly touches your left middle finger. Then your right hand slides from your left middle finger toward your left inner elbow, while your left forearm remains straight. From above, when your two middle fingers touch, your arms will look like an equilateral triangle with one side always collapsing toward its opposite corner, pivoting back and forth, back and forth.

It's confusing. But you've done this so much by now that you just feel it. As you go on, your hands slap the dough in a curvy crisscross motion, making it turn, making it stretch into a larger circle. A circle big enough now to toss.

And this is what a tosser does. (Yes, you will sauce the skin of dough, and put the pie in the oven, and set the timer for 3 minutes, maybe 30 seconds more or less depending on how cool or hot the ovens are that day. And after the pies have cooled, you'll cut some of them into halves and quarters, while leaving a few pies whole.) But what really defines you as a tosser is not the patouts or the flouring or the cutting, but the tossing. It sounds so simple, but you're a tosser because you toss. And this, this is it:

You drape the dough over your left forearm like a dishrag. No, not a dishrag. That's too much like a waiter. And you're so much more than that. You think, How many people in the world know how to do something so particular?

You're not even in the restaurant when you toss. You're elsewhere. It's you and the dough, like matador and bull. You can imagine that flap of dough like a cape. And since you imagine the dough to be a cape, you can imagine the rest of it all as sport, too. And the dough hangs down, slung low, where your right hand cups the heaviest, lowest edge. Your left hand will spring up and out, and your entire left arm will straighten as your shoulder locks, then your elbow, then your wrist, so that your arm shoots out like a discus thrower's.

But before that, your body winds up by corkscrewing down: your left arm lurches to your hips and curls behind your back, your torso twists, and you're crunched down with so much potential energy that when you come up, it all goes into your right hand, which whisks the dough off your wrist like it's a Frisbee. And if you snapped a picture of this moment, your left hand would be turning over, palm-side up, opening. That same swimming hand that slapped the dough now ready to receive it when it comes back like a boomerang. That dough spinning, spinning, spinning in the air, its beauty summed up by little kids who come to the counter to watch. You know they want to ask you how you do it, but instead of asking, maybe because you're an adult, they point and then explain to you, or the parent holding them up, or especially a younger sibling: "It's magic!"

You know exactly what these kids mean, because every time you are here under the dough, you remember back—way back—to kindergarten. When you were out on the playground for recess, away from the dull pounding of the fluorescent lights. The best days of recess were when you all played parachute with the extraordinarily large multicolored nylon circle. You and all the rest of the kids got hold of a spot and, together, lifted the parachute up and then down, trapping air under it, like catching a big empty cloud. But what you really loved was when everyone lifted the parachute up again, releasing the air, and before the parachute floated down, one by one, you all got a turn to run under its stained-glass canopy.

You come out of the zone. You glance at the clock. Its red block numbers blink 10:55. You're on your last pie. The others are on the rack, cut, and logged in. And this one will only take 3 minutes in the oven. It doesn't take you longer than 2 minutes and change to toss and sauce a pie. You've almost played a perfect game. 11 by 11. One hour. Just one more.

And you take this last circle of dough, slap it back and forth, and wind up and toss it so that the dough nearly brushes one bulb of the draped Christmas tree lights strung from the ceiling tiles. And as you're under the dough—for a second you feel trapped, because you realize after this you can't ever be better—you wish you could be back in school, having fun like a kid again with no expectation of something perfect never being better. But you're here, on this last pie, with your left arm open and ready and waiting as it spins and spins and spins above you, about to come down.

Personal Tastes

Meet the Parents

By Eddie Huang

From *Fresh Off the Boat*

Food was always a flashpoint in the cultural mash-up that produced Taiwanese-American Eddie Huang—streetwear mogul, laid-off lawyer, stand-up comic, blogger (thepopchef.blogspot.com), and founder of the Lower East Side hotspot Baohaus. He sets the scene in his hiphop-flavored memoir *Fresh Off the Boat.*

The soup dumplings are off today!" Grandpa said.

"Should we tell the waiter? We should send these back."

"No, no, no, no, no, don't lose face over soup dumplings. Just eat them."

My mom always wanted to send food back. Everything on the side, some things hot, some things cold, no MSG, less oil, more chilis, oh, and some vinegar please. Black vinegar with green chilis if you have it, if not, red vinegar with ginger, and if you don't have that, then just white vinegar by itself and a can of Coke, not diet because diet causes cancer.

Microwaves cause cancer, too, so she buys a Foreman grill and wears a SARS mask because "oil fumes can ruin lungs," says the woman who smokes Capri cigarettes and drives an SUV wearing a visor. That's my mom.

I couldn't eat with my mom; she drove me crazy. But she never bothered my grandfather. He was always above the trees. Like 3 Stacks said, "What's cooler than cool? Ice cold." That was Grandpa: a six-foot-tall, long-faced, droopy-eyed Chinaman who subsisted on a cocktail of KFC, boiled peanuts, and cigarettes. Thinking back on it, my grandfather created the ultimate recipe for pancreatic cancer. At the time we had that lunch, he'd been battling it for a while, but we tried not to talk about it. That day, we just ate soup dumplings.

"It's the meat, did they not put enough ginger? *Mei you xiang wei dao.*"

"Eh, there's ginger, it's just heavy-handed. Who cares, just eat them! The rest of the food is on the way."

Xiang wei is the character a good dish has when it's robust, flavorful, and balanced but still maintains a certain light quality. That flavor comes, lingers on your tongue, stays long enough to make you crave it, but just when you think you have it figured out, it's gone. Timing is everything. Soup dumplings, sitcoms, one-night stands—good ones leave you wanting more.

The perfect soup dumpling has eighteen folds. Taipei's Din Tai Fung restaurant figured this out in the mid-eighties. While Americans had Pyrex visions, Taiwan was focused on soup dumplings. My grandparents on my father's side lived right on Yong Kang Jie, where Din Tai Fung was founded. To this day, it is the single most famous restaurant in Taipei, the crown jewel of the pound-for-pound greatest eating island in the world. Din Tai Fung started off as an oil retailer, but business took a dive in the early eighties and they did what any Taiwanese-Chinese person does when they need to get buckets. You break out the family recipe and go hammer. Din Tai Fung was like the Genco Olive Oil of Taipei. Undefeated.

The dough is where Din Tai Fung stays the hood champ. It's just strong enough to hold the soup once the gelatin melts, but if you pick it up by the knob and look closely at the skin, it's almost translucent. They create a light, airy texture for the skin that no one else has been able to duplicate. I remember going back to Din Tai Fung when I was twenty-seven and saying to myself, They're off! It's just not as satisfying as I remember it to be! But two hours later, walking around Taipei, all I could think about was their fucking soup dumplings. Across the street from Din Tai Fung was another restaurant that served soup dumplings and made a business of catching the spillover when people didn't want to wait an hour for a table. They were really close to the real deal. Like the first year Reebok had AI and you thought that maybe, just maybe, the Questions with the honeycomb would outsell Jordans. A false alarm.

Grandpa Huang put on for Yong Kang Jie and never cheated on the original. On the other hand, Grandpa Chiao, my mother's father, had money on his mind and really didn't have time for things like soup dumplings. He was the type of guy who would go across the street without thinking twice. He would be fully aware Din Tai Fung was better, but he was a businessman. He had things to do and never lost sight of them. Everything was calculated with my grandfather. On his desk, there was always this gold-plated abacus. Whenever something needed to be calculated, the other employees would use calculators, but Grandpa beat them to the punch every time. With his fingers on the abacus, he looked as slick as a three-card monte hustler. I loved hearing the sound: *tat, tat, tat, rap, tat, tat, tat.* After tapping the beads, he'd always reset them all with one downward stroke, *whap*, and out came the answer. He'd much rather save an hour, eat some perfectly fine soup dumplings, and go on his way.

Mom had other plans. She was my grandpa's youngest and loudest child. Mom claims she was his favorite, and I can't say I don't believe her. Grandpa loved her because she was entertaining and full of energy. As a kid, she took the Taiwanese national academic exam and got into all the best schools in Taipei. After she came to America as a seventeen-year-old, she managed to graduate as the salutatorian of her high school, even though she barely spoke English. On top of that, she's still the best cook in the family. My cousins love talking about things they don't know about and everyone claims their parents are the best, but even the aunts admit my mom goes hard in the paint.

That day, my uncle Joe from my dad's side was with us at Yi Ping Xiao Guan. I think he actually discovered the spot, because it was in Maryland, where he lived. Earlier that day, Grandpa had asked me where I wanted to go for my sixth birthday. He figured I'd say Chuck E. Cheese or McDonald's, but Momma didn't raise no fool. Chuck E. Cheese was for mouth breathers and kids with Velcro shoes. "I want to go where they have the best soup dumplings!"

"Where's that?"

"Even Uncle Joe knows! Yi Ping Xiao Guan."

I really liked Uncle Joe. He built three of the major bridges in DC and wore these big, thick black-rimmed glasses. I was into glasses, especially goggles, because Kareem wore them and he had the ill sky hook.

After we ate, I was kinda pissed with the shitty soup dumplings. It was my birthday! Yi Ping Xiao Guan, you can't come harder than this for the kid? Chuck E. Cheese can serve shitty food 'cause you get to smash moles and play Skee-Ball after lunch. But all you have are soup dumplings! How could you fuck this up? Yi Ping Xiao Guan was like Adam Morrison: your job is to slap Kobe's ass when the Lakers call time out. If you can't do that, shoot yourself. As I sat there, pissed off, I saw a waiter pouring off-brand soy sauce into the Wanjashan Soy Sauce bottles. Corner cutting, bootleg, off-brand-soy-pouring Chinamen!

"Mom! Mom!"

"Eddie, stop it, I'm talking to Grandpa. Talk to Uncle Joe!"

If someone was talking to Grandpa, you couldn't interrupt, but apples don't fall far from the tree. My mom was the youngest and never followed rules in the family. She enforced them on everyone else, but she never followed them herself.

"MOOOMMM! Listen!"

"Huang Xiao Wen!"

That was the signal. Black people use the government name when shit hits the fan, and my family would bust out the Chinese. It hurt my ears to hear the Chinese name. Not only did it seem louder and extra crunchy, but it usually meant you were about to get smacked the fuck up. Luckily, Uncle Joe was a nice guy who actually thought it was possible that a child might have something important to say.

"Uncle Joe, I know why the soup dumplings are bad."

"Really? Tell me!"

"Look over there: the waiter is putting the cheap soy sauce in the bottles. They must be using it in the dumplings, too."

"Genius! Genius! *Aya, Rei Hua, Rei Hua, zhu ge Xiao Wen tai cong ming le!*"

Rei Hua was my mother's Chinese name, so Uncle Joe got her attention when he used it.

"Eddie figured it out. They're using that cheap heavy soy sauce now. Look over there, he's putting it in all the bottles!"

"Oh my God! Too smart, too smart, I told you, this one is so smart!"

"Whatever, Mom, you never listen!"

"Shhh, shhh, shhh, don't ruin it for yourself. You did a good thing, just eat your food now."

I think my mom is manic, but Chinese people don't believe in psychologists. We just drink more tea when things go bad. Sometimes I agree; I think we're all overdiagnosed. Maybe that's just how we are, and people should leave us alone. My mom was entertaining! If you met my family, you'd prescribe Xanax for all of them, but then what? We'd be boring.

When the Kids Make You Breakfast for Mother's Day

By Kim Foster

From kim-foster.com

Author of *Sharp Knives, Boiling Oil: My Year of Dangerous Cooking With 4-Year-Olds*, NYC-based Kim Foster sends out SOS dispatches from the parenting front lines on her blog Kim-Foster.com. Ah, the idyllic soft-focus image of Mother's Day—prepare to see it shattered.

My kids made me breakfast last Mother's Day. There's a pretty good chance they'll do it again this year.

I'd be stupid to say they did it for me, really. Mother's Day was an excuse to get in the kitchen and go crazy without having me in there butting in with my rules and safety concerns, my constant nagging not to stick their fingers in their eyes after they chop the jalapenos, my desire to use one bowl and not five.

Lucy was seven, Edie was five and, having served as my sous-chefs since they could stand on the family "cooking stools," they were hankering for some kitchen autonomy. Mother's Day meant they could force me to stay in bed under the guise of relaxing.

I'm not going to lie. I was freaking out.

I imagined what every mother/home-cook imagines from her bed/prison on Mother's Day—my kitchen being dismantled piece by piece, my progeny unloading cabinets, burrowing through spices, dishes breaking, boxes and bins clattering to the floor, a completely upended kitchen that would require a half-day of heavy cleaning and reorganization

I imagined how I would react when I heard Lucy say to Edie, "I think your hair is on fire!" or "I think Mommy needs another spoonful of cumin in her coffee."

I wondered if I'd be able to just lie there in my bed, silently not helping, all the while hearing them search the kitchen for the bowl I know is right there in the dishwasher, also the only place they won't think to look, ever. I prepared myself to enjoy whatever crazy concoction they served, no matter how awful it smelled, no matter how it turned my stomach, even if it was ice cream drowned in fish sauce. I practiced my smile, like I really meant it, and repeated the words, "mmm . . . yummy."

Mother's Day, and all its required relaxing, is stressful.

The neighbors had sent us over a dozen eggs from their ever-productive backyard chickens, and this made Lucy and Edie focus on eggs. Eggs for Mother's Day.

Lucy decided that I would eat two eggs, fried sunny-side up, super-runny yolks, covered in chives and a little cheese, either cheddar or raclette. It was chef's choice, but I could get behind it. Lucy grabbed the egg carton and inspected: blueish, brownish, greenish, speckled. She picked out Puff Ball's eggs, the bluish ones—her favorite chicken and her favorite color. She set those aside for herself.

Then she chose eggs for me. The ones from the chicken named, "Gwen" because, as I heard Lucy tell it, "Gwen is older, like Mama." Edie didn't care which eggs she got because she hates eggs and most breakfast foods in general. She would make eggs for Daddy. She thought Daddy would like the speckled ones.

From the bed/prison, I heard the clatter of pans hitting the stove.

David, my husband, was relegated to procurer of things from the unreachable top shelf of the fridge—butter, herbs, cheese. He took his orders, fetched what they asked for, and kept his head down. If he even got near the stove, or tried to suggest something about the cheese, or how high the gas was, Edie stopped him and reminded him that he didn't know how to cook (this is true) and so could not offer any advice.

He told me later she gave him the "the hand."

I gamely pulled the *New Yorker* up on my Kindle and started "Shouts and Murmurs." I was going to get into this. I embraced the bed/prison. I didn't think I'd have a realistic shot at finishing the *New*

Yorker Fiction—too long, too much quiet time required—but "Shouts & Murmurs" seemed doable. I went with that.

I heard David reminding them not to let the butter burn. Edie told him to shush. It was harsh. But he took it well and next thing I know he was next to me, handing me a cup of coffee, flipping through magazines on his iPad.

"I've been kicked out of the kitchen," he told me, nearly gleeful.

Mother's Day was looking up.

The girls cracked their eggs. Lucy is very particular about her yolks so, when Edie's yolk broke, they stood over the bowl, and held a summit about how to handle it. Should they throw away the egg and start over? That would be a waste. But they couldn't make a proper sunny-side up egg this way. Maybe Ju-Ju the cat would eat it. Ju-Ju likes people food. More discussion. More peering into the bowl trying to make the egg yolk come back together.

Finally, they decided Edie would make a frittata, or even better an omelette, depending on whether she felt she could flip it. They would decide on the fly.

Done. Summit over.

David had laid everything out on the cutting board. Lucy grabbed the big knife from the drawer and sampled the cheeses and, deciding on cheddar, cut slivers of it, and hacked away at a handful of chives.

About the big knife. Our kids use knives: steak knives when they were toddlers, our knives now. By six, kids who have been cooking alongside their parents are pretty adept at not chopping off their fingers. They understand that knife cut = bloody trip to the hospital in an ambulance, hours in the ER waiting room, possibly stitches and a long needle full of local anesthetic. Kids will do just about anything to avoid that. So we trust them to use real knives.

And I've told them, over and over, what I believe is fundamentally true—if you're going to cook, you're going to get cut. You're going to burn your hand getting the cast iron pan out of the oven. You'll get lime juice in your paper cut. You'll itch your nose after dicing a jalapeno, and in the most jarring manner possible, clean out your entire sinus cavity. Or like Lucy when she was two, you might scrape your tongue on a box grater trying to lick off the cheese.

If you cook long enough, it'll happen. You can minimize the pain with safety measures, a policy of no fooling around and attentiveness, but make no mistake—cooking, when done correctly, is a full-body contact sport.

And to prove that point, a kid-on-kid smack-down was happening in my kitchen. It was the chives. Edie hogged them. Lucy wanted them for my eggs. (She's a purist, liking her eggs oozingly runny, with a little salt, nothing else.) Edie, working on the omelette, felt she needed most of the cheese and chives in hers.

Lucy found the "Omelette Defense" severely out of bounds and, from what we could gather from under the covers, Edie elbowed her in the face. Lucy pushed her back. There were accusations and whimpering, then all out screaming.

"I hate you, Lucy!"

"I hate you, too!"

David peeked out the door. "No fighting at the stove, girls."

To which both girls ratted each other out furiously, and Edie started to cry.

"Mommy!"

David, God bless him, said simply, "It's Mother's Day, girls. Figure it out."

The girls looked irritated by his lack of support. Lucy walked over and pulled the bedroom door shut.

Cooking can make people cranky.

Then, there was an eerie silence. For a long time. I presumed eggs were cooking, cheese was being shared and sprinkled, herbs falling like a light rain over the food.

Or they were dead.

I finished "Shouts & Murmurs." There was nothing more to do. Silently and slowly I cracked open the door.

What I saw amazed me. A kind of intuitive cooking was happening.

They were looking at each others' pans, deciding when the eggs were done. They were checking whether the whites shook all jelly-like, which meant they weren't quite ready, or if the yolks were getting too solid and pale at the edges, which meant they were over-cooking and wouldn't be messy-runny. Lucy saw that bits of stray cheese were frying a little in the pan. She leaned in and shut off the gas.

They weren't following a recipe. They weren't even cooking the way they had seen me do it. It was their own thing, all intuition and senses—sight and smell, the sound of eggs sizzling in butter, the sight of edges crisping up. It's exactly the way I had hoped they'd learn to cook.

I notice they defer to me when I'm in the kitchen. They ask me questions about doneness, when food is ready to be turned, flipped or stirred. Sometimes they just hand the egg to me because they might break the yolk, but they know I won't. I'm the sure bet.

It's easy to take over and have them do less.

But when they are alone, and there is no one to defer to, they have to figure it out themselves. I cannot hog the process. There is no safety net, so they simply depend on themselves to make decisions about the cooking.

David, unsure of why I was peeking through a crack in the door, came over to mock me, but ended up hooked on the action.

When they could tell the whites were not like jelly anymore, and the yolks were still a jiggly molten orange, they grabbed the spatulas from the jar on the counter. Lucy worked her eggs and mine onto plates.

Edie got her eggs on the spatula but couldn't quite negotiate the flipping. Lucy stepped in—all hurt feelings forgotten—positioning her spatula on the other side of Edie's eggs. The omelette flipped up and landed sort of lopsided in the pan.

Close enough.

They let it sit for a moment and then, they each put a spatula under a side of the omelette. They were already moving when they realized the plate was not on the counter where it should be. So they carried the omelette, balanced across two spatulas, as if it were a hurt kitten on a pillow, cautious step after cautious step, across the kitchen. It was like watching a high wire act.

No one took a breath until the omelette made it unscathed onto the plate.

David and I both realized Edie had forgotten to shut off the gas, but we refrained from saying anything. Although it was killing me. I had this thought that maybe we'd be gassed to death. I felt the urge to cough a little.

That's when I heard Lucy, rummaging for forks and napkins.

"Dude, turn off the gas."

Edie ran over, switched off the knob. And like her neurotic mother, (apple meet tree, tree meet apple) Lucy walked over and worked the knob again to make sure it was off.

Ah yes, a family tradition of OCD.

David, seeing an opportunity, went out for coffee refills. They frowned at him a little, but he assured them he was simply on a coffee run. Lucy said he should cover the left side of his face, so he couldn't see her eggs. He obliged and poured us more coffee, one-handed, shielding one whole side of his face.

I got back into bed. I pretended to read my Kindle. I waited to be called for breakfast.

But the call never came.

I expected a beautifully-calibrated table setting, maybe a cloth napkin, a wilted, hand-picked dandelion in a glass milk bottle, a hand-drawn card with hearts. What I got was much less refined. The girls brought their masterpieces to the bedroom. They shoved plates and forks into our hands and plopped themselves on the bed. Lucy flipped on the TV with the remote and Edie settled into my lap.

"Eat Mama," was all she said.

This was it. Mother's Day.

Eggs and *iCarly.*

We ate our eggs, all lumped up on the bed together, watching bad kids TV. Edie ate nothing.

My eggs were lovely, a little over-salty (in a good way) with runny yolks that puddled neon-yellow, a mad scattering of chives and melted cheese. Lucy has a heavy hand, so there was never any hope for a light dusting. The omelette must have been pretty good because David inhaled it before I could get a taste of it.

Edie wanted to know if I was planning on licking the plate. I was, so I did.

It was Mother's Day. I could lick the plate if I wanted to.

This made Lucy smile.

Is there anything better for a little kid? To cook something, completely by themselves, and watch their parent love it so much they throw all manners to the wind and lick the plate spotless?

David cleaned the kitchen, washed the dishes. The girls jumped on the trampoline in the back yard. I could hear them laughing as I started to read the *New Yorker* Fiction. I knew I wouldn't finish it, but even the start of it was good, freeing. A few minutes for Mom.

It was a good Mother's Day.

Which makes me wonder what they'll make this year.

Maybe I'll finish the Fiction this year. Maybe I'll relax and enjoy the sounds of them in my kitchen—our kitchen—making something for me with their own sweet hands.

Yes, that's it.

Still, I'm keeping the fire extinguisher by the bed/prison. Just in case.

Coke and Peanuts

By Carol Penn-Romine

From *Leite's Culinaria*

From her home base in Los Angeles, food writer and cooking teacher Carol Penn-Romine roams the globe, leading culinary tours and blogging about world cuisine at HungryPassport.com. But she's also a native Tennessean—and scratch a Southerner, you'll always find a hankering for Southern food.

Back when I was a preschooler in the '60s, I'd beg my daddy to let me tag along with him on his weekly trips to the farmers' co-op in town. Okay, I didn't so much beg as I did scurry into his truck and wait with the certainty that he couldn't possibly say no. The reasons behind my insistence on going along on this excursion were twofold. It was an escape from our quiet Tennessee farm for a taste of the city (Kenton, population 1,495 at the time), an outing I otherwise made only on Sunday mornings, when we went to church and everything else in town was closed. It also meant I got to indulge in my Coke-and-peanuts habit.

Daddy and I would pull into the gravel lot of the co-op, park alongside the other dirt-encrusted pickup trucks, and make our way to the low building with a dull corrugated-metal roof and walls that smelled of burlap and old wood. There we'd find a handful of farmers sitting around, their tractor allegiances displayed on their caps. (My daddy was a John Deere man.) Aside from selling seed and fertilizer, the co-op constituted the only social outlet most farmers had outside of church. We usually found them discussing crops, either mourning the lack of rain or lamenting its excess. It wasn't a place to linger all afternoon. Just a place to sit for a spell.

But before taking a seat on the odd chair or packing crate, my daddy, just like every other farmer, would first drop 15 cents into the cigar box on the counter. He'd pull a glass bottle of Coke from the chest-style vending machine that'd forgotten how to accept change and grab a pack of Lance's Spanish-Roasted Peanuts from the rack on the wall. Then he'd lean back and luxuriate in the break from the vagaries of an occupation that relied on the good graces of the Lord, all while taking part in one of the South's true culinary eccentricities.

The ritual, a sweet Southern tradition, is simple: Open the bottle of Coke and take a couple of swigs. Tear off the corner of the cellophane sleeve—one of those single serving-size packages that contain no more than a handful of peanuts, the ones with the rusty skins still attached—and shake some nuts into the bottle. Then drink. The first few sips are the best, when the Coke is at its coldest and the peanuts at their salty crunchiest. If you linger, the Coke gets warm, the peanuts turn soggy, and the whole thing is about as appealing as drinking from an old bottle that's been dredged from the bottom of a pond. This treasured custom is, to us Southerners born before LBJ took office, what the tea ceremony is to the Japanese.

Somewhere around the age of six, I decided I was big enough to quit sharing with my daddy, who, I'm quite certain, was happy to be free of my backwashing ways. My first try, I grabbed both sides of the bag and ripped the top completely open, which left me with no way to corral the peanuts into the narrow bottle opening. Most of the nuts missed their mark, bouncing off my legs and onto the rough wooden floor, where they remained—the three-second rule not being applicable in a place where people wear the same boots they used to tromp through pig droppings. Sacrificing those few peanuts was just as well, seeing as I hadn't yet figured out that I had to first sip some of the soda so as to make room in the bottle for the nuts. Still, enough of the nuts made it in for me to succumb to this early experience of mixing sweet and salty.

Witness to this first feeble attempt was our sometimes farmhand Kinch (Mr. Kinch, to me). The next time my daddy and I came in, Mr. Kinch bought me a Coke and a pack of peanuts, squatted down alongside me, and sat me on his knee. "This here's how you do it, Sister," he said, taking my tiny hands into his large, roughened ones and gently guiding me through the requisite steps.

It wasn't long before I became adept at assembling this Southern-bred cocktail. Bottle in hand, I'd lean back against a mound of seed corn or cottonseed sacks, propping the rear legs of my chair the way I'd seen the men do. I'd take a languid swig and pick at the rusty red peanut skins that clung to my mouth in a studied fashion with my thumb and ring finger, imitating the grown-ups I'd seen picking bits of tobacco from their lips while smoking unfiltered cigarettes.

Coke and peanuts wasn't something we indulged in at home. Sipping "Co-Cola," as it was called in the South—we Southerners never having met a syllable we wouldn't lop off to conserve energy—to quench one's thirst was considered wasteful. My mother actually kept a couple of bottles on hand at all times, but they were strictly for medicinal purposes, much like aspirin, calamine lotion, and Merthiolate. If you had an upset stomach, Coke was the cure. Despite this, I never connected it with being sick, but rather with the promise of feeling better.

I once tried substituting canned Coke, but it was patently absurd—it's nigh unto impossible to make peanuts flow out of a can. I'd never even consider diminishing the tradition by pouring Coke and peanuts into a glass. I don't think people outside the South understand unless they are, in fact, displaced Southerners, but there's something about gripping that curvy green glass bottle and tilting it just so, at that perfect 40° angle that offers up a trickle of Coke with an attendant peanut or two in each swig, that makes for one of the most satisfying sensations imaginable.

I still approach the Coke-and-peanuts ritual with reverence, though I consider myself a Californian these days. It takes me straight back to those excursions into town with my daddy, when the two of us shared a little together time riding in the pickup with the windows down, watching for wildlife along the roadside, the clean Tennessee air wafting through the cabin. Completing these trips with Coke and peanuts was ritual. Sacramental, even.

Eating the Hyphen

By Lily Wong

From *Gastronomica*

A recent graduate of Williams College who majored in Asian Studies, Boston native Lily Wong now teaches English in Hong Kong, where she explores the mysteries of dim sum. It's all part of piecing together a cultural identity that makes sense.

Fork? Check. Knife? Check. Chopsticks? Check. It may seem odd to have all three of these eating utensils side by side for the consumption of a single meal, but for me, there's just no other way. Oh, and ketchup, that's key. Definitely need to have the ketchup, pre-shaken to avoid an awkward first squirt of pale red water. There's no place for that on my plate, not when I'm eating dumplings. Yes, that is what I said: I need a fork, a knife, a pair of chopsticks, and ketchup before I eat my dumplings.

Now I've just looked up "dumpling" on the online *Oxford English Dictionary* and discovered that it is "a kind of pudding consisting of a mass of paste or dough, more or less globular in form, either plain and boiled, or enclosing fruit and boiled or baked." I am definitely not talking about whatever unappetizing-sounding food that dumpling is supposed to be. I'm talking about Chinese dumplings, pot stickers, Peking ravioli, *jiaozi*, whatever you want to call them. Do you know what I mean yet? Maybe you've gotten a vague idea, but let me explain, because I am *very* picky about my dumplings.

To begin with, the skin has to be thick. I mean really thick. Thick and chewy and starchy and the bottom should be a bit burnt and dark golden brown from the pan-frying. Have you ever had *gyoza*, the Japanese dumplings? Yes, those thin, almost translucent skins just won't do it for me. Hands-down, no question, until my dying day, I will vouch that the skin is the make-or-break feature of a dumpling. Bad skin equals bad dumpling. Those boiled dumplings that are also a type of Chinese dumplings? The skin is too thin, too soggy, and frankly, rather flavorless. If I had to call it names, I'd say it was limp and weak and characterless. The thick-skinned dumplings that I know and love absorb more of the meaty-flavored goodness inside the dumplings. Also, because they are pan-fried (a key aspect of delicious dumplings), the bottom gets its own texture—a slightly charred crispiness to add that perfect smidgen of crunch. So, if you were to eat just the skin of the dumpling, it would be simultaneously chewy and crispy, with a bit of savory meat flavor mixed in with a burnt taste off the bottom—a wonderfulness that the words of the English language are hard-pressed to capture.

But what about the filling? To me, it's a bit peripheral. The dumplings I'm talking about have a standard pork filling with "Chinese vegetables." I've never been entirely sure what these elusively named Chinese vegetables actually are, but I imagine that they are some combination of leeks and Chinese cabbage. They're not too salty and they don't have cilantro. These dumplings also have enough savory broth secretly sequestered inside the skin so that when you cut them open, you get some oil spatterings, pretty much all over your clothes, plate, and table. That's the sign of a good, moist, and juicy meat section.

I should mention before you envision me slaving away in a kitchen to create the perfect dumplings that the ones I like come out of the freezer. In plastic bags of fifty each. Imported to my house from Boston's Chinatown. It's strange, considering that most days I like the homegrown version of foods more than the store-bought version, but these are the exception. Even though I know they're handmade by a small company, so you get that same small-batch feel as if you made them at home, they're still store-bought and frozen rather than fresh.

But enough about finding the right dumplings; you're probably still confused as to why it's so imperative that I have a fork, knife, chopsticks, and ketchup. Here is your step-by-step guide to an entirely new dumpling eating experience:

1. On a large white plate, place six or seven dumplings (or more if you're particularly ravenous) and add some broccoli or beans for color and nutrition.
2. Squirt a glop of ketchup in one of the empty white spaces on your plate (as in not touching the broccoli or the dumplings). This is where it's key that the ketchup has been shaken a bit, otherwise that red ketchup juice runs all over your plate ruining everything.
3. Take that fork and knife on the side and cut each dumpling in half width-wise. Make sure to cut completely through the skin and meat.
4. Take the backside of your fork and push down on the top of each dumpling half until the meat abruptly pops out in a pool of brothy juice.
5. Once you've finished systematically cutting and squishing, you'll have lots of skins and meat pieces separated and you can put that knife and fork away. Grab the chopsticks.
6. Pick up a piece of the meat (just the meat now, no trying to get some skin in on this too) and dip it into the ketchup. Eat and repeat. If at any point you want to indulge in that steamed broccoli, it's a good idea. You wouldn't want to leave it all to the end. But don't dip it in ketchup. That's weird.
7. Now this is the best part. Use your chopsticks to one-by-one eat every last half dumpling's worth of skin. Savor every part because this is what it's all really been about. No ketchup or meat to obscure the flavor and chewiness, just pure starchy goodness.

And that's how it goes. Every single time. Confused? So was I the first time I really sat down to think about how I eat dumplings. It sounds a little like a grand mutilation of how a dumpling should be eaten for it to be "authentic" (using only chopsticks and with the dumpling left whole and dipped in black vinegar, no ketchup in sight). And I have unabashedly criticized and ridiculed Americanized Chinese food for being fake and something of a disgrace to "authentic" Chinese food. Yet here I am, still eating my dumplings with ketchup and a fork, unceremoniously and quite literally butchering my dumplings before I eat them. My grandmother meanwhile takes small bites out of whole dumplings, careful not to lose any of that broth from inside (with a face only three-quarters filled with disgust as I rush from the table to grab my ketchup from the fridge).

Bottled up in this entirely strange ritual is my status as a Chinese American. It is unclear to me where I ever came up with the idea that dumplings should be cut in half, or that the meat would taste better with ketchup (particularly since this is literally the only time that I use ketchup). Perhaps this combination has something to do with the fact that since both my parents grew up in the States, we've embraced many American traditions while abandoning or significantly modifying many Chinese ones. But even so, I have always embraced my Chinese culture and heritage. It gives me something larger to cling to when I'm feeling ostracized by American culture for looking "different." The suburb I grew up in is mostly white, but it's not as if I didn't have Chinese people around me; after all, there was always Chinatown. But Chinatown was full of people who spoke the language—whether Cantonese or Mandarin—who somehow just seemed so much more Chinese than I ever could be. And perhaps that's true. Maybe that's why I feel so gosh-darned American when I eat my dumplings with ketchup while holding my chopsticks "incorrectly." The notion that this somehow takes away from my ability to identify with Chinese culture is, I rationally understand, flawed. But in my pursuit to try and discover who I am, it's taken an oddly large place.

I'm not sure why I often think that to be a Chinese American means that you relish authentic Chinese food—and by authentic I mostly mean strictly what your grandmother cooks for you—but I do. I've told friends that they don't know what real Chinese food is because all they know is Panda Express. I pride myself on my Cantonese background, which leads me to look favorably on pig's ears and fungus of all shapes and sizes. My innate territorialism regarding my particular definition of what Chinese food is makes the choice to continue eating my dumplings in such a strange fashion slightly fraught. I'm not even sure that anyone besides my family knows that this is how I eat dumplings. In part, I think my reticence derives precisely from a fear that it would make me "less" Chinese.

Somehow, I've come to strange terms with these contradictions. Somewhere along the way, dumplings, cut in half with ketchup on the meat and the skin separated as a special entity of its own, have become my comfort food. So whether or not it perverts some thousand-year-old tradition of the "proper" way to eat dumplings, this is what makes me happy. Although I sometimes catch myself overcompensating with extra delight in Chinese delicacies involving jellyfish and sea cucumber that cause most Americans to squirm, eating dumplings in my own style has become the hyphen between Chinese and American in my identity.

Variations on Grace

By Paul Graham

From *Graze*

A professor of writing and literature at upstate New York's St. Lawrence University, Paul Graham dwells on the meaning of our daily rituals in fiction (*Crazy Season*, 2012) and essays in literary journals such as *Alimentum* and the new semi-annual *Graze*. Here he ponders: when was the last time you said grace before eating?

Easter Sunday. It's just my wife and me in the numb yearning of another North Country spring, and I have suddenly remembered a similar afternoon when I was ten years old. I had observed to my mother that because family rarely visited us on holidays, and friends never did, holidays felt like any other day of the week except that we ate more. Her reaction was a shrug.

Seeking a remedy for this nagging feeling, I reach into my mother's bag of tricks. I move dinner to the dining room. Sweep the tumbleweeds of dog fur off the floor. Get the linen napkins. Light tapers. It's only window-dressing, though. I think for a moment that it might be easier to go back, to prepare instead of vanilla crème brulée a dessert iconic of my youth—maybe a no-bake banana crème pie with layers of smashed Graham crackers and Cool-Whip. At least the contrast would be striking.

Here is the thing I am up against: when you have honed your skills and become a very good cook; when you think nothing of spending two hours on a weeknight preparing, say, seared lamb loin on a bed of lentils, which you parboil in homemade chicken stock and then finish in a pan with diced bacon and onions and herbs, and pair with a Barossa shiraz because you know the affinities between lamb and that varietal; when your kitchen is always stocked with exotic spices and your freezer contains several different cuts of meat; when your wine cellar is respectable; when you have within your reach, both economically and geographically, some of the best produce available; well, then you have that much further to go to create a special or graceful meal. To make dinner spiritual rather than merely gustatory.

That is when, freed from the memories of long-forgotten Sunday-school lessons at the United Methodist Church in Andover, New Jersey, not to mention the fates of the wealthy and social-climbing characters who appear under one of the greatest themes of the greatest Western novels—*money*—that is when the question, unsettling and smelling slightly of curdled crème, wafts from the pan of reducing *jus*: Could *this* be why it's easier to fit a camel through the eye of a needle? Could it all come down to dinner?

To be more direct, I'm sometimes dogged by the possibility that my meals are soulless.

I'd thought I was a palsy of Calvinism until I read an essay by Charles Lamb, a Londoner who wrote in the first half of the nineteenth century. Lamb writes in "Grace Before Meat" that holidays, feast days, and other elaborate gatherings to eat are antithetical to the true spirit of grace. The anticipation of the meal, the exotic aromas, the food itself, and—Lamb would not note this, having kept a cook (his sister), but let's admit it since most of us no longer do—the sheer exhaustive effort of preparation (to say nothing of the impending doom of cleanup!) all combine to distract the diners from the powerful truths attendant to the meal. That someone dedicated time and energy to making it, for example. That one can pay for it. That one has a house in which to eat it. That many people do not. That an animal died for it. All of these facts and more are elusive enough because of their obviousness, unpleasantness, or both. Introduce a current of fragrant steam, Lamb says, and the truths simply float away. They cannot hold up to the turkey done to a turn, the steaming ham, the oysters on their bed of ice—and we haven't even reached dessert yet.

Call Lamb a killjoy if you like. Essayists as a breed practice contrariety; it's the currency in which they trade. If you resist, you can hedge a little and say instead that feasts simply prove we *are* animals, often more driven by our appetites than anything our hearts and minds might have to tell us. And if you don't believe *that*, think back to your last food coma or hangover, or the day after you stayed up just a little too late with your partner, or ran a little too far in the heat, that time when you knew better but went and did whatever it was to excess anyway, then paid the price. On the other hand, rarely do we say over a morning cup of coffee, clutching our temples, "I read/thought/prayed/painted/petted my dog way too much last night, and man, do I feel like crap."

Ironically, or maybe predictably, it was *only* at feasts for Christian holidays that my father's family, eager though not devout northern Methodists, ever said grace. My immediate family never said grace at all, no matter what the occasion. My father knew how but was too reticent. Find your own path, he seemed to say, which makes me wonder now if at heart he's really a Unitarian with a Methodist hymnal. And while I remember my grandparents saying grace when the whole family gathered, my grandfather did not ask the blessing, as he called it, when my brother and I stayed with them for a weekend and we sat down to beef stroganoff or pork chops at the small, blue-lacquered table in their kitchen. I suspect that grace works like this for many, though I have known some who said grace before every dinner (which raises the question, why only the evening meal? Is a cup of coffee and toast in the morning worth any less?), including a Catholic family of eight who murmured one sentence, as ritual as genuflection, in one breath: *blessusoLordandthesethygiftswhichweareabouttoreceivefromthybounty throughChristourLordamen.* There was something reassuring about that ritual, something I liked.

Lamb believes that simpler suppers, eaten in a quiet and mundane atmosphere, offer the opportunity for true grace. This is especially true for the poor, because the poor man may not know where his next meal will come from. Or, if he does have work, he knows *exactly* where the food on his table comes from and knows it is still a combination of good fortune, or blessing, and toil. The sanctity of such a simple meal, Lamb writes, is not obscured by a feast's luxurious food. One's attention, when not compelled outward to the dishes on the table, may turn inward. Uncertainty breeds introspection, and the introspection breeds true gratitude. The famous line from Flannery O'Connor's Misfit may apply here, O'Connor having been a Catholic and interested in grace, though like almost all things relating to

O'Connor's fiction, the Misfit's words are a model of grotesquery: "She'd of been a good woman if it had been someone to shoot her every moment of her life." We'd be more graceful eaters if there were something to snatch the food from our hands.

I'm middle aged, now, yet I can count on one hand the number of blessings I have asked. A few years back we began having my wife's family to Thanksgiving, and I believe that since this tradition started, I have asked the blessing only once. We were in our house, I was the principal cook, but I conceded the duty gladly, my pride about my spirituality bristling even as I did it. Hypocritical, I know, but family relations are complex. I know the words. I feel the words. But I have never been one who, to borrow James Baldwin's expression, sings the tune just because he knows the words (in fact, the more confident my knowledge of the tune, the less likely I am to sing at all). So I just sat at the table, resigned to the Almighty's disappointment. I remember the relief I felt when I discovered, on a January evening, that Lamb had figured out the confusion I felt for me. After the hours of preparation, coordinating cooking times, attempting to make sure the bird reached the table not raw but not dry either, exhausted and buzzed on *half a glass* of third-rate American pinot noir (a pathetic showing for someone who can hold up his end of a bottle), and the kitchen looking like a construction site—well, small wonder that all I wanted was a loaf of homemade bread and a block of good cheese, and maybe some Burgundy. And just the two of us at the table. All that pageantry! I couldn't think.

"I am no Quaker at my food," Lamb confesses, before going on to describe an appetite that would see him a happy man in today's epicurean culture. "I quarrel with no man's tastes"—unless, it seems, the tastes be insipid. It is not the feast itself he faults; instead, Lamb wonders if the spirit of grace might be more honest if practiced at some time other than immediately before the meal. I remember one afternoon when my mother, for instance, turned to me as she restocked the pantry after the biweekly, hour-long sortie to the grocery store that was known, in our house, as Big Food Shopping, and saying, "I know it sounds corny, but this, for me, is Thanksgiving." At the time, I had no idea what she was talking about. The food simply appeared in the pantry, and then it appeared on my plate.

My wife and I belong to no church, but we are dedicated locavores. I've come to hate that word, along with other trendy labels, even those that don't apply to me. How locavorism works is, by now, old news: Take out a map. Draw a circle with a radius of fifty or one hundred miles from your town. Eat within that circle. Try it for a week, a month, as long as you can. Accept that explorers from Magellan forward have spoiled us; from that moment when the first ship's hold was emptied in a London harbor of its vanilla, coconuts, and tea, we've craved things we have no hope of growing in our native soil. Keep your coffee, your olive oil, your lemons, your vanilla; I keep mine. A healthy percentage of what you eat will do.

Living this way, you dust your own soil from the potatoes. You taste the same sunlight that comes through your morning window in the lettuce. You taste last week's rains in the melon. You exchange money with the hands that yanked those beets, picked those tomatoes, drove the hatchet down on the chicken's neck, or, if you're lucky enough to live on the coast, dug the clams. But be careful, lest we drift into sentimentality or sanctimoniousness. These are all the precious reasons people love farm shares and farmer's markets. Yet, admit it: There is something purifying about buying a sweet potato or bag of apples without swiping a gas-rewards card. There's also the unavoidable fact that local food always tastes better (a consideration Lamb likely never entertained). Then, there are the setbacks and limitations.

We have a share with farmers who are always apologizing for crops that underperform, or even crash, due to factors well beyond the control of people whose philosophy is organic and then some. Occasionally our farmer writes long letters about pests, wind, hail, and the inefficiency, as he sees it, of his acres. This man has the essayist's drive toward honesty without the essayist's insulating irony, which is always bad news for the psyche. I tell him to pipe down about the strawberries killed by a late frost, or tomatoes in short supply because there was a blight after some fool burned his ruined foliage instead of burying it, turning a localized disappointment into a regional crisis. I say the same to farmers at the market who don't have what I'm looking for, even as I reach for what they do have. A table with generous but not unlimited options is how it *should* be. Surely living in a state where scarcity is scarce has consequences for your soul. Betimes, more wolves, literal and metaphorical, roamed the boundaries of our imagination. They kept us honest. We seem to have convinced ourselves we've removed the wolf from our doorstep. We've tranquilized him, loaded him into a cage, trucked him forty miles into the woods, and let him out to sniff around a bare hill on wobbly legs as he waits for the narcs to wear off and wonders what the hell happened.

But if you pursue locavorism to its depths, eating every meal as far off the industrial food chain as possible, accepting both the disappointments and surprises of your agricultural community, you cannot help but see that a sacred trust exists there. *My life is in your hands.* The farmer feeds me, and in return I pay him from the expenditure of my energies in different fields. We know this, though inevitably we forget it. But once you acknowledge that sacred trust, you see that you cannot ignore a deeper truth: *I probably need the farmer more than he needs me.* This is especially the case if you're trading on literature to buy your carrots, but that is another essay.

Four years of a mostly local diet has taught me lessons about grace that an equivalent amount of Sunday School had only barely begun to suggest, and which Charles Lamb saw on the bulging tables of his friends: Grace can issue from many places, but one of them is certainly from the honest recognition and expression of vulnerability. Grace is born of fragility, from acknowledging the wellspring of provisions that maintains the thinnest barrier against disaster. And finally, grace is one's humble, deep, and constant hope that those provisions continue to arrive.

As a rule, human beings—animals in general—don't like to feel vulnerable. We'll do anything to end, or at least temporarily forget, a feeling of physical vulnerability in particular as quickly as possible. I say this risk aversion is mostly a good thing. It keeps us from playing in the traffic. And yet it was Rilke (a killjoy if ever there was one) who observed that, given the chance, human beings will also orient themselves toward the easiest of the easy. Historically speaking, in this country at least, our feelings of vulnerability—*mortal* vulnerability—may be at an all-time low. Or maybe nothing regarding our vulnerability has changed, and our powers of distraction are greater. That's partly the story of technology, and innovation, and progress, but it's also a story of human behavior. Some of the least graceful people I know are the most strident, loathe to show any vulnerability at all.

If the locavore movement, which is now burning comet-like across our country with all the sizzle of a fad, has a deep virtue, it's an invitation to vulnerability, and, with it, mindfulness. Perhaps even grace. That CSA farmers and growers' cooperatives are doing this in a country that excels at oblivion—in general, but especially when it comes to food—is no small thing. And if such mindfulness *is* a small thing, well, we have to start somewhere. Brillat-Savarin argued that a country's fate rests on how it eats. In many ways—economically, environmentally, physically, and yes, spiritually—we're just now beginning to see how right he was.

That Easter Sunday, as I prepared the chicken for roasting, I thought about the farmers down the road who had raised and killed it. The wild leeks, and the garlic, too, had come out of the ground not too far away, and I considered the miracle of spring, how everything keeps happening more or less when it should, in spite of us. Someone, somewhere, had produced a miracle of salad greens—in a cold frame or greenhouse, I couldn't tell. It hardly mattered; we hadn't eaten a salad in months. The onions and potatoes were fall storage crops. The carrots too. All grown and washed by a neighbor, or that's how I've come to think of the growers scattered across this muddy, brown, and sparsely-populated place: friends and neighbors. As I cooked, I thought of these people and how different life would be without them. I realized that I do this often. I had never thought of that recognition as something like grace, seeing it, instead, as a practice that kept me honest. Life would be less savory for sure without them. Less healthy, too. Sadder? Absolutely.

When my wife and I sat down to eat, even though it was just the two of us, I still did not ask a blessing. Shyness, I guess. Reticence. More like my father every year. To be sure, I could do worse. I felt nonetheless aware, and awake, and grateful.

The neighbors and friends, as Lamb might have predicted, vanished from my mind before I even put the first bite in my mouth. As I've said, it had been months since we tasted romaine. The candles sputtered. The music played. I can't remember what we talked about, though I remember the chicken had roasted well and the white Burgundy was good.

IN SUSAN'S KITCHEN

By Elissa Altman

From *Poor Man's Feast*

Falling in love is a complicated dance. In her tender, funny memoir, *Poor Man's Feast,* Beard-award-winning food writer, editor, and blogger Elissa Altman (PoorMans Feast.com) describes how she learned the dance with her new partner Susan—a dance that always seemed to come back to food.

In the way that some people believe you can always tell the nationality of a tourist by looking at their shoes or their underwear, I've always thought you could do the same by digging around in someone's kitchen. You can tell who they are, existentially speaking, just by opening cabinet doors, poking around their refrigerator, and pulling open a few utensil drawers.

I tested this theory years ago, long after my parents' divorce, on a visit to my mother's house: she was in the bedroom, on the phone, and I was alone in her kitchen, just looking around at her slightly peeling 1980s silver-and-white wallpaper, opening the odd food cabinet to see what, if anything, she was eating—six small cans of tuna packed in water, a one-thousand-packet box of Sweet 'n' Low—when I opened her lower cabinet doors. There was an electric knife in one of those cracked black cardboard boxes with red felt lining. I opened the box, and there was the white-and-gold plastic electric knife handle—still lightly coated with the gunk of an ancient holiday rib roast—but no actual knife. There was the fondue pot top to my mother's brown-and-white Dansk fondue set, and a box of fondue forks containing just one, lone, slightly bent one, but the base—the contraption on which the fondue pot sits—was missing.

"Your *father* must have taken them," she said, ruefully, when I asked. But it didn't make any sense: Why would my father want the bottom of the fondue set but not the top? Why would he take the knife part of the electric knife, but not the handle?

"Just for spite," she added, with an angry gimlet eye.

"Come on, Mom," I said. "You're being silly."

"Then they just disappeared. Who knows what happens to these things?"

In my mother's world, inanimate objects are always developing minds of their own. When they get good and tired of being neglected and ignored, they simply say *goodbye, good riddance* and off they go, stomping away in the middle of the night like a knife and fork dancing across the screen of a 1950s drive-in movie: a single fondue fork and the top part of the electric carving knife, marching out the door in a conga line. She had even managed to lose an entire set of flatware that I once bought for her when she somehow, inexplicably, was running low. If you aren't a party-thrower, and you don't have dinner guests over on a regular basis, how do you lose flatware? But for my mother, it makes sense: she doesn't cook—she is fearful of food and every morsel that passes her lips sends her careening backward in time to the days before she lost all the weight and became a television singer, back to when she was a fat child—so the idea of caring for, of coddling cookware like it was a baby or a prized pair of Chanel pumps was utterly, ridiculously crazy.

But crazy is relative. And so on the other hand, I was equally insane about what lived in my kitchen, and I doted on its contents the way you would a small, brokenhearted child: In my house, no knife ever sat in the sink. No pot filled with baked-on mess ever traveled through my tiny, eighteen-inch-wide dishwasher. No cast-iron pan ever saw a rinse of soapy water or a damp sponge, or even soap.

"This is *disgusting*," my best friend Abigail once said when she came over for brunch, picking up the Lodge cast-iron pan I'd bought specifically for making a honey-glazed, blue-corn corn bread I'd once eaten at an uptown, neo-Southern restaurant. She ran her finger along its surface and made a face.

"It's just age," I said. "And the fact that you're never supposed to wash it."

"And I just ate something cooked in this thing? How the hell are you supposed to clean it?"

"With salt," I answered.

"Salt? Just *salt*?" She was aghast.

"Yes," I said. "It's the way it's been done for centuries. The coarser the better. Like maybe, a nice flakey Maldon sea salt from England."

"So you scrub your pans with imported English sea salt. Tell me that's not completely nuts."

"It's not," I told her, waving a copy of Edna Lewis's *The Taste of Country Cooking* in her face. If it was good enough for Edna, it was good enough for me.

"Honey," Abigail snorted, "you may have noticed: you're not exactly a six-foot-tall black woman who likes to do things the way her great-grandma did back when she was a slave. Go out and buy yourself some dish soap."

In truth, the idea of using salt to scrub a pan thickly caked with baked-on food was something that I had always found secretly terrifying, especially after my first bout of food poisoning ended with a doctor friend coming to my house to hook me up to an IV for a few hours while we watched daytime television together in between my unhooking myself and racing for the bathroom. Scrubbing cast iron with salt was one of those mildly upsetting, romantic constructs, like threading adorable, tiny birds on a skewer and roasting them whole in a wood fire, like Richard Olney used to do in his tiny, sweet, sun-drenched house in Provence. It was like a ride through culinary fantasy land until you stopped and thought about it for a minute.

When I better-examined Auntie Et's nested set of jet-black, clean-as-a-whistle Griswold pans sitting on the counter, I couldn't imagine for the life of me how they'd gotten that way, or if they were just so old that the stuck-on food had disintegrated and fallen off over the years, like the now-empty can of rubbed sage from 1953 that Susan's mother still kept in her spice rack over her sink, having evaporated into light-green dust sometime during the Tet Offensive.

"Et must use a *lot* of salt on these babies," I said to Susan later that day, holding one of the smaller pans up to the light and running my finger along its surface.

"Are you kidding?" she barked. "Her secret is *far* more subversive."

"What is it?" I whispered, leaning in close.

"Soap and water. And a good, long soak in the sink," Susan said, matter of factly. "Salt is just so—I don't know—*twee*."

Earlier that morning, when the alarm went off at eight, I threw the covers back and raced down the stairs with MacGillicuddy following me, sounding like a stampeding herd of cattle in the otherwise still house.

"What are you doing?" Susan groaned from upstairs.

"I'm making dinner," I yelled back.

"*Now*?"

"Yes—*now*. It'll go in at eleven and be ready at three, you can take me to the station at 4:30, and I'll be back on the train home to New York by six. So, *now*—"

At eight on this mid-December Sunday morning, with my still-new love interest drowsing away upstairs, her slobbering dog following me around the kitchen hoping I'd drop something, and the *braciole* that Arnaud had cut for me on Friday, it was now or never. I wasn't going to freeze meat as gorgeous as this, so I got up to make supper, roughly an hour after the white, wintry sun had come up.

Susan's refrigerator, a mammoth black side-by-side Kenmore, so immense that the moving men had to slide it through the living room and over the counter on blankets—like an obese Pasha perched on a flying carpet—had a reputation for swallowing up anything you happened to be looking for at the very moment you needed it. I opened it, and cheese—soft, hard, harder, some white, some yellow, some blue—fell out at my feet, draped in varying degrees in plastic wrap. A small, blue-striped yellow ware bowl from the 1930s containing beige, cardboard-colored ground turkey and covered with foil sat precariously close to the edge of one of the sliding glass shelves. I searched and looked, lifting up packages of deli meat and containers of yogurt like a child does on a scavenger hunt. But no *braciole*.

"Where's the meat?" I yelled up the stairs.

"What?" Susan was still half asleep.

"The beef—*THE BEEF, DAMMIT*—from Arnaud," I shouted, anxiously, like I was having a dinner party in a few hours to which Russian royalty might be in attendance.

"It's there," Susan pleaded. I heard her get up, her feet hitting the floor above me. "I didn't touch it!"

"I don't see it!"

"Look behind the shaker," she shouted.

I stomped back to the fridge, removed the cocktail shaker still half-filled with the watered-down remnants of the bourbon Manhattan that we'd sucked down before running to Et's house for the chicken slop, and there, nestled between a loaf of Pepperidge Farm white bread and a Tupperware container of leftover macaroni and cheese, was my outrageously expensive beef.

I rummaged around the kitchen cabinets for a small platter and came up with one—part of a whole set of blue-and-white Anne Hathaway's Cottage service for twelve—that would allow the two pieces of *braciole* to come to room temperature comfortably and slowly without daring to touch each other, which, if they did, would result in unacceptable, uneven, oxidized spotting. I covered them with foil and set them aside, out of reach of the dog, and went back to the fridge to search for the handful of wild mushrooms—golden chanterelles, hen of the woods, and brown spongy morels—that I'd dropped fifteen bucks for at Dean & DeLuca. By the time Susan trudged down the stairs, I was sitting at the counter, gingerly rubbing and patting the dirt off of them with the dry piece of raw white silk that I'd neatly folded up, wrapped in a white handkerchief, and tucked into my coat pocket before leaving my apartment on Friday. Soft, delicate, and with the tiniest amount of nap, raw silk is the perfect tool for cleaning mushrooms without bruising them.

"Good morning, honey," Susan said, giving me a sleepy peck on the cheek.

"Good morning," I said, with an edge, looking at her out of the corner of my eye.

"Can I ask what is it that you're doing?" She filled up the tea kettle at the sink, and glared at my little patch of silk.

"What does it *look* like I'm doing?"

"Dusting? Drying the tears of a weeping morel that misses its mother?"

"Very funny," I replied, putting the last of the mushrooms on Susan's small tag-sale wooden chopping board that was in the shape of an apple. "I need a knife—do you have anything sharper than this?"

I held up a five-inch chef's knife with a plastic handle that I'd found in a drawer near the sink; a full quarter-inch of its tip was missing, sheared clean off, like it had been circumcised.

"They're all in here," she said, opening up a narrow drawer near the stove. I poked around and pulled out a paring knife that had a thin crack in its plastic handle. There was a long, heavy chef's knife, and both of them had seen better days and were about as sharp as limp celery.

"Do I need to bring my knife roll up next week?" I asked.

"What wrong with *these*?" she said, holding up the paring knife.

"What year are they from?"

"My mother gave them to me. Or they might have belonged to one of the aunts; I can't remember."

I snorted. I prized my knives, which I never, ever let rest in the sink, or ever see the rough vulgarity of a dishwasher.

Susan shook her head, exasperated.

"I don't understand what the difference is—if it's a good knife, it's a good knife."

"But don't you think you should take better care of them? I mean, look at this one." I held it up, and nodded at the missing tip. Susan swooned, and took it out of my hands.

"I love that knife. I think I found it at a tag sale, at the bottom of a box. I felt badly for it—it just needed a little love."

"You sound like Linus at the end of *A Charlie Brown Christmas*, when he gets down on his knees and wraps the tree in his blanket."

I was involved with a woman who had rescued a stray knife from a tag-sale FREE box because it needed a little love. My knives came from Bridge Kitchenware in the East Fifties, back in the day when the infamous owner, Fred Bridge, was considered the Soup Nazi of professional cookware. If you wanted to buy a bird's-beak paring knife from him and you weren't planning on using it to carve roses out of baby radishes like Jacques Pépin, he wouldn't sell it to you. My knife roll contained an eight-inch chef's knife, a six-inch carbon-steel Sabatier that rusted in mild springtime humidity, four paring knives, a Japanese cleaver, a nine-inch slicer, and a seven-inch filleting knife. And all of them were kept in pristine condition: the moment I saw a ding in one of them, I hurried it to a specialty sharpener on the

Lower East Side, like an hysterical mother who rushes her baby to the emergency room after a sniffle.

"Tell me what you need chopped," Susan said, sipping on a steaming royal-blue mug of odorous Lapsang souchong, a tea so simultaneously sweet and pungent and smoky that it made the dog throw up.

I looked at her.

"Come on—I'm really *good* at chopping—I'm a designer, remember?"

I reached into the vegetable drawer in the fridge and extracted a large onion, two celery stalks, and two carrots.

"Can you chop me a mirepoix?"

I was so fucking haughty about it, and she didn't even bat an eyelash.

"No problem," she said, putting her mug down. She took a scuffed plastic cutting board from behind the faucet and set it down on top of a lightly dampened paper towel, to keep it from moving around. I just stared at her, my arms folded.

"You gonna ask me what a mirepoix is?" I said.

"You gonna keep talking?" she replied, looking at me over her reading glasses.

And with that, she began to chop everything using that sad, tipless tag-sale knife. When she was done, she dumped the carrots, celery, and onion into three Anne Hathaway's Cottage soup bowls, pushed them toward me, picked up the newspaper and her tea, went into the living room, and sat down on the couch. The vegetables were perfect eighth-inch cubes and lovely. I remembered the day we met, when she touched the tiny scar on my right hand.

Details.

Two hours later, while the *braciole*—paper-thin slices of Arnaud's prime beef rolled around black truffle–scented wild mushroom duxelles, parsley, and Pecorino di Pienza, and then browned in olive oil and butter—sat braising in red wine and San Marzano tomatoes in Susan's only high-sided sauté pan, Susan began to rummage around the fridge.

"I'm hungry," she said, gazing into it like she was expecting a human voice to spring forth from its depths.

"I'll cook," I announced, putting the newspaper down, certain that she would somehow manage to change the oven temperature and turn the *braciole* into shoe leather.

"Sit," she said, pointing at the oven. "You're making dinner, remember?"

"Okay. So, what will we have? Grilled cheese? God knows we have enough pecorino to feed a small village in Tuscany."

I moved to the other side of the counter so I could keep an eye on things.

She pulled a small, dented Revere Ware saucepan out from the drawer under the oven, filled it with water and a few tablespoons of Heinz vinegar—the sort that my grandmother used to mix with water to clean the windows—and brought it to a simmer. She placed the smallest of the Griswold pans over a burner, heated it dry over medium heat, and set down four overlapping slices of Canadian bacon in it, like an edible Venn diagram.

"Stop!" I shouted, leaping up. "You're not using oil? You're going to destroy that pan!"

"You need to not talk so much," she said without looking up, carefully breaking four eggs into four small ceramic pudding ramekins. She put four slices of plain white bread into the toaster, stirred the simmering water to create a vortex, and one by one, using a slotted spoon, gingerly lowered each egg into the water, simultaneously reaching over and pressing the lever down on the toaster. The Alessi timer—the one shaped like a lady in a dress, that she'd brought back from a work trip to Italy the year before along with holy water from Lourdes and a Pope John Paul bottle opener—was set to three minutes. When it pinged, so did the toaster.

Susan set down on two lovely, hand-painted Italian breakfast plates golden slices of toast topped with Canadian bacon and four magnificent, firm, buxom white orbs, the most perfect, perfectly poached eggs I had ever seen. I sliced gently into one, and its great gush of deep yellow yolk slowly flooded the plate and the meat and the bread. She pushed a small ceramic bowl of coarse salt and freshly ground black pepper in my direction. I took a pinch between my thumb and forefinger, rubbed them carefully together, and released a slow shower of tiny flakes over the eggs.

When people over the years have asked me, "When did you know you were falling in love with Susan," the answer is an easy one: just the simple, thoughtful action of having coarse salt in a small bowl instead of iodized dreck in a shaker was enough to make my heart careen from one side of my chest to the other. The tactile, ancient process of taking a pinch of salt from a tiny bowl between human fingertips, and rubbing it, sprinkling it, thoughtfully, on food, connects the diner with what is on the plate with a sense of immediacy. There is no need for a grain of rice to keep the salt dry in the humidity and the shaker clear.

Bowl of salt. Fingers. Food.

Susan began slicing up both pieces of her toast, bacon, and eggs into miniscule squares, like the mother of a small child would do for her baby who has just learned to use utensils, and I laughed out loud.

"What's wrong with it?" she asked. "It lets me read the paper and eat without having to use both hands."

Details.

When we were done—it was early in the afternoon on a frigid Sunday—Susan got up and put the tiny cast-iron Griswold in the sink, filled it with soapy water, and let it rest.

"Salt," she said, "is for eating. Not for scrubbing."

The *braciole*, which filled the house with the earthy essence of tomato and truffle and wild mushrooms, cooked in a very slow oven for the rest of the day, and when it was time for me to leave for the city, was not quite finished. I left it to Susan's hands, to slice into perfect roulades, which I was sure she could do expertly, since her mirepoix was so goddamned precise.

"Promise me you'll toss the sauce with the fresh tagliatelle I brought," I said, as we drove to the train station in Hartford.

"I promise," she agreed, glancing over at me.

"And that you'll let the meat rest for ten minutes before slicing it exactly an inch thick."

"Oh for god's *sake*, I *promise* already."

But it wouldn't matter: without my being there, I was sure that the first meal I'd ever made for Susan was going to be an abject failure, and I wasn't even going to be around to ask forgiveness. Or to make excuses.

"How was it?" I asked that night when I called to say I was home. It was after nine.

"Good," Susan said, "but maybe a little tough. So I chopped up the meat and stuffing and tossed it all together with the pasta. And it was so much better."

Poached Eggs with Canadian Bacon on Toast

In every new relationship, one dish emerges that becomes synonymous with love, safety, and goodness. Silly me, I thought it would be my *braciole*, but no; it was Susan's miraculously cooked, splendidly perfect poached eggs. Soft, runny—but not too runny—they scream comfort and howl happiness. And today, years later, when I'm either feeling frisky or like I want to crawl under a blanket and suck my thumb, it's Susan's poached eggs that I crave. Forget the fancy poaching devices and tools that I used to sell at Dean & DeLuca: all you'll need is a wooden spoon, a small saucepan, and a timer. Note to self: the fresher the eggs, the less the whites will hold together, so if your friendly neighborhood urban chicken-farming hipster rushes over with a few newly laid ones for you, give them a few days before you make this.

Serves 2

2 not-so-fresh eggs
1 tablespoon distilled white vinegar
2 slices Canadian bacon
2 slices bread of your choice (white is best, raisin is not)
Coarse salt and freshly ground black pepper

1. Carefully crack each egg into a small ramekin and set aside. In a small saucepan filled three-quarters of the way with water, add the white vinegar and bring it to a simmer over medium heat. While it's simmering, place the Canadian bacon slices in a medium, dry cast-iron pan over medium-low heat; cook on one side for 4 minutes and flip.

2. When the water comes to a rolling simmer, gingerly slide the eggs into the pan, and with the dowel end of a wooden spoon, flip the white over onto the yolk two or three times. Slap a cover onto the pan, remove it from the heat, and set your timer for exactly 3 minutes.

3. Meanwhile, cook the bacon on the other side for 2 minutes, and simultaneously toast your bread. When the bread is done, the bacon will be done. As soon as the timer goes off, and using a slotted spoon, carefully remove each egg to a ramekin.

4. Top each piece of toast with a slice of bacon, and top each with a poached egg. Serve with a bowl of coarse salt and freshly ground black pepper.

What I Know

By Diane Goodman

From *Eating Well*

In Diane Goodman's aptly-titled short story collections—*The Genius of Hunger, The Plated Heart*, and *Party Girls*—her characters' lives revolve around food, nurturing, and desire. Her day job as a Miami-area caterer provides rich material—and sometimes it also leads her to make surprising friends.

I met Edith two years ago when her daughter Ruthie hired me to cook her 30th birthday dinner. Ruthie had said, "Don't be offended if my mother doesn't seem appreciative. She's a little . . . gruff. And she doesn't like people cooking in her house." *Now you tell me?*

When I rang the doorbell, Edith called out, "Who's there?" It was 3:00 and Ruthie wouldn't arrive until 5:00 but I thought her mother would be expecting me. I said "the caterer?" as if I didn't know who I was.

I had imagined a big, intimidating woman, but what I saw was the reason I was there: Edith was ill. She was not old, maybe in her late 50s, but she was tiny and bent, thin and bird-boned. Her fingers on both hands were gnarled nearly into fists. She didn't invite me in.

"I hope you brought your own pans because you're not using mine," she said. "And what are you making anyway?" I stood on the porch and told her the whole menu, including her own Braised Chicken; Ruthie had given me her mother's recipe.

"That's Ruth's favorite dish. I invented it. You don't know how to make that," she snarled.

I had all the ingredients it required. I knew how to braise. But

I said, "I'm really sorry, Mrs. Kassenbaum. I know this is intrusive, but . . . "

"You don't know anything," she said.

I knew one thing: I was in for a long night.

Edith stepped aside and then hobbled behind me as I made my way to her kitchen. Her breath was short, but I could hear her swearing under it. She sat down at her table, glowering while I unpacked the ingredients.

Edith said. "Are those leeks? Did you take the sand out?"

I had. Of course I had. I almost said as much.

"Don't you know anything? You have to rinse the sand out of leeks," she said again, but this time in a quieter voice. I thought maybe her fury had exhausted her but when I turned to answer, she was crying. She was so hunched over her face was practically on her knees. I walked toward her and when she didn't react, I knelt down and put my hand on her back.

She tried to shake me off. Edith didn't trust me. She didn't know me. She didn't even know my name. I was a stranger in her home, about to cook her recipe for her family. In her own kitchen.

"What can I do?" I asked. "How can I make this easier?"

She said, "You? You're making everything worse. It's my daughter's birthday. I make the Braised Chicken for her every year. Almost 30 years. Who are you? I don't know what you're doing here!"

But she did. Edith's hands were so deformed from her illness that she could no longer cook. She didn't know what she would lose next.

"I understand," I said.

She said, "What? You understand? What do you know?"

I knew I was petrified and didn't want to do anything else to upset her, especially not being able to make her dish exactly the way she did.

"I'm sorry," I said. "I don't know . . . how do you make your Braised Chicken? Can you walk me through it?"

And out of my fear came the fix. Edith sat up and used her twisted hand to gesture me back to the stove. Then she walked me through every step of her recipe until it was simmering and the house smelled delicious. I covered it and sat down with her at the table. She looked completely spent. But she was smiling.

"Can I get you something?" I asked. "Water? Tea?"

"Didn't you bring any wine?"

Edith is confined to a wheelchair now and she rolls herself into her bedroom; I follow, carrying two glasses of Merlot. Tonight we are cooking her Beef Stroganoff and she will walk me through it, as she has for hundreds of meals in the last two years. We clink glasses, then drink.

"So go pick out my clothes," she says.

I select a lilac dress that matches the table linen and the tulips. Ruthie and her dad will be home soon. Edith does not leave her house anymore.

She lets me undress and then dress her. She lets me comb her hair, apply some lipstick. She tells me where to find her pearl earrings and I put them in her ears while she finishes her wine.

"You look beautiful," I tell her.

"What do you know?" she says. But she's smiling.

When There Was Nothing Left to Do, I Fed Her Ice Cream

By Sarah DiGregorio

From *GiltTaste.com*

In various stints as a food reporter/editor/reviewer—at the *Village Voice*, *Food Network Magazine*, and now *Parade*—Sarah Di Gregorio focuses on gourmet trends and the latest developments in the national food scene. But there are some moments in life when all that becomes irrelevant.

Cape Cod, where I grew up, is practically the ice cream capitol of the world, and my mother took full advantage of her adopted home. Unlike many women, my mother had an uncomplicated relationship with ice cream. She loved it and she ate it often, sometimes as a meal. She never missed an opportunity for soft serve, always chocolate-vanilla swirl. Her favorite summer lunch was a mud pie cone from the Whistle Stop in Monument Beach. That's what growing up on a farm in Kansas will do for you: Food is for growing, cooking and eating, not for worrying about.

The very idea that any woman would feel guilty about food was weird to her. Of course, it was easy for her to say, since she naturally hovered around 100 pounds. She looked at me like I might be adopted when I started hating my inner thighs—she claimed that, as a scrawny teenager, she would have given anything for her thighs to touch at the top. (She was probably the first woman in history to actually wish this.) She found any talk of dieting or aging boring and maybe even morally suspect. As woman after woman wailed about turning 40 or 50, she would quietly ask, "What's the alternative?"

She treated her cancer with the same pragmatism. She swelled with fluid; she shrunk to bone; she shook uncontrollably. If there was nothing that could be done about it, we didn't talk about it. What was the alternative?

We never managed to acknowledge to each other that this was not going to end well. Her silence on the matter was a non-acceptance, a refusal to go gently. It was also her deeply ingrained, farmwoman way of coping—and she was a master of coping. She could cope anyone under the table. If today was a day that demanded the insertion of a permanent catheter into an artery above her heart, the better to mainline chemo, well, that was just what we were doing today. Maybe we could stop for ice cream after. Meanwhile, I became an expert in magical thinking, a maker of deals with the universe.

So at the end, when there was nothing else I could do, I sat by her bedside and fed her Hoodsie Cups, half chocolate, half vanilla. After all her other pleasures—even reading—abandoned her, this one remained. I'd get an armful of the single serving cups from the hospital refrigerator and just keep spooning them into her mouth, stashing the empties under the bed so she wouldn't see how many she'd eaten. The ice cream acquired an imaginary power, like a garland of garlic or a nightlight. I thought it probably wasn't possible to die mid-bite.

About two weeks before she died, an occupational therapist came to her room. "I see you were a children's librarian," she chirped, consulting the chart. "I *am* a children's librarian," replied my mother. "Well," said the therapist, flustered, "I see your daughter has been feeding you. Do you want to work on eating on your own?" "I like her to feed me," said my mother. "But I can actually do it myself." To my surprise, she then demonstrated that she could.

Even after I knew she could do it herself, I couldn't stop dishing out those Hoodsie Cups, like they were some kind of sweet miracle drug, and she never stopped me. I loved the reassuring *schliiiick* of the cardboard lid lifted from the plush ice cream underneath, the miniature wooden spoon that came with each cup.

I don't know if it made my mother think of the big, creaky wooden ice cream maker she grew up with, packed with rock salt and chunks of ice. I don't know if it made her remember taking turns cranking the iron handle in the sticky heat of a Kansas summer, afternoons heavy with the hum of cicadas. I don't know if it made her remember that barely frozen sweet cream, of licking it directly from the paddle. It's one of the many questions I never asked her, one of the many things I'll never know. But I hope it did.

Recipe Index

Permissions Acknowledgments

Grateful acknowledgment is made to all those who gave permission for written material to appear in this book. Every effort has been made to trace and contact copyright holders. If an error or omission is brought to our notice, we will be pleased to remedy the situation in subsequent editions of this book. For further information, please contact the publisher.

Kliman, Todd. "The Meaning of Local." Copyright © 2013 by *Washingtonian Magazine*. Used by permission of the publisher.

Goulding, Matt. "Confronting a Masterpiece." Copyright © 2012 by Roads & Kingdoms. Used by permission of the author.

Wells, Pete. "The View from West 12th." From *The New York Times*, May 22, 2013, © 2013 *The New York Times*. All rights reserved. Used by permission and protected by the Copyright Laws of the United States. The printing, copyng, redistribution, or retransmission of this Content without express written permission is prohibited.

Froeb, Ian. "Takaya or Leave Ya: Didn't New Asian Get Old, Like, Ten Years Ago?" Copyright © 2013 by *Riverfront Times*. Used by permission of the publisher.

Shilcutt, Katharine. "I Ate My First McRib, and I Regret It." Copyright © 2012 by *Houston Press*. Used by permission of the publisher.

Barry, Dan. "Back When a Chocolate Puck Tasted, Guiltily, Like America." From *The New York Times*, November 17, 2012, © 2012 *The New York Times*. All rights reserved. Used by permission and protected by the Copyright Laws of the United States. The printing, copyng, redistribution, or retransmission of this Content without express written permission is prohibited.

Jacobsen, Rowan. "Forgotten Fruits." Copyright © 2013 by Rowan Jacobsen. Originally published in *Mother Jones*. Used by permission of the publisher.

Byers Murray, Erin. "Earth Mothers." Copyright © 2012 by *Edible Boston*. Used by permission of the publisher.

Moskowitz Grumdahl, Dara. "The Cheese Artist." Copyright © 2012 by *Minneapolis-St. Paul Magazine*. Used by permission of the publisher.

Watson, Molly. "A Snail's Tale." Copyright © 2013 by *Edible San Francisco*. Used by permission of the publisher.

O'Donnel, Kim. "Yes, We Can." © GRACE Communications Foundation. Used with permission.

Estabrook, Barry. "Hogonomics." Estabrook, Barry, "Hogonomics," in *Gastronomica*, vol. 12, no. 2, Summer 2012. © 2012 by the Regents of the University of California. Published by the University of California Press.

Kessler, John. "The Upstart Cattleman." From *The Atlanta Journal-Constitution*, February 14, 2013, © 2013 *The Atlanta Journal-Constitution*.

All rights reserved. Used by permission and protected by the Copyright Laws of the United States. The printing, copyng, redistribution, or retransmission of this Content without express written permission is prohibited.

Hayward, Tim. "The Ibérico Journey." Copyright © 2013 by *Financial Times.* Used by permission of the author.

Brouilette, Alan. "Beer and Smoking in Danville, Illinois." Copyright © 2013 by Blood and Thunder. Used by permission of the author.

Sula, Mike. "Chicken of the Trees." Copyright © 2012 by *Chicago Reader.* Used by permission of the publisher.

Rinella, Steven. "Tasting Notes: Heart." From *Meat Eater: Adventures from the Life of an American Hunter* by Steve Rinella, copyright © 2012 by Steven Rinella. Used by permission of Spiegel & Grau, an imprint of The Random House Publishing Group, a division of Random House, Inc. Any third party use of this material, outside of this publication, is prohibited. Interested parties must apply directly to Random House, Inc. for permission.

Shaw, Hank. "An Awful Mercy." Copyright © 2012 by *Hunter Angler Gardener Cook.* Used by permission of the publisher.

Hamilton, Gabrielle. "Guess Who's Coming To Dinner." Copyright © 2013 Condé Nast. All rights reserved. Originally published in *Bon Appétit.* Reprinted by permission.

Lopez-Alt, J. Kenji. "How To Make Real New England Clam Chowder." Lopez-Alt, J. Kenji. "How To Make New England Clam Chowder." Copyright © 2013 by SeriousEats.com. Used by permission of the publisher.

Pollan, Michael. "Step Two: Saute Onions and Other Aromatic Vegetables." From *Cooked* by Michael Pollan, copyright © 2013 by Michael Pollan. Used by permission of The Penguin Press, a division of Penguin Group (USA) LLC.

Arnold-Ratliff, Katie. "Cooking with Friends." Copyright © 2013 by Katie Arnold-Ratliff. Originally published in *Tin House.* Used by permission of the author.

Manning, Joy. "The Swedish Chef." Copyright © 2013 by *Table Matters.* Used by permission of the publisher.

Carman, Tim. "The Gingerbread Cookie Reclamation Project." From *The Washington Post,* December 11, 2012, © 2012 Washington

Post. All rights reserved. Used by permission and protected by the Copyright Laws of the United States. The printing, copying, redistribution, or retransmission of this Content without express written permission is prohibited.

Procopio, Michael. "Hortotiropita & the 5 Stages of Restaurant Grief." Copyright © 2013 by Michael Procopio. Used by permission of the author. Originally appeared on FoodforTheThoughtless.com.

Crapanzano, Aleksandra. "Lobster Lessons." From *The Cassoulet Saved Our Marriage* by Caroline M. Grant and Lisa Catherine Harper, © 2013. Reprinted by arrangement with Roost Books, Boston, MA. www.roostbooks.com.

Herman, Bernard. "A Bountiful Shore." Originally published in *Saveur.* Used with permission of Saveur Copyright © 2013. All rights reserved.

Swansburg, John. "Empire of the Burning Tongue." Copyright © 2012 by New York Media LLC. Originally published in *New York Magazine*, December 3, 2012. Used by permission of the publisher.

Gold, Jonathan. "The King of Food Trucks Hits Hawaii." Copyright © 2012 by Jonathan Gold. Originally appeared in *Food & Wine.* Used by permission of the author.

Barrett, Peter. "Fish & Game." Copyright © 2013 by *Edible Manhattan.* Used by permission of the publisher.

Pang, Kevin. "His Saving Grace." From *Chicago Tribune*, 2/14/2013 © 2013 Chicago Tribune. All rights reserved. Used by permission and protected by the Copyright Laws of the United States. The printing, copying, redistribution, or retransmission of this Content without express written permission is prohibited.

Lam, Francis. "Spin the Globe." Copyright © 2013 by Francis Lam. Originally published in *AFAR Magazine*, May 2013. Used by permission of the author.

Barichievy, Karen. "To Serve and Obey." Copyright © 2013 by *Fire & Knives.* Used by permission of the author.

Wiewiora, Chris. "This is Tossing." Copyright © 2013 by Chris Wiewiora. Used by permission of the author.

Huang, Eddie. "Meet the Parents." From *Fresh Off the Boat: A Memoir* by Eddie Huang, copyright © 2013 by Eddie Huang. Used by permission of Spiegel & Grau, an imprint of The Random House Publishing Group, a division of Random House, Inc. Any third party use of this material, outside of this publication, is prohibited. Interested parties must apply directly to Random House, Inc. for permission.

Foster, Kim. "When the Kids Make You Breakfast for Mother's Day." Copyright © 2013 by Kim Foster. Used by permission of the author.

Penn-Romine, Carol. "Coke and Peanuts." Copyright © 2012 by Carol Penn-Romine. Used by permission of the author.

Wong, Lily, "Eating the Hyphen," in *Gastronomica*, vol. 12, no. 3, Fall 2012. © 2012 by the Regents of the University of California. Published by the University of California Press.

Graham, Paul. "Variations on Grace." Copyright © 2012 by Paul Graham. Used by permission of the author.

Altman, Elissa. "In Susan's Kitchen." From *Poor Man's Feast* © 2013 by Elissa Altman. Used with permission of Chronicle Books LLC, San Francisco. Visit ChronicleBooks.com.

Goodman, Diane. "What I Know." Copyright © 2013 by Diane Goodman. Used by permission of the author. Originally published in *Eating Well®* magazine February 2013.

DiGregorio, Sarah. "When There Was Nothing Left to Do, I Fed Her Ice Cream." Copyright © 2012 by Gilt.com. Used by permission of the publisher.

About the Editor

Holly Hughes is a writer, the former executive editor of Fodor's Travel Publications, and author of *Frommer's 500 Places for Food and Wine Lovers.* Her website is hollyahughes.net

Submissions for
Best Food Writing 2014

Submissions and nominations for *Best Food Writing 2014* should be forwarded no later than May 15, 2014, to Holly Hughes at *Best Food Writing 2014*, c/o Da Capo Press, 44 Farnsworth Street, 3rd Floor, Boston, MA 02210, or emailed to best.food@perseusbooks.com. We regret that, due to volume, we cannot acknowledge receipt of all submissions.